RETHINKING THE MEDITERRANEAN

RETHINKING
THE
MEDITERRANEAN

Edited by

W. V. HARRIS

OXFORD

UNIVERSITY PRESS

OXFORD
UNIVERSITY PRESS

Great Clarendon Street, Oxford OX2 6DP

Oxford University Press is a department of the University of Oxford.
It furthers the University's objective of excellence in research, scholarship,
and education by publishing worldwide in

Oxford New York

Auckland Cape Town Dar es Salaam Hong Kong Karachi
Kuala Lumpur Madrid Melbourne Mexico City Nairobi
New Delhi Shanghai Taipei Toronto

With offices in

Argentina Austria Brazil Chile Czech Republic France Greece
Guatemala Hungary Italy Japan Poland Portugal Singapore
South Korea Switzerland Thailand Turkey Ukraine Vietnam

Oxford is a registered trade mark of Oxford University Press
in the UK and in certain other countries

Published in the United States
by Oxford University Press Inc., New York

© Oxford University Press 2005

British Library Cataloguing in Publication Data

Data available

Library of Congress Cataloging in Publication Data
Rethinking the Mediterranean / edited by W.V. Harris.
p. cm.
Papers from a conference organized by the Columbia University Center
for the Ancient Mediterranean September 21-22, 2001.
Summary: "This text examines the ancient and medieval history of the
Mediterranean Sea and the lands around it"–Provided by publisher.
Includes bibliographical references and index.
ISBN 0-19-926545-3 (alk. paper)
1. Mediterranean Region—Civilization—Congresses. I. Harris, William V.
(William Vernon) II. Columbia University. Center for the Ancient Mediterranean.
DE2.5.R48 2004
930—dc22   2004025112

Typeset SPI Publisher Services, Pondicherry, India
Printed in Great Britain
on acid-free paper by
Biddles Ltd., King's Lynn, Norfolk

ISBN 0-19-926545-3   978-0-19-926545-9
ISBN 0-19-920772-0 (Pbk.)   978-0-19-920772-5 (Pbk.)

1 3 5 7 9 10 8 6 4 2

PREFACE

How useful is the Mediterranean Sea as an intellectual construct? And how should it be studied? Nearly sixty years after
the publication of Fernand Braudel's first great book, and some
forty years after the Mediterranean became a major category in
anthropology, these questions continue to trouble and intrigue
us. For those of us who study the ancient world or the Middle
Ages, the questions are particularly pressing. In consequence,
they have in recent times figured quite often in the merry-
go-round of academic conferences. One such conference was
organized by the Center for the Ancient Mediterranean at
Columbia University on 21 and 22 September 2001.

The book you have before you consists for the most part of
the proceedings of that meeting. All of the orally delivered
papers have been revised, in some cases substantially. Three
others are additions: I was fortunate enough to find David
Abulafia, whose work I have long admired, willing to contribute
a paper, even though he had not been among the attendees in
New York (the cast consisted mostly of *antichisti*); Peregrine
Horden and Nicholas Purcell have written an extra essay in
response to the reviewers of their recent book *The Corrupting
Sea* (2000). Finally, I have taken the opportunity provided by
the period of revision to crystallize my thoughts on this subject
and put them together as an introduction; I thank Susan
E. Alcock in particular for helping me to do this.

In the interests of preventing further delays, matters have
been so organized that none of the contributors saw either my
introduction or Horden and Purcell's response to critics before
they finished their own contributions. Horden and Purcell did
not read my essay, and I have not altered it since I read theirs.
So there will no doubt be plenty of material for later responses.
But we have already been compelled by various circumstances
to wait quite long enough. And it was never of course our
intention to produce an agreed body of doctrine. If there are
unresolved conflicts between some parts of the book and

others—and there certainly are—there is not the least reason to apologize for them.

The immediate occasion for the organization of our conference was the establishment of Columbia University's Center for the Ancient Mediterranean, which we devised in 1999 and brought into being in 2000 with the intention of fostering exchange between the exponents and students of a number of different disciplines which our university, like all or virtually all others, tends to separate. No sooner had we done this, however, with no thought much deeper than that the ancient Mediterranean would serve as a useful practical focus (cf. the title of Michael Herzfeld's paper), than some of us found ourselves thinking more systematically about the intellectual, as distinct from institutional and pedagogic, advantages and disadvantages of concentrating on the Mediterranean. As is well known, sharply divergent views have been expressed—and the debate goes on, in these pages and elsewhere.

The contributors were generally told nothing more specific than that they could put forward any Mediterranean thoughts or research that might be of interest to other scholars with Mediterranean interests, history being the broad umbrella. They rode off, as will be seen, in three general directions, which, I think, complement each other nicely, and reflect some of the current thinking on the subject very well. Some chose to present particular pieces of research in ancient or mediaeval history, attempting to evaluate the nature and importance of the Mediterranean context (Chaniotis, Horden, Purcell). Others have written about perceptions of the Mediterranean world in antiquity (Bowersock), or about its creation, in scientific, literary or fantastic minds, in post-antique times (Armstrong, Herzfeld, Marshall, Said). Still others have mainly attempted to describe and evaluate the current state of the ancient history of the Mediterranean (Alcock, Bagnall, Bresson, Harris, Horden and Purcell together, Van De Mieroop) or to contextualize Mediterranean history by reference to other Mediterraneans (Abulafia). Yet every one of these papers branches out far beyond these categories—and of course there is constant reference, often admiring, sometimes critical, to *The Corrupting Sea.*

I am sharply aware of what has been left out. The plan was to engender some reflection about the field and its intellectual tropes by scholars with a historical mentality (even though some of them do not see themselves primarily as historians). All the present authors are, I think, alert to what is going on in contiguous fields, particularly archaeology, but Susan Alcock is, I suppose, the only contributor who can claim the actual title of archaeologist. There is no geographer here. These and other gaps I most sincerely regret: one does what one can with the resources available at a particular moment.

Finally, some pleasurable expression of gratitude. All of the distinguished contributors are busy people, and I should like to thank them for making the journey to New York, for sending in their revised papers in good time, and in general for effective cooperation.

I also wish to thank those who have cared for the Center for the Ancient Mediterranean in its infancy, and those who helped the conference to take place. Among the former I should single out in particular my colleagues Roger Bagnall, Clemente Marconi, and Suzanne Said. How sad it is that we can no longer thank John H. D'Arms, at the time of his death President of the American Council of Learned Societies, who was a member of the original steering committee of the Center: it was shortly before our conference that he was struck by what proved to be a fatal illness. I extend sincere thanks too to crucial figures in the university administration at that time, Jonathan Cole, Provost, and David Harris Cohen, Vice-President for Arts and Sciences: without their imaginative understanding the Center could never have come into being at all. I believe that the nearly simultaneous publication of this book and of *Greek Vases: Images, Contexts and Controversies*, edited by Clemente Marconi, the proceedings of another conference of Center for the Ancient Mediterranean, will demonstrate the Center's vitality.

W.V.H.

New York
December 2003

CONTENTS

List of Maps   xv
List of Illustrations   xvii
List of Tables   xviii
List of Abbreviations   xix
Notes on Contributors   xxi

1. The Mediterranean and Ancient History   1
   W. V. HARRIS
   1. Introduction.   1
   2. Towards a history of the Mediterranean,
      3500 BC–AD 1000.   3
   3. Unity?   20
   4. 'Ruralizing' ancient history.   29
   5. Categories, dynamic processes, causation, and avoiding
      conclusions.   34
   6. Mediterraneanism and ancient history:
      in favour of a wider ethnography.   38

THE BIG CANVAS

2. Practical Mediterraneanism: Excuses for Everything,
   from Epistemology to Eating   45
   MICHAEL HERZFELD
   1. On the ontological persistence of a shrinking sea.   45
   2. Comparing the comparisons: power, authority,
      and classification.   46
   3. Stereotypical permutations of a civilizational ideal. 48
   4. Strategies of self-stereotyping.   52
   5. Mediterraneanism and the politics of humiliation.   59

Contents

3. Mediterraneans   64

   DAVID ABULAFIA

   1. The Mediterranean and the Mediterranean Sea.   64
   2. The Classic Mediterranean and its sub-Mediterraneans.   67
   3. Neighbouring Mediterraneans:
      the Saharan Mediterranean Desert.   75
   4. The Mediterranean of the North.   76
   5. The Mediterranean Atlantic.   80
   6. A trans-oceanic Mediterranean: the Caribbean.   82
   7. The Japanese Mediterranean.   85
   8. The Indian Ocean as a Braudelian problem.   90
   9. Comparative Mediterraneans.   91

4. Ecology and Beyond: The Mediterranean Paradigm   94

   ALAIN BRESSON

   1. One or several? Zones and unity in the ancient
      Mediterranean.   95
   2. Forms of connectivity.   104
   3. Mediterranean connectivity: inside and outside.   108

ANGLES OF VISION

5. The Eastern Mediterranean in Early Antiquity   117

   MARC VAN DE MIEROOP

   1. Introduction.   117
   2. The states of the eastern Mediterranean world.   119
   3. Political evolution in the second half of the
      second millennium BC.   123
   4. Social structure.   128
   5. War and diplomacy.   131
   6. Cultural and mercantile interactions.   134
   7. An eastern Mediterranean system.   137

6. Ritual Dynamics in the Eastern Mediterranean:
   Case Studies in Ancient Greece and Asia Minor   141

   ANGELOS CHANIOTIS

   1. Mediterranean rituals.   141
   2. From meanings to functions.   143
   3. Rituals and cultural transfer.   146
   4. The elusiveness of rituals.   149

5. Artificial revivals. 152
6. Misleading analogies: the Daidala of Plataia and its
   modern exegetes. 155
7. Rituals and the physical environment. 160
8. The role of religious idiosyncrasies. 162
9. The manifold character of ritual transfer. 164
10. Contextualizing Mediterranean rituals. 166

7. The East–West Orientation of Mediterranean Studies
   and the Meaning of North and South in Antiquity 167
   G. W. Bowersock

8. Travel Sickness: Medicine and Mobility in the
   Mediterranean from Antiquity to the Renaissance 179
   Peregrine Horden
   1. Introduction. 179
   2. Mobility and fixity. 181
   3. Travel as therapy. 186
   4. Regimen for travellers. 190
   5. Free-standing regimens. 195

9. The Ancient Mediterranean:
   The View from the Customs House 200
   Nicholas Purcell
   1. On the usefulness of the history of taxation. 200
   2. Taxation and mobility. 203
   3. Three phases of Mediterranean evidence. 206
   4. Managing interdependence: the nature of the network. 215
   5. Progressive regression? 220
   6. Athens and Rome: Mediterranean and other
      hegemonies. 222
   7. The edges of the system: conclusion. 228

THE ARCHAEOLOGY OF KNOWLEDGE

10. Travel and Experience in the Mediterranean
    of Louis XV 235
    Christopher Drew Armstrong
    1. Introduction. 235
    2. Constructing the scientific traveller-observer. 236

3. The Mediterranean Sea and Enlightenment science.   242
4. The *voyage philosophique* in the Aegean Sea.   253
5. Conclusion: Chabert and Choiseul-Gouffier.   263

11. The Mirage of Greek Continuity: On the Uses and
    Abuses of Analogy in Some Travel Narratives from
    the Seventeenth to the Eighteenth Century   268
    SUZANNE SAÏD
    1. The first wave.   269
    2. Spon and Wheler and their successors.   274
    3. The Romantic sensibility.   287
    4. Conclusion.   290

12. Mediterranean Reception in the Americas   294
    FRANCISCO MARSHALL
    1. The Amazon.   297
    2. Bernardo Ramos: myth and epigraphy.   301
    3. Epilogue.   311

13. Alphabet Soup in the Mediterranean Basin:
    The Emergence of the Mediterranean Serial   314
    SUSAN E. ALCOCK
    1. Introduction.   314
    2. Chronological patterning.   316
    3. Where, who, and in whose language?   322
    4. A good cover.   324
    5. Mission and agenda.   326
    6. Covering the Mediterranean.   333

LAST WORDS

14. Egypt and the Concept of the Mediterranean   339
    ROGER S. BAGNALL

15. Four Years of Corruption: A Response to Critics   348
    PEREGRINE HORDEN AND NICHOLAS PURCELL
    1. *Quid eis cum pelago?* The response by discipline. 348
    2. *Les auteurs ne se noient jamais dans leur
       Méditerranée:* theory and scope.   355

Contents

3. Doughnuts in cyberspace: finding the metaphor.   359
4. Falsifiability.   361
5. Monstrous squid or calamari?   367
6. Doing without towns.   369
7. Managing monotheisms.   371
8. Render unto Caesar: in quest of narrative,   372

Select Bibliography   377

Index   407

LIST OF MAPS

1. The eastern Mediterranean in Early Antiquity   xxiii
2. The spread of bronze   xxiv
3. The Mediterranean in Greek, Roman,
   and medieval times   xxvi

LIST OF ILLUSTRATIONS

10.1. Corrected map of Italy and Greece, from
Guillaume Delisle, 'Justification des mesures
des anciens en matiere de geographie',
HAS, 1714, Mém. pl. 8   245

10.2. 'Projet d'une Carte reduite de la Méditerrannée
assujetie aux Observations Astronomiques les plus
certains Comparée avec la carte du Sr. Berthelot
hydrographe du Roy, le 15 Jan 1735'. Paris,
Bibliothèque Nationale de France, Cartes et
Plans, portefeuille 64, pièce 12   249

10.3. 'A Head of Homer. From the Collection of Lyde
Browne Esq' (J. B. Cipriani, d.; Engrav'd by
J. Basire), from Robert Wood, *An Essay on the
Original Genius and Writings of Homer*
(London, 1775)   256

10.4. 'View of Ancient Troas together with the
Scamander and Mount Ida, as taken anno
MDCCL' (Borra delin; Major Sc), from Robert
Wood, *An Essay on the Original Genius and
Writings of Homer* (London, 1775)   257

10.5. 'Plan de la Plaine d'Athenes, et de quelques lieux
qui l'environnent' (Littret de Montigny, sculpt.),
from Julien-David Leroy, *Les Ruines des plus
beaux monuments de la Grèce* (Paris, 1758), part 1,
pl. 9   260

10.6. Detail of capitals and entablature of the Parthenon
(Pierre Patte, sculpt.), from Julien-David Leroy,
Les Ruines des plus beaux monuments de la Grèce
(Paris, 1758), part 2, pl. 9   261

10.7. 'Vue du Temple de Minerve Suniade' (Philippe
Le Bas, sculpt.), from Julien-David Leroy,
Les Ruines des plus beaux monuments de la Grèce
(Paris, 1758), part 1, pl. 15   262

10.8. 'Ruines du Temple de Mars' [at Halicarnassus] (Dessiné par J. B. Hilair; Gravé à l'eau forte par Marillier et terminé au burin par Dambrun), from Choiseul-Gouffier, *Voyage Pittoresque de la Grèce*, i (Paris, 1782), pl. 99   264

10.9. 'Détails de ce monument' [Temple of Mars at Halicarnassus] (Dessiné et Mesuré par Foucherot; Gravé par Sellier), from Choiseul-Gouffier, *Voyage Pittoresque de la Grèce*, i (Paris, 1782), pl. 101   265

10.10. 'Carte détaillée de la route de l'Auteur depuis le Méandre jusqu'au Golfe d'Adramyhtti' (Rédigée sur les Lieux par le Cte de Choiseul Gouffier; Gravé par J. Perrier; Ecrit par L. J. Beaublé), from Choiseul-Gouffier, *Voyage Pittoresque de la Grèce*, i (Paris, 1782), pl. 117   266

12.1. The primitive and figurative variants of Greek script according to Bernardo Ramos   304

12.2. Marajoara ceramics yield Greek   306

12.3. A 'Greek inscription' from the Amazon   307

12.4. The same markings interpreted by Bernardo Ramos   308

13.1. Number of 'Mediterranean serials', 1960–2002   315

13.2. Number of US periodicals, in history and in anthropology/sociology, 1970–2000   321

LIST OF TABLES

Table 13.1: List of 'Mediterranean serials' considered in the text.   317

LIST OF ABBREVIATIONS

Braudel, *MMW*	F. Braudel, *The Mediterranean and the Mediterranean World in the Age of Philip II*, 2 vols. (trans. S. Reynolds, London and New York, 1972–3) (original edn.: *La Méditerrannée et le monde méditerranéen à l'époque de Philippe II*, Paris 1949; second edn., Paris, 1966)
CMG	*Corpus Medicorum Graecorum*
FGrH	*Die Fragmente der griechischen Historiker*, ed. F. Jacoby
Horden and Purcell, *CS*	P. Horden and N. Purcell, *The Corrupting Sea: A Study of Mediterranean History* (Oxford, 2000)
I. Cret.	*Inscriptiones Creticae*
IG	*Inscriptiones Graecae*
IGRRP	*Inscriptiones Graecae ad Res Romanas Pertinentes*
IGSK	*Die Inschriften der griechischen Städte Kleinasiens*
ILS	*Inscriptiones Latinae Selectae*
JRA	*Journal of Roman Archaeology*
OGIS	*Orientis Graeci Inscriptiones Selectae*
SEG	*Supplementum Epigraphicum Graecum*
*SIG*³	*Sylloge Inscriptionum Graecarum* (3rd edn.)
SGDI	*Sammlung der griechischen Dialekt-Inschriften*, ed. H. Collitz *et al.*
TAM	*Tituli Asiae Minoris*
ZPE	*Zeitschrift für Papyrologie und Epigraphik*

NOTES ON CONTRIBUTORS

DAVID ABULAFIA is Professor of Mediterranean History at Cambridge University. His books include *The Western Mediterranean Kingdoms* (1997), and he has edited *The Mediterranean in History* (2003).

SUSAN E. ALCOCK is John H. D'Arms Collegiate Professor of Classical Archaeology and Classics at the University of Michigan. Author most recently of *Archaeologies of the Greek Past: Landscape, Monuments and Memories* (2002), she is a 2001 recipient of a MacArthur Fellowship.

CHRISTOPHER DREW ARMSTRONG is currently a post-doctoral fellow in the Department of Fine Art at the University of Toronto, where he is preparing a book on architectural theory in the French Enlightenment.

ROGER S. BAGNALL is a professor in the History and Classics Departments at Columbia University and author of, among other books, *Egypt in Late Antiquity* (1993) and *Reading Papyri, Writing Ancient History* (1995).

GLEN BOWERSOCK is Professor of Ancient History at the Institute for Advanced Study in Princeton. He has published over a dozen books on the Roman Empire, Late Antiquity, and the Ancient Near East.

ALAIN BRESSON is professor of Ancient History at the University Michel-de-Montaigne Bordeaux 3. Among his recent publications is *La Cité marchande* (2001); he is preparing a new work of synthesis on the economy of ancient Greece.

ANGELOS CHANIOTIS is Professor of Ancient History and Vice-Rector at the University of Heidelberg. He is co-editor of the *Supplementum Epigraphicum Graecum*, and with Pierre Ducrey has recently edited *Army and Power in the Ancient World* (2002).

W. V. HARRIS is Shepherd Professor of History at Columbia University. His latest book is *Restraining Rage: The Ideology of Anger-control in Classical Antiquity* (2002).

MICHAEL HERZFELD, Professor of Anthropology at Harvard University, is the author of among other books *Anthropology: Theoretical Practice in Culture and Society* (2001) and *The Body Impolitic: Artisans and Artifice in the Global Hierarchy of Value* (2004).

PEREGRINE HORDEN is Reader in Medieval History, Royal Holloway College, University of London. He is currently writing a comparative study of early medieval health care.

FRANCISCO MARSHALL is Associate Professor of Ancient History in the Federal University of Rio Grande do Sul, Brazil, author of *Édipo Tirano, a tragédia do saber* (2000), and head of the Projeto Apollonia: Archaeology and History of the Ancient City.

NICHOLAS PURCELL is Fellow and Tutor in Ancient History at St John's College, Oxford. His next book is *The Kingdom of the Capitol*, a study of Roman culture and society.

SUZANNE SAID, who is a professor of Classics at Columbia University, has published extensively on Greek literature from Homer to Basil the Great. Her most recent books have been *Histoire de la littérature grecque* (with M. Trédé and A. le Boulluec)(1997), which has also appeared in English, and *Homère et l'Odyssée* (1998).

MARC VAN DE MIEROOP is a Professor in the Departments of Middle East and Asian Languages and Cultures and of History at Columbia University. His most recent book is *A History of the Ancient Near East*, ca. *3000–323* BC. (2004).

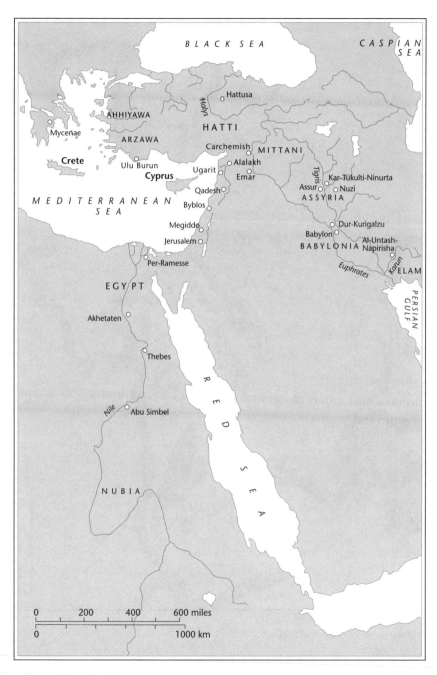

Map 1. The eastern Mediterranean in Early Antiquity

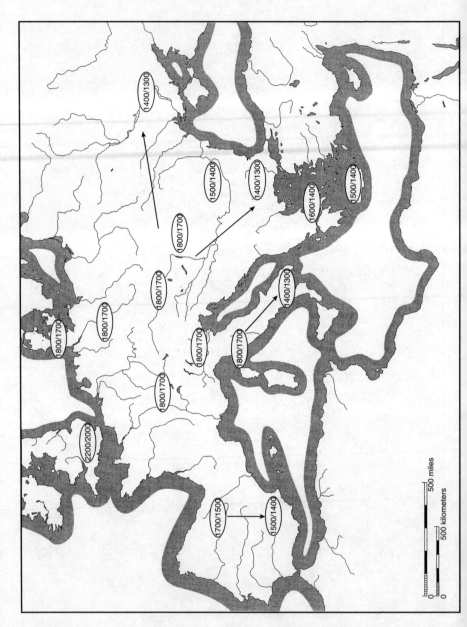

Map 2. The spread of bronze

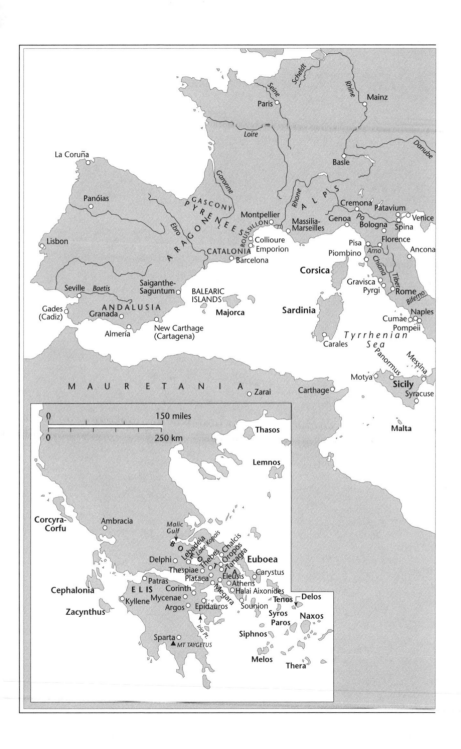

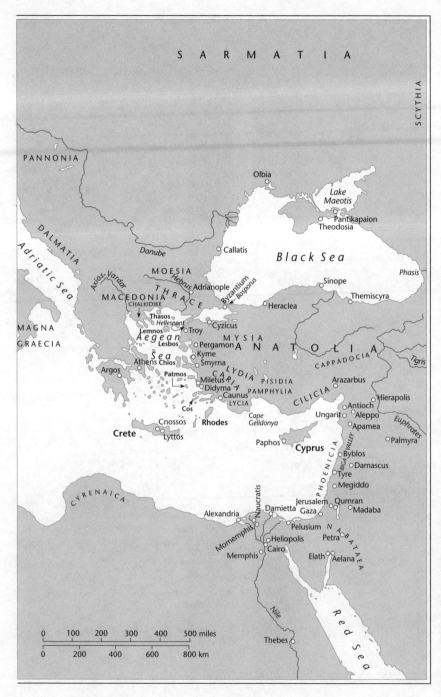

Map 3. The Mediterranean in Greek, Roman, and medieval times

1

The Mediterranean and Ancient History

W. V. Harris

1. INTRODUCTION

Historians, and probably anthropologists too, are destined to write a great deal more about both the Mediterranean and Mediterraneanism—the doctrine that there are distinctive characteristics which the cultures of the Mediterranean have, or have had, in common. And whatever the importance of the Mediterranean may be for earlier or later history, those of us who study the history of the Greeks and Romans have a particular need, for obvious reasons, to get the subject straight.

With practised one-upmanship, one of those most responsible for opening up the debate about Mediterraneanism, my friend Michael Herzfeld, has implied (in his contribution to this volume) that it is now *vieux jeu*, an unexciting leftover (if not hangover) from the 1980s and 1990s.[1] In other words, concen-

---

[1] According to the anthropologists V. A. Goddard, J. R. Llobera, and C. Shore, 'Introduction: The Anthropology of Europe', in Goddard, Llobera, and Shore (eds.), *The Anthropology of Europe* (Oxford and Providence, RI: 1994), 1–40: 4, 'the Mediterranean' was invented in 1959, and had already outrun its usefulness in the 1980s (pp. 20–3). But there was a touch of wishful thinking when J. De Pina-Cabral wrote in an important article in 1989 that there was 'an increasing awareness that something is wrong with the notion of the Mediterranean as a culture area' ('The Mediterranean as a Category of Regional Comparison: A Critical View', *Current Anthropology* 30 (1989), 399–406: 399). In reality, the Mediterranean is a concept with a long and somewhat shady modern history; see, for example, G. Sergi, *La decadenza delle nazioni latine* (Turin, 1900). For a balanced assessment of 'culture areas' in general see R. Lederman, 'Globalization and the Future of Culture Areas', *Annual Review of Anthropology* 27 (1998), 427–49. This introduction aims to set out a positive programme, and to criticize certain general intellectual trends. Criticism of *CS* is incidental. It may in any case not be very opportune, since Horden and Purcell promise a second volume in which they will consider

trating on the Mediterranean may not only be a romantic delusion or a piece of Eurocentric cultural imperialism—thoughts which we have grown rather accustomed to—it may, worse still, be a recipe for boredom. The other side of that coin is presented by Susan Alcock in her revealing survey of 'Mediterranean' periodicals: there are more and more players. Thousands, no doubt, receive the electronic information service H-Mediterranean. Something of an illusion is involved, however, for while there has been a wave of important new work on the ancient Mediterranean environment in recent years—and a lot of thought about what the term 'Mediterranean' denotes—it has scarcely been a wave of tidal proportions, and much of what is being published in 'Mediterranean' journals is in fact old-fashioned local history, archaeology, or antiquarianism of little general significance.[2] And 'Mediterranean' has often been a synonym for 'Greek and Roman, plus such other ancient cultures as I may happen to pay attention to'. Yet as far as ancient historians are concerned, there are still important Mediterranean questions to answer—some of them arguably quite crucial for the understanding of the ancient world.

There is admittedly something a little old-fashioned about almost all recent writing about the ancient Mediterranean. The modern scholar gazes upon that world with scientific detachment, all the more self-confident because he/she is often borrowing from the notoriously objective natural sciences. This volume breaks away from that tradition to some extent, and subjects the observer to some observation from time to time.

What I mainly plan to discuss in this chapter are two very difficult questions that can be framed quite simply. How should the history of the ancient Mediterranean be written—if it should be written at all? And is Mediterraneanism of much use to ancient historians, or is it alternatively something of a danger (and in effect a cousin of Orientalism)?

climate, disease, demography, and relations with the outside world (p. 4). Debate must continue, however.

[2] The new journal *Ancient West and East* (2002) might be thought to point in the opposite direction, since it wishes to reinstate the periphery—but that implicitly keeps the Mediterranean at the centre.

2. TOWARDS A HISTORY OF THE MEDITERRANEAN 3500 BC–AD 1000

We are in one sense only at the beginning. Until AD 2000 no one ever published a book about the ancient history *of* the Mediterranean as distinct from history *in* the Mediterranean (to borrow a distinction from Peregrine Horden and Nicholas Purcell which, as we shall see, is not without problems).[3] In other words no one had written a book in which the sea and its coastlands had been the central object of enquiry, as distinct from the human activities that took place there in ancient times. What *might* have turned out to be such a book was published in 1998, Braudel's *Les Mémoires de la Méditerranée*,[4] a book about antiquity written some thirty years earlier. Braudel had died in 1985, and a questionable kind of piety towards the dead decided to publish what the author himself did not, apparently, consider ready for the press. Braudel had written that his own research covered (at the time of writing) only the period 1450–1600, and although he indicates that the Mediterranean Sea is the book's subject[5] that body of water receives rather casual attention in what is in essence a conventional, albeit certainly intelligent, summary of ancient history from the palaeolithic down to Constantine. If one had thought that the author regarded this book as an original work of scholarly research, one would have been seriously disappointed. It was in any case Braudel's first book, *The Mediterranean and the Mediterranean World in the Age of Philip II*, that provided the challenge for Horden and Purcell.

The response, ambitious in both scale and tone, was *The Corrupting Sea: A Study of Mediterranean History*. Their sub-

---

[3] I have not been able to trace this distinction beyond J. Beckett's comment in *Current Anthropology* 20 (1979), 85. Shortly after *CS* there appeared A. T. Grove and O. Rackham, *The Nature of Mediterranean Europe: An Ecological History* (New Haven and London, 2001).

[4] *Les Mémoires de la Méditerranée: Préhistoire et antiquité* (Paris, 1998), trans. by S. Reynolds as *The Mediterranean in the Ancient World* (London, 2001). The book was apparently written (quite quickly) in 1968–9, thus before the work which many historians regard as Braudel's greatest, *Civilisation matérielle, économie et capitalisme* (*Civilization and Capitalism*).

[5] All this: *Les Mémoires* 17. Not that one should doubt the depth of Braudel's knowledge of ancient history (at the Sorbonne his teachers had included Maurice Holleaux: Braudel, *MMW*, i. 22 n. 1).

ject is the 'human history of the Mediterranean Sea and its coastlands' during roughly three millennia, to AD 1000.[6] Thus the period is vastly longer, although as we shall see, the subject-matter is more circumscribed; in particular, it is important to notice that most of the central questions of economic history are *not* being addressed. Fair enough. But a perilous element of vagueness in the authors' programme is summed up in the word 'coastlands', and indeed *The Corrupting Sea* does not concern itself only with what can easily be called coastlands. Hinterlands and inland mountains are often, understandably, in the foreground. So we immediately recognize that there is a problem of delimitation, a problem accentuated by the fact that the human history of the Mediterranean in these 3,000 years was often intimately linked to power centres far away from the coastlands, in Mesopotamia, for example, or up the Nile.

Horden and Purcell declare their intention of establishing the 'unity and distinctiveness' of the ancient–medieval Mediterranean world. On a cultural plane, this is a hard question indeed, to which we shall return (Sections 3 and 6), offering in the end some limited assent but of a possibly unwelcome kind. On the ecological plane, matters seem rather simpler. The Mediterranean is, obviously, a construct, but it is a construct with something of a natural basis. The region is the historic home of *vitis vinifera* and *olea europaea*, and the exploitation of the vine and the olive-tree seems to provide both unity and distinctiveness. There is a unified climactic zone, and in addition relatively easy navigability: the famous obsidian of Melos was already being fetched to the mainland in the palaeolithic (eleventh millennium BC?), so it is believed;[7] deep-hulled sailing ships from Egypt sailed up the Levantine coast in the mid-third millennium,[8] and in the second millennium such ships began to cross the open sea, where the mariner could not see land—hence spasmodically increasing medium-distance and eventually

---

[6] *CS* 9.

[7] C. Broodbank, *An Island Archaeology of the Early Cyclades* (Cambridge, 2000), 110–11. For sea-borne carriage of obsidian in the Italian Mediterranean in the Neolithic see G. Camps and A. d'Anna, 'Recherches sur les navigations préhistoriques en Méditerranée occidentale', in *Navigation et gens de mer en Méditerranée de la préhistoire à nos jours* (Paris, 1980), 1–16: 5.

[8] Broodbank, 96 (the whole chapter is important).

long-distance exchange of commodities (and of course the exchange of cultural influences). The very uneven distribution of resources, especially metal resources, greatly encouraged a system of long-distance exchange. Much later, in the era of the Arab conquests, when to a superficial gaze the Mediterranean became more of a frontier than a unity and new non-maritime capitals became important, the natural basis at least remained much the same.

Quite how strong an ecological construction this is we shall consider in Section 3. And whether the Mediterranean world can really be said to have had a natural barrier to its east during antiquity is an awkward question. Given the quantity of interaction with Mesopotamia, with Arabia and with the Indian Ocean over the millennia, the answer may well be more 'no' than 'yes'. Horden and Purcell meanwhile maintain that there were 'intrinsically Mediterranean factors in the history of primary production';[9] we shall want to identify them and evaluate them.

Bloch once warned: 'l'unité de lieu n'est que désordre. Seul l'unité de problème fait centre'.[10] For a historian, the unity of the place can only be a preliminary. All sorts of interesting books have been written more or less about the Mediterranean and its coastlands as a place, but how often have they been history books? What we can imagine—and what it would have been difficult to imagine, say, seventy years ago—is a history of the Mediterranean world which would essentially be a history of the interaction of that environment and the human beings within it. Here we can return to the scholastic-sounding distinction between history *of* and history *in*. Horden and Purcell distinguish between their own subject and what is put forward in part 1 of the *The Mediterranean and the Mediterranean World* ('The Role of the Environment') by proclaiming their allegiance to 'microecologies' (due for some further definition), though they agree that this will bring in, in a subordinate way, 'political, social, economic, religious' history, which according to them is history *in*.[11]

---

[9] *CS* 176.
[10] In a review, *Annales d'histoire économique et sociale* 6 (1934), 81–5: 81.
[11] *CS* 2.

The Corrupting Sea differentiates itself from *The Mediterranean and the Mediterranean World* in several other ways too. The authors accuse their predecessor of 'a strong leaning towards environmental determinism'—as others had done before—,[12] but whether the defendant should be convicted is not wholly clear, as I think Horden and Purcell recognize. Braudel pleaded his innocence,[13] and the great synthesis, *Civilization and Capitalism*, lends him support. Like many economic and political historians before and since, Braudel struggled to establish the right causal balance between physical environment and human decision-making. He did not succeed, but at least his three rhythms of time are an exceptionally imaginative attempt to counter the problem. We can hardly blame *Annales* historians for seeking the long-term determinants of action, and it was they after all who gave *mentalités* an important role in history. Adopting the standard contemporary view that human beings and the environment act upon each other, Horden and Purcell claim to allow more room for the agency of humans,[14] but it is hard to see that there is much difference. When they discuss their four chosen microregions, they do not seem to diverge greatly from Braudel in this respect.[15]

[12] *CS* 36. And see 41–2. This is a little like accusing Aquinas of not knowing Latin.

[13] See for instance *MMW*, i. 267; but see also ii. 1244.

[14] See for instance A. Ruiz Rodriguez, M. Molines, and M. Castro López, 'Settlement and Continuity in the Territory of the Guadalquivir Valley (6th Century B.C.—1st Century A. D.)', in G. Barker and J. Lloyd (eds.), *Roman Landscapes: Archaeological Survey in the Mediterranean Region* (London, 1991), 29–36: 29.

[15] In the case of the Biqa valley, we have a brief reference to the settlement of Roman veterans (*CS* 58); in the case of southern Etruria, the absence of the human actors is still more marked because here at least Etruscans and Romans made a serious difference to the carrying capacity of the land by constructing and maintaining the drainage *cuniculi* (duly mentioned later, *CS* 247); Cyrenaica is handled a little differently, for we are told something about silphium production and about the invasion of the Hilali nomads in the eleventh century (pp. 65, 74); Melos, finally, presents especially difficult problems to an ancient environmental or economic historian, in spite of the ground-breaking study *An Island Polity* (C. Renfrew and J. M. Wagstaff (eds.), Cambridge, 1982), and though Horden and Purcell make as much as they can out of that book we do not see in *CS* much of the human influence on the island's ecology. The concept 'microregion' is plainly central to *CS*, but its meaning is not defined: is every inhabited Greek island a microregion, every river valley?

The line between human intervention (admissible, according to *The Corrupting Sea* as part of history *of*) and history *in* (inadmissible) is next-to-impossible to maintain. Think of a concrete example of a humanly generated ecological change— say Roman hydraulic engineering in the plain of the Po—and it seems obvious that the phenomenon cannot be discussed intelligently in isolation from its economic and its social and probably its political history. It is an important achievement of Horden and Purcell to have put the physical environment at the centre of their analysis, but we assume that it is not their ambition to be geologists or oceanographers.[16]

Would it, incidentally, be possible to write a satisfying history of pre-modern man's interaction with the environment in other more-or-less self-contained seas within the Mediterranean or nearby? Why not? There is certainly no shortage of environmentally interesting facts and theories about, say, the Aegean or the Tyrrhenian Seas. And now that a more strictly environmental history has come into being, there is no reason not to write about the history *of* any number of smaller stretches of water. Indeed, there is a terrific advantage: you can be thorough. The suspicion returns that the Mediterranean as a whole has a more powerful attraction as a subject partly for a reason that is only remotely related to environmental history: it has simply been the scene of several of the principal power conflicts of Western history, Greeks against Persians, Romans against Carthaginians (and everyone else), Christians against Muslims. Even Braudel found the contingent hard to resist, and in *The Mediterranean and the Mediterranean World* he of course provided a part 3 on events ('Events, Politics and People'), including a fifty-page chapter on the Battle of Lepanto (mainly about diplomacy, presumably reflecting the earliest phase of his research).

---

[16] Horden and Purcell write (464–5) that they have tried to show how their 'microecological approach can be brought into relation with the "textbook" ingredients of political, social, religious and economic narrative [sic]', but few readers, one suspects, will have noticed this. It can be assumed that they do not think that 'all analyses of culture and social relations dissolve into an all-embracing ecology' (R. Ellen's way of describing an error which environmental anthropology should avoid, *Environment, Subsistence and System: The Ecology of Small-scale Formations* (Cambridge, 1982), p. xi).

For years now scholars have been discovering Mediterraneans in other parts of the world. Later in this volume David Abulafia's paper, a notable tour de force, surveys this literature. It should warn us that fragmentation and diversity are to be expected in a region of such a size, whether it is the South China Sea or the Caribbean. The real Mediterranean region is not surprisingly rather variegated in some respects, but that should hardly earn it special historiographical respect ('La Toscana è...una regione fondata sulle diversità', says my guide-book, not blushing at the cliché). Connectedness—'connectivity' in the electronic patois of *The Corrupting Sea*—is a very different matter, and the factors that have brought it into being, or inhibited it, in any particular case, are a fascinating, we might say urgent, question.

Another thing the environmental historian cannot skimp on is time. *The Mediterranean and the Mediterranean World* constantly struggles to express the relationship between the author's three levels of time, in particular between those that have the clearest identity, the *longue durée* and the time of contingent events. *The Corrupting Sea* bravely assumes responsibility for a good long period—though in the end the Bronze Age is much neglected.[17] It requires quite unusual scholars to manage even two thousand years, let alone three or four.[18] Unfortunately it is hardly possible to argue about pre-modern ecology with any more restricted horizon.[19] By 2000 BC the vine and the olive-tree had already been domesticated. (From a prehistoric archaeologist's point of view, the proposed time-limits will still not seem very impressive: 20,000 years is a normal horizon, and the earliest firmly dated human settlement in Europe, Isernia La Pineta, used to be located *circa* 750,000 BP,[20] when rhinoceroses

[17] Even the Minoans and Mycenaeans receive much less attention than might have been expected, not to mention the other (majority) inhabitants of the coastal Mediterranean in the second millennium BC.

[18] My dream is that one day doctoral candidates in American history will be required to take an exam on the *longue durée*.

[19] Criticism of *The Corrupting Sea*, on a variety of grounds, for not embracing a longer period: L. Nixon, *Journal of Roman Studies* 92 (2002), 196.

[20] G. Barker, with R. Hodges and G. Clark, *A Mediterranean Valley: Landscape Archaeology and* Annales *History in the Biferno Valley* (Leicester, 1995), 85–7. I have been told that there is now a still earlier site.

and elephants roamed in Molise). Not that the matter is at all simple, since it was only in Mycenaean times that the western Mediterranean, or part of it, began to have contacts with the east, and well into the first millennium BC there were plenty of western areas which, like the Biferno Valley, seem to have been untouched by people or cultigens from further east.

It is admittedly a reasonable strategy for any historian of pre-industrial times to argue that little if anything changed from one century to the next, all the more so if the focus is on demography, subsistence agriculture, pastoralism, the environment—rather less so, fairly obviously, if the focus is on, say, exchange, migration, acculturation, *mentalités*, or power. But the case for immobility has to be argued—and the changes that did occur need to be measured. Immobility can be so relative. The changes in the Mediterranean economy and in Mediterranean navigation between 400 BC and 100 BC were slow if compared to those that have taken place in the last 300 years, but rapid indeed by the overall standards of the millennia we are now considering.

The sheer length of the time which a historian of the Mediterranean is more or less constrained to consider will probably be an enduring obstacle. Van De Mieroop's chapter in this book is particularly welcome because it makes us think about the kinds of people who inhabited the eastern shores of the Mediterranean *c.*1500 BC His paper may also help to inoculate us against historical generalizations about this region based on Italy and Greece, two fragments of a vastly larger whole.

The question about immobility and change in antiquity is, once the terms have been defined, fundamentally one of degree. But that puts us in a difficult, not to say desperate position, because almost nothing to do with the environmental history of the ancient Mediterranean world can be measured. 'All is mutability', say Horden and Purcell.[21] Fair enough; but they do not offer us any ways of measuring or evaluating ecological or economic change. Here is one of the frontiers of our subject: shall we ever, for example, be able to measure the pace of that controversial but probably crucial process, deforestation, in the

---

[21] *CS* 464.

ancient Mediterranean?[22] It was certainly not a process that advanced at an even steady speed in all periods.

Then there is the question of immobilism between the end of antiquity, or alternatively the Middle Ages, and the ethnographic present. The temptation to identify the past and the (pseudo-)present, or rather to find the former in the latter, has often proved irresistible. It is enshrined in at least one of the great works of twentieth-century literature—*Cristo si è fermato a Eboli*. There he (or she) is—*homo Mediterraneus*, patient, tough, fantastically superstitious, clannish, full of hatred for his/her neighbours, unchanging. Is it a true portrait, or merely a convincing one? Of course Carlo Levi never pretended, unlike some of those who have quoted him, that the ecology or economy of 'Gagliano' was really untouched by the outside world: indeed one of the chief sufferings of the Gagliano peasants consisted of a stupid new tax on goats thought up far way in Rome. And the most important social fact about Lucania at that time was quite massive male emigration to other continents.[23]

We shall return later (Section 6) to the more general question how ancient historians should use ethnographic evidence. *The Corrupting Sea* attempts to reach a balanced assessment of what should be done with Mediterranean ethnography: its authors raise the hope that 'a judicious combination of anthropology and nineteenth-century history might take us back to just before the unexampled tumult of "modernization" began'.[24] They appear to hope that by getting back to say AD 1800, they will virtually have arrived at their ancient/medieval period, a

[22] We shall return to this question later, but I must say at once that I lack the scientific knowledge needed to reach an independent conclusion.

[23] What is really extraordinary is to see this immobilism embraced by Braudel, *MMW*, ii. 1239, 1242–43—largely on the basis of Lawrence Durrell and a careless reading of Carlo Levi. For a much better reading of the latter see *CS* 468–70. R. S. Bagnall, *Reading Papyri, Writing Ancient History* (London, 1995), 70–1, comments well on the importance of resisting the temptation to see the contemporary Egyptian countryside as timeless and unchanging. M. Fotiadis, 'Modernity and the Past-still-present: Politics of Time in the Birth of Regional Archaeological Projects in Greece', *American Journal of Archaeology* 99 (1995), 59–78, is essential reading here, but his paper would have benefited from more attention to, precisely, politics.

[24] *CS* 466–74; the passage quoted: 471.

view they rightly qualify as 'optimistic'.[25] They quote with approval the following from Bloch:[26]

> But in the film which he [the historian] is examining, only the last picture remains quite clear. In order to reconstruct the faded features of the others, it behoves him first to unwind the spool in the opposite direction from that in which the pictures were taken.

But to be blunt, this has almost nothing to do with what historians did in Bloch's time or do now, certainly not ancient historians. And it does not represent Bloch's own method, though it stems from his much more limited belief that a French historian could learn a vast amount from the French landscape.[27]

What then are the essential elements in a history *of* the Mediterranean (to accept, for the sake of discussion, the validity of the *of/in* distinction)? The following could not properly be omitted, I suggest:

- *Some delimitation of the area in question.* While no canonical definition is possible, there really do have to be some boundaries, for each period; otherwise we shall seem neurotic (there will be no great difficulty, however, in treating peripheral zones as intermediate or transitional). Plato saw, as other Greeks had doubtless seen for many generations before him, that there was a single sea that stretched 'from the River Phasis [i.e. the land at the far eastern end of the Black Sea] to the Pillars of Heracles' (*Phaedo* 109ab), which admittedly leaves a great deal indeterminate. The question of delimitation can become in part a question about river valleys or basins, Danube, Rhine, Baetis, Mesopotamia—not to mention the great rivers that actually flow into the Mediterranean—but also about uplands. Where are the places substantially untouched by man's

---

[25] *CS* 474.

[26] *The Historian's Craft*, trans. P. Putnam (New York, 1953); original edn.: *Apologie pour l'histoire, ou Métier d'historien* (Paris, 1949), 46, quoted *CS* 461 and approved 484.

[27] Note the force of 'first' in the passage quoted. Earlier in the same paragraph Bloch wrote a counterbalancing sentence: 'Not, indeed, that there could be any question of imposing this forever-static picture, just as it is, at each stage of the journey upstream to the headwaters of the past.' But rewinding the film recurs in Braudel, *The Structures of Everyday Life* (*Civilization and Capitalism*, 1), trans. S. Reynolds (London 1979); original edn., *Les Structures du quotidien* (Paris, 1979), 294.

interaction with the Mediterranean environment? And can it really be true that Egypt is 'outside [the Mediterranean] ecologically'?[28] How indeed would we argue the case for that, one way or the other? The southern border of the Mediterranean world can be the line between 'the desert and the sown',[29] but that leaves the Nile valley inside. And in other directions the flora are not so cooperative: should we really, for instance, hang a great deal upon the northern limits of the cultivation of the olive tree? If we neglect this matter of delimitation, we may end up like a recent writer by denying that there was major deforestation under the Roman Empire (a question I do not claim to answer in this essay) on the grounds that almost all the evidence for it comes from such places as 'the southern Alps' and 'some northern parts of modern Greece'[30] which we might very well on other grounds consider to be part of the Mediterranean world (and in any case they were part of the Roman Empire).[31]

- *The natural history, articulated through periods.* It would do no harm to set out, for botanically and biologically ignorant historians such as many of us are, what is known to have been domesticated and growable in the whole area; pests, viruses, and bacteria are also highly relevant.[32] We should think not only of foodstuffs but of the three other physical necessities too, fuel, clothing, and shelter. Of course there has been a

[28] As claimed by *CS* 397. Not that the authors are consistent: ancient Alexandria is out, but medieval Cairo is in (the ancient Nile makes a brief appearance, 239; and see Map 21). See R. S. Bagnall's chapter later in this volume. B. D. Shaw, reviewing *CS* in *JRA* 14 (2001), observes (p. 444) that Egypt's 'whole ecology stands at odds with the authors' model of the Mediterranean'.

[29] Shaw 423.

[30] O. Rackham, 'Ecology and Pseudo-ecology: the Example of Ancient Greece', in J. Salmon and G. Shipley (eds.), *Human Landscapes in Classical Antiquity* (London, 1996), 16–43: 31. See further below, p. 35.

[31] Roman imperial history, it may be added, needs a quite different map, covering not the Mediterranean or that familiar area corresponding to the provinces as they were in the reign of Trajan, but a much wider area where the Roman Empire had economic connections, from Poland to Sri Lanka to Zanzibar.

[32] Rat studies have now been put on a new footing by M. McCormick, 'Rats, Communication, and Plague: Toward an Ecological History', *Journal of Interdisciplinary History* 34 (2003–4), 49–61.

tremendous amount of science on most of these subjects,[33] and a recent volume about Pompeii marks an important step forward.[34] It would be extraordinarily useful to have Frayn's *Subsistence Farming in Roman Italy* writ larger, on a Mediterranean-wide scale, with all the enrichment provided by modern palaeobotany and palaeozoology. It is so easy for historians to assume that things grew only where they grow now—hence the frequent adaptation of Braudel's map of the northern limits of olive cultivation, in spite of the evidence that, for fairly obvious reasons, it was cultivated further north in antiquity and the Middle Ages.[35] Closely related to all this is of course the question of water. One of the most important achievements of *The Corrupting Sea* is to formulate an approach to the history of water management and irrigation (with intriguing information about the Orontes), and together with other recent work, this book now begins to give us a clearer idea of ways in which water dictated the limits of ancient and medieval land use and urbanization.[36]

[33] Cf. *CS* 111–12, Grove and Rackham, *The Nature of Mediterranean Europe*, esp. chs. 4, 10, and 11. On the very neglected subject of fuel see S. Pignatti, 'Human Impact in the Vegetation of the Mediterranean Basin', in W. Holzner, M. J. A. Werger, and I. Ikusima (eds.), *Man's Impact on Vegetation* (The Hague, 1983), 151–61: 152–3, H. Forbes, 'The Uses of the Uncultivated Landscape in Modern Greece: A Pointer to the Value of Wilderness in Antiquity?', in Salmon and Shipley, *Human Landscapes*, 68–97: 84–8, W. Smith, 'Fuel for Thought', *Journal of Mediterranean Archaeology* 11 (1998), 191–205. Concerning textiles see especially E. J. W. Barber, *Prehistoric Textiles: The Development of Cloth in the Neolithic and Bronze Ages* (Princeton, 1991), and *CS* 352–63.

[34] W. F. Jashemski and F. G. Meyer (eds.), *The Natural History of Pompeii* (Cambridge, 2002); note especially Jashemski, Meyer, and M. Ricciardi, 'Plants' (pp. 80–180), and A. King, 'Mammals' (pp. 401–50).

[35] The only writer who seems to have noticed the unhistorical nature of Braudel's map is D. J. Mattingly, 'First Fruit? The Olive in the Roman World', in Salmon and Shipley, *Human Landscapes*, 213–53: 215–16, and even he misses the Italian aspect of the matter. For olive cultivation in eighth-century Lombardy see L. Schiaparelli (ed.), *Codice diplomatico longobardo* (Rome, 1929), documents 123, 167, 231, 234, 257 (and possibly others).

[36] See *CS* 237–57, 585–8 (but for their view of the role of the state see below, p. 37). For some striking recent contributions see J. P. Oleson, 'Water-lifting Devices at Herculaneum and Pompeii in the Context of Roman Technology', in N. de Haan and G. C. M. Jansen (eds.), *Cura aquarum in Campania* (*Bulletin Antieke Beschaving*, Suppl. 4) (Leiden, 1996),

● *What population burdens could this region carry*—in all the circumstances relevant at particular times, such as degrees of afforestation and marshiness, available crops and methods of land management, likely animal populations, availability of meat and fish, known methods of food distribution, food storage and food preparation? This too is an extremely complex question, and one of the most pressing tasks awaiting the environmental historian of the ancient Mediterranean. It has proved difficult to establish prehistoric population sizes on the basis of carrying capacity, and such attempts need to take account of the 'welfare' standards of the population in question.[37] Horden and Purcell tell us that estimates of carrying capacity 'are clearly impossible',[38] but their own Chapter VI helps to lay some of the foundation for an answer.[39]

The underlying questions concern Malthus's positive checks, and how ancient populations reacted to them, and further whether there were 'preventive' checks, and beyond that again whether there was any possibility in antiquity of sustained economic growth. A merely environmental history cannot be expected to answer such questions in full, but it can be expected

67–77, P. Kessener, 'The Aqueduct at Aspendos and its Inverted Siphon', *JRA* 13 (2000), 104–32, D. Amit, J. Patrich, and Y. Hirschfeld (eds.), *The Aqueducts of Israel* (*JRA*, Suppl. 46) (Portsmouth, RI, 2002). Once again we need long-term chronology: the Bronze Age can be seen as the time when large-scale water management began in the Mediterranean region—see G. Argoud L. I. Marangou, V. Panagiotopoulos, and C. Villain-Gandossi (eds.), *L'Eau et les hommes en Méditerranée et en Mer Noire dans l'antiquité* (Athens, 1992).

[37] T. Bayliss-Smith, 'Prehistoric Agriculture in the New Guinea Highlands: Problems in Defining the Altitudinal Limits to Growth', in J. L. Bintliff, D. A. Davidson, and E. G. Grant (eds.), *Conceptual Issues in Environmental Archaeology* (Edinburgh, 1988), 153–60: 153.

[38] *CS* 47. But on the carrying capacity of islands cf. *CS* 381. Renfrew and Wagstaff (eds.), *Island Polity*, 145, credibly set the maximum population of Melos in classical times at about 5,000, 'a ceiling some 40–60% above the levels likely to have been attained in practice'. On the difficulties of calculating carrying capacity see Ellen, *Environment*, 41–6, R. Sallares, *The Ecology of the Ancient Greek World* (London, 1991), 73–7, Grove and Rackham, *The Nature of Mediterranean Europe*, 70–1.

[39] It is difficult to see how they will be able to avoid conclusions of some sort, however tentative, when in volume 2 they finally reach the subject of demography.

to link itself to such other areas of enquiry as the history of migration and colonization—these to be seen not in the classic fashion as the filling of empty spaces but as the *occupation* of space.

• *What did the inhabitants of the ancient Mediterranean region think was the identity of the part of the world in which they lived?* If human intervention is to have a role in our history of the Mediterranean, we need to know how the coastland inhabitants (at least) regarded it. How they imagined its size, shape and other characteristics, and even how they named it, is of significance.[40] To say that in the Semitic languages the Mediterranean was 'quite widely' called 'the Great Sea' by 1000 BC, and to imply that this was later the standard Greek term[41] is scarcely to say enough. Some Akkadian documents use such an expression,[42] but it is not likely that they refer to the whole Mediterranean. It is hard to imagine that when the Phoenicians and Greeks were travelling the length of the Mediterranean in the ninth and eighth centuries BC they did not invent names for it. Hecataeus, as it happens, is the first Greek known to have called it 'the great sea' (*FGrH* 1 F26), and he meant something like the whole of it. More interesting, perhaps, is the expression 'our sea', *he hemetera thalassa* (Hecataeus F302c), and the variant *he kath'hemas thalassa*, 'the sea in our part of the world' (Hecataeus F18b).[43] Whatever it was called, it was the sea around which 'we' (an undefined 'we') live, like ants or frogs around a pond, according to the Platonic Socrates (*Phaedo* 109b). Had all Greeks domesticated the Mediterranean Sea to this extent? As for the Mediterranean *world*, however, neither Greek nor Latin had a special expression for

---

[40] The article of O. A. W. Dilke, 'Graeco-Roman Perception of the Mediterranean', in M. Galley and L. Ladjimi Sebai (eds.), *L'Homme méditerranéen et la mer* (Tunis, 1985), 53–9, does not live up to its title. On the other hand V. Burr, *Nostrum Mare. Ursprung und Geschichte der Namen des Mittelmeeres und seiner Teilmeere im Altertum* (Stuttgart, 1932), is still very useful. He reviewed the ancient names for no fewer than 27 component parts of the Mediterranean as well as for the sea itself.

[41] *CS* 10–11.

[42] Burr, *Nostrum Mare*, 89 n. 50.

[43] There is no need to discuss here whether these expressions were really as old as Hecataeus. 'Mediterraneum Mare' first appears as a name of the sea in Isid. *Etym.* 13. 16. 1.

it: Greeks could call it the *oikoumene* but they also used that word for the entire world, which of course they knew to be much larger.[44]

● *Did those who lived around the ancient Mediterranean regard it—or their own part of it—as a potential link or a barrier or both at once?* What kinds of people were so drawn to the sea that they overcame the fear of pirates and lived by the shore? Who knew the risks and opportunities? Was there a small-islander *mentalité*? (The questions quickly proliferate). And let our answers not be too Greek; ancient near-eastern texts would need to be constantly in our hands. And what did the illiterate ship-hand think, or the peasant who might or might not migrate, or that favourite of Braudel, also of Horden and Purcell, the coastal trader, the *caboteur*? These are not wholly impossible questions: after all, we know that Phoenicians and Greeks emigrated in considerable numbers, while others did not, and it is not likely to have been simply a matter of who possessed the necessary maritime technology.

For many Greeks, plainly, the sea was at the centre and proximity to the sea was an essential condition of economic life and of civilized life: you knew that you had reached a different world when on your travels you met 'men who do not know the sea, and do not eat salt with their food' (*Od.* 11.122–3). Hesiod turns naturally, though diffidently, from the land to the sea (*Works and Days* 618–94). But how much these attitudes were representative, or duplicated by other Mediterranean populations, is still a subject for investigation.

A phenomenon of the ancient world which expanded and contracted was the long-distance transport of basic commodities such as the Mediterranean triad and metal ores. All concerned had come to regard the practical problems of long-distance commodity transport as manageable ones. We seem to lack any systematic account of how this came about.

● *Exploiting the natural environment versus making sensible use of it.* Facing the question whether the classical Greeks 'had

---

[44] Even the clear-headed Polybius is inconsistent: in i. 1–4, ii. 37, iii. 3, etc, the term means something like the Mediterranean world, but in iii. 1, iii. 58, viii. 2, etc., it refers to the wider world, and in iii. 37 and elsewhere the Mediterranean world is *he kath'hemas oikoumene*. For the view that civilization centres around the Mediterranean see Strabo ii. 122.

an attitude' towards ecology, Rackham understandably replied 'I do not know',[45] and proceeded to point out the methodological difficulties. For the Roman period, there is at least a competent study by P. Fedeli of ancient notions of what damaged nature.[46] But the main question to start from, I suppose, is how people treated the natural world when the available technology provided them with choices, or seemed to do so. It is hardly surprising that the inhabitants of the Roman Empire cut down immense numbers of trees (the effects are hotly disputed), but it *is* surprising to a certain degree that the government of Tiberius once planned to make the River Chiana flow northwards into the Arno instead of southwards into the Tiber, in order to lessen flooding in the capital (Tac. *Ann.* i. 79, etc.). Ambitious hydraulic engineering, often in the service of a city, is a constant theme.

● *Which elements in the natural environment brought into being systems of plunder and exchange over distance?* And what happened when such systems weakened, when piracy was reduced (if it ever really was for any extended period),[47] and when long-distance trade slowed down? Bronze-Age trade in the Mediterranean has been very carefully studied in recent decades,[48] but we may need some more theorizing about its diachronic development. What led Greek mainlanders to Melos and its obsidian in the first place? We may suppose that Bronze-Age men initiated efforts to obtain specific materials such as copper, tin, and obsidian from relatively far-off. Later on, pirates and merchants, largely indistinguishable from each other, began to gather merchandise, including human beings, for opportunistic exchange.[49] Later still, cities began to seek

[45] Rackham, 'Ecology', 33.

[46] P. Fedeli, *La natura violata: ecologia e mondo romano* (Palermo, 1990).

[47] D. C. Braund, 'Piracy under the Principate and the Ideology of Imperial Eradication', in J. Rich and G. Shipley (eds.), *War and Society in the Roman World* (London, 1993), 195–212, argues cogently that even under the Roman emperors piracy went on largely unabated.

[48] See for instance N. H. Gale (ed.), *Bronze Age Trade in the Mediterranean* (Jonsered, 1991), E. H. Cline, *Sailing the Wine-dark Sea: International Trade and the Late Bronze Age Aegean* (Oxford, 1994).

[49] Except that, it now appears, they sometimes covered long distances to obtain materials that were available close to home, such as iron in Euboea (the

more systematically for agricultural surpluses which they might import—thus we need to divide the Mediterranean environment into places capable and incapable of producing such surpluses, and once again we come back to demography. The places from which such agricultural surpluses might be obtained would normally not be very distant,[50] which underlines the extraordinary nature of the Roman power which could import grain in huge quantities from Egypt to the capital. Innumerable facts underline the importance of water-borne transport: in Bronze-Age Italy, for instance, that was how metals made their journeys, by river or along the coast.[51] Since we still do not have a first-rate map of the Mediterranean mineral resources that were exploitable in antiquity,[52] we have quite a way to go before we understand the effects of their distribution.

That of course leaves us with some fifteen hundred years of ancient history still to go, including the high period of Mediterranean exchange dating from the second century BC to the

'coals to Newcastle' problem): see D. W. Tandy, *Warriors into Traders: The Power of the Market in Early Greece* (Berkeley and Los Angeles, 1997), esp. p. 64, and D. Ridgway, 'Final Remarks: Italy and Cyprus', in L. Bonfante and V. Karagheorgis (eds.), *Italy and Cyprus in Antiquity: 1500–450 B. C.* (Nicosia, 2001), 379–93: 380.

[50] Cf. the map in M. E. Aubet, *The Phoenicians and the West*, 2nd edn., (Cambridge, 2001), 124, showing the 'Main products of exchange in Tyrian trade in Ezekiel'.

[51] Barker, *Mediterranean Valley*, 152.

[52] The best one I know of even now is provided by M. Lombard, *Les Métaux dans l'ancien monde du Ve au XIe siècle* (Paris and The Hague, 1974), 10–11 (with other useful maps too). Cf. also R. Shepherd, *Ancient Mining* (London and New York, 1993). The kind of work we need more of is represented by N. H. Gale, Z. A. Stos-Gale, and T. R. Gilmore, 'Alloy Types and Copper Sources of Anatolian Copper Alloy Artifacts', *Anatolian Studies* 35 (1985), 143–73; Z. A. Stos-Gale and N. H. Gale, 'New Light on the Provenence of the Copper Oxhide Ingots Found on Sardinia', in *Sardinia in the Mediterranean: Studies in Sardinian Archaeology Presented to Miriam S. Balmuth* (Sheffield, 1992), 317–37, etc. (the full bibliography is too long to give here). For a useful overview see A. B. Knapp, 'Ethnicity, Entrepreneurship, and Exchange: Mediterranean Inter-island Relations in the Late Bronze Age', *Annual of the British School at Athens* 85 (1990), 115–53: 129–41. For sources of tin see C. F. E. Pare, 'Bronze and the Bronze Age', in Pare (ed.), *Metals Make the World Go Round* (Oxford, 2000), 1–38: 25.

second or third century AD. Horden and Purcell have many trenchant things to say about ancient trade—including a vigorous critique of the view Hopkins baptized as 'static minimalism'—,[53] but there is much more to say, even now, especially about intensification and decline.

• *The technical means developed by all the peoples in the region to deal with the nuts and bolts of all this connectedness.* We should include here nautical technology,[54] the diffusion of information,[55] and development and spread of the skills, for instance in textile production and in mining, which the Bronze- and Iron-Age Mediterranean region required. Further down the road, but outside the realm of environmental history, we will come to the social changes that followed from adapting to such forms of connectedness as migration, external markets, and the importation of basic commodities.

• *How much economic interdependence was there among Mediterranean (coastal and hinterland) populations at any given period?* Finley claimed in one of his last works that the ancient economy was not 'integrated', even under the Roman Empire, which is both true and untrue.[56] It would be more fertile to ask about interdependence, since lack of 'integration' may mainly have resulted from the relative slowness of communications. Interdependence, like carrying capacity, needs to be seen in the context of perceived needs. We should consider here not simply the widespread dependence on imported commodities, but the widespread use, especially by Phoenicians, Greeks and

[53] The view, that is, that economic life experienced minimal development from one period of antiquity to another, never provided more than a bare subsistence livelihood to the vast majority of the population, and never witnessed any but the simplest economic institutions. Against static minimalist views of ancient Mediterranean commerce: *CS* 146–52. Not that I can agree with the authors' characterization of 'existing approaches to Mediterranean trade' (p. 144).

[54] For basic bibliography see *CS* 565.

[55] See among other recent publications J. Andreau and C. Virlouvet (eds.), *L'Information et la mer dans le monde antique* (Rome, 2002).

[56] M. I. Finley, *The Ancient Economy*, 2nd edn. (Berkeley and Los Angeles, 1985), 177–9; for some discussion see W. V. Harris, 'Between Archaic and Modern: Some Current Problems in the History of the Roman Economy', in Harris (ed.), *The Inscribed Economy* (*JRA*, Suppl. 6) (Ann Arbor, 1993), 11–29: 18–20.

Romans, of colonization for the maintenance of population equilibrium.[57]

● *To what extent was there ever a cultural unity?* It is evident that scholars set the bar at very different heights. For some the supposedly Mediterranean-wide and millennia-long preoccupation with honour has seemed sufficient; others, taking the one period of ancient history in which a single power imposed itself on the whole Mediterranean, the Roman Empire, have argued that the Romans did *not* succeed in producing cultural unity, even of a bi-cultural Graeco-Roman kind. That is a vital question in Roman history (that is to say in history *in* the Mediterranean), but we should probably be content if we could show that there were any widely shared and characteristic features. We shall return to honour in the following section. According to P. Brown, on the other hand, the centrepiece of the ancient Mediterranean was the city,[58] in the Greek sense of course. This is a traditional and reasonable point of view—which *The Corrupting Sea* has now in effect attempted to demolish (though not without equivocations); more will be said about this too in the next section. The question for us in this context should rather be whether the Mediterranean environment, and the immediate human reaction to it, brought about any noteworthy commonalities of culture. And if there were such features, how distinctive were they?

3. UNITY?

A brief essay such as this cannot discuss any of the above questions in full, but in order to deal with the issue of Mediterraneanism (Section 6), I must at least discuss unity. For the

---

[57] The long debate about the functions and nature of ancient colonization continues of course. See, for instance, G. Cawkwell, 'Early Colonisation', *Classical Quarterly* 42 (1992), 289–303; G. R. Tsetskhladze and F. De Angelis (eds.), *The Archaeology of Greek Colonization: Essays Dedicated to Sir John Boardman* (Oxford, 1994); Aubet, *The Phoenicians*, 76–9. A convincing model now has to include early Greek migration and such phenomena as the early Euboean settlers in Chalkidike (cf. A. M. Snodgrass, 'The Euboeans in Macedonia: A new Precedent for Westward Expansion', in *Apoikia. Scritti in onore di Giorgio Buchner* (= *Annali di archeologia e storia antica* NS 1, Naples, 1994), 87–93).

[58] P. Brown, *Society and the Holy in Late Antiquity* (London, 1982), 169.

claim that the Mediterranean region possessed or possesses unity is linked, though not in a neat logical fashion, to the notion that it is distinctive. The focus here will continue to be on antiquity. In a weak sense at least, there was always of course a degree of unity. There is a climactic zone after all, with a partial natural boundary to the east in the shape of the Syrian-Arabian desert, as well as boundaries to the south and north (which is not to say that these boundaries are easy to define, or that the internal differences, in precipitation for example, are negligible[59]). This is an area of relatively moderate temperatures, except at high altitudes, an area in which, although aridity is an extremely common problem,[60] there is usually enough water to support agriculture and towns. In a similar climate, and with similar fauna and flora, the means of survival inevitably demonstrate similarities and continuities. And ever since men learned to cover considerable distances in boats, in the Bronze Age, a network of maritime connections covering all or most of the bodies of water between Phoenicia and Cadiz has virtually always existed.

Many scholars have wanted to discover a Mediterranean ecology with characteristics more specific than these. The classic zone of the vine and more particularly of the olive tree have long served as rough approximations; the southwards boundary can be found in the northern limit of the palm tree growing in compact *palmeraies*.[61] So far so good, and no one will want to underestimate the impact of wine and olive oil on ancient Mediterranean lives or landscapes. Braudel, as is well known, argued for a much wider concept of the Mediterranean, more

[59] On this point cf. J. D. Hughes, *Pan's Travail: Environmental Problems of the Ancient Greeks and Romans* (Baltimore, 1994), 10. For Braudel's view of the climactic and ecological unity see *MMW*, i. 234–48.

[60] The point is made repeatedly: see ibid. 238–39; J. Davis, *People of the Mediterranean: an Essay in Comparative Social Anthropology* (London, 1977), 41, etc. Other places in the world have Mediterranean climates—significant parts of Australia, California, Chile, South Africa; for some useful comparisons see F. di Castri, 'An Ecological Overview of the Five Regions with a Mediterranean Climate', in R. H. Groves and F. di Castri (eds.), *Biogeography of Mediterranean Invasions* (Cambridge, 1991), 3–16.

[61] Cf. Braudel, *MMW*, i. 168.

historical than ecological, though he took account of three physical frontier zones, the Sahara, 'Europe', and the Atlantic (with the Middle East apparently subsumed under the Sahara). But it is symptomatic that even Braudel found it practically impossible to define his 'greater Mediterranean': 'we should imagine a hundred frontiers, not one, some political, some economic, and some cultural'; according to this logic, Goethe was in the Mediterranean even before he left Frankfurt.[62]

Wine and olive oil will in fact serve us quite well as defining features of the ancient Mediterranean, in spite of the Mesopotamian anomaly. Consumption may be a more useful indicator than production, and thanks to the archaeology of amphorae we can produce at least an approximate map of olive oil consumption in the period of the Roman Empire.[63] Archaeobotany can now present a much more elaborate picture of all the domesticated plants known in this general region in ancient times,[64] as well as describing the spread of vine and olive tree cultivation from east to west. Two questions seem to need answering now: can we determine more precisely what proportion of the caloric needs of the Mediterranean population was met by wine and by olive oil? And which structural features of ancient societies and economies can be attributed to the logic of vine and olive tree cultivation? Horden and Purcell say that we should not see trade in olive oil as 'a harbinger of a commercial economy',[65] but it is most unclear why not.

Another much-studied feature is transhumant pastoralism, widespread virtually throughout Mediterranean lands over several millennia. Like the vendetta, it appeals to scholars through

---

[62] Ibid. 170. Horden and Purcell attempt to evade the problem of defining their Mediterranean by relying on the concept of microregions (*CS* 80), but this is a distraction or an escape mechanism rather than a solution.

[63] See D. P. S. Peacock and D. F. Williams, *Amphorae and the Roman Economy* (London, 1986), esp. figs. 8, 21, 82, 102, 105, 108. For production, the best guide is M.-C. Amouretti and J.-P. Brun (eds.), *La Production du vin et de l'huile en Méditerranée* (*Bulletin de Correspondance Hellénique*, Suppl. 26) (Athens and Paris, 1993). See further *CS* 209–20.

[64] See D. Zohary and M. Hopf, *Domestication of Plants in the Old World: The Origin and Spread of Cultivated Plants in West Asia, Europe and the Nile Valley* (note the choice of area) 3rd edn. (Oxford, 2000); and cf. *CS* 210, 262.

[65] *CS* 213. *CS* 211–20 discusses the implications of widespread vine and olive cultivation.

being so obviously deep-rooted in time, and it is often said to be distinctively Mediterranean.[66] Which may suggest that a practice can be distinctive but at the same time not defining. What Horden and Purcell insist on as the peculiarity of Mediterranean food production is that it was especially full of risk.[67] The risks are clear enough: the difficulty is that risk is also the chronic condition of pre-modern farmers (and not only pre-modern ones), in plenty of other places, such as, purely for the sake of example, China and tropical Africa.[68] 'It is the frequency of change from year to year, in both production and distribution, that makes Mediterranean history distinctive', it is said.[69] That would be hard to establish. 'In France, there were sixteen nation-wide famines between 1700 and 1789'.[70]

A stronger meaning of Mediterranean ecological unity depends on whether local economies are solidly *connected* to the wider Mediterranean (and disconnected from other parts of the world?). If a great many people who lived on the Mediterranean's shores at any particular time were autarkic fishermen or pastoralists or farmers, then the Mediterranean was not in this sense a unit. And in that case we should rate the Mediterranean less important at the date in question than other realms of connectedness such as the micro-microregion (if such a phrase is allowed) or a great river valley. But what in any case constitutes a connection? Not only *cabotage*, long-range trade, piracy and migration, but many other forms of human and also non-human movement, including the spread of plants and of diseases.

---

[66] See for instance P. Garnsey, *Famine and Food Supply in the Graeco-Roman World* (Cambridge, 1988), 201.

[67] *CS* 178, 287. The notion that it was environmental risk that led ancient Mediterranean communities to communicate with one another seems particularly unsupported.

[68] In a survey of world pastoralism, the only region where risk management, rather than profit maximization, is said to be the aim is as it happens the Andes: D. L. Brownan, 'High Altitude Camelid Pastoralism of the Andes', in J. G. Galaty and D. L. Johnson (eds.), *The World of Pastoralism: Herding Systems in Comparative Perspective* (New York and London, 1990), 323–52: 325–6.

[69] *CS* 74.

[70] M. J. Daunton, *Progress and Poverty: An Economic and Social History of Britain 1700–1850* (Oxford, 1995), 56.

It can also be argued that, for a large part of the three millennia we have under consideration, the people of the Mediterranean were very effectively linked by warfare, for the people they fought against, at least until the moment when Caesar invaded Gallia Comata, were very often Mediterranean too (no need to point out all the exceptions). And all this had quite a series of effects on the environment, even if we leave out of the account the subsequent effects of empire. The records of ancient Mediterranean warfare suggest that it was usually carried out with as much destruction of the enemy's natural resources as could possibly be achieved with the technology available[71]—with the important proviso that some conquerors (but how many?) may have taken thought for the future productivity of their putative future subjects. A change of political masters might have little impact on ordinary life, but prolonged periods of warfare could destroy fixed capital, diminish trade and reduce agricultural productivity—some of the main events in the history of the late-antique economy.[72]

One of the central theses of *The Corrupting Sea* is that the 'connectivity' was always there to some degree even when the Mediterranean world seems to have been most fragmented.[73] That is undoubtedly true to some extent, but the important question must be how far the potential was realized from one age to another: this is the essence of a historical account of Mediterranean connections. We want to know how and why the connections strengthened in the second millennium BC, supplementing those that already existed in the Middle East, and strengthened much more from the time of the expansion and colonization by the Phoenicians and Greeks that began in the ninth and eighth centuries. These questions lead inevitably

[71] No need here to refer to the large literature on this topic. According to W. G. Sebald, 'the innermost principle of every war ... is to aim for as wholesale an annihilation of the enemy with his dwellings, his history, and his natural environment as can possibly be achieved' (*On the Natural History of Destruction*, trans. A. Bell (London and New York, 2003; original edn. *Luftkrieg und Literatur*, Munich, 1999), 19). I imagine that some would disagree, but they are more likely to be lawyers or classicists than historians.

[72] See M. McCormick, *Origins of the European Economy* (Cambridge, 2001), 25–119.

[73] *CS* esp. 160–72.

to the relative importance or otherwise of other, non-Mediterranean connections. Consider, for instance, how the use of bronze is now thought to have spread across Europe from the Middle East: to judge from a recent study by C. F. E. Pare (Map 2), the Mediterranean was not the sole or even a crucial vector.[74]

In the period of the Twelfth Dynasty (1991–1786 BC), though Egyptian ships could have reached the Aegean, they seem not to have done so; during the Eighteenth Dynasty (1575–1308), on the other hand,—or perhaps during the period of the Hyksos in the seventeenth century BC—the two areas were in contact.[75] In the second millennium BC the western half of the Mediterranean was mostly untouched by the peoples of its eastern half until Mycenaeans reached South Italy, Sicily, and Sardinia—a by now very familiar story.[76] When the network of connections grew stronger, in the age of colonization, it of course affected the western Mediterranean environment profoundly, not only by means of vines and olive trees, but through intensified mineral extraction, urbanization, hydraulic engineering, and in other ways too. How these connections came into being, and how they weakened in late antiquity, are much-studied problems, hardly to be eliminated by the thought that they were *always* there potentially. It was especially disappointing that *The Corrupting Sea* did not really address the evidence, simply enormous in extent, for a prolonged period of late-antique and early medieval economic decline, except to say in effect that it is a historiographical commonplace (in part traceable back to Ibn Khaldun); not all historical commonplaces are false,[77] and much of the evidence is in any case material.

[74] Pare, 'Bronze and the Bronze Age', in Pare (ed.), *Metals*.

[75] For the first two dates see D. O'Connor, 'Egypt and Greece: The Bronze Age Evidence', in M. R. Lefkowitz and G. M. Rogers (eds.), *Black Athena Revisited* (Chapel Hill, 1996), 49–61: 54, 55. For the other chronology see Cline, *Sailing the Wine-dark Sea*, 5–8.

[76] See among others D. Ridgway, 'The First Western Greeks and their Neighbours, 1935–1985', in J.-P. Descoeudres (ed.), *Greek Colonists and Native Populations* (Canberra and Oxford, 1990), 61–72; K. Kilian, 'Mycenaean Colonization: Norm and Variety', ibid. 445–67; O. Dickinson, *The Aegean Bronze Age* (Cambridge, 1994), 249–50.

[77] Much of the evidence which an economic historian would adduce to show that economic connections tended to decline between AD 200 and 700 is mentioned by McCormick, *Origins*. Ibn Khaldun: *CS* 154. This is a huge

But for many scholars Mediterranean unity has meant much more than all this: it has meant primarily or indeed exclusively *cultural* unity. And thereby hangs a many-sided dispute which has flickered on for decades. My concern here is limited to ancient history and once again to the methodological question as to how one might establish the existence of a cultural unity in the ancient Mediterranean. It is not enough any more to write about 'the basic homogeneity of Mediterranean civilization'.[78] I will make five observations (and later allow the discussion to spill over into Section 6 below):

• There is no longer any point in discovering that ancient Mediterranean people shared some particular social-psychological characteristic, such as an intense devotion to honour (in some sense or other of that long-suffering word) or to female chastity (in some sense or other), *unless* you can make at least a plausible case that the rest of humanity has usually been less interested. Herzfeld and De Pina-Cabral demonstrated years ago that the old favourite honour was a very opaque lens through which to inspect the twentieth-century Mediterranean world.[79] That may also be true, in spite of the undoubted importance of honour for many Greeks and Romans, for the region's ancient history and for the *longue durée*: the question is

topic: my objection is that *CS* has not found an acceptable methodology for settling the truly outstanding issues.

[78] Brown, *Society*, 168, admittedly with the important proviso 'deep into the early Middle Ages' (the passage is quoted with approval in *CS* 33). Brown was emphasizing another point, the supposed continuity from antiquity to the Middle Ages. What he found most characteristic of the Mediterranean was urban civilization (see below). The deep desire some scholars feel to assert the cultural unity of the (present) Mediterranean can be observed in F. H. Stewart, *Honor* (Chicago and London, 1994), 75, who, although he professes not to believe in Mediterranean unity, asserts that 'it is undoubtedly true the peoples of southern Europe, and especially the rural peoples, resemble in some ways those of the Levant and North Africa more than they do those of northern Europe', and then admits that he cannot say in which ways!

[79] Which is obviously not to deny that honour *in a particular sense* could be extremely important. The crucial contributions here are M. Herzfeld, 'Honour and Shame: Problems in the Comparative Analysis of Moral Systems', *Man* 15 (1980), 339–51, and J. De Pina-Cabral, 'The Mediterranean'. D. Gilmore's response to the latter, 'On Mediterraneist Studies', *Current Anthropology* 31 (1990), 395–6, is insubstantial.

familiar but still needs re-examining.[80] Dover caustically wrote that as far as honour and shame are concerned, 'I find very little in a Mediterranean village which was not already familiar to me from a London suburb'.[81] What is honour in any case? Is it exclusively the property of men of standing? Does it primarily concern war? Or sexual codes? Is it mainly a feature of face-to-face societies? And so on.[82] How can we decide how much importance it possesses in any given society? Obviously not without making comparisons.

• A historical work cannot legitimately address this question of the cultural unity of the Mediterranean on the level of the ethnographic present, recent writers notwithstanding.[83] The methodology concerned is wholly inadmissible: we cannot extrapolate the ancient Mediterranean from the ethnographic Mediterranean (the modern Mediterranean is yet a third phenomenon). All suggestions of cultural continuity between the ancient and the recent Mediterranean are to be regarded with

[80] For the Greeks see H. Lloyd-Jones, 'Ehre und Schande in der griechischen Kultur', *Antike und Abendland* 33 (1987), 1–28, repr. in English in *Greek Comedy, Hellenistic Literature, Greek Religion, and Miscellanea* (Oxford, 1990), 253–80; for Rome J. E. Lendon, *Empire of Honour: the Art of Government in the Roman World* (Oxford, 1997) (who sees, p. 32 n. 5, that his evidence concerns people of high status). But neither account has the necessary comparative dimension. I return to this matter in the next section.

[81] Reviewing D. Cohen, *Law, Sexuality and Society*, in *Gnomon* 65 (1993), 659. A similar point is made by Stewart, *Honor*, 76–7.

[82] For the enormous multiplicity of meanings cf., in addition to the works cited in n. 79, Davis, *People of the Mediterranean*, 77 ('it is derived from the performance of certain roles, usually domestic ones'), 89–101 (supporting a materialist view); D. D. Gilmore, 'Introduction: The Shame of Dishonor', in D. D. Gilmore (ed.), *Honor and Shame and the Unity of the Mediterranean* (Washington, 1987), 2–21: 3–4 (what is distinctive about the Mediterranean variant of honour is 'its relationship to sexuality and gender distinctions', and the supposed fact that 'in the Mediterranean world women are often non-productive materially' (!)); P. Sant Cassia, 'Authors in Search of a Character: Personhood, Agency and Identity in the Mediterranean', *Journal of Mediterranean Studies* 1 (1991), 1–17: 8 (anthropologists mean a type of 'touchy individualism, of self-regard, and a concern with one's reputation'); Stewart, *Honor*, esp. 29–47 (above all, honour is a right, p. 29).

[83] *CS* 522–3. They conclude that 'honour and shame are indeed deeply held values across the region' (p. 523), without clarifying either terms or tense. A similar lack of attention to tense can be seen in Sant Cassia, 'Authors', 7 ('culture contact was significant' (is, has been?)); Shaw, 451–2.

the greatest suspicion; *The Corrupting Sea* vividly summarizes the many types of disruption that throughout their period (and since, it may be added) disturbed rural life, from invasions of settlers to the manipulations of the powerful.[84]

One of the most lucid and persuasive ancient historians who have made use of Mediterranean anthropology in recent times has been David Cohen. The crucial point in his theoretical argument is the *faute-de-mieux* gambit (no one has found a better model than the ethnographic Mediterranean)[85]—which comes close to circularity. What we need is what Cohen in fact attempts to provide in his later work, a much wider ethnography which can be applied to specific historical problems (see below, Section 6).

● If we are going to engage in the comparative history of Mediterranean or other cultures, we should pay more attention to difficulties of translation and to linguistic nuances, concerning honour among other subjects.[86] Translation problems can be quite fundamental.[87] An ethnography of Mediterranean honour that failed to analyse the vocabulary of the subject in Arabic would have little value.[88] The vocabulary of honour in

[84] *CS* 275–7. The authors' belief in 'mutability' was referred to earlier. Their practice, however, verges on the inconsistent: they often 'turn to the recent past for illumination of remoter periods' (*CS* 465, with cross-references). They claim to have used Mediterranean anthropology 'selectively' (ibid.), and they can at the very least be credited with having dedicated two lengthy chapters to discussing the issue (XI and XII).

[85] *Law, Sexuality, and Society in Classical Athens* (Cambridge, 1991), 38–41. It must be added at once that Cohen was concerned with a specific set of historical problems which he in my view succeeded in illuminating brilliantly. He also maintains that his model is immune to Herzfeldian objections because it is based on many different Mediterranean societies; but that is simply a technical improvement. Later, Cohen seems to have modified his approach (below, p. 40).

[86] Cf. J. A. Pitt-Rivers, 'Honour', *Proceedings of the British Academy* 94 (1997), 229–51.

[87] As in the cross-cultural study of the emotions: W. V. Harris, *Restraining Rage: the Ideology of Anger Control in Classical Antiquity* (Cambridge, Mass., 2002), 34–6.

[88] On *sharaf* and other concepts in a particular (and atypical) population see still A. Abou-Zeid, 'Honour and Shame among the Bedouins of Egypt', in J. G. Peristiany (ed.), *Honour and Shame: The Values of a Mediterranean Society* (London, 1966), 243–59.

Hellenistic and Roman–imperial Greek still needs attention, the Latin words even more;[89] and once again let us not make the Mediterranean too Graeco-Roman.

• Can we legitimately say that ancient Mediterranean culture was urban? This has been widely assumed, and the doctrine has been the foundation for whole programmes of research.[90] Horden and Purcell have now contested the notion and presented an interesting alternative way of looking at patterns of Mediterranean settlement. But their doctrine seems to have fallen on somewhat stony ground,[91] and we shall re-consider the issue (though all too briefly) in the following section.

• Nothing like cultural unity in more general terms was ever reached in the coastlands of the ancient Mediterranean prior to the Roman conquests, that is obvious, but it remains a central and open question of Roman history how much the populations of these territories, and not just their elites, shared social forms, productive technology, languages, artistic forms, religious practices and beliefs, and many other cultural features. Horden and Purcell claim that such cultural unity as there was lasted into the Middle Ages;[92] be that as it may, the study of cultural unity has to be the study of its formation and disintegration.

4. 'RURALIZING' ANCIENT HISTORY

The most original aspect of *The Corrupting Sea* may be its attempt to 'ruralize' ancient and medieval history (the authors' quotation marks). The whole category of town or city is made to shrink into insignificance. These terms are not being wholly wished out of existence, but neither is this simply a shift of

[89] Lendon, *Empire*, 272–9, gathers some material, but his analysis of the Latin vocabulary is a model of how such things should not be done: in particular he forces a number of different concepts into the straightjacket of English.

[90] The Copenhagen Polis Centre, founded by M. H. Hansen. Its publications have been extensive.

[91] Shaw, 444–6; E. and J. Fentress, rev. of *CS*, *Past and Present* 173 (2001), 203–19: 211–13; H. Driessen, rev. of *CS*, *American Anthropologist* 103 (2001), 528–31: 530.

[92] Yet in *CS* this doctrine is set about with so many reservations that one may be confused as to where the authors finally stand.

emphasis.[93] Towns, in the view of Horden and Purcell, are simply microregions writ small (or large?), and there is no 'urban variable' that made town life 'qualitatively... different from that of other settlements'.[94] Now we see why Rostovtzeff, Pirenne, Goitein, and Braudel were singled out at the beginning of the book as the four historians to undermine. It was a slightly odd line-up for the year 2000, for none of them, not even Braudel, could be said to represent what scholars currently think about the history of the ancient or medieval Mediterranean—a subject that has inevitably passed into other hands;[95] but, as historians, they were all lovers of cities.

Here Horden and Purcell are almost symmetrically at odds with the dominant trend in anthropology, and their approach seems *retardataire*, since it echoes what De Pina-Cabral has called 'the ruralist emphasis of social anthropology'[96] characteristic of the 1950s—and still detectable in the 1990s.[97] Meanwhile, the anthropology of consumption and a variety of other interests have led anthropologists more and more to town.

In the end, I think that this 'ruralization' is misguided, but it has an immediate attraction. Most ancient and medieval people are widely believed to have lived in the countryside. What proportion is of course unknown, and estimates will partly depend on defining such terms as 'town' and 'village'. Hopkins has guessed that the urban population of the Mediterranean provinces of the Roman Empire might have made up 10 to 20 per cent of the total.[98] Horden and Purcell conjecture, for the pre-industrial Mediterranean, an urban population of '3, 5, 10 per cent: a figure of that order'.[99] It would make no sense,

---

[93] *CS* 92.

[94] *CS* 96. But they hold that 'the Mediterranean has been the most durably and densely urbanized region in world history.... The major cities have... been the sites... in which the fortunes of its populations have principally been determined' (CS 90). The town drives the authors to a shameless display of verbal bravura: *incastellamento*, densening, tentacular.

[95] *CS* 91 says that these four 'dominate modern thinking about the Mediterranean'. It is the tense that is wrong.

[96] De Pina-Cabral, 'The Mediterranean', 405.

[97] See, for instance, Sant Cassia, 'Authors in Search', 10.

[98] K. Hopkins, 'Rome, Taxes, Rent and Trade', *Kodai* 6/7 (1995/6), 41–75: 46.

[99] *CS* 92.

obviously, to apply a single figure both to the Bronze Age and to the high Roman Empire, and the highest of their figures is presumably what they hypothesize for the Roman world.

There is in fact a glaring and fascinating problem here. Many scholars might be inclined to suppose that survey archaeology has demonstrated the truth of the Horden–Purcell hypothesis. 'Traditionally', so one writer observes, 'most of the rural population of the Mediterranean has lived in nucleated villages or towns, far from the majority of their fields'—but his belief is that survey archaeology has shown that in classical antiquity much more of the population lived on scattered farms.[100] There are certainly arguments for supposing that in some areas of the Roman Empire, at least, the population was very dispersed.[101] Yet the traditional pattern, according to which the great majority, at least in some parts of the Mediterranean region, dwelled in large villages or small towns, may often have obtained in antiquity too. Here is a scholar with an unsurpassed knowledge of the ancient Greek countryside: 'for most periods of antiquity the Greeks preferred to live in such nucleated settlements, even when they were supporting themselves primarily from agriculture'.[102] The whole issue—too complex to be entered into here—needs reconsideration on as large a canvas as possible.[103]

Nonetheless this 'ruralization' has some visceral appeal, at least as an experiment and as a change of perspective. Not that the approach is entirely new, and there has been no great

[100] P. Halstead, 'Traditional and Ancient Rural Economy in the Mediterranean: Plus ça change?', *Journal of Hellenic Studies* 107 (1987), 77–87: 82–3 ('relatively dispersed pattern of settlement'), with plentiful bibliography.

[101] W. V. Harris, *Ancient Literacy* (Cambridge, Mass., 1989), 192.

[102] M. H. Jameson, 'Private Space and the Greek City', in O. Murray and S. Price (eds.), *The Greek City from Homer to Alexander* (Oxford, 1990), 171–5: 173. He goes on to say that 'in certain, quite limited periods (especially the century or so after about 375 BC ...) there were also substantial structures scattered over the countryside; the latter are not accompanied by a diminution of population in nucleated settlements, but were occupied entirely or partly by the same people who maintained homes in the towns or villages.'

[103] See also A. Snodgrass, 'Survey Archaeology and the Rural Landscape of the Greek City', in Murray and Price (eds.), 113–36: 125–28; S. E. Alcock, J. F. Cherry, and J. L. Davis, 'Intensive Survey, Agricultural Practice and the Classical Landscape of Greece', in I. Morris (ed.), *Classical Greece: Ancient Histories and Modern Archaeologies* (Cambridge, 1994), 137–70: 147–8.

shortage, over the last generation, of studies of the Greek and Roman countryside and its inhabitants.[104] 'Ruralization', however, could have the valuable effect of concentrating extra attention on any number of interesting historical problems. The history of Greek and Roman religion, for instance, almost always has an excessively urban focus, and *The Corrupting Sea* does well to counteract this tendency in its chapter on the geography of religion. There are many other questions to explore, from characteristically rural forms of dispute and cooperation to rural metallurgy.[105]

A town, say Horden and Purcell, implicitly contradicting the experience of many ancient historians, is not 'a particularly helpful category'. They add, still more provocatively, that 'there is no particular quality of urban space that automatically colours belief and action within it...a town is an address, an arena, an architectonic agglomeration'.[106] Urban history has its place, they agree with decided reluctance, and there is 'scope for a history of the region which starts from its countryside and, as it were, looks inwards to the town';[107] but they have left their readers with the strong impression that towns and cities are extraneous to their account. The arguments in favour of this position are scarcely cogent.[108] I still prefer the Braudel

[104] Especially worthy of note: R. Osborne, *Classical Landscape with Figures* (London, 1987); C. R. Whittaker (ed.), *Pastoral Economies in Classical Antiquity* (Cambridge, 1988) (*Proceedings of the Cambridge Philological Society*, Suppl. 14); Barker and Lloyd (eds.), *Roman Landscapes*.

[105] There is naturally a sizeable existing bibliography on both of these themes. For some comments see respectively *CS* 283–84 and 184.

[106] Both quotations: *CS* 90. The word 'automatically' is something of a red herring. In my view, the authors have allowed themselves to be unduly influenced by R. J. Holton, *Cities, Capitalism and Civilization* (London, 1986), who had a specific aim in mind when he diminished the city's historical role. To the many works that maintain the importance of the city can now be added J. W. H. G. Liebeschuetz, *The Decline and Fall of the Roman City* (Oxford, 2001).

[107] *CS* 91. They are willing to talk about 'settlements', however (108–12).

[108] There is little point in asserting that scholars do not agree very well how 'town' and 'city' should be defined (*CS* 92–6; see rather Fentress and Fentress, 212)—by that route you could argue that such categories are useless in modern history too. We deserve instead a careful analysis of what in fact differentiated ancient settlements, taking into account all that valuable French work about 'agglomérations secondaires'. One wonders whether Horden and

of *Civilization and Capitalism*: 'towns are like electric trans-formers'.[109]

We may agree that ancient history often used to be too urban in outlook, but what is needed now is not paradox or exaggeration but a balanced approach which recognizes the crucial element that towns represented—even in the Bronze-Age Mediterranean and certainly later. Starting in the Ancient Near East, and even more emphatically from the eighth century BC onwards, towns in various degrees conditioned the economic life of vast numbers of Mediterranean people, and helped to determine the course of the entire history of ancient culture. There is no end to describing and defining the relationship between town and country, and once again the story varies from period to period, but the central point is too obvious to bear much repetition. Even from the most narrowly environmental perspective, the town was of central importance. Does anyone think that the Phoenicians or Greeks would have been able to colonize the Mediterranean if they had not possessed urban settlements? Leveau showed long ago how, in the western Roman Empire, the location and nature of towns profoundly affected patterns of rural settlement, from Algeria to Britain.[110] Even if for some obscure reason the complex term 'Romanization' were to be rejected by informed historians, the fact would remain that the spread of Roman power really did mean a measure of urbanization,[111] and of a specific kind, with environmental as well as other consequences.

It was in towns that specialist workers of almost all kinds came into existence, it was in towns that wealth was accumulated, it was in towns that decisions were made about peace and war (Horden and Purcell's Mediterranean world is too peaceful). As for qualitative differences, it was in town that most literacy was imparted, it was mainly in town that Romans

Purcell would like to expel the town from the history of pre-modern Asia as well (on the environmental aspects of Indian Ocean urbanization prior to 1750 see K. Chaudhuri, *Asia before Europe* (Cambridge, 1990), 368–74).

[109] The opening words of ch. 8 of *The Structures of Everyday Life*.

[110] P. Leveau, 'La Ville antique et l'organisation de l'espace rurale: *villa*, ville, village', *Annales ESC* 38 (1983), 920–42: 924.

[111] Cf. S. Keay and N. Terrenato (eds.), *Italy and the West: Comparative Issues in Romanization* (Oxford, 2001).

benefited from aqueducts, it was in town that if they were very poor they sought casual work. And so on. And then there are the big cities, Rome, Alexandria, and one or two others. It was not their population that mattered most, but their consumption power and the huge numbers of workers, agricultural and otherwise, that it took to maintain them.

5. CATEGORIES, DYNAMIC PROCESSES, CAUSATION, AND AVOIDING CONCLUSIONS

The Corrupting Sea has other major points of interest in addition to 'ruralization'. All scholarly readers have appreciated its theoretical and empirical erudition, which spans several traditionally separate disciplines. It is also refreshing to read a book about ancient history in which the physical places and mankind act upon each other. Another great strength resides in the book's close attention to local differences in topography, environment, and economic practice. An excellent example, a model of its kind to a certain degree, is the account of Cyrenaica,[112] bringing out the great environmental differences within this microregion (not so very micro: the plateau is some 400 kilometres long); yet this is generally acknowledged to be an *exceptionally* variegated environment. The conclusion is that 'topographical fragmentation' and 'the connectivity provided by the sea itself' are 'the two key environmental ingredients' in Mediterranean history.[113] This seems at once familiar and yet arbitrary—what of the scattered incidence of crucial resources, in particular minerals, and what of the capacity of certain areas for producing sizeable grain surpluses?

The purpose of *The Corrupting Sea*, the authors say, is to discover how far the region showed, over three millennia, unity and distinctiveness, and secondly 'what kinds of continuity could have been involved'.[114] This distinctiveness, in their view, consists mainly in risk and response to risk,[115] a conclusion we have already commented on briefly in Section 3. The continuity, they argue, is provided by an environment that in spite of all vicissitudes, never experiences 'catastrophe'.[116]

[112] *CS* 65–74.   [113] *CS* 101.   [114] *CS* 9.
[115] *CS* 287, etc.   [116] *CS* 338–41.

This is a strange kind of conclusion. What counts as a catastrophe? Presumably nothing in the way of ordinary misery or ordinary climatic events is going to qualify. There seems to be plenty of evidence for microregional famines in the better documented eras of antiquity.[117] And if we want major catastrophes, the candidates are very few—the eruption of Thera, the end of the Mycenaeans (perhaps a mainly military event), the epidemics that troubled the Roman Empire in the second and fifth centuries AD, deforestation. As for epidemics, Duncan-Jones and others have reinstated the demographic importance of the smallpox epidemic that began under Marcus Aurelius,[118] and a strong case can be made for seeing it as a catastrophic event. In the case of deforestation, Horden and Purcell, while allowing that there was periodically over-felling of woodland, choose to support the 'optimistic' case repeatedly stated by O. Rackham.[119] But the reader familiar with, among other things, the remarkable evidence from Greenland about the level of copper-smelting in the Roman Mediterranean, or with the vast consumption of wood in the Roman Empire—not least for heating baths—requires a fuller and more balanced presentation of the evidence to be convinced.[120] The notion that the Roman

---

[117] Garnsey, *Famine and Food Supply*.

[118] R. P. Duncan-Jones, 'The Impact of the Antonine Plague', *JRA* 9 (1996), 108–36; W. Scheidel, 'Progress and Problems in Roman Demography', in W. Scheidel (ed.), *Debating Roman Demography* (Leiden, 2001) (*Mnemosyne*, Suppl. 211) 1–81: 74–5, etc. For some doubts, not very substantial it seems to me, see the papers by J. Greenberg and C. Bruun in *JRA* 16 (2003), 413–34.

[119] *CS* 182–6, 338 (there is a Panglossian tone to these passages). The authors are prepared to admit that there were 'fewer dense woodlands ... in the nineteenth century than there had been in the Bronze Age' (p. 339), but what I have in mind is a difference between (say) the fifth century BC and the first century AD For O. Rackham's views, which cannot unfortunately be discussed in full here, see 'Ecology and Pseudo-ecology'. It is interesting to see what a role timber shortage plays in a recent (much-debated) comparative history of the eighteenth-century economies of north-west Europe and China (K. Pomeranz, *The Great Divergence: Europe, China, and the Making of the Modern World Economy* (Princeton, 2000), 219–42).

[120] Greenland: S. Hong, J.-P. Candelone, C. C. Patterson, and C. F. Boutron, 'History of Ancient Copper Smelting Pollution during Roman and Medieval Times Recorded in Greenland Ice', *Science* 272 (1996), 246–9, etc. For wood consumption under the Roman Empire *CS* 185 adopts an estimate by H. N. le Houérou ('Impact of Man and his Animals on Mediterranean

Empire as a whole managed its timber resources sensibly is not realistic.

The primary analytic choice of Horden and Purcell is to dissolve or dispense with a number of seldom-questioned categories. They claim that their argument is directed against typologies,[121] but the attack goes much further than that. It is never unmotivated, but seldom if ever does it succeed (so it seems to me). Towns we have already considered. More fundamentally still, the authors wish away periods, and in particular any divide between ancient and medieval. Lines of 'connectivity' were never truly broken, they say. They speak instead of 'a complex tangle of abatements'.[122] Now, no historian doubts that major changes of period are complex affairs—hence all those interminable arguments, more beloved of continental scholars than of Anglo-Saxons, about continuity and discontinuity. But the Mediterranean world underwent vast economic and social as well as political and religious changes in late antiquity. What appears to be the key section of *The Corrupting Sea* simply does not face the evidence for major changes, let alone explain them.[123]

It is perhaps less clear what *The Corrupting Sea* wants to do to the distinction between private enterprise and the state: the authors simply say they want to 'by-pass' it.[124] That is to be

Vegetation', in F. di Castri, D. W. Goodall, and R. L. Specht (eds.), *Mediterranean-type Shrublands* (Amsterdam and Oxford, 1981), 479–521: 514) for the 1980 consumption by 50 million people living in developing Mediterranean countries—27 million tons a year; but even this estimate is quite likely, for reasons (climactic among others) that cannot be entered into here, to be too low.

[121] *CS* 101.   [122] *CS* 154–5.

[123] *CS* 263–70. But see Fentress and Fentress, review, *Past and Present*, 214–17: 215: 'the fact that we cannot pin down a moment when the change takes place does not prove that it never happened.... Between the third and the end of the seventh century many Roman landscapes disappeared for ever [details follow].' Compare the overview of the late-antique/early mediaeval city in G. P. Brogiolo and B. Ward-Perkins (eds.), *The Idea and Ideal of the Town between Late Antiquity and the Early Middle Ages* (Leiden, 1999), pp. xv–xvi: there was no mere transformation, 'the changes that occurred in urban life generally look more like the dissolution of a sophisticated and impressive experiment in how to order society . . .'.

[124] *CS* 338. For the 'systemic linking of state and private enterprise' in the ancient Mediterranean world see Shaw, review (n. 28), 441–2 (Roman republican *publicani*, etc.), and cf. Van De Mieroop, below p. 136.

regretted, for all over the region, through much, though not all, of its history, there are unresolved historical problems about the role of the state in all sorts of matters which Horden and Purcell consider to be part of their subject, such as economic connectedness and water management. To argue that the role of the state was always trivial, in the face of such phenomena as state management of, or at least involvement with, major rivers (the Nile above all, but not only the Nile), the creation under the Roman Empire of a large number of truly extraordinary aqueducts[125] and an equally extraordinary network of public roads, and the more-or-less constant anxiety of ancient governments about the grain supply, would be to distance oneself quite far from the evidence.[126]

More generally, all forms of power, state power and individual power over other individuals, tend to be eliminated from this account. Neither empire nor social class receives much attention. When the power of the state comes back in,[127] it is only for a moment. It is consistent with this that our authors seem to take a quite optimistic view of human nature: they use such phrases as 'sensible and responsible way of managing', and 'niches, exploited with tenacity and ingenuity since time immemorial'. The fittest, those who survive, are those who 'review . . . their portfolios frequently', a surprising metaphor.[128]

Horden and Purcell's strong tendency to reject categories appears to be part of a general reluctance to draw historical conclusions,[129] or to give shape to historical change. Their

---

[125] It is impossible to resist mentioning the extreme case, the aqueduct of Roman Apamea, which was about 150 kms long: J.-C. Balty, 'Problèmes de l'eau à Apamée de Syrie', in P. Louis, F. Métral, and J. Métral (eds.), *L'Homme et l'eau en Méditerranée et du Proche Orient* (Paris and Lyon, 1987), iv. 11–23: 16–21. Later, a delightful Arabic story about a beautiful princess was necessary in order to explain it.

[126] On the state and the Roman economy cf. W. V. Harris, 'Roman Governments and Commerce, 300 BC–AD 300', in C. Zaccagnini (ed.), *Mercanti e politica nel mondo antico* (Bari and Rome, 2003), 279–309.

[127] *CS* 86, 87, for instance.

[128] *CS* 221, 75, 58.

[129] According to *CS* 74 you cannot therefore properly generalize about the prosperity or desolation of regions. Or (more plausibly) you cannot generalize about the economies or societies of mountain regions (pp. 80–1). But of course

avowed purpose is to produce a more dynamic account,[130] but the effect is to produce one so atomized that the great changes involving man and the environment that did occur within their 3,000-year, or 2,000-year, period seem to lack all explanation. Humans went on being tenacious and ingenious (or not, as the case might be), which explains nothing. Yet the authors see clearly that the 'static minimalist' account of the economic world of Graeco-Roman antiquity is now most definitely untenable.[131]

6. MEDITERRANEANISM AND ANCIENT HISTORY: IN FAVOUR OF A WIDER ETHNOGRAPHY

Mediterraneanism was defined earlier as the doctrine that there are distinctive characteristics which the cultures of the Mediterranean have, or have had, in common—from which it has been thought to follow that one may extrapolate the importance of social practices and their meanings from one Mediterranean society to another. It might be accounted optimistic to expect much from a theory so obviously related both to a quasi-Orientalist desire to assert cultural superiority (*they* have amoral familism) and to touristic nostalgia. But I will attempt to weigh it in the balance.

First of all, we should take note of the fact that Mediterraneanism is often nowadays little more than a reflex. The Mediterranean seems somehow peculiarly vulnerable to misuse. 'A deep familiarity with the dream-images of his fellow Mediterraneans assured Artemidorus of the iconistic verity of these gods as dreams' is simply rather sloppy prose.[132] Another author picks phrases from Friedl's description of the people of

---

you can do both, if you make room for necessary exceptions and there are not too many of them (whether Braudel was right about mountain regions, *MMW*, i. 25–53, we need not decide, but Horden and Purcell simplify his analysis).

[130] *CS* 464.

[131] *CS* 146–7.

[132] P. C. Miller, *Dreams in Late Antiquity* (Princeton, 1994), 29. Artemidorus of Daldis claimed to have listened to immense numbers of dreams in Greece, Asia, Italy 'and in the largest and most populous of the islands' (*Oneir.* i, proemium, p. 2 in Pack's edn.).

Vasilika and transfers them to 'the Romans'.[133] But this kind of thing should not be especially difficult to guard against.

The alternatives to Mediterraneanism are now two. One is to ignore comparative history altogether, and it is this option that many ancient historians fall into in their year-to-year practice. The other choice is to pursue broader comparisons and a less restricted ethnography. The authors of *The Corrupting Sea* assert that their book is 'as comparative as anti-Mediterraneanism recommends'. But at the same time they maintain not only that living in this region was, in antiquity, peculiarly a matter of managing risk (a matter we discussed earlier), but that 'honour and shame are indeed deeply held values right across the region'; this, they say, is guaranteed by the fact that some of the evidence comes from 'indigenous scholars'.[134] If this were simply an assertion about the validity of certain ethnographic conclusions, it would be left on one side here, my concern being ancient history, but the implication seems clear that the film can be rewound (*à la* Bloch), or at least that Mediterranean unity in one period makes it more plausible in another.[135]

The point here is not whether the 'indigenous scholars' have it right when they detect honour and shame as deeply held values in particular regions: they are after all scholars, and therefore as vulnerable to academic topoi as anyone else. The fact is that we still have no reason to think that honour is a *distinctively* Mediterranean preoccupation. Given the downright superficial attitude of most Mediterraneanists towards the Arab world, we are scarcely in a position to define Mediterranean honour, let alone proclaim it to be different from the honour which we may encounter in Ireland, Iceland, or Indonesia. And still less do we have reason to impose these particular hypothetical characteristics of the modern Mediterranean world on the ancient Mediterranean world.

But let us consider some particular historical problems, in order to illustrate the principal argument of this final section. In recent years there has been a lively debate concerning Athenian

---

[133] C. Barton, *Roman Honor* (Berkeley and Los Angeles, 2001), 271.

[134] These quotations: *CS* 523.

[135] The authors say (p. 523 again) that what they are engaged in here is a 'primarily historical enquiry into Mediterranean unity'.

notions about revenge, and there is more to learn, without any doubt, about both Greek and Roman attitudes and what may underlie them. In the course of this debate, Mediterranean comparisons have raised some interesting questions—but it has been *difference* that has been most intriguing: while vendetta (in the English and French sense, i.e. a long series of killings and counter-killings) has been characteristic of certain regions such as Sicily and Corsica (that is to say, as they were in ethnographic time), it was arguably a rare phenomenon in Graeco-Roman antiquity. The *Oresteia* was a particularly horrific story.[136] The fact is, however, that if you want to study how any given society has dealt with the apparently innate human desire to inflict revenge, a matter which forces itself into the consciousness of all communities everywhere, there is not the slightest advantage in limiting oneself to the Mediterranean.

Or consider again the question how much of the Greek or Roman population lived in the countryside (above, p. 31), which many scholars probably regard as an open question, within certain broad limits. The comparative Mediterranean evidence from early modern times is instructive, but it is not definitive. A wider ethnography would certainly help: we need to know about more cases in which pre-modern farming populations lived in town, more about which occupations besides farming and flock-grazing kept pre-modern populations almost all the time in the countryside, more about how much rural (or urban) crime was too much to bear. The wider our angle of vision the better.

What is needed in the study of the ancient world is a wide frame of reference that accepts structural similarities from any-

---

[136] D. Cohen, *Law, Violence and Community in Classical Athens* (Cambridge, 1995), 16–21, makes use of comparative evidence to illuminate the trilogy's significance on the subject of feuding (cf. also Harris, *Restraining Rage*, 161–2). In this book Cohen in fact moved away from the heavily Mediterraneanist model he had employed in *Law, Sexuality, and Society*. Some of the material he invokes is of marginal relevance, but that does not invalidate the method (which is not represented accurately in G. Herman's review, *Gnomon* 70 (1998), 605–15: 606). M. van de Mieroop's 'Revenge, Assyrian Style', *Past and Present* 179 (2003), 3–23, raises other questions which cannot be pursued here.

where whatsoever while respecting the great divides such as the emergence of agriculture and of industrialization. I do not refer primarily to other areas of the ancient world well away from the Mediterranean—northern Europe, south Russia, Mesopotamia, Nubia—though it will scarcely have escaped anyone's attention that many of the questions set out above in Section 2 are *not* in fact exclusively Mediterranean questions at all. It is the rest of the world I have in mind. This world-wide ethnography—which is full of risks of course—is an old tradition, which it is easy to trace back past E. R. Dodds to Frazier and Tylor and to 'a deep-seated conviction that human nature [is] fundamentally uniform'.[137] No such conviction is necessary, however. Some limited patterns of cause and effect can sometimes be enough to bring about real progress.[138]

One's views about historical comparativism are certain to be coloured by one's own scholarly experience. I will describe one case only, without suggesting that it should be taken as typical, but at the same time in the conviction that it is methodologically instructive. For generations a certain type of classicist liked to insist that the mass of the population in the Greek and Roman worlds was able to read and write. There was nothing surprising about that: the literary evidence was limited in extent and not overwhelmingly clear (though it was clear enough to enable some scholars to get the matter right).[139] Many ancient historians were in any case prevented from reaching a reasonable conclusion by their obsession with writing history from above. The papyrological evidence, a complicated though not especially mysterious body of material, was only brought into the matter in a useful fashion—by H. C. Youtie—from 1966 onwards,[140]

[137] M. Herzfeld, *Anthropology through the Looking-Glass* (Cambridge, 1987), 71–2.

[138] I take it that comparative historical *method* mainly serves the purpose of validating or invalidating historical models. But historical comparison can serve many other purposes (cf. among others W. H. Sewell, 'Marc Bloch and the Logic of Comparative History', *History and Theory* 6 (1967), 208–18: 215–16; M. Herzfeld, 'Performing Comparisons: Ethnography, Globe-trotting, and the Spaces of Social Knowledge', *Journal of Anthropological Research* 57 (2001), 259–76).

[139] Harris, *Ancient Literacy*, 10, 94 n. 135.

[140] His five most important papers were all reprinted in *Scriptiunculae* (Amsterdam, 1973) or *Scriptiunculae Posteriores* (Bonn, 1981).

which was in part the fault of ancient historians who were too inclined to treat Egyptian evidence as being irrelevant to the main questions of Greek and Roman history. There existed, in short, no credible model of the history of literacy in the Graeco-Roman world: we were supposed to believe that there was majority or mass literacy even though no one could produce adequate evidence for a system of popular education, or explain what the functions of all that literacy could have been. Meanwhile the history of literacy had made giant strides in other, better-documented, periods and places (from England to Liberia to Brazil).[141]

This story should not be oversimplified, and to some extent we can accommodate a Greek *Sonderweg* with respect to the written word. Indeed it is plain that many Greek communities harboured ideas about the ability to write that were quite different from those of most other pre-modern societies. What matters here, however, is that the optimum model for understanding pre-modern literacy—a model that explains the necessary and sufficient conditions for the increase of literacy (of various kinds) to various levels—can only be constructed out of materials from parts of the world where illuminating work has previously been done. The first three important pieces of research, in chronological order of publication, described England, France, and New England. The Mediterranean as such had nothing to do with it.

---

[141] For a basic bibliography of such work down to that time see Harris, *Ancient Literacy*, 367–9.

The Big Canvas

2

Practical Mediterraneanism: Excuses for Everything, from Epistemology to Eating

Michael Herzfeld

1. ON THE ONTOLOGICAL PERSISTENCE OF A SHRINKING SEA

At the beginning of a new century, I confess to a feeling of astonishment that we are still talking about the utility, or otherwise, of the concept of 'the' Mediterranean. I do not mean that I am astonished to find that the Mediterranean Sea is still there, although the ecological mess we seem to be making of the planet might give one pause before accepting even this apparently simple certainty (and certainly the fish that were once a defining feature of the diet to which it has given its name appear to be getting ever scarcer and more expensive). Indeed, if Horden and Purcell are right to see a nexus of 'environmental opportunism' and 'frequency of change' as what constitutes the basis for acknowledging some degree of systemic and chronologically deep distinctiveness in the region,[1] these latest vicissitudes would seem to offer a magnificent test from which their thesis may well emerge in good order even if the place itself does not.

Nor do I mean that I am astonished to find anthropologists and historians recognizing common cultural characteristics in the countries bordering this shrinking sea; with not only that physical shrinkage but with the conceptual shrinkage of the world into a 'smaller place' widely attributed to new technologies of communication, the people of the relevant countries are themselves apt to encourage precisely such sweeping essentializing of 'their' cultural area, and this, as I shall argue below, constitutes an important reason for treating the idea of regional unity with the

[1] *CS* 67, 74, 80.

respect due to a research object even if we continue to harbour doubts about its utility as analytic tool. Indeed, its methodological utility is reduced to the same degree that this exponentially intensifying self-stereotype interests us as a cultural and political phenomenon. Epistemology is at the heart of the matter. For the idea that the Mediterranean is more interesting as a local category than as an analytic tool is hardly novel any more. What I find extraordinary, then, is the curious circumstance that, in an age in which just about every other category has been deconstructed or reconstructed, or at least has self-destructed, 'the' Mediterranean has shown a remarkable tenacity in the face of a barrage of critiques—indeed, that barrage has at times seemed simply to confirm its general importance. And that, in my view, is a thoroughly weighty reason for taking it seriously.

I shall take my lead here from two highly significant studies, one an enormous and encyclopedic review of the Mediterranean itself, the other a brief but suggestive overview of a very distant but surprisingly analogous area. The weighty tome is Horden and Purcell's *The Corrupting Sea*. I am impressed by the seriousness with which these authors have broached their complex field as well as the generosity with which they treat the ideas of those, including myself, with whom they disagree on key issues. More substantively, I find some surprising common ground in our divergent positions, and would like to reciprocate their engagement here.

2.   COMPARING THE COMPARISONS: POWER, AUTHORITY, AND CLASSIFICATION

The physically lighter (but intellectually no less interesting) work is Rena Lederman's essay, 'Globalization and the Future of Culture Areas'.[2] This position paper is an overview of the current status of Melanesianist writings in modern anthropology. Much as anthropologists have had to wrestle with the exoticism of much of the earlier Mediterraneanist writing, while recognizing its very substantial ethnographic and comparative

---

[2] Rena Lederman, 'Globalization and the Future of Culture Areas: Melanesian Anthropology in Transition', *Annual Review of Anthropology* 27 (1998), 427–49.

richness, Lederman—who also acknowledges the Mediterranean/Melanesian epistemological parallel—argues for the importance of the Melanesianist tradition as an ideal test case for examining 'situated disciplinary discourses'.[3] She thus brings the role of anthropologists themselves into critical view, showing how their mutual neighbourliness (both geographic and intellectual) can generate comparative and critical insights that can then be further projected into more global comparisons. Such comparisons will also then inevitably include the role of anthropologists and those whose thinking has been affected by these scholars as data relevant, not so much to mere disciplinary introspection, as to an active inspection of the engagement of theory with the political realities of a world in which epiphenomenal globalization may mask persistent cultural specificity.[4]

My intention is not to argue—as some believe I have done in the past—for a dismantling of the category. I have never claimed that the Mediterranean did not exist; indeed, like facts themselves, such culture-area categories have an existence by virtue of being articulated, and this is the key point to which I address my remarks. To say that the Mediterranean 'does not exist' is as silly as to argue that facts themselves 'do not exist'. They exist in the sense that they are representations of something experienced in the phenomenal world.[5] Thus, too, the Mediterranean has impinged on many forms of consciousness, of which the academic may be a paltry reflection but is a reflection nevertheless. Thus, to deny its existence is as obtuse as to treat it as an obvious fact that needs no further comment. These apparent ontological truisms become interesting—but then they become extremely interesting—when we ask who makes them and why. They serve as a point of entry into a politics of knowledge that includes in its purview the constitution of what we are pleased to call 'the West'.

[3] Ibid. 442.

[4] See, for example, James L. Watson, 'Introduction: Transnationalism, Localization, and Fast Foods in East Asia', in J. L. Watson (ed.), *Golden Arches East: McDonald's in East Asia* (Stanford, 1997), 1–38.

[5] See the argument I have made on similar grounds, derived substantially from Vico, to the effect that, inasmuch as facts are constructions of reality, they have the same ontological status as other perceived realities (M. Herzfeld, 'Factual Fissures: Claims and Contexts', *Annals of the American Academy of Political and Social Science* 560 (1998), 69–82).

My intention is thus to ask why the category is so persistent—why it survives, whose interests its maintenance serves, and what are the consequences of its continuing importance. I have often been represented as both a critic of the very idea of the Mediterranean and as a student of typically Mediterranean cultures—and, not infrequently if decidedly paradoxically, as both. But my criticisms have been directed against 'Mediterraneanism', a coinage that I have modelled unashamedly on Edward Said's 'orientalism' and the follow-up converse of 'occidentalism'.[6] This Horden and Purcell clearly understand, and I do not think we disagree on the evidence that, whatever else we may say about its utility, the idea of a vast Mediterranean culture has frequently served the interests of disdainful cultural imperialism. I certainly find myself in harmony with their historically grounded evocation of Bismarck's crack that 'Europe' was no more than a 'geographical expression',[7] but ask why, hyperbole (which they also attribute to Said's critique of 'orientalism') aside, we cannot say the same of 'the Mediterranean'—but say it with exactly the same degree of realization that such dismissals and their objects are alike the products of the desire to promote a different configuration, with a different political advantage, in each case.

3.   STEREOTYPICAL PERMUTATIONS OF A CIVILIZATIONAL IDEAL

This is a problem of horizons. In the past, as Horden and Purcell correctly note, I have criticized Mediterraneanism as a comparative exercise in part because it falls between the two stools of global comparativism and ethnographic precision. Yet to leave my criticism at that is to miss the point. I can agree with John Davis's early call for a comparative study of the Mediterranean cultures and societies[8]—but only on condition that we may then, in the style that Lederman has recommended for Melanesia, expand that study both to include the scholars'

---

[6] See Edward Said, *Orientalism* (New York, 1978), and compare James G. Carrier (ed.), *Occidentalism: Images of the West* (Oxford, 1995).

[7] *CS* 18.

[8] J. Davis, *People of the Mediterranean: An Essay in Comparative Social Anthropology* (London, 1977).

own engagements and to embed the regional in wider forms of comparison.

Otherwise, in the rather limited version proposed by Davis, a perfectly reasonable exercise turns into a circular argument. Intermediate comparisons of this type have a tactical rather than a substantive advantage. Inasmuch as they may reveal differences within a framework of undeniable contiguity rather than of pre-emptively conceived similarity, I am all in favour. Greece and Italy, for example, while sharing the mantle of the classical past, are radically and starkly different in important respects: while in Italy all cultural roads appear to lead away from Rome, a city viewed by other Italians as a provincial place where people speak an ugly dialect, and while nevertheless national policy recognizes local variation everywhere including the capital, in Greece Athens remains the object of passionate 'city mania' (*astifilia*) and is the cultural capital of a self-homogenizing polity, a lone European Union member state in the extent of its foot-dragging on the principle of minority self-determination.

Let me explicate this point a little further. Greece and Italy are contiguous and have long and at many levels experienced the phenomenon that produced what Horden and Purcell,[9] perhaps rather too sociomorphically, call the 'interactionism' of some earlier (and indeed ancient) writers. The question that interests me is why, in two countries that are so manifestly different from each other but have 'interacted' so intensively and extensively, we so often find the same images of 'the Mediterranean'. Can we link the respectively different uses of such stereotypes to the structural and institutional differences between the two countries? If so, can we also, by analogy, extend the same mode of analysis to all those countries where a significant segment of the populations invests time and effort in claiming a Mediterranean identity? Such a project, I suggest, would have enormous heuristic value for understanding the current international politics of taste and might, again by analogy, shed some light on modern scholars' use of the label 'Mediterranean' for describing past societies as well. It is a concern that would not necessarily prove incompatible with the 'ecological' interests of Horden and Purcell or with the more generically materialist ones of

---

[9] *CS* 12.

Davis, but it offers the added advantage of providing a factual, historical, and political framework for taking seriously what people in the area itself have had to say about these matters. Indeed, I suggest, it would ground the study of regional culture and society more, not less, empirically.

I have said that the Mediterranean category is an example of the larger representational category known as 'fact', but I would like to qualify that remark by suggesting that factuality itself is always a constitutive act. Claims that the Mediterranean 'exists' are performative in Austin's sense;[10] they do not so much enunciate facts as create them. Our task is then to determine what conditions make these utterances persuasive as statements of fact. My first suggestion is thus that we treat attributions of Mediterranean culture, not as literal statements, however literally they may be intended (and it is not for us to attribute motives to colleagues any more than we would to those whose cultures we have been studying), but as performative utterances that can, under the right 'felicity conditions', actually create the realities that people perceive. This is a crucial move: it allows us to see claims of Mediterranean unity as a number of things: excuses expressive of, and enmeshed in, a global hierarchy of value in which 'Mediterranean' comes somewhere between 'modern' and 'primitive';[11] political moves aiming to unify weaker countries behind a strong regional leader such as France; the rhetorical moves of publicity campaigns designed to exploit lingering exoticism among consumers or awaken their mystical leanings toward new diet fads;[12] and scholarly classifications shoring up the boundaries of existing disciplines or, more kindly, for defining new alliances and agglomerations capable of generating novel and interesting heuristic options (which is where I would locate Horden and Purcell's impressive tome). It also allows us finally to get away from the tiresome ontological debate and to focus instead on issues of power and hierarchy.

---

[10] J. L. Austin, *How To Do Things with Words*, 2nd edn. ed. J. O. Urmson and M. Sbisà (Cambridge, Mass., 1975) (1962).

[11] Davis, *People of the Mediterranean* 7. And see also n. 26 below.

[12] See now Vassiliki Yiakoumaki, '"The Nation as Acquired Taste": On Greekness, Consumption of Food Heritage, and the Making of the New Europe' (Ph.D. diss., Department of Anthropology, The New School University, New York, 2002).

My business here, then, is epistemological provocation. In that spirit, I shall not deal with the detailed ethnographic issues to which my usual inclinations lead me. The evidence for what I have to say will be deliberately eclectic and impressionistic. I certainly do not intend to claim high originality or conclusive insight, but offer these comments in an intentionally and heuristically iconoclastic spirit. Nevertheless, the result may be quite radically ethnographic—that is, if we end up talking about what (for want of a better term) we might call a 'Mediterranean consciousness': why does it matter to people to 'be' Mediterranean, or to lump others together under that title? That is perhaps something that Durkheim might have recognized as a total social fact; it is also something to which performative approaches to taxonomy will allow us critical and analytic access.

I want to spend a few sentences on the word 'practical' in my title. It is in part a recognition of 'practice' as a key element of social theory that emerged in the 1960s and has flourished especially since the mid-1970s,[13] but it is a recognition of a peculiar kind. In earlier work, I have written about 'practical orientalism' and 'practical occidentalism'.[14] Inasmuch as 'Mediterraneanism' is coined on the model of orientalism,[15] it too can be treated as much more than an ideology—as, in fact, a programme of active political engagement with patterns of cultural hierarchy. It is important not to leave matters there.

Said, for all his original praise of anthropology and his later recriminations against it, was heavily textual; for a writer speaking for the oppressed, and this may be one source of the hyperbole with which Horden and Purcell have taxed him, he seems curiously uninterested in ordinary people's engagements with the images about which he writes so powerfully. We must not fall into the same trap; besides, ethnography of the kind I am

---

[13] An especially useful assessment of this development is Sherry Ortner, 'Theory in Anthropology in the Sixties', *Comparative Studies in Society and History* 26 (1984), 126–66.

[14] See, for example, Michael Herzfeld, *A Place in History: Social and Monumental Time in a Cretan Town* (Princeton, 1991) and *Cultural Intimacy: Social Poetics in the Nation-State* (New York, 1997).

[15] Michael Herzfeld, 'The Horns of the Mediterraneanist Dilemma', *American Ethnologist* 11 (1984), 439–54.

proposing here encloses researchers and researched in a common frame of analysis, one that reflects their common humanity and their common subjection to symbolic modes of political entailment. To be a 'Mediterraneanist'—whether in the academic sense or in the rather more fundamentally political sense to which I am alluding here—is to insert oneself in a global hierarchy of value,[16] and to calibrate specific moments of experience to that hierarchy. These moments, the stuff of which experiential reality is made,[17] may be quite fleeting. For modish young men to justify their predation on young tourist women as an act attributable to the 'hot Mediterranean temperament', for example, is a tactical move,[18] one that might subvert a larger desire to be taken seriously by more obviously powerful representatives of those 'cold' northern peoples. The complicity that self-ascription of Mediterraneanism can imply is hardly unrelated to the larger geopolitical inequities in which it is embedded, any more than are (for example) the defensive posture and habit of blaming the 'foreign finger' for national woes with which Greece is often taxed by commentators from those very countries that have held Greece accountable to their own uncompromising ubiquitous political and ethical values.

4. STRATEGIES OF SELF-STEREOTYPING

The curious element in all this is not that circum-Mediterranean cultures share some features: that is only to be expected as the result of all those millennia of contact; I have no quarrel with the Braudelian *longue durée* in this sense. What is more, they share these features with many other societies as well; even leaving aside the evidence that more of what was hitherto taken as indigenous to pre-Columbian Latin America was instead

[16] See Michael Herzfeld, *The Body Impolitic: Artisans and Artifice in the Global Hierarchy of Value* (Chicago, 2004).

[17] See Michael Jackson, *Paths Toward a Clearing: Radical Empiricism and Ethnographic Inquiry* (Bloomington, 1989); M. Jackson (ed.), *Things As They Are: New Directions in Phenomenological Anthropology* (Bloomington, Ind., 1996).

[18] Michel de Certeau, *The Practice of Everyday Life*, trans. Steven F. Rendall (Berkeley, 1984), p. xix.

Iberian (and so Mediterranean?) in origin,[19] we could hardly subsume all of the Indian subcontinent under a Mediterranean rubric unless we were to grant the Moghuls a more sweeping or durable cultural hegemony than even their own chroniclers claimed for them,[20] or unless we are to surpass Greek nationalists in attributing the entire gamut of Indian culture to Alexander of Macedon.

What initially seems paradoxical is the consistency with which the stereotype appears within the area itself. From Morocco to Turkey, from Thessaloniki to Toulouse, we hear more or less the same list of traits that supposedly characterize Mediterranean peoples. As an anthropologist, I am less interested in arguing about the truth or falsehood of these characterizations than in examining the play that local social actors give them in everyday encounters.[21] Indeed, my complaint is precisely that anthropologists and others who are shy of seeming to embrace stereotypes have sometimes been dangerously reluctant to tackle them analytically as an ethnographic phenomenon, as a speech act that can be tracked across a wide array of social contexts and historical periods, and as both the instrument and the expression of power in a struggle to determine the global hierarchy of value. In an age in which globalization has become a popular theme of conversation and analysis, moreover, it is precisely this globalization of the regional that ought to command our attention. Who stands to gain from it?

We can best begin by trying to define the stereotype. Honour and shame form the underlying binary here, at least as far as the anthropological literature is concerned.[22] In passing, I would simply remark that I have not so much opposed recognizing the ideas that have been glossed as 'honour and shame' as I have

[19] See Paul H. Gelles, 'Equilibrium and Extraction: Dual Organization in the Andes', *American Ethnologist* 22 (1995), 710–42.

[20] This is the move that Carroll Quigley ('Mexican National Character and Circum-Mediterranean Personality Structure', *American Anthropologist* 75 (1973), 319–22) notoriously did for Mexico, linking such generic stereotypes very clearly to the equally reductive notion of 'national character'; cf. James W. Fernandez, 'Consciousness and Class in Southern Spain', *American Ethnologist* 10 (1983), 165–73, for a critique.

[21] Herzfeld, *Cultural Intimacy* 156–64.

[22] J. G. Peristiany (ed.), *Honour and Shame: The Values of Mediterranean Society* (London, 1965).

tried to show that this concern with the play of concealment and intimacy may undergo transmutations, within the global hierarchy of value, that are intially at their most recognizable around the Middle Sea but that eventually compel us to cast a much wider net. But another pair, noted early by Davis, is the tension between town and country, between an ancient urban tradition and its rural hinterland.[23] Here we immediately encounter a model for hierarchies of value: if what is created in the cities is considered to be politically superior (although perhaps morally inferior) to the supposed simplicity of the rural, this is less a matter of different dwelling systems or modes of subsistence than of a hierarchy of taste—the urbane versus the rustic, rather than the urban versus the rural. It was the imperial powers that spread what they interpreted as the Roman ideal of civilization throughout the known world, reimporting it into the Mediterranean—not only into obviously colonial situations such as those of Cyprus, Malta, and Gibraltar, but also into countries like Greece, already subject to its imperious judgmentalism through the proximity of Italian models of considerable historical depth. In the British Ionian Islands, as Thomas Gallant has shown,[24] the Italian and northern European models fused, to the great discomfiture (but also long-term political advantage) of the local Greeks. This value hierarchy was thus less Mediterranean than an imposition on Mediterranean peoples of values that their self-appointed protectors from further north thought Mediterranean peoples should embrace. Much as classical Greek culture was filtered back to Greece through German philology and art history, so the civic morality of civlization came full circle through imperial recensions of an imagined ancient Rome.

Much of the anthropological literature about Mediterranean cities emphasizes the fear of the city's open spaces. Notions of exposure and moral degeneracy, expressed through metaphors

---

[23] In addition to the discussion in Davis, *People of the Mediterranean*, 7–8, see especially Sydel Silverman, *Three Bells of Civilization: The Life of an Italian Hill Town* (New York, 1975); Paul Stirling, *Turkish Village* (London, 1965), 283–8.

[24] Thomas W. Gallant, *Experiencing Dominion: Culture, Identity, and Power in the British Mediterranean* (Notre Dame, Ind., 2002), 5–6.

of 'open' (morally suspect) and 'closed' (morally safe) space,[25] are common, and reproduce the deliberate architectonics of concealment characteristic of many rural societies in the region.[26] In Muslim countries, the veil and the latticed balcony afford greater protection in large public spaces, but are often less frequently observed in cities than in the countryside. The dialectics of openness and closure are heavily gendered; they are also associated with the control of personal information— indeed, in Greece the literature clearly indicates a parallel between sexual and other forms of moral continence on the one hand and the regulation of gossip and demeanour on the other. It is interesting to note Horden and Purcell's adoption of the 'Corrupting Sea' label in this context,[27] for clearly the Mediterranean was especially significant inasmuch as it appeared to dissolve the firm boundaries of a lost golden age. All classification systems, including bureaucracies, treat poorly defined entities as polluting or corrupt;[28] and so it was with 'the Mediterranean'. And it is also relevant that 'corruption' is associated in popular images in the First World with the idea of a 'typically' Mediterranean society.

Thus, while urbanity might provide a model for a powerful culture, it also provided a speculative account of its eventual ruin. This is an old theme, and not only in the Mediterranean.[29] Nazi hatred of the Jews, in particular, was argued partly on the basis that the Jews' allegedly urban proclivities—deriving from that same Mediterranean Sea where the Nazis also claimed ancestry from Hellas—were *ipso facto* corrupt and polluting.[30] It is a sad confirmation of such ideas that we soon find an elected Canadian government rejecting Jewish refugees from

[25] See, e.g. Renée Hirschon, 'Open Body/Closed Space: The Transformation of Female Sexuality', in Shirley Ardener (ed.), *Defining Females* (London, 1978), 66–88.

[26] e.g., Ernestine Friedl, *Vasilika: A Village in Modern Greece* (New York, 1962), 14.

[27] *CS* 278.

[28] Here I am invoking a notion that has been taken as virtually a commonplace ever since the publication of Mary Douglas's magisterial *Purity and Danger: An Analysis of Concepts of Purity and Taboo* (London, 1966).

[29] Raymond Williams, *The Country and the City* (London, 1973).

[30] George L. Mosse, *Respectability and Abnormal Sexuality in Modern Europe* (New York, 1985).

the Holocaust on the grounds that these were urban people who consequently would be incapable of filling the country's need for agricultural labour—a need that in fact had already been met to excess.[31] (The fundamental selectivity of such characterizations was also demonstrated, ironically, both by the new Israelis' eager and dramatically effective embrace of agriculture and by their subsequent refusal to acknowledge long Palestinian engagement in the same activity on the same land.) And yet, as Raymond Williams's *The Country and the City* has made us particularly aware, the term 'culture' is itself entailed—dare I say 'rooted'?—in the practices of agriculture, a metaphor that is reproduced in academics' models of 'the field'. The town–country duality is tense with historically embedded ambiguities, and these reflect both the existing cultural evaluations to be found all around the Mediterranean and beyond, and the discontents of civilization that afflict countries claiming Mediterranean sources for their own hegemonic models of high culture.

In Greece today, the notion of culture has bifurcated; in partial contrast with the neoclassical *politismos*, the more ironic and self-mocking model of a cosmopolitan *koultoura* marks the Greek intelligentsia's engagement with an international economy of taste. *Koultouriaridhes*, culture vultures, are often those who today most disdainfully reject the neoclassical in favour of the folkloristic and the Byzantine—concessions, respectively, to an international trade in picturesqueness and a religiously neo-Orthodox desire to return to pre-Cartesian ontologies in roughly equal measure.[32] Those Mediterranean origins of Western civilization are now transposed from the neoclassical to a reworking of the noble savage and the oriental mystic. Zen Buddhism and yoga seem to thrive in Athens almost as luxuriantly as neo-Orthodoxy and the revival of folk systems of belief and practice as well as the creation of a traditionalist Greek *nouvelle cuisine*.

Doubtless it is no coincidence that this phenomenon has occurred at the same time as Greece has begun to shift from

[31] Irving Abella and Harold Troper, *None Is Too Many: Canada and the Jews of Europe 1933–1948* (Toronto, 1982), 54–5.

[32] On the latter, see Chrestos Giannaras (Yannaras), *Ορθοδοξία και Δύση στη Νεότερη Ελλάδα* (Athens, 1992).

British and American hegemony to incorporation into a Europe in which the Greeks' fast-developing new economy can conceivably bury the humiliations of yore. This vision is compatible with the view of Horden and Purcell, who rightly argue that the idea of European unity represents a political ideal based on the idea of a transcendent but infinitely variable genius[33]— though there is an irony in their return to a similar idea in their invocation of Mediterranean distinctiveness on the grounds of an enormous degree of variation.

Local people invoke the idea of a shared Mediterranean identity for a variety of reasons. One such reason may simply be the desire to represent themselves as exercising cultural choice in parallel with other, neighbouring populations doing exactly the same thing. Another may be a genuinely expanded access to resources of knowledge about local and regional culture that were simply not available under the more repressive regimes of the past. For many others, however, the idea of a Mediterranean identity may be as much of a trap as its predecessors, nativist demoticism and neoclassical folklorism.[34] For, by conforming to a model of Mediterranean peoples as unreliable, imprecise, and spontaneous—all virtues that are highly regarded in the inside spaces of Greek cultural intimacy—they are also providing both an excuse for their own failures in the larger spheres of competition and an excuse for others to despise them. And so the self-fulfilling quality of earlier stereotypes, once again, may all too easily fulfil itself.

It is instructive, in this sense, to compare the way in which Italians invoked the idea of being Mediterranean. For them, inhabitants of a culturally and linguistically more fractured land, there is less reason to invoke the stereotype at the national level. Romans, to be sure, accept that they are 'of the south' (and even embrace a cultural hierarchy that rates the Neapolitan dialect as superior to the Roman, and Magna Graecia as more venerable culturally than their own johnny-come-lately capital

---

[33] *CS* 16; see also Michael Herzfeld, *Anthropology through the Looking-Glass: Critical Ethnography in the Margins of Europe* (Cambridge, 1987), 77–81.

[34] See, respectively, Dimitris Tziovas, *The Nationism of the Demoticists and its Impact on their Literary Theory (1881–1930)* (Amsterdam, 1986); Michael Herzfeld, *Ours Once More: Folklore, Ideology, and the Making of Modern Greece* (Austin, 1982).

city). They may attribute Mediterranean characteristics to themselves; but they do so, not as Italians, but as Romans—they are often quick to point out, with an odd mixture of envy and contempt, that Milanese are not of the same ilk at all. At the same time, the Romans' use of such stereotypes of exclusion from 'Europe' is specific to Italy, being quite unlike what one encounters in Greece. They will, for example, point to their unwillingness to get excited about things that cannot be avoided or start fights over petty matters, here contrasting themselves with Sicilians and other southerners as well, implicitly, as with Greeks—whose more aggressive social style often provokes deep astonishment in Italian tourists. These Italians are consequently all the more bemused by popular Greek clichés that are designed to suggest cultural commonalities between the two peoples.

Indeed, it is much easier to talk about 'the' Greek response than 'the' Italian response. This is not simply a matter of relative size, Greece having about one-sixth the population of Italy, although size presumably does have something to do with the differences that we can observe. I believe that the Greek response arises much more precisely from a Greek concern with cultural intimacy that is more national than its Italian counterpart, which is more regional in focus. This contrast is the result of very different national political histories. If Greeks agree more generally about 'being Mediterranean' than do Italians, what does this tell us about the respective degrees of confidence and independence with which each country goes about the negotiation of its position in the era of globalization? It is this kind of comparison, rather than the more old-fashioned but also compelling sets of similarities between Mediterranean and Melanesian worlds (androcentrism, segmentary social relations, occasionally violent nationalism, ideas about witchcraft, and so on), that makes what Lederman suggests so appealing. The idea of a Mediterranean culture area, recast as a heuristic device in which its inherent limitations are turned to advantage, gives way to a sophisticated rethinking of globalization from the perspective of the regionalisms invoked by those who see various levels of local cultural unity as the only available source of resistance to domination by a few powers and cultures.

Such comparisons incorporate the sources of doubt about the regional project itself, making that project, paradoxically, much more valuable. One should be wary of taking Mediterranean self-stereotypes too literally; but that is all the more reason for comparing the conditions under which they are used. Romans, for example, often comment that the aggressiveness they encounter in Greece is also characteristic of southern Italy, thereby contrasting themselves with southerners (rather than with non-Italians, who similarly serve to underscore by association how non-*Roman* these other Italians are). They describe themselves as relatively resigned (*rassegnati*) and attribute this both to the brutal nineteenth-century police state run by the Vatican and still very much alive in popular memory and, paradoxically, to a besetting southern character that embraces a life of ease even if it brings no material rewards—a life, indeed, of *dolce far niente*. This is doubly paradoxical because, on the one hand, it entails ignoring the equally repressive histories of the Bourbons in the south, and, on the other, it overlooks the contradiction between this relaxed image and that of the southerner quick to avenge the slightest insult to personal dignity.

5. MEDITERRANEANISM AND THE POLITICS OF HUMILIATION

For decades the literature on prejudice has focused on its apparent illogic.[35] That literature misses the point: that stereotyping is always both practical and contextual. The important thing is to move it from the impenetrable domain of belief to the more accessible one of social practice. It is not that speakers hold mutually contradictory convictions (although for all we know that may also be true). The crux of the matter is that they will use these stereotypes to organize their lives and actions around what Peter Loizos has clarified as political alignment (as opposed to belief or conviction).[36] When a Roman wishes to justify doing nothing, this is 'Mediterranean'; when the same

---

[35] For a famous example, see Gordon W. Allport, *The Nature of Prejudice*, abridged edn. (Garden City, NY, 1958).

[36] Peter Loizos, *The Greek Gift: Politics in a Cypriot Village* (Oxford, 1975), 138 n. 5.

Roman wishes to justify a furious reaction, this, too, is 'Mediterranean'.

Being 'Mediterranean', however changeable its semantic load, is also not without a heavy load of entailments. For those powers for which the Mediterranean has traditionally been the zone of terrorist states, the mafia, and 'amoral familism',[37] all of these characteristics interlinked as the basis of a vicarious fatalism, the two elements of aggressive touchiness and indolent non-involvement are 'proof' of supposedly innate characteristics that justify paternalistic and oppressive responses. That such characterizations are an unfortunate but common feature of the present-day geopolitical landscape is sometimes a hard point to get across. When I recently taught a large undergraduate course on 'Cultures of Southern Europe', several students accused me of endorsing crude stereotypes—because, apparently, they had missed the point that these stereotypes exist 'on the ground' as well as in the earlier scholarly literature and that an honest empirical appraisal could hardly leave them out. There is a useful object lesson here, and it concerns the pragmatics of stereotyping itself—an activity that does not admit much irony or humour.

Mediterranean stereotypes are not always, or automatically, demeaning. For the more powerful nation-states that today at times claim a Mediterrnanean identity—France among them—historical rights to the mainstream of European history are what is more likely to be emphasized. But note that this is the first mention of France in this essay. Is France, which after all has an extensive Mediterranean coast, ever mentioned in the classic anthologies of Mediterranean ethnography? Portugal, with a far weaker geographical claim, appears much more often. Here I suspect that we are dealing with political hierarchy again: France, while geographically Mediterranean, belongs to a different category of countries—imperial, northern, universalist, and rationalist, a country that—unlike Portugal, Spain, Greece, and sometimes Italy—does not generate 'ethnic food' in North America but is instead the authoritative source of *haute cuisine*.

---

[37] This phrase gained considerable notoriety after its proclamation by E. C. Banfield in *The Moral Basis of a Backward Society* (Glencoe, Ill., 1958).

In an article that otherwise faithfully reproduces the classic Mediterraneanist position, Anton Blok makes the very interesting point that ideas about honour in industrial societies tended to disappear from the local level and become instead part of the apparatus of national identity.[38] National identity became the only legitimate kind. Blok clearly sees this as a sort of Eliasian civilizing process, one that can be plotted along a more or less unilinear model of evolutionary progression. (Contrary to what they appear to think, Horden and Purcell and I are actually in agreement in rejecting this kind of evolutionism.) On that logic, we may suppose, once certain Mediterranean countries become powerful modern states in their own right, we should expect the same development to occur there as well. The point is not that it does so as a matter of (evolutionary) course, but that the evolutionary argument becomes part of the overall logic of the assumption of state power—and this is a rhetoric that the most absurdly self-Mediterraneanizing of regimes, that of the Greek colonels (1967–74), was very happy to use, with its defensive posture rejecting every exposure of internal cultural intimacies as an insult to national pride. The expression of outraged dignity is clearly the privilege of those with the power to do something about it, while those whose power is literally emasculated by a repressive system appear to 'compensate' by competing in a game of honour.[39] That game, while it allows weaker players to gain small stakes in a face-to-face game, condemns them to perpetual marginality on larger stages. In this sense, what works for the rural poor facing a national elite also works for weak countries facing international power brokers; and at both levels, too, the mantle of 'tradition' becomes instead the dead weight of 'traditionalism,' the honour of past glory transmuted into the opprobrium of present backwardness. This is a non-evolutionary and discursive adaptation of Blok's argument that will, I think, work quite well in explaining why the stereotype of Mediterrnean culture and society has continued to

[38] Anton Blok, 'Rams and Billy-Goats: A Key to the Mediterranean Code of Honour', *Man* (NS) 16 (1981), 427–40.

[39] See especially David D. Gilmore, 'Introduction: The Shame of Dishonor', in David D. Gilmore (ed.), *Honor and Shame and the Unity of the Mediterranean* (Washington, 1987), 14.

exercise such fascination over many who could reasonably be seen as its victims.

It is when such attributions begin rather obviously to look like excuses that we see most clearly how this dynamic works. For it is in trying to 'explain away' certain features that in the global hierarchy of taste have become generically undesirable that Mediterrnean dwellers reveal how they perceive both the real contours of that hierarchy and their own position within it. That is why their evocation of self-stereotypes, empowering though they may seem to be in an immediately contingent sense, ultimately achieve the opposite effect. They reveal expectations—the basis of that very concern with 'honour' that has been so fundamental to the Mediterraneanist project[40]— that give massive play to the dynamics of humiliation. To say that Mediterranean life must be spontaneous because nothing is predictable, for example, may recognize the ecological realities that Horden and Purcell have emphasized, but it is also to yield, at the level of everyday life and in terms of its practical essentialisms, to an ecological determinism that turns part of the early scholarly literature into a formidable weapon of present-day *Realpolitik*. To accept the self-image of cultures tainted by a 'corrupting sea' is to play into the hands of a 'new world order'—with its distinctive hierarchy of purity and pollution—that was already old before George Bush *père* claimed the term.

This is not to suggest, of course, that scholars who have promoted the idea of a Mediterranean area, defined by a common and distinctive history, deliberately endorse that seedy cosmology. To the contrary, their efforts today, like mine, appear to me more directed toward acknowledging what (in the somewhat rebarbative terminology of an older style of anthropological writing) we would recognize as an 'emic' perspective—the perspective of local social actors trying to make sense of an environment in which they are often chastised for the very characteristics that have also allowed more powerful

[40] See Michael Herzfeld, 'Honour and Shame: Some Problems in the Comparative Analysis of Moral Systems', *Man* (NS) 15 (1980), 339–51. For an extended discussion of the dynamics of the global hierarchy of taste and value, see Michael Herzfeld, *The Body Impolitic: Artisans and Artifice in the Global Hierarchy of Value* (Chicago, 2004).

countries to foist upon them, and to live with the consequences. This is a spectacular case of visiting the sins of the children upon the fathers. A critical study of Mediterranean identities is not necessarily and should not be, an act of 'Mediterraneanism'. It can instead be a critical response to such essentializing discourses. To become that response, however, it must entail full recognition of the extent to which it is itself enmeshed in political and ideological processes. There is no value in emphasizing the excesses of critique if the alternative is to retreat into another, no less totalizing and politically insensitive discourse. For better or for worse, the history of even the most distant Mediterranean pasts is always already politicized—indeed, one might argue that its distance is precisely what allows politicians to have their way with the past-in-the-present. And that engagement is part of what creates both the distinctive peculiarities of the microregions of the Mediterranean and the occasionally compelling sense that it does, after all, have quite a lot in common. Here, too, the discursive community of disciplinary practitioners, in Lederman's sense, exemplifies the trade-offs between conceptual expediency and critical knowledge that we can none of us entirely sidestep, but toward which we must always maintain a critically vigilant and politically sceptical stance. In that sense, we do indeed have a lot to talk about.

3

Mediterraneans

David Abulafia

1. THE MEDITERRANEAN AND THE MEDITERRANEAN SEA

We talk of the Mediterranean and of the Mediterranean Sea, and we often assume we mean much the same thing. But here lies the root of a significant confusion. 'Mediterranean' means that which is between the surrounding lands. Yet histories and geographies of 'the Mediterranean' may concern themselves mainly with the lands that surround the Mediterranean Sea and the peoples who have inhabited them, to the extent of paying rather little attention to the bonds that have linked the opposing shores of the Mediterranean world: studies of Mediterranean Europe, for example, that are more concerned with the inner history of Provence or Catalonia than with the impact of the Great Sea upon the societies that developed in such regions. Many associations of 'Mediterranean historians' are really concerned with research on the lands that border the Mediterranean, and the Society of Mediterranean Studies based in the United States goes even further afield, taking in all those societies that trace their cultural origins back to the ancient and medieval Mediterranean, including not merely Portugal (which for various reasons has often been counted as an honorary Mediterranean land) but Brazil and Spanish South America. This is certainly defensible: the impact of the cultures formed around the shores of the Mediterranean on the wider world has quite simply been enormous. And indeed those who lived close to its shores in the Middle Ages generally saw it, and not the outer Ocean, as the central sea of the world, the *Yam Gadol*, the 'Great Sea' of the rabbis.

The intention here is to shift the emphasis back to the role of the relatively empty space between the lands that surround the sea, and to look at the ways in which the waters create links between diverse economies, cultures, and religions. But the intention is to go much further afield as well, setting out a series of comparisons with other Middle Seas in other parts of the world, as far distant as Japan and the Caribbean. This is not a vague exercise in comparative history. The argument being pursued here is that 'Mediterraneans' have played an essential role in the transformation of societies across the world by bringing into contact with one another very diverse cultures, which have themselves emerged in very diverse environments. The argument is also that these Mediterraneans are not necessarily seas in the sense that we normally understand the term. Space must also be found for the desert wastes that function like seas and that are traversed by caravans, often camel caravans, bringing not just goods but ideas across inhospitable and empty areas of the earth. Deserts, like seas, have their islands, or oases, and they have their established trade routes, their navigators and their own very limited resources for which nomads can 'fish'. The obvious cases of sand- and scrub-filled Mediterranean deserts are the Sahara and the Gobi, which were both crossed by important trade routes in the Middle Ages; but the Arabian desert, on the northern and western edges of which three great religions emerged, also functioned as a vector for goods and ideas in the same period.

The concept of a Mediterranean being adopted here is, then, rather different from that of Fernand Braudel, whose Mediterranean was to a great extent formed by the physical setting in which its inhabitants were forced to make a living; this also serves as the essential background for the conception of the Mediterranean developed by Peregrine Horden and Nicholas Purcell, with its welcome emphasis on local resources and the short-distance exchanges of vital necessities available in one area but hard to produce in another. They have rightly emphasized the importance of the micro; here, without challenging that approach, we will be concerned with the macro. Indeed, where Horden and Purcell have been more reluctant to offer opinions is in looking at the nature of cultural and religious exchanges, and the relationship between those exchanges and trade. Here a comparative perspective can be revealing: to see how medieval Japan acquired Buddhism along with Chinese trade goods, to see, indeed, how its rulers and nobles long sought to model their culture on that of China, is to observe a phenomenon not so very different in its essential aspects from the receptivity of al-Andalus to eastern Mediterranean Islamic culture, or the spread of Byzantine models outwards from metropolitan Constantinople to Italy, the Slav perimeter, and beyond. Questions can also be asked in all these cases about the relationship between trade and tribute, about the spread of technology (in all these instances, in fact, sericulture features prominently), and about the relationship between conquering elites and older native populations.

Another theme that will be addressed here is the relationship between these different Mediterraneans. The emphasis throughout will be on the later Middle Ages, a period when, in many cases, these contacts between Mediterraneans were particularly intense and profitable. In certain cases, most obviously the desert Mediterranean of the Sahara and the 'Mediterranean of the North' comprising the Baltic and the North Seas, the commercial networks and even certain key cultural strands were linked across the landmass to the trade and civilization of the Classic Mediterranean, as the Mediterranean Sea will be called here. (The term 'Northern Mediterranean' employed by Lopez to describe the Baltic-North Sea complex has been altered slightly here, since his own terminology is confusing). Constantinople, for its part, acted as a bridge between two Mediterraneans, the Classic Mediterranean and the Black Sea or Pontus. In the period we shall mainly be examining here, the central and late Middle Ages, these Mediterraneans were far from being closed worlds. This, of course, was stressed by Braudel, whose Mediterranean extended at times as far as Cracow and Madeira, as its merchants searched for raw materials, foodstuffs, and luxury items. Yet some of the Mediterraneans under examination here, in particular the Indian Ocean Mediterranean described by Kurti Chaudhuri, had open sides as well as coastal flanks, and the same applies to the 'Mediterranean Atlantic' (or 'Atlantic Mediterranean') which was created by Iberian navigators in the late Middle Ages around the islands of the eastern Atlantic. Mediterraneans thus flowed into one another, literally and figuratively, and that flow carried goods, cultures, even religions.

Written in these terms, the maritime history of the Classic Mediterranean, or any other Mediterranean, ceases to be simply the history of naval encounters between rival powers, of trade and piracy, but becomes the history of human encounters. It is not just the history of what happened on the sea, but the history of the way the inhabitants of the opposing shores of the sea interacted across the sea. In this way we can hope to restore one of the missing elements in the Braudelian Mediterranean: human beings.

2. THE CLASSIC MEDITERRANEAN AND ITS SUB-MEDITERRANEANS

Of all these Mediterraneans, the Classic Mediterranean is perhaps the most complex, for, as Purcell and Horden observe, the Classic Mediterranean is itself a group of interconnected seas, sub-Mediterraneans with their own history of cross-cultural exchange. Thus the Adriatic Sea is a miniature Mediterranean; the Adriatic has, since the early Middle Ages, brought the inhabitants of Italy face-to-face with Slavs, Albanians, and other Balkan peoples, and the linguistically and ethnically mixed societies created along the Dalmatian coast reflect these contacts. The Adriatic was a special theatre of operations for Venice, which relied on the region for wood, salt, foodstuffs, and raw materials, dominating Adriatic navigation from the eleventh century onwards: it was known to late medieval writers as 'The Venetian Gulf'. Yet the Adriatic had long been a route by which eastern goods reached the West, and in that sense it was indeed well integrated into the trade networks of the rest of the Mediterranean: the Etruscan port of Spina was already importing prodigious numbers of Greek vases in the fifth century BC.

The Aegean too, from the time of the Ionian colonization of Asia Minor, is rich in evidence for the exchange of goods, ideas, and literature between its western and eastern shores, and indeed it was a city close to its north-eastern shore, Troy, that would provide the greatest theme in the literature of the Greek and Roman world. But these little Mediterraneans within the

greater Mediterranean were also passageways through which
goods passed back and forth across the Mediterranean: nothing
demonstrates this more clearly than the trade axis between
Venice and Constantinople, two cities which themselves functioned as commercial intermediaries between the Mediterranean world and the areas beyond: the Black Sea and the edges
of the steppes, in the case of Constantinople, and the western
European landmass in the case of Venice. The Black Sea,
though connected to the Mediterranean via Constantinople
and the Dardanelles, had its own active trade routes, its own
political rivalries, its own religious and ethnic confusions which
were distinct from those of the Mediterranean Sea. Constantinople blocked access to the Jewish Khazar Empire when the
Spanish courtier Hasdai ibn Shaprut sought to make contact
with fellow Jews in the steppes. Constantinople discouraged
Venetian traders from entering the Black Sea even when, in
1082, it appeared to grant the Venetians almost unlimited
trade rights in the Byzantine Empire. These became less obviously separate worlds once the Byzantine Empire came to
depend on Genoese trade and aid after 1261, only to revert to
separation from contact with the western Mediterranean after
the Osmanli Turks asserted control of the entire region in the
fifteenth century. Indeed, in the fourteenth century several
Mediterranean cities, notably Genoa, regularly consumed
large amounts of grain from the Crimea and the western Black
Sea coasts.

We can thus agree with Braudel that the Mediterranean
possessed a basic commercial unity, while also agreeing with
Horden and Purcell that the intense regional variety of the
Mediterranean lands acted as a vital stimulus to the creation
of lasting exchange networks; indeed, this unity began to be
created as early as the eighth century BC, as the Phoenicians and
Etruscans carved out markets in southern France, Spain, and
the larger Mediterranean islands, while the Greeks too established trading bases that grew into substantial cities in southern
Italy ('Magna Graecia') and Sicily, as well as seeking to obtain
the iron of Etruria from such bases as Pyrgi and Gravisca on the
Tyrrhenian coast. This is not to deny that the different groups
entered into frequent conflict with one another, with Etruscans,
for example, meeting defeat at the hands of the Syracusan

tyrant Hieron off Cumae in 474 BC, even while Attic products were ever more keenly favoured in the markets of Etruria. Trade engendered trade wars then and later; but trade wars often engendered truces and treaties that enabled free commerce to resume, generally on better terms than previously. However, part of the interest of the often debated argument that the disintegration of the Roman Empire in the West and the rise of Islam shattered the unity of the Mediterranean lies precisely in the fact that the Mediterranean had possessed such a high measure of unity for well over a millennium already, ever since long-distance trade linked the shores of Lebanon to the *Qart Hadasht* or 'New City' known now as Carthage, and then moved further west to reach the Mediterranean shores of Spain and even Cádiz beyond the Straits of Gibraltar. In other words, the extreme antiquity of commercial networks in the Mediterranean is not in doubt.

Bearing this in mind, any discussion of the unity of the Mediterranean in post-classical times has to confront two problems. One is that of the confrontation between Islam and Christendom in the Mediterranean, which was generally characterized by intense conflict and wars of conquest. The other problem is the difference in the character of the economies of the western and eastern Mediterranean, a distinction that also has some significance for our understanding of the conflict between Islam and Christendom. Yet even the conflict between the two religions needs to be re-examined from the perspective of trade; here we see continuing contacts, even, for example, in the twelfth century, between the aggressive Almohads of north Africa and Spain and unlikely partners, the Italian merchants, at a time when the Almohads were busily suppressing Christianity and Islam in their own lands. Papal fulmination against Italian and Catalan merchants who sold armaments, or raw materials for the arms industry such as iron and pitch, provides (of course) the surest evidence that contraband trade was regular and easily arranged. Piracy interfered with free intercourse between the Christian merchants and their Muslim business partners, but, seen in the round, piracy was also a profitable and even well-controlled part of the Mediterranean economy, by the end of the Middle Ages. Pirate states such as Piombino, on the Tuscan coast, maintained a delicate balance in their relations with Muslim Tunis and other centres, aware that they could choose between licit and illicit ways of making a profit from trade with the Islamic lands. Thus the great paradox is that, at the very moment when military conflict between Christians and Muslims reached a new intensity in the early crusades, the trade routes linking East and West became ever more active thanks to the involvement of Pisans, Genoese, and Venetians, sometimes as commercial intermediaries with Islam, and sometimes as eager crusaders who sought to prise the cities of the Levant from Islam. But the essential point is that the unity of the Mediterranean Sea as a place of commercial exchange had been restored.

At the heart of this relationship between Christendom and the Islamic or Byzantine lands lay the differences in economic structures between East and West. It would obviously be an exaggeration to see the western Mediterranean as primarily rural in character and the eastern Mediterranean as primarily urban. Islamic lands in the western Mediterranean, notably Morocco, shared with Christian ones a propensity for grain production and the rearing of animals; eleventh-century Muslim Spain was more urbanized than contemporary Morocco. But a long-standing reality was that towns counted for more in the eastern Mediterranean: a greater percentage of the population was urbanized; urban industries provided employment for significant numbers of people; these industries themselves were supported by elaborate exchange networks, so that, under Islam, the artisan products of Egypt could be found as far afield as Spain and Iraq.

From the tenth to the twelfth centuries, these trade routes appear to have been favourites of the Jewish merchants of Old Cairo (Fustat) whose letters survive in the famous Cairo Genizah; these merchants were the members of a 'Mediterranean Society' vividly brought to life by Shlomo Goitein in his close studies of the Genizah letters. What is noticeable is that the Christian lands of western Europe barely feature in the Genizah trading networks, while Muslim merchants were often instructed by their religious leaders not to enter Christian lands. Thus until the late eleventh or twelfth century commercial contact between the Christian shores of the Mediterranean and the Islamic shores remained rather limited. And yet the development of urban life in the Islamic lands was closely related to the lack of sufficient agricultural resources to feed the cities; towns in the arid lands of the eastern Mediterranean needed to buy in grain and other vital goods, and as they expanded so did the scale of the trade in primary goods. Indeed, agriculture itself became increasingly specialized, as exotic goods could be exported for high profit (later, the crops themselves were transplanted westwards: asparagus, artichokes, lemons, bitter oranges, sugar, rice). When Christian conquerors overwhelmed lands such as Sicily and Majorca their instinct was to turn away from the production of specialized crops, back to the wheat and other grains they knew so well as sources of rent in cash and kind. The result was a diminution in production of sugar, indigo, and henna in thirteenth-century Sicily, and appeals by its ruler, Frederick II, to the Jews of north Africa to bring back the forgotten agricultural knowhow.

Despite the existence of large grain estates in parts of the eastern Mediterranean—in large tracts of Byzantine Greece, as well as along the Nile—it was in western Europe that reasonably self-sufficient grain-based local economies had always predominated; they were not a by-product of the 'fall of the Roman Empire', though the loss of foreign markets and political confusion undoubtedly led to urban contraction in the western Mediterranean, leaving only a few centres trading actively with the East by the eighth century. Naples and Marseilles had never ceased to function as intermediaries between East and West, joined later by the new trading centres established at Amalfi south of Naples, and by the nominally Byzantine inhabitants of a marshy set of lagoons in the Upper Adriatic, whose many settlements coalesced by the tenth or eleventh century into a city built around the Rialto or 'high bank'. The skills of the settlers as fishermen and salt-makers provided a sound basis for the creation of a great trading empire linked to Constantinople, the mother-city that was soon to be effectively a colony.

This interaction between a lightly urbanized West and a more heavily urbanized East raises a theoretical question of some importance. To what extent did trade alter the character of the societies in western Europe that were visited by Italian and Catalan merchants bearing either luxury goods or raw materials they had acquired from the Mediterranean islands and coasts? (Of course, most of the spices came from much further away, as far away as Indonesia; but access to the Red Sea was closed to the Italians and they had to obtain these goods in Alexandria and other Levantine towns). Cotton from Sicily, Malta and Egypt undoubtedly fed the looms of the Lombard, Tuscan, and Catalan cities. Grain from Sicily, Sardinia, Crete and, eventually, the Black Sea, undoubtedly fed the stomachs of those who worked the looms, at least in Barcelona, Genoa, Pisa, and Florence. Mediterranean trade enabled these and other cities to grow: not just the luxury trade in fine dyestuffs, silks, slaves, and gold, but the more modest trade in wheat and wine from the Italian South, which also sustained Tunis, itself home to a massive population of Italian and Catalan traders. We can thus see the trade of the Mediterranean in this period as a source of wealth both to an expanding group of western merchants based in the Mediterranean towns of Italy, Spain, and southern France, but also as a source of livelihood to the artisans of those cities and satellite towns in the hinterland. The 'commercial revolution' began on the seaboard, but had a knock-on effect inland: the greatest exponent of this effect was Florence, a city some way from the sea that still came to depend significantly on grain brought to Tuscany by sea from Apulia, Sardinia, and Sicily, and a city whose woollen cloth (partly made of fibres also imported by sea) became a prized article of trade throughout the Mediterranean.

Still, we must be careful about interpreting these developments as the emergence of a 'bourgeoisie', as a middle-class revolution: the elites in the Italian cities were generally formed out of old landed families who intermarried with bankers and wealthy traders to form an aristocratic mercantile upper class unlike anything in the Islamic world, possessing political power and passing on wealth and property within the extended family; the key to survival was, indeed, to vary one's portfolio, to combine trade and banking with the purchase of tax farms and bonds, the management of cloth workshops, urban property, lands in the countryside. If the commercial revolution produced a middle class, it was more properly the skilled artisans who were the rank and file of the guilds; but even the guilds were often dominated by the patrician families. Thus, rather than trying to apply a Marxist framework to the effects of trade on the society of Mediterranean western Europe, it is more helpful to emphasize the very distinctive forms of social structure that emerged in the Italian city-states, structures that fit uneasily into any preconceived models. All the more so, indeed, when one turns to Barcelona, whose trading elite seems to have been much more town-based, much less rooted in an out-of-town petty aristocracy, than was the case in Italy. This, in any case, was a capital city for rulers who came to dominate much of the western Mediterranean in the thirteenth and fourteenth centuries, the seat, as well, of a substantial Jewish community which, contrary to the easy stereotype, had no special interest in overseas trade or in large-scale moneylending. And finally there is Venice, whose patriciate was once again not significantly wedded to the land (apart from urban property) until the fifteenth century, and whose plebs was apparently so convinced of the manifold economic benefits of good government by aristocrats that the city largely avoided the social tensions rampant elsewhere in northern Italy.

A significant characteristic of the merchants who dominated Mediterranean trade was that, although Christian in the main (there were some Jewish merchants active in Provence and Catalonia, but very few in Italy), the merchants were riven apart by disputes between cities, trading companies, and family loyalties; rivalry between clans and political factions, notably Guelfs and Ghibellines, was one of the less savoury exports from the Italian cities, other than Venice. On the ground, in places such as Tunis and Alexandria, even this did not prevent a remarkable degree of cooperation between, say Pisans and Genoese when it seemed advantageous for profit, or because of personal ties that transcended the rivalries. Yet the city governments which claimed the right to protect the merchants were jealous of others who appeared to have gained better trading privileges in overseas ports, while merchants themselves could occasionally solve the problem of the appearance of new rivals by going out and sacking their quarters (as happened to the Genoese in Constantinople in 1162). Rulers who did not cooperate with the merchants might also have their harbour sacked as a sign of displeasure. In other words, the commercial revolution was the product of cut-throat competition and frequent violence: sometimes the word 'cut-throat' has to be taken literally, as when in the early fourteenth century Catalans and Genoese ruthlessly slaughtered passengers on one another's boats, innocent victims of the battle for control of Sardinia. In such an atmosphere of underlying violence it is perhaps not so surprising that Christian merchants learned little of the culture of the lands they visited and played only a limited role in the transmission of texts and ideas from East to West; the contrast with the role of merchants in transmitting culture from China to Japan in the same period is striking.

If we are looking for a general theory to apply to this evidence, its outlines would perhaps be these. Trade can indeed act as a 'solvent' (to use a word familiar to Marxist historians), transforming societies once they come into intense, regular contact with very different economies and polities; and Mediterraneans facilitate this by enabling contact between unlikely partners which have developed largely independently of one another but are, once the sea is discounted, actually near neighbours. (This is to ignore for the moment the phenomenon of transplanted societies, colonies which may even be clones of the mother-city, to which we shall return in a later section). Sometimes complementary relationships develop across the Great Sea, as between Sicily and Tunisia in the age of the Genizah merchants, and between Sicily and northern Italy in later centuries, or as between al-Andalus and Morocco throughout the Middle Ages. Here, regions well supplied with foodstuffs were able to offer essential supplies to towns that sought to concentrate on the production of industrial goods; and this occurred across cultural and political boundaries, notably that between Islam and Christendom, no less than within the political spheres of the rival religions. As vectors of change, we can single out Jewish merchants, who had relative freedom of movement compared to Muslims and Christians, though by 1200 the Christians themselves had seized the initiative and become the master mariners of the Mediterranean. What they offered was a combination of nautical and commercial skills, whereas the Jews could only offer the latter.

3. NEIGHBOURING MEDITERRANEANS: THE SAHARAN MEDITERRANEAN DESERT

The Jews are often seen as experts in the trade of a neighbouring 'Mediterranean' which needs consideration at this point, in view of its close interrelationship with the Classic Mediterranean: the Sahara Desert. A network of contacts enabled Jewish merchants to make payments in Sijilmasa for purchases as far away as Walata, and Walata, deep in the interior, was a transit post in a great sandy sea with a similar entrepôt function to, say, Majorca in the western Mediterranean. These were critical stages, islands if you like, along the caravan trade routes that brought gold northwards and salt and textiles southwards. Sijilmasa was the home of the famous Jewish merchant Solomon ben Amar, who was favoured with privileges by King James I of Aragon, and came to live in newly conquered Majorca, where his business deals are well reflected in the notarial registers of the years around 1240. The Sahara was a true Mediterranean in the sense that it brought very different cultures into contact, and across the open spaces they brought not merely articles of trade but ideas, notably religious ones, and styles of architecture appropriate to the Muslim culture they implanted on the northern edges of Black Africa. There they established trading centres which were sometimes physically separate from the ceremonial cities of the Black African kings, as in Mali, whose emperor Mansa Musa went on a great trek to Mecca in the fourteenth century, literally scattering gold on his way. The double entities consisting of trading city and ceremonial city were sometimes also distinguished by religion, however, and the penetration of Islam into Black Africa was a slow process, not helped by an occasionally disdainful attitude among the northern visitors to their Black interlocutors. Yet Timbuktu, with its Muslim religious elite and madrasas, became a major centre of Muslim learning, and its libraries still survive, dating back to the fourteenth century; here, on the north bend of the River Niger, it was possible to tap into the gold reserves of the lands to the south of the Sahara. In the same way, Catalan and Genoese merchants arriving in, say, Bougie on the Algerian coast were able to tap into the caravan routes that crossed the Sahara and buy the gold dust that had been brought from the Niger. In the middle of the fifteenth century there were one or two brave attempts by Italians to penetrate deep into the Sahara, and Antonio Malfante crossed to Timbuktu in 1447. However, this was largely a closed 'sea', dominated by the Tuareg nomads who knew how to navigate it and live off its resources.

The contact between the Maghrib and Black Africa was not all one-way, since slaves were brought from the south and there was a degree of ethnic mixing in the Maghrib. Indeed, we can see the Maghrib as a fascinating example of a territory caught between two Mediterraneans, and well able to make use of the resources of both, a bridge between worlds. Thus in the thirteenth century cowrie shells from the Indian Ocean, in demand as currency in Black Africa, passed into the Mediterranean, as far as Marseilles, then down via Majorca into north Africa, whence they weighed down the camels bound for the 'Sudan', the land of the Blacks. These interrelationships did, however, begin to change when the routes leading to the southern Sahara were diverted around the outer edges of this 'Mediterranean', after the Portuguese opened up the Atlantic sea routes and began to extract gold, slaves, and forest products out of Black Africa through their trading bases at Elmina and elsewhere. This did not mark the end of the trans-Sahara trade, by any means; but it marked the beginning of fundamental changes in the nature of the relationship, political and economic, between Black Africa and southern Europe, which no longer depended on Berber, Jewish, Catalan, and Genoese intermediaries passing goods to one another.

4. THE MEDITERRANEAN OF THE NORTH

This relationship between the Classic Mediterranean and the Saharan Mediterranean calls to mind another example of Mediterraneans that interacted strongly in the late Middle Ages. The eminent historian of medieval Genoa, Roberto Lopez, described the North Sea and Baltic, taken together, as a 'Northern Mediterranean', with boundaries set by Britain, Flanders, northern Germany and the present-day Baltic States, as well as the Scandinavian kingdoms.[1] The roots of the late medieval trading networks must be traced back to the Frisian and Viking navigators of the early Middle Ages, and it is clear that Danish and Swedish expansion along the coasts of the Baltic in the thirteenth century shared many common features with the raiding and conquests of the Vikings and Varangians in the tenth and eleventh centuries. Overall, this was an area characterized to a much greater degree than the Classic Mediterranean by cooperation between merchants, particularly with the creation of the trading networks of the German Hansa, which stretched from the steelyards of London and Lynn to Bergen, Bruges, Cologne, Bremen, Lübeck, Visby, Riga and even as far as the Peterhof in Novgorod. This is only to name some of the most famous trading destinations of Hanseatic merchants, but a whole host of smaller towns along the Dutch and German coasts and in the hinterland (such as Dordrecht) were, at various times, linked to the Hansa; the towns just listed were in some cases members of the League, in others only hosts to Hanseatic warehouses and trade counters. However, it would be an error to suppose that the Hansa possessed quite as complete a control over Baltic and North Sea trade as has often been suggested; it was possible to survive outside the Hansa, and even to challenge its power, as Bristol and several Dutch towns did in the fifteenth century. Yet the presence at the Hansa diets of the deputy of the grand master of the Teutonic Knights underlined the fact that the Hansa was linked to the territorial power of a crusading military order, willing to offer rye and other basic commodities to the towns of the German seaboard in return for weaponry and shipping services.

We can thus see a complementary relationship developing between the lands of the eastern Baltic under Teutonic rule and the towns of the south-western Baltic, and even the German flank of the North Sea, a relationship which continued to flourish despite the knocks and blows of the Black Death and subsequent attacks of plague. The towns that grew up on the shores of Livonia and Estonia existed to service the needs of

[1] Robert S. Lopez, *The Commercial Revolution of the Middle Ages, 950– 1350* (Englewood Cliffs, NJ, 1971), 20, 23, 95, 113–17, 136.

trade with cities much further to the west, above all Lübeck; indeed, the main motor of urban growth in the Baltic Far East was German trade and migration. Outside the towns, the fifteenth century saw an intensification of control by landlords over the peasantry of eastern Europe, which reduced the agricultural workforce to a 'second serfdom', and ensured the continued importance of the rye lands as a source of grain for the Dutch and other consumers well into the seventeenth century.[2] In other words, this Mediterranean of the North remained a lively economic theatre well into the early modern period.

Just as the other Mediterraneans saw alongside the expansion of trade an intensification in cultural contacts across the water, so too in this area we can observe a process of Christianization, accompanied by human migration, that transformed the societies of the coasts of the Mediterranean of the North: the process begins, indeed, in the Viking age, with the Danish and Norse settlement of northern England and the outer isles of Great Britain, but rapidly the direction of cultural influences reversed, as Norway's rulers accepted the Christian faith and as Christianity also spread into the Baltic region;[3] there, a certain amount of competition between Catholic and Orthodox Christianity occurred, though one area, Lithuania, proved very resistant to formal Christianization, retaining a pagan elite until the end of the fourteenth century.[4] This made Lithuania (which came to rule over a vast area reaching almost from the North Sea to the Black Sea) not a more but a less closed world: it was home to Catholics and Orthodox, Jews and Muslims, as well as a diversity of pagans.[5] In Finland, on the other hand, Swedish

---

[2] W. Kula, *An Economic Theory of the Feudal System: Towards a Model of the Polish Economy 1500–1800*, trans. L. Garner (London, 1976); D. Kirby, *Northern Europe in the Early Modern Period: The Baltic World 1492–1772* (London, 1990), 3–23.

[3] G. Turville-Petre, *The Heroic Age of Scandinavia* (London, 1951), 130–64.

[4] On this process see the two volumes of collected essays published by the Pontificio Comitato di Scienze Storiche, *Gli Inizi del Cristianesimo in Livonia-Lettonia* and *La Cristianizzazione della Lituania* (Vatican City, 1989); S. C. Rowell, *Lithuania Ascending: A Pagan Empire within East-Central Europe, 1295–1345* (Cambridge, 1994).

[5] Cf. a similar scenario in Hungary: N. Berend, *At the Gates of Christendom: Jews, Muslims and 'Pagans' in Medieval Hungary*, c.1000–c.1300 (Cambridge, 2001).

royal campaigns, under the banner of crusades, established trading bases such as Porvoo (Birka) and brought Scandinavian culture to a land that offered furs and amber. Intensive exchanges with Norway also characterize this region: German merchants brought grain to Bergen, in return for which they were permitted to export fish; English merchants likewise, for the intensity of Anglo-Norwegian commercial and cultural exchanges must not be underestimated well after the Viking period.

The hinge around which this network turned was the large and wealthy city of Bruges, a centre of textile production and later of high finance without equal in late medieval northern Europe, the seat of countless warehouses catering to the needs of Scottish, Portuguese, Florentine, Genoese, and many other merchants. The crucial point is that Bruges was also the major link between this Mediterranean of the North and the Classic Mediterranean, for, as Fernand Braudel made plain in his great work on the Mediterranean in the age of Philip II, the terminal point of the great medieval trade routes leading up from the Mediterranean was this Flemish city. The interaction between the Mediterraneans of North and South was of critical importance in the take-off of the medieval European economy, for northern textiles conveyed by land and river to Italy were then diffused widely through the Mediterranean by Genoese, Venetian, Tuscan, and Catalan merchants. Once again, we can see a process at work by which navigators began to sideline the traditional trade routes, at first sight similar to the sidelining of the Saharan trade routes visible during the phase of Portuguese exploration of the Guinea coast. However, the opening of the Atlantic sea routes past Gibraltar actually reaffirmed the ties between the two Mediterraneans, by making easier the bulk transfer of wool into the Classic Mediterranean and of alum into the Northern Mediterranean, with the result that textile industries were further able to expand in Tuscany, Catalonia, northern and southern France, Flanders, and eventually England. Again, this relationship was of considerable cultural importance, for the transfer of artistic methods and even exact iconographic themes between Flanders and Italy (or the other way) was a marked feature of fifteenth-century painting; one could cite the debt of the Neapolitan painter Colantonio to very precise models from the workshops of the van Eycks and their contemporaries, or the experience gained by Antonello da Messina in northern workshops.

It is hard not to be struck by the structural similarities between the Classic Mediterranean and the Mediterranean of the North, regions which constituted frontiers between Christians and non-Christians, and which therefore were the theatre of holy wars, Mediterranean crusades and Baltic ones, but also of commercial penetration by town-based merchants, predominantly Low German in the north and predominantly north Italian or Catalan in the south. In both areas, trade and crusade went hand-in-hand. In both, the exchange of luxury goods for raw materials was the foundation of trade, though of course there was a massive difference between doing business as a guest of the Mamluk sultan or caliph of Tunis and trading in forest products along the barely developed shores of Estonia and Livonia. The distinctive style of brick-built gabled housing, suitable for warehouses and living quarters combined together, spread from the Netherlands and northern Germany eastwards across the Baltic, along with the Low German languages. This created a degree of cultural homogeneity among the trading elites, not dissimilar to the way that Catalan trade brought Catalan building styles and pockets of Catalan settlers speaking the Catalan tongue to Sicily, Sardinia, and even in some measure Greece, or to the way that the towns of Sicily became impregnated with the culture of northern Italy, to which a significant proportion of the population traced their ancestry.

5. THE MEDITERRANEAN ATLANTIC

The interest of the waters beyond the Straits of Gibraltar lies, in part, in the way that western European colonists adapted the islands they found (principally the Madeira group, the Azores, the Canaries, with southward extensions to the Cape Verdes and São Tomé) to the needs of the European economy, at a time when access to eastern Mediterranean goods was being hindered by the advance of the Ottomans. The area is defined not by coasts, except to the east, but by the lines linking the island archipelagoes that make up this region. Still, this has not dissuaded historians such as Verlinden from describing the region as a sort of Mediterranean. The interchangeable terms 'Mediterranean Atlantic' or 'Atlantic Mediterranean' have thus come into use to describe the area; Fernández-Armesto justifies the terms by arguing that this was a 'middle sea' surrounded by mainlands and archipelagos which constituted, for a while, the practical limits of navigation, but also because what was trans-planted into this zone was 'traditional Mediterranean civiliza-tion'.[6] The Mediterranean Atlantic could thus be characterized as in part an artificial Mediterranean, constructed around pre-viously uninhabited islands under the rule of Portugal, with one important exception: the Canary archipelago, which was al-ready populated by Neolithic cultures and which was eventually conquered and held by the Castilians. The physical boundary in the west was a technological one: the difficulty of penetrating further than the Azores before the time of Columbus and Cabot. Before the end of the fifteenth century, even attempts to go further west, such as that of Ferdinand van Olmen in the 1480s, were apparently guided by the belief that there were more islands in the Ocean (Brazil, the Antilles, etc.) rather than continents, whether these might be Asia or a New World.

This region took advantage of its ease of access not merely to the Classic Mediterranean but also to the Mediterranean of the North, with which the Portuguese merchants of Madeira and the Azores developed intensive relations via Middelburg, Ant-werp, and other towns. The eastern flanks of this Mediterra-nean were also important: Lisbon, and Lagos in the Algarve itself, provided command centres for operations by Portuguese merchants, as did Seville and Cádiz for the Castilians. The colonizers had some contact, too, with the African coast oppos-ite the Canaries, though the trade with that area was probably dominated by the purchase of slaves. There was a highly de-veloped inter-island trade by 1500, dealing in grain, animal products, and wood, the article that gave its name to Madeira itself. But the prize export, particularly from Madeira, was sugar, though later wine took the lead instead, a product trad-itionally sold to western merchants in large quantities in the

[6] F. Fernández-Armesto, *Before Columbus: Exploration and Colonisation from the Mediterranean to the Atlantic, 1229–1492* (London, 1987), 152.

eastern Mediterranean, but now available within the Mediterranean Atlantic to consumers in Iberia and northern Europe.
After 1500, this region underwent a further change in character
as it became a staging post for access to the newly discovered
Americas; in that sense, its existence as a homogeneous 'Mediterranean' was rather brief. That the region saw the introduction of Iberian culture and religion from its north-eastern flank
goes without saying: the Canary islanders were Christianized
before they died out, and the Portuguese islands were settled by
a solely Christian population, at least in theory; the reality was
that Iberian conflicts were played out in the islands, including
the Canaries, and the presence of crypto-Jews, with a Canary
Inquisition to deal with them, comes as no great surprise. São
Tomé was specifically chosen as the home for deported Jewish
children from Portugal, who were to be brought up as Christians far from parental influence. The conquest of the islands
was even given a modest crusading dimension, though how
Henry the Navigator could claim that in conquering empty
Madeira he had scored a victory against Islam is a mystery.

6. A TRANS-OCEANIC MEDITERRANEAN: THE CARIBBEAN

The opening of the Atlantic achieved its next phase with the
discovery by Columbus of the Caribbean. This is a sea that
exhibits many of the obvious physical characteristics of a Mediterranean: like the Classic Mediterranean it is a space between
continents, North America and South America, following,
indeed, the joins between continents rather as the shores of
the Classic Mediterranean trace the limits of Europe, Asia,
and Africa. Its eastern boundary, however, consists of a line of
islands, close enough to be in easy contact with one another, and
forming a great semicircle from Cuba and the Bahamas down to
Trinidad, which is effectively an offshore extension of the
South American landmass. Cuba itself reaches out towards the
peninsula of Yucatán, though by the fifteenth century it had no
contact with the residue of Maya civilization on the mainland.
However, there was apparently limited contact with the Timi-
cua and other peoples of what was to become Florida; the
Florida Indians included communities that depended on the

sea, and the middens containing hundreds of thousands of shellfish remains provide rich archaeological evidence of this dependency. Florida itself closes off a second space, the Gulf of Mexico, which forms a second Mediterranean; this, however, seems to have been a quieter area from the perspective of maritime contacts in the pre-Columbian period, even if around its shores some sophisticated cultures had developed. Thus, as with the ancient Mediterranean, we can speak of a double area partly closed off by a major island (in this case, Cuba), in which commercial activity was more intense in one area than in another.

In Pre-Columbian times, this area had further characteristics of a Mediterranean, as migrants moved up the chain of islands, with Taínos moving north from the Arawak lands of present-day Venezuela and the Guianas, displacing the more primitive, possibly legendary, Ciboneys, who were supposedly pushed into the western extremities of Cuba; and with Caribs raiding into the islands, spreading fear with their propensity for fattening up male captives and feasting on human meat (hence the new meaning of their corrupted name, cannibals). To Columbus and his Italian contemporaries Amerigo Vespucci and Peter Martyr, thinking in the black-and-white terms then current in the original Mediterranean from which they came, the Taínos were the victims of a sort of Carib jihad, and the answer was to win permission for the war against the Caribs to be classed as a holy war. But this image of conflict has been subtly modified by scholars, some of whom have been deeply doubtful (too much so, probably) about the veracity of tales of man-eating Caribs; in any case, a new consensus reveals that Caribs and Taínos shared more cultural attributes than had been assumed. Nor were the Taínos themselves entirely homogeneous. Most archaeologists attribute a higher level of technology and more elaborate social institutions to the 'Classic Taínos' of the larger islands, especially Hispaniola, while those who first greeted Columbus, the Lucayan Indians of the Bahamas, appear to have lived in less complex societies, even though they had contact with the 'Classic Taínos'. As far as evidence for state formation is concerned, we can observe small political entities on the bigger islands, dividing up the territory (sometimes in rivalry with one another); large political entities comprising a whole major island or a group of minor ones did not come into being. This is obviously very different from the centralized states with massive public works (palaces, temples, great mounds) coming into existence in central America, and as far south as Peru and as far north as the Mississippi valleys. Curious, though, is the importance both in Central American high cultures and in the Caribbean of ceremonial ball games; maybe this indicates some cultural contact, going back to the South American origins of the Taínos. Even so, the ball games played by the Taínos appear to have lacked the intensity of those of Maya and Aztecs: in the Caribbean they did not result in the losers being selected for ritual execution, and, at the risk of oversimplifying what one sees, one could say that they appear to have had a social but not so much a religious function.

However, what is certain is that news and goods travelled rapidly along the trade routes. Columbus was surprised to find that some of the simple trade goods such as hawks' bells and buttons that had been handed to the Indians of the Bahamas actually preceded him on his journey down the edges of the Caribbean; canoe traffic was fast and intense, and there are signs that communities traded both luxury goods and basic foodstuffs, such as manioc, the staple foodstuff of South American origin whose cultivation spread northwards as the Taíno Indians moved through the island chain. However, the Florida Indians did not adopt the distinctive agricultural methods of South America, relying instead on seed crops of the sort also cultivated along the coasts of the Gulf of Mexico; in this sense the Florida Channel, though navigable, constituted a cultural frontier between two worlds.[7]

This was thus a Mediterranean with invisible boundaries. Moreover, rumours of high civilization which percolated to Columbus in Hispaniola and Cuba may have been founded on very little, and were probably not based on any exact knowledge of the land-based civilizations of Mexico. Even in Veragua, along the Central American coast, clues to the existence of city-based cultures with a higher level of technology than that of the Caribbean Indians were vague; still, by noticing (for

[7] Carl E. Sauer, *The Early Spanish Main* (Berkeley and Los Angeles, 1966), 51–3.

instance) the much more extensive use of textiles in that region it was possible to deduce that the Spaniards were on the edges of an exotic and opulent world.

7. THE JAPANESE MEDITERRANEAN

This exotic and opulent world was not supposed (according to Columbus) to be an undiscovered civilization but Cathay and Cipangu, China and Japan, though he relied for the latter only on the vague words of Marco Polo, who portrayed a highly luxurious society rich in silks and precious metals. In fact, the real medieval Japan fits well into the theme of societies tranformed by their contacts across a 'Mediterranean'. Japan's Mediterranean consists of two main parts: in the north, there are the waters between the main island, Honshu, and the Asian mainland, including the eastern coast of Korea and the early medieval kingdom of Parhae between Harbin and the sea; in the south, the Korea Strait acted as a bridge between the southern Japanese island of Kyushu and Korea, while to the west of Kyushu lay the Yellow Sea and the East China Sea, bordered by the chain of the Ryukyu islands, the best known of which is Okinawa, and, at the southernmost point of the chain, the larger island of Taiwan. This 'Mediterranean' offers some of the richest parallels to the Classic Mediterranean as far as the medieval period is concerned, just as the evolution of Japanese society as a whole has certain striking resemblances to that of 'feudal' Europe; it therefore makes sense to look at the evidence quite closely.[8]

What is interesting about the Japanese case is that the flow of ideas and artistic influences was primarily into Japan in the Middle Ages, though trade between Japan and Asia was naturally a two-way process. The Japanese, though often keen to assert their political autonomy, were influenced in the way they articulated the idea of that autonomy by Chinese models; they acquired texts and part of their writing system from China;

---

[8] For what follows, I have relied on Jean-François Souyri, *The World Turned Upside Down: Medieval Japanese Society*, trans. K. Roth (New York, 2001/London, 2002), and on Charlotte von Verschuer, *Le Commerce extérieur du Japon des origines au XVIe siède* (Paris, 1988) who have themselves built on exciting new archival work by Japanese scholars.

the religious influences from the mainland became exceptionally strong as Buddhism gained a hold in Japan during the early
Middle Ages, coexisting fairly easily with native beliefs and
rituals, though one of the major effects of the Buddhist implantation was the creation of large monastic estates with all that
implied for the organization of Japanese society. The Japanese
Mediterranean was thus a channel by which Japan was brought
deeper into the cultures of East Asia. The appetite in aristocratic circles for Chinese goods was almost insatiable, though
the finest silks from China were kept for rare occasions, and the
Japanese developed their own very fine traditions of silk production.

The meeting of cultures is well represented in the extraordinary collections of palace artefacts and works of art preserved at
the Shoso-in repository attached to the Todai-ji temple in Nara;
here influences from lands to the west can be traced both in
designs imitated from Persian, Indian, and Chinese models (for
example in painted screens that recall T'ang iconography), and
in actual objects brought across the seas (for example lapis lazuli
belt ornaments from Afghanistan). Even Chinese tea bowls
were in massive demand, at a time when tea drinking had not
actually taken off in Japan; in fact, the Japanese, despite a very
long ceramic tradition, found it hard to imitate the superb
celadon wares which were imported in vast quantities in the
twelfth century. During the excavation of the metro at Fukoaka,
the city on Kyushu which incorporates the medieval port of
Hakata, 35,000 fragments of native and Chinese pottery were
found, the latter coming mainly from centres of production on
the Chinese coasts. The white pottery of Yue zhou was known
sometimes under the name *hisoku* or 'forbidden object' because
it was originally reserved to the imperial family alone. Particularly prized were Chinese books, including Buddhist religious
texts such as the Lotus Sutra and collections of T'ang poetry; in
the early eleventh century the regent Fujiwara no Michinaga
was given the T'ang anthology three times, and in 1010 he gave
a printed copy, with commentary, to the emperor. Although the
Japanese sent back to China ornamented boxes and fine cloths
of silk and canvas, only a few of the islands' products had
particular renown across the sea: one was Japanese paper,
which was manufactured from different plants and by slightly

different processes from that used in China, and was admired for its smoothness and delicacy; there were also decorated screens (themselves partly made of paper). But Japan was also known as a richer source of gold than China, and as a major source of pearls, aspects of 'Cipangu' that were readily appreciated by Marco Polo and by Christopher Columbus.

This trade between Japan and the mainland underwent a series of distinct phases in the Middle Ages. From the sixth and seventh century, the assumption in China was that Japan was another vassal state, and objects received were treated as tribute, with gifts sent in return. At the Japanese end, trade was treated as a state enterprise, which was not the case in eleventh-century China, even though the Chinese government took a close interest in its encouragement and taxation. By the eleventh and twelfth centuries, there is fuller evidence for regular commercial exchanges, and it is thought that at least one well-laden vessel a year reached Hakata full of luxury goods for the Japanese elite. Hakata was the one official port for trade with China, well placed for access to the Asian mainland, though standing at some remove from the centres of power at Kyoto and Nara, and even further from the power base at Kamakura which became particularly significant after 1185. The island of Tsushima, halfway across the Korea Strait, provided a base en route to Korea, and the straits also contained an important cult centre for mariners. But contact was so intense that there even developed a Chinese commercial colony in Kyushu, and in the eleventh and twelfth centuries several prominent merchants seem to have had mixed Chinese-Japanese parentage.

Despite the burgeoning trade, the imperial court was also keen to maintain its distance and dignity; visiting merchants could be kept waiting for many months while the central administration slowly reflected on whether it did or did not wish to receive a consignment of goods, and what could be sent in return that would uphold the dignity of the Japanese court. In the early Middle Ages, the Japanese court set out a well-spaced timetable to ensure that visits from Korea and China were not too frequent (the interval could be as much as six years for the Chinese, and twelve years for Parhae, while in the period 922–40 visitors from the Koryo kingdom of Korea were regularly rebuffed and made to return home without even being received). However, this practice vanished by the late twelfth century, when the military government based at Kamakura was less well able to control the day-to-day affairs of Kyushu island. Chinese coins became widespread in both Japan and Korea, leading to a drainage of bullion out of China, and an attempt in 1199 to prevent Japanese and Korean merchants from acquiring Chinese money (there were even attempts by customs officials to inspect departing ships for illicit bullion); but this had no real effect. Another effect of the commercialization of Japanese society as a result of its trade links was the appearance of more elaborate credit arrangements and of moneylenders.

At the same time, there was evidently a growing private trade between China and Japan, and also between Korea and Japan. A wreck of a Chinese junk dating from 1323 provided eloquent testimony to this trade expansion: over 18,000 pieces of pottery, predominantly Chinese, were found on board, as well as tons of Chinese copper coins; and it appears that the ship was sailing from Ningbo on the Chinese coast to Japan, on the account of the Tofukuji Zen Buddhist monastery of Kyoto, which had burned down a few years earlier and was seeking to finance its rebuilding programme. However, this trade was increasingly compromised by the activities of pirates; this became a particularly severe problem from the fourteenth century onwards, and indeed it may be taken as further evidence that trade was flourishing, since there was clearly good business to be done by interlopers. The Inland Sea through which shipping had to pass to reach the outports of Kyoto from Hakata was a particularly pirate-infested area. However, there is plentiful evidence of lively trade out of one of those outports, Hyogo, in a customs register of 1445, which reveals that nearly two thousand vessels passed through one tollgate in a year, heading in the direction of Kyoto. Charlotte von Verschuer speaks of the twelfth to the fourteenth centuries as a time of 'un commerce actif et liberalisé', culminating in the fifteenth century in a balance of trade that was favourable to the Japanese.

A distinction remained between official and unofficial trade, but by this period it was clearly impossible to prevent the movement of unauthorized vessels. Under shogun Yoshimitsu, legitimate shipping bound for China was provided with official seals, and under this scheme two ships each year crossed to the mainland between 1401 and 1410. The shoguns and the monasteries such as the Kofukoji at Nara were great patrons of such large-scale enterprises throughout the fifteenth century. The political price, in the fifteenth century, was an occasional admission that even the Japanese emperor was a vassal of the Chinese one, an admission for which Yoshimitsu was roundly condemned by his son and successor; but this admission could bring great dividends: at the time of the early Ming voyages, when the Chinese sought to take tribute from a vast swathe of East Asia and the Indian Ocean, the Japanese were compliant and were rewarded with gifts of silk, silver, and lacquer, but were able to maintain their exports of horses and armaments to the mainland. Later, in 1432–3, these included over 3,000 sabres, and nearly 10,000 sabres in 1453. This was a period in which control of the shipping routes off the Asian coasts shifted away from the Chinese, who had dominated navigation for centuries, into the hands of other peoples, including Japanese mariners. A particularly important role was acquired by the autonomous kingdom in the Ryukyu islands, with its centre at Okinawa, on the southern edge of this Japanese Mediterranean; this region provided southward links, connecting the Japanese Mediterranean to some of the longer-distance trade routes as far as the Malacca Straits (home to Malacca, Palembang, and Temasek, the modern Singapore), which had become once again a very significant centre of the spice trade in the fifteenth century, the focal point, indeed, of a Malay Mediterranean around the South China Sea, the Java Sea, and the eastern Indian Ocean. Thus the Japanese Mediterranean was becoming less and less isolated by 1500.

Although the focus of the Japanese trade in luxury items was the court and the great monasteries, the impact of trade on the wider economy of medieval Japan should not be underestimated. Jean-François Souyri places some emphasis on the role of trade in late medieval Japan as an element that helped transform quite a conservative society. To this should be added the overwhelming impact of Asian religion and the exceptionally powerful influence of Chinese culture: books, images, social values. All this had been carried across Japan's Mediterranean, and had been carefully filtered, in the formative period of the early Middle Ages, by government control and by attempts to keep contact with the mainland within carefully prescribed limits. The result was the creation of a distinctive society that combined indigenous with mainland Asian features. By the late Middle Ages Japanese society was able to produce significant quantities of goods that were in demand on the mainland and to reverse the balance of trade, which was now in favour of Nippon.

8. THE INDIAN OCEAN AS A BRAUDELIAN PROBLEM

Finally, we can look at a very large-scale example of a 'Mediterranean', that of the Indian Ocean in late medieval and early modern times. Since this area has already been analysed in overtly Braudelian terms by Kurti Chaudhuri, it is not essential here to spell out all the ways it can be compared to the Classic Mediterranean: the importance of wind and waves, the impact of climate (with the effects of the monsoons across a wide swathe of the region), and the economic and cultural links that enabled goods and ideas to move from the Muslim to the Hindu and Buddhist spheres and back again. All the other Mediterraneans examined here are more or less closed seas, and the Indian Ocean obviously does not meet that criterion; its south-western extremities are reasonably well defined (the coasts of East Africa down to Moçambique or even further), and at the north-west the Red Sea forms a tight funnel linking Indian Ocean trade to the Mediterranean, though of course this still necessitated a relatively short overland journey until the building of the Suez Canal. Its eastern end can best be defined as the Malacca Straits and the series of maritime passageways between Malaya and the East Indies that lead to the Spice Islands, though Chaudhuri extends it further towards China and Japan in the era of Portuguese hegemony that followed the voyages of Vasco da Gama and Cabral, and the eventual creation of Portuguese trading bases in Goa, Diu, and Macao, as well as relatively short-lived attempts to create bases in Japan. Thus this was an area that possessed a certain degree of economic unity in the years either side of 1500, for even before the Portuguese arrived Arab and Indian merchants created a chain of communication linking the Spice Islands to the Red Sea.

Malacca was a sort of East Indian Alexandria, inhabited by merchants speaking what appeared to be every language in Asia; even the parrots were multilingual, an early Portuguese visitor insisted. Moreover, the early fifteenth century had seen the ambitious attempts of the Chinese imperial fleet to take home tribute from almost every corner of the Indian Ocean.[9]

The sheer scale of the Indian Ocean trading region, and the fact that a significant proportion of its luxury trade consisted of the carriage of goods from the eastern extremities to Egypt and into the Mediterranean, before the Portuguese deflected part of that business into the Atlantic, does give the region a very distinctive character compared to the more obviously closed seas that constitute other Mediterraneans examined here. Chaudhuri's impressively coherent interpretation is deeply indebted to Braudel, with its strong emphasis on the slowness of change and on the importance of the physical setting; he cites with distinct approval Braudel's characterization of the Mediterranean as a place 'in which all change is slow, a history of constant repetition, ever-recurring cycles'.

9. COMPARATIVE MEDITERRANEANS

Space precludes consideration of more examples of 'Mediterraneans': the Caspian region, the Gobi Desert, even perhaps Lake Victoria, might all qualify for analysis as areas of water or desert across which trade routes have carried migrants, religions, commodities, and cultures. It is clear, too, that some of these comparisons with the 'Classic Mediterranean' are more meaningful than others: the 'Mediterranean of the North' and the Saharan Desert Mediterranean, with their links to the Classic Mediterranean, illuminate important aspects of the economy and indeed the culture of the Classic Mediterranean in the late Middle Ages. The Japanese Mediterranean, though physically remote from the Classic Mediterranean, poses similar questions about the relationship between trade and cultural or religious influences. And that, after all, is the main virtue of comparative

---

[9] I have no time at all for the theories of G. Menzies about these expeditions: *1421: The Year China Discovered the World* (London, 2002), retitled *1421: The Year China Discovered America* (New York, 2003) in its US edition!

history: that the questions one may ask about another culture can easily be taken for granted when looking at what, to Western historians, is the much more familiar one of the Mediterranean Sea. At another level we have perhaps identified, in the broadest outline, a fundamental characteristic of Mediterraneans: the relative proximity of opposing shores, but the clear separation between shores, enables different cultures to interact with one another across what may at times seem almost impermeable cultural barriers, such as the Christian–Muslim divide in the Mediterranean Sea or the political suspicions which sometimes led the medieval Japanese to hold the Chinese and Koreans at arm's length, while still enjoying a close rapport with Chinese and Korean culture. In the case of the Mediterranean of the Sahara ships of the desert brought the Islamic north into contact with Black Africa, leaving a cultural and commercial imprint that lasts to this day.

Yet it might all seem to be a truism. Of course seas divide as well as link. And in a certain sense the early modern Atlantic, opening out far beyond the 'Mediterranean Atlantic' described here, became a vast Mediterranean in its own right, tying together Spain and its colonies; superimposed on this was a second Mediterranean, the western trading world of Portugal, which shared parts of the same space, but had different priorities and economic structures. And in the twenty-first century the entire world could be said to be one Mediterranean, a globalized Mediterranean, with the United States playing the role that China had played in Japan's Mediterranean, as both a cultural idol and (to some) a suspect political force. Plotting the routes taken by passenger and cargo planes, one could describe a new worldwide Mediterranean characterized by exceptionally intense trans-Atlantic contacts tying together Europe and North America, and other very intricate webs around Singapore, Hong Kong, Taipei, and Tokyo.

So what is special about past Mediterraneans? In part it is a question of scale, of ease of movement, which is a good reason for arguing that the global Mediterranean is something only created by air travel and other forms of rapid communication (electronic as well as physical). Mediterraneans conjure up the history of coexistence—commercial, cultural, religious, political, as well as that of confrontation between neighbours aware of their often powerful ethnic, economic and, again, religious differences. This too, though Braudel did not always remember the fact, was one theme of Braudel's book on the age of Philip II, as indeed of Goitein's opus on the Genizah merchants: a human history of the Mediterranean Sea and of other Mediterraneans expressed through commercial, cultural, and religious interaction.

4

Ecology and Beyond:
The Mediterranean Paradigm

Alain Bresson

One of the fundamental notions put forward by P. Horden and N. Purcell in their important book *The Corrupting Sea* is the necessity of separating history *in* the Mediterranean from a history *of* the Mediterranean.[1] The former was Fernand Braudel's purpose in his famous book *The Mediterranean and the Mediterranean World in the Age of Philip II*. The latter is Horden and Purcell's ambition. They hold that such an approach can isolate what might be called the nucleus of a Mediterranean paradigm. With this purpose in mind, they provide an account that covers a very long period of history from the prehistoric period up to the beginning of industrialization. This is a necessary foundation for an analysis that aims to provide trans-periodical definitions.

Although it will not refrain from presenting short comments on more recent periods, this chapter will focus mostly on antiquity, with only brief glances at more recent periods. However, these 'ancient times' will begin far earlier than usual, that is in the neolithic period, thus allowing us to take into account the *longue durée* required for an exercise in conceptualization. According to the *Corrupting Sea*, the nucleus of the Mediterranean paradigm consists in an exceptional fragmentation of landscapes and countryside as well as in an extreme instability and unpredictability of the climate, which thanks to the presence of the sea provided the conditions for a connectivity that reached a

I should like to express warm thanks to William Harris for improving my English, and to all the participants in the conference for our exchange of ideas.

[1] Horden and Purcell, *CS,* with the sensitive review by B. D. Shaw, *JRA* 14 (2002), 419–53.

level unknown in other climatic or regional zones. It is the forms of this connectivity that will be addressed here. This paper will be in three parts. First we shall explore the purely regional forms of this connectivity and their consequences. Then some reflections on the nature of this connectivity will be presented, and on what it implies for the long-term history of the Mediterranean world. In the third part, a comparison will be drawn with two other maritime zones, the Atlantic and the Indian Ocean.

1. ONE OR SEVERAL? ZONES AND UNITY IN THE ANCIENT MEDITERRANEAN

Sea transport offered an advantage in terms of cost and speed. This has been stressed quite often. Without any doubt, the rule prevailed for any kind of commodity but presented a special advantage for the transport of heavy goods. In this respect, it has for long been recognized that the Mediterranean Sea potentially provided an exceptional space of connectivity. This observation applies by definition to every coast of the Mediterranean, but especially to the peninsulas of Greece and Italy, insofar as in their case the coast is exceptionally long. Thus it is clearly no accident that they played the role which they did in ancient times. It should be added that the major Mediterranean islands provided an additional supplement of potential connectivity. In the Aegean space, this characteristic reaches its highest point, with the existence of a series of smaller islands, thus creating an archipelago that finds only rare parallels on the surface of the earth.

The fragmented configuration of the Mediterranean Sea also deserves special attention. That the Mediterranean is highly compartmented is well known and deserves little mention in itself: the existence of two Mediterranean basins, east and west of the Sicilian straits, was commonly observed in antiquity, for instance by Polybius and Strabo. But several sub-zones also have their own identity, such as the Tyrrhenian Sea between Italy, Sicily, Sardinia, and Corsica, the Adriatic, the Aegean Sea, and of course the Black Sea, to mention only the principal ones.

The first level of this connectivity, purely local, was obviously very important, but does not require a lengthy presentation here. When we consider local transport beyond the very local indeed, say beyond ten miles, the starting point could be one of the many examples offered by Horden and Purcell, and quite a humble one: the exchange of dung against pottery on the coast of Lebanon.[2] A series of such microregional connections can be found throughout the history of the Mediterranean, and a series of examples comes immediately to the classicist's mind. One of our first epigraphic testimonies on the coast west of Marseille is a lead document from Pech-Maho in Languedoc, dated around 470–440 BC, which mentions freight coming from Emporion, situated about 70 miles further south on the same coast.[3] Another such document, this time found in Emporion, mentions the city of 'Saiganthe' (Saguntum), some 270 miles to the south.[4] Pseudo-Demosthenes, in the 340s BC, provides the example of short-distance transport between Panticapaion and Theodosia, two neighbouring towns in the southern Crimea about 70 miles apart by sea; the goods are poor-quality wine and salt fish as food for workers on a landed property.[5] The accounts of the construction of the sanctuary of Epidauros show or presuppose a local origin for some things, for instance for rough-textured stone, or imports from Argos, Corinth, or Athens for higher quality stone (tiles came from Corinth).[6] At Delos, transports of bricks or tiles from neighbouring islands seems to have been the rule.[7] All this shows the permanent connectivity, by way of *cabotage*, that existed between neighbouring ports.[8] The primary market for many commodities was the nearby city or village, which could more easily be reached

---

[2] M. E. L. Mallowan, 'Phoenician Carrying-Trade, Syria', *Antiquity* 13 (1939), 86–7; cf. *CS* 371.

[3] H. van Effenterre and F. Ruzé (eds.), *Nomima: Recueil d'inscriptions politiques et juridiques de l'archaïsme grec*. (Rome, 1995), no. 74, ii. 268–71, and J.-Cl. Decourt, 'Le Plomb de Pech-Maho: État de la recherche 1999', *Archéologie en Languedoc* 24 (2000), 111–24.

[4] *Nomima*, no. 75, ii. 272–5, with Decourt 112–13 for more recent bibliography.

[5] Pseudo-Demosthenes 35. 32 and 34.

[6] A. Burford, *The Greek Temple Builders at Epidauros* (Liverpool, 1969), 167–84.

[7] G. Glotz, 'Le prix des denrées à Délos', *Journal des Savants* (1913), 16–29: 18.

[8] X. Nieto, 'Le Commerce de cabotage et de distribution', in P. Pomey (ed.), *La Navigation dans l'Antiquité* (Paris, 1997), 146–58.

by sea. Archaeological evidence offers many other examples, such as the recently explored case of the small port of Aperlae in Lycia, which exported *murex* from which purple dye was made.[9]

Some remarks can already be appended to this presentation of a microregional exchange. First, it should be stressed that beyond a few miles these relatively short-distance transports by sea required nonetheless a form of specialized activity and a comparatively elaborate ship technology. Representations of ships might already appear on the 'frying pans' of Syros. They show ships of considerable size, with seemingly elaborate equipment.[10] It has rightly been supposed that a division of labour existed as early as the Bronze Age.[11] Already in that period we must assume the existence of 'professional sailors', that is of people for whom sailing was perhaps not the only occupation, but at least an activity that occupied a large part of their time. These people had acquired specialized know-how. In the Aegean, for instance, they were able to sail from the island of Melos to the continent. The Bronze Age was clearly a period of innovation in the construction and manning of sailing ships.[12] A counter-example might seem to be provided in a later period by the seventh-century BC Greek poet Hesiod (after the Bronze Age). In his *Works and Days*, he presented the case of a peasant whose experience at sea was quite limited.[13] But precisely the point he makes shows that others were far more experienced than he was: a Boeotian peasant on his small bark could sail across the gulf to reach Corinth or Sikyon, but he could not expect to go any further. This form of small-scale sea-transfer may always have existed, but was nothing else than a purely local *cabotage*.

And we should not lose sight of the fact that land transport always played a very important role. From the neolithic and the

[9] R. L. Hohlfelder and R. L. Vann, 'Cabotage at Aperlae in Ancient Lycia', *International Journal of Nautical Archaeology* 29 (2000), 126–35.

[10] J. Guilaine, *La Mer partagée: La Méditerranée avant l'écriture 7000–2000 avant Jésus-Christ* (Paris, 1994), 52–7.

[11] Ibid. 61–2.

[12] S. Wachsmann, *Seagoing Ships and Seamanship in the Bronze Age Levant* (College Station, Tex., 1998).

[13] Hesiod, *Works and Days*, 618–94.

Bronze Age onwards, exchange and diffusion by land has played a major part in diffusing raw materials, manufactured products, and—no less important—techniques. But this micro-diffusion was also the vehicle of important long-distance diffusion. Such is the case with the basic introduction of cereal production and with the domestication of draught animals, which gradually spread from the southern Turkish and Syrian region to the western parts of the Mediterranean, in a process of one and a-half millennia, between *c*.7500 and 6000 BC.[14] However, it is also striking that, in the west, the coastal regions of the northern Adriatic, of southern Italy, and southern Spain, seem to have been the first to be concerned by the introduction of these new techniques. It should be added that from the earliest phase, facing the coast of Levant, Cyprus participated in this movement, as did Crete, Sicily, Corsica, and Sardinia later, islands in which the so-called 'Neolithic Revolution' went at the same pace as on the continent which faces them.

A second, more elaborate level of connectivity could be styled the truly regional one, which embraces a whole sub-zone of the Mediterranean. It is obviously a natural extension of the first level. There are already some examples in the neolithic period. Take the case of obsidian. In the Tyrrhenian Sea and beyond, obsidian produced at different sites in Sardinia and Italy can be found as far away as northern Africa, Spain, southern France, and Corsica. It is true that it is not easy to prove direct transport and contact. As for the Aegean Sea, archaeological artefacts testify to a high degree of connectivity as early as the Bronze Age. For the diffusion of Melian obsidian, the hypothesis of some kind of transport by professional carriers is an attractive one.[15] In the zone of Cyprus and the Levant, as previously mentioned, a high degree of connectivity is attested very early, and it never stopped. In some other sub-zones, such as the Black Sea, the golden age of connectivity began comparatively late, when Greek colonists settled on the coasts all around it, that is in the seventh and sixth centuries BC.

The consistency and/or the persistence of some sub-zones, sometimes notwithstanding dramatic transformations in cultural or political frameworks, show that configurations of the

---

[14] Guilaine, *La mer partagée*, 8–50.   [15] Ibid.

coast, of the streams and of the winds played a crucial role. The Black Sea provides the best example perhaps. It was a Greek lake from archaic times down to the later Roman period. This high degree of connectivity expressed itself for instance in the exchange of wine and perhaps also olive-oil amphorae between the different coasts of the Black Sea, for instance from the southern towards the western or northern littorals (containers of Herakleia in Callatis, of Sinope in Olbia and in other sites of the northern Black Sea, etc.).[16] In the Tyrrhenian Sea, the Etruscans established a wide process of exchange with Sardinia and Carthage.[17] Later the lead was taken over by Rome, and the famous treaties between Rome and Carthage (Polybius 3.22–5) testify to the continuation of the same process. After comparatively short periods of war, which in the end saw the destruction of Carthage in 146 BC, Roman colonization in Africa led to the development of a new and intensive exchange relationship between Rome and its province of Africa. Along the coast of Languedoc and Spain, in the sixth and fifth centuries BC, the Etruscans regularly exported their wine amphorae and their bucchero ceramics.[18] An east–west sea route from Sicily to Iberia through the Balearic Islands existed before the Roman conquest, attested for instance by the wreck of El-Sec in the first part of the fourth century BC.[19] The Roman conquest of Spain intensified these east–west relations, with massive imports to Rome of Dressel 20 oil amphorae, salt fish, mineral products, etc. Spain and Carthage were key provinces for imperial Rome, as was proved when the invasion of Africa by the Vandals in the fifth century AD. cut the supply of African grain to the capital of the empire. This is of course history *in* the Mediterranean, but set against the background of the *longue*

---

[16] L. Buzoianu, 'Types d'amphores hellénistiques découverts à Callatis', in Y. Garlan (ed.), *Production et commerce des amphores grecques en mer Noire* (Aix-en-Provence, 1999), 201–14, and Y. Garlan, 'Réflexions sur le commerce des amphores grecques en mer Noire', in the same volume, 131–42, with bibliography, esp. 138–9.

[17] M. Gras, *Trafics tyrrhéniens archaïques* (Rome, 1985).

[18] L. Long, P. Pomey, and J.-Chr. Sourisseau, *Les Étrusques en mer: Épaves d'Antibes à Marseille* (Marseilles, 2002).

[19] A. Arribas, G. Trias, D. Cerdá, and J. de Hoz, 'L'Épave d'El Sec (Mallorca)', *Revue des Études Anciennes* 89 (1987), 3–4, 13–146.

durée these developments transform themselves into a framework that becomes part of the history *of* the Mediterranean.

A third and fourth level must now be addressed, which are on the one hand the connectivity inside each of the two basins of the Mediterranean, and on the other hand the connectivity that could exist in the whole Mediterranean. It is easy to prove that the basic norm was sub-zone and/or west- or east-basin exchange, rather than general internal connectivity all over the Mediterranean. This holds true even in the framework of the Roman Empire, at a time when the Mediterranean connectivity was probably at its maximum. During the neolithic and early Bronze Age, the lack of technology that would have made very long sea journeys possible seems to have prevented the development of a direct exchange between the eastern and the western basins. This is why, for instance, it has so far been impossible to prove the direct arrival of third-millennium Cypriot ceramics or metal artefacts in the western basin, be it in Malta, Sicily, or Sardinia.[20]

It would be a caricature to present exchange within the Mediterranean as an ever-growing connectivity zone, gently leading to a complete unification under the Roman Empire, then to a final collapse, followed two centuries later by a strange north–south partition of the Mediterranean which is still operative today. Matters were vastly more complex. Yet this scenario is not wholly misleading. A big issue for a macro-history would be to understand why this seemingly 'ideal state' of general connectivity did not survive. Addressing this point would be going too far, or rather, would be going far beyond the ecological approach to which a conceptualization of 'Mediterraneism' invites us. Perhaps these considerations also show the limits of a purely ecological approach, but that is another story.

If we consider the phases and forms of connectivity, it should be stressed once again that direct connectivity between very distant parts of the Mediterranean came into being comparatively late, being well attested only in the second millennium BC. Then it developed rapidly in the first millennium up to the final unification by Rome. In the East, in the third and second millennia, the permanent great power was Egypt, which under

---

[20] Guilaine, *La mer partagée*, 82–4.

the New Kingdom showed great interest in the control of Cyprus and of the coast of the Levant. However, Egypt was anything but a sea-oriented country. As for exploration and the acquisition of prestige commodities, its interest focused on the Red Sea or further south to East Africa, but not on the West. Other powers, like the Hittites, whatever may have been their great achievements in eastern and southern Asia Minor, never seem to have had any interest in the far west. In fact, the Mycenaeans were probably the first people to be involved in a relationship both with Asia Minor, Cyprus, the Levant, and Egypt on the one hand, and with the west (Italy and Sicily) on the other.[21] But this is better seen as a relationship which allowed them, as a people situated in a key position at the junction of the two zones, to be present in both of them, rather than as a real connectivity between the two basins themselves. In other words, this does not show that the Mycenaean Greeks played the role that was to be later that of their descendants of the first millennium. At the end of the second millennium, a new phenomenon was the invasion by sea of the Shardanes, who definitely seem to have come from Sardinia, and other Sea Peoples who represented a direct form of connectivity, if a violent one, between the two horizons. Their failure to invade Egypt did not prevent the installation of some of these people on a portion of the coast of the Levant, to which they gave the name of Palestine. We could define this connectivity as a transfer of men instead of a transfer of goods.

Then the tempo became ever quicker. The Phoenicians and the Greeks soon became the two go-between people *par excellence* of the whole Mediterranean Sea. As early as the beginning of the first millennium, Phoenicians founded settlements in southern Spain and even Portugal, and also the new city of Carthage and its surrounding cities in north-east Africa. The closeness of the links between these western settlements and their mother cities has been an object of discussion. Some have argued that the mention of Tyre in the second treaty between

---

[21] On the Mycenaean presence in the West, see L. Vagnetti, 'Les Premiers Contacts entre le mende égéen et la Méditerranée occidentale', in G. Pugliese Carratelli (ed.), *Grecs en Occident: De l'âge mycénien à la fin de l'Hellénisme* (Milan, 1996), 109–16.

Rome and Carthage (Polybius 3.24) must be to another, homonymous, city situated in the west. However, this relationship is beyond doubt. If the connection between the Phoenicians of the west and their motherland is not as obvious as expected, this is basically because of the Greeks, who did not let the 'Phoenician connection' develop to a greater degree. More prosaically however, the present state of our archaeological knowledge for Phoenician sites in Phoenicia itself, as compared to the far better situation which prevails in the west, especially in Spain and Portugal, may also play a role, depriving us of the required information.

As for the Greeks, their expansion began as early as the tenth and ninth centuries BC, first following the same routes as the Mycenaeans, but extending their efforts up to the farthest Mediterranean horizons. They reached their zenith at the end of the archaic period and the beginning of the classical period, when, apart from zones where there already existed states with a firm control of their coastal area, the Greeks settled on most of the coasts of the Mediterranean Sea. It seems that this is the ideal case of connectivity: through the mediation of the Greeks or the Phoenicians, any point on the Mediterranean coast was now potentially in connection with any other. It should also be stressed that the two networks, the Phoenician and the Greek, were not ignorant of each other. Contrary to the view that formerly prevailed, Greeks were numerous in Carthage and in Motya in western Sicily. Conversely, groups of Phoenicians or Carthaginians were present in Athens in the classical period, and excavations in Corinth have proved the existence of direct commerce with Carthage. This was a situation hitherto entirely unknown in the history of the Mediterranean. The Greeks and Phoenicians thus raised to an unprecedented level the degree of connection between the peoples of the Mediterranean. While the Etruscans were to some extent active at sea on the coasts of Italy, Sardinia, Spain, and even Carthage,[22] for long-distance

---

[22] Long *et al.*, *Les Étrusques en mer*, esp. 55–62, with a new wreck of possibly more than 1,000 Etruscan amphorae; and see also an Etruscan lead letter from Languedoc of the same period analysed by M. Cristofani, 'Il testo di Pech-Maho: Aleria e i traffici del V secolo a.C.', *Mélanges de l'École Française de Rome: Antiquité* 105 (1993), 833–45.

trade in the western Mediterranean they let the western Phoenicians and above all the Greeks play the main role.[23] Nevertheless, the Etruscans were fully up-to-date in agriculture and metal-working technology, and they could benefit from all the achievements of eastern and Greek civilizations. Thus the Etruscans could develop their own alphabet derived from the Greek, and fully participate in the artistic achievements of the Orientalizing period. In different ways and at a different time, the cultures of Iberia also benefited from the impulse that gave them both the West-Phoenicians and the Greeks.

This role of go-between people was not sufficient to ensure the Greeks an everlasting domination. Through conquest by Alexander, they managed to gain control over the eastern basin of the Mediterranean—that is another story. But it was just then that a specific cycle of their culture, represented by the city-state, began to come to an end. In fact, it soon appeared that in this role of middlemen the Greeks were no longer needed; and the heritage of their specific city-state organization even proved to be a radical handicap when it came to competing with the territorial state that Rome developed in Italy. Then the two basins of the Mediterranean were at last united and this time a general connectivity could come into being. At first this connectivity mainly benefited Rome and Italy, as both texts and archaeology testify. But under the Empire this one-sided situation changed. We now know that the Roman world was more 'multi-polarized' than was previously thought,[24] though Rome and Italy long remained the centre. In any case this general connectivity in the Mediterranean world was not 'the end of History': several very serious internal difficulties brought about a first crisis in the third century AD, then the final collapse in the fifth century of the western part of the empire.

[23] On the maritime contacts of the Phoenicians see A. Millard, 'The Phoenicians at Sea', in G. J. Oliver, R. Brock, T. J. Cornell, and S. Hodkinson (eds.), *The Sea in Antiquity* (Oxford, 2000), 75–9; and, more generally, the articles in S. Moscati (ed.), *The Phoenicians* (Milan, 1988). On the Greek presence in the western basin of the Mediterranean see the many different studies in the collective volume edited by Pugliese Carratelli.
[24] K. Hopkins, 'Rome, Taxes, Rents and Trade', *Kodai* 6–7 (1995/6), 41–75; H. W. Pleket, 'Models and Inscriptions: Export of Textiles in the Roman Empire', *Epigraphica Anatolica* 30 (1998), 117–28.

The key to this progressive integration is that the forced connectivity rightly adduced by Horden and Purcell as a way of coping with the risks inherent in the Mediterranean zone also in fact allowed a quick accumulation of profit. Far from being a factor of stability, this added to 'ecological' instability and to the unpredictability of the local ecology. It should also be stressed that accumulation of profit also made possible new and longer travels throughout the Mediterranean Sea. Financing trade across the Mediterranean presupposed significant capital, which previous accumulation made possible, thus making sea transport more frequent. It was sea connectivity that made all this possible. An aspect of the role of capital in maritime trade is the size of the bigger ships, much more important under the Empire than in the classical and even the Hellenistic period.[25]

2. FORMS OF CONNECTIVITY

The first question concerns the link that could exist between small-scale transport, by land or by sea, and overseas transport. The problem has been well addressed by Horden and Purcell. The myth of complete self-sufficiency should now be rejected:[26] autarky was an ideal, not a reality. In view of the risks inherent in an unpredictable environment, the trend was of course to make sure that a maximum of commodities was at hand. This was true not only of individuals, but also of states, and it was not by chance that in the classical period large cities like Athens managed to secure themselves a regular supply of grain by means of political control, either via the occupation of other territories or via the creation of checkpoints on the main sea routes. It should also be stressed that in Plato or Aristotle an autarkic city was not conceived of as a completely closed zone but rather as a state that managed to organize regular trade with a small number of cities with which it could mutually supplement basic needs, for example by the exchange of wine against grain.[27]

---

[25] L. Casson, *The Ancient Mariners*, 2nd edn. (Princeton, 1991), 113–14, 191, and *Ships and Seafaring in Ancient Times* (London, 1994), 122–24.
[26] *CS* 369.
[27] A. Bresson, *La Cité marchande* (Bordeaux, 2000), 109–30.

Then it should be clear that the hinterland was not deprived of connection with the coast. Thus, in the case of Greece, Horden and Purcell point out, with regard to Arcadia, in the centre of the Peloponnese, that the Aeginetans could communicate with the people there 'by means of track animals from the port that they had established at Kyllene' (it should be stressed that Kyllene, near Elis, was located on the *west* coast of the Peloponnese).[28] Since Herodotus already mentioned that as early as 480 BC the Aeginetans exported grain to the Peloponnese,[29] the fourth-century dedication of the Arcadians to the Spartokid Leukon, dynast of Bosporus, would ideally be explained by exports in grain from their ports towards the Peloponnese.[30] Arcadian access to Cyrenaean grain in the 320s confirms the existence of these imports.[31] These Arcadian examples have many parallels. It should be clear that even inland regions had normal access to Mediterranean trade.

A recent view of the economy of Athens and of its grain trade unfortunately leaves the impression of a complete separation between the town and the countryside.[32] It is explained that in the countryside people lived in a face-to-face society, exchanging only commodity for commodity, without the use of money. True, when forced to live inside the walls of the city during the Peloponnesian war, the Acharnian in Aristophanes, complaining about his lot, longs for his village where he was not constantly badgered *to buy*.[33] But it is a bold assumption to consider that the town was, economically speaking, completely separated from the countryside. It has been argued that transport costs within Attica were so high that in town local barley or wheat could not compete with their imported Black Sea counterparts, the reverse being true in the countryside.[34] All the same, it is assumed that a

---

[28] Pausanias 8.5.8, with *CS* 370.   [29] Herodotus 7.147.

[30] M. N. Tod, *A Selection of Greek Historical Inscriptions*, 2nd edn. (Oxford, 1949), no. 115A, ii.

[31] *SEG* 9.2, with A. Laronde, *Cyrène et la Libye hellénistique: Libykai Historiai* (Paris, 1987), 30–4; P. Brun, 'La Stèle des céréales de Cyrène et le commerce du grain en Égée au IVe s. av. J.-C', *ZPE* 99 (1993), 185–96, and Horden and Purcell's map (*CS* 73).

[32] V. J. Rosivach, 'Some Aspects of the Fourth-Century Athenian Market in Grain', *Chiron* 30 (2000), 31–64.

[33] Aristophanes, *Acharnians* 33–6.   [34] Rosivach, 'Some Aspects', 59.

new taste for bread rather than for the traditional *maza,* a taste
that the Athenians acquired during the Peloponnesian War,
would also explain why people preferred imported wheat instead
of barley. Unfortunately, this viewpoint is difficult to accept. It
contradicts all the information we may have about the Greek city
and its link with its countryside. Furthermore, as pointed out by
Horden and Purcell, Thucydides (7.28.1) informs us that grain
was transported by land from Oropos, which occupied a key
position on the canal of Euripos.[35] It sometimes seemed more
convenient (for instance for security reasons during a war) to
disembark grain in Oropos, and then to transport it to Athens.
This shows at least that transport costs were not so high as to
prevent any such transfer. In fact nothing disproves the existence of a connection between the city and its *chora.* The very idea
of a fully autarkic Athenian peasant is a myth. Some basic
exchange may have been made in kind. But from the land leases
from Athens and different parts of the Greek world, we know
that in the classical and Hellenistic period most rents on land
were to be paid in cash, not in kind.[36] Also, the assumption that
there existed no *agora* outside those of Athens and Piraeus
cannot be admitted: other *agorai* existed in Eleusis, Halai Aixonides, and Sounion.[37] The too-simple idea of an autarkic and
motionless Mediterranean countryside should be rejected.

The second point concerns what might be called virtual
connectivity. Before the time for which we possess written
documents, this type of connectivity is very hard to prove. Yet
as early as the second millennium BC, there already existed in
the Mediterranean a kind of common international behaviour, if
not shared law. This is proved by the famous report on the
Travel of Unamon, which has been the object of a recent
re-evaluation from an international law perspective.[38] The

[35] Horden and Purcell, *CS* 128, who stress the role of Oropos as a centre of
connectivity.

[36] R. Osborne, *Classical Landscape with Figures: The Ancient Greek City
and its Countryside* (London, 1987), 42–3.

[37] Eleusis: *IG* II^2 1188; Halai Aixonides: *IG* II^2 1174; Sounion: *IG* II^2
1180; D. Whitehead, *The Demes of Attica* (Princeton, 1986), 96–7 and n. 51.

[38] R. De Spens, 'Droit international et commerce au début de la XXIe
dynastie: Analyse juridique du rapport d'Ounamon', in N. Grimal and B.
Menu (eds.), *Le Commerce en Égypte ancienne* (Cairo, 1998), 105–26.

text is to be dated to the eleventh century BC, between the XXth and XXIst dynasties. A certain Unamon (Wen-Amun) was in charge of furnishing wood for renovating the bark of Amon, the great god of Upper Egypt. After his arrival in Dor, on the southern Phoenician coast, he is deprived of a portion of his goods by one of the men of his own ship, who were Phoenicians. Arriving in Byblos, he had to conduct a difficult commercial negotiation to obtain the wood he needed. Then on his way back, his ship was wrecked on the coast of Cyprus, and he had to negotiate with local authorities to avoid being the victim of the *ius naufragii*. The papyrus then stops. The basic nature of the document has been much discussed. Is this the authentic report of real travel or a piece of a novel? Some consider that an authentic report may have been preserved as a teaching document, for it presented a lot of difficulties that future travellers would have to cope with. In any case, the text is highly interesting insofar as it shows the conclusion of a true international sales contract (with the prince of Byblos), the existence of a commonly accepted principle of collective responsibility even in the absence of personal fault, and the role of written documents for the identification of the parties (Unamon is supposed to have credentials with him).

The Unamon document has led to far-reaching speculation about long-distance commerce in the Bronze Age. Were the ships of which wrecks have been found the product of such an 'oriented trade', organized by states for the benefit of the elite of rulers? Or did it already exist as 'free trade' independently of states? The question also arises in connection with three Late Bronze Age wrecks : (1) Ulu Burun near Kaş in Lycia (dated about 1325 BC), which carried at least 18 tons of freight (a very valuable and varied cargo, including copper and glass beads; the ship was bound from Ugarit/Cyprus to the Mycenaean world); (2) the Cape Gelidonya wreck in Lycia (1200–1150 BC, also with a load of copper); and (3) the Point Iria wreck (in Greece, *c.* 1200 BC—the ship came from Cyprus);[39] but for now at least no firm conclusion seems possible.

So it should be stressed that the form of common international law which emerged in the Greek world, and which

---

[39] *CS* 347, 607, and 613.

later the Roman Empire transformed into the law of a single state, finds a predecessor in the Late Bronze Age. As early as the second millennium, connectivity had reached a high level of sophistication, at least in the eastern part of the Mediterranean. This is also an element in the *longue durée* which is a part of the history *of* the Mediterranean.

3. MEDITERRANEAN CONNECTIVITY: INSIDE AND OUTSIDE

We can now draw a parallel with other zones that have a sea as a basic defining quality. Recent research on other zones such as the Atlantic and the north-western part of the Indian Ocean tries to elaborate concepts like those which have long been applied to the Mediterranean case. These studies provide a helpful comparison with the Mediterranean paradigm.

As for the Atlantic, it is immediately apparent that a basic difference lies in the enormous distances between its two coasts, so important that it long prevented any communication between them. It was a great technical achievement to master the sea routes between one side and the other. More than that, on the European-African side of the ocean as well as on the American one, it was in the same period, and basically for the same reasons, that general communication was established along the coasts themselves. It seems for instance that on the American side contacts between the different civilizations of central or South America were limited. The Phoenician circumnavigation of Africa launched by Necho II (*c*. 600 BC) was a brilliant success. Starting from Carthage, Hanno's voyage along the coast of West Africa (*c*. 425 BC) may have reached the region of Mount Cameroon. In the second century BC, Eudoxus of Cyzicus also made explorations in the same area, although he probably did not go as far as his Phoenician predecessors. Yet these fascinating experiments had no lasting consequences. Beyond the coast of present Morocco, no permanent relation was established with local people. If trading posts were established, which may have been the case with Hanno's exploration, they had no future that we know of.

Curiously enough, the reason why Eudoxus, who had first been in the service of Ptolemy VII, envisaged a circumnavigation of Africa was the same as that of the Portuguese in the fifteenth century AD.: direct access to India, to avoid the power(s) controlling the Mediterranean route, namely Ptolemaic Egypt for Eudoxus, the Italian cities and the Islamic powers for the Portuguese.[40] But a long-distance voyage differs from general connectivity. Large parts of the western coast of Africa offer inhospitable conditions: deserts in tropical regions alternate with dense forests with no easy access to the hinterland. As early as the sixteenth century, the Portuguese had contacts on the west coast of Africa to obtain gold, slaves, and ivory.[41] But it was the achievement of the Spaniards to build a truly integrated network.[42] The same conditions prevailed in modern times and explain why the Portuguese, then the Dutch, could establish trading posts in the Indian Ocean without significant contact with Africa, apart from the region of the Cape of Good Hope. In the seventeenth and eighteenth centuries, western Africa was integrated for good into the general economy of the Atlantic, but through the terrible interface of the slave trade, with its devastating consequences for local peoples. The process of acculturation of African societies began comparatively very late, in the nineteenth century, and took the form of European colonization, not of an autonomous and progressive transformation of local societies through their contact with the outer world. If there is no ecological unity on the western coast of Africa, this is all the more true for the European and African coasts taken together.

There is however an undisputable unity on the Atlantic coast of Europe. Under the influence of the Gulf Stream, which warms this part of the Atlantic, a mild climate prevails, quite unlike the irregularities of the Mediterranean. The ancient peoples facing the Atlantic in these regions were richly supplied with all kinds of fish. The littoral also 'provided a buffer of food reserves', making a general shortage unlikely under normal political conditions, as has been convincingly shown by B. Cunliffe.[43] But the predictable environment of the Atlantic

[40] Casson, *The Ancient Mariners*, 168–9.
[41] P. Butel, *The Atlantic* (London and New York, 1999), 39–44.
[42] Ibid. 62–77.
[43] B. Cunliffe, *Facing the Ocean: The Atlantic and its Peoples* (Oxford, 2001), 555.

littoral does not mean that there was no connectivity and that
the Atlantic peoples were self-sufficient and closed communities. It must be assumed that as early as the fourth and third
millennia BC a dense network of exchange of rare raw materials
developed from Shetland down to Morocco. Axes, first made of
stone, then of bronze, were a prominent exchange item and
were widely circulated. Displaying a large quantity of axes
obviously was a privilege of the 'Atlantic elites'. The exchange
of some more common commodities has left no archaeological
trace but is likely to have been no less active. Beliefs and cultural
attitudes also travelled from one place to another. But the most
striking feature of this 'Atlantic civilization' is precisely its
homogeneity and stability over time. The predictable environment of the Atlantic peoples did not force them to engage in the
general process of connectivity that for Mediterranean communities was vital.

Another difference in the form of connectivity is worth
stressing. Whereas Mediterranean societies, as early as the
Bronze Age, experienced regional navigation embracing a
whole sub-zone of the Mediterranean, a process that culmin-
ated in a general connectivity in the first millennium, it seems
that a simple overlapping of purely local and restricted circuits
characterized connectivity in the Atlantic. Even in the Roman
period, when the greater part of it came under the authority of
one single power, the Atlantic littoral was not a zone of general
and autonomous circulation. The Roman amphorae of Dressel
IA type that reached Brittany in the first century, before
Caesar's conquest, came through the isthmus of Gascony.[44]
Even at that time, the western littoral of Europe did not transform itself into a large commercial highway. The existence
of the lighthouse of La Coruña proves that some traffic took
place on these coasts, but the main way to Britain from the
Mediterranean started from Massilia, used the Rhône, then
the Scheldt or Rhine valley, and finally crossed over the
North Sea, as is proved among others by the diffusion of
Dressel 30 amphorae.[45]

[44] B. Cunliffe, *Facing the Ocean: The Atlantic and its Peoples* (Oxford,
2001), 389.
[45] Ibid. 418–19.

And if one takes into account the European, African, and American coasts as a whole, there is no global ecological unity in the Atlantic. It was only in the northern, European-American part of the Atlantic Coast that a form of general connectivity could develop, but at a very late date. When it was established, it obeyed mainly the rule of capital, not the full constraints of the ecological milieu: the difference with the Mediterranean could not be sharper.

With respect to the Indian Ocean zone, A. Wink has stressed its main characteristics.[46] Rivers and river plains shaped as deltas define the ecological milieus, whereas in the Mediterranean area only the Nile and Egypt can provide a parallel. The Tigris and the Euphrates, the Indus, Ganges, Brahmaputra, Irrawaddy, and Mekong rivers, to cite only the main ones, each gave birth to different civilizations with histories of their own. These plains of high seed-yield ratio agriculture and of high population densities sharply contrast with the neighbouring desert zones, where pastoral life and low density is the rule. Hydrological instability explains the frequent and important changes in the environment and thus the frequent movement of settlements. This also contributes to the characteristic fragility of the Indian Ocean cities, which are not in any case clearly differentiated from their rural context.

If all the ecological milieus of the Indian Ocean do not fit with this general scheme (for instance the mountains of Yemen, which benefit from the monsoon, are a comparatively high density zone), its main features hold true. A consequence of this is the contrast between the scarcity of the population in large tracks of the coastal areas and comparatively highly populated zones, such as Yemen, East Africa, or large sectors of western India and, more recently, of Indochina and the Indonesian archipelago. This is also of course an element of discontinuity. Another characteristic is the general lack of good natural harbours. Most of the time the great ports were situated at the mouths of large rivers. In sofar as the rivers were not navigable over long distances, traffic into the hinterland depended on caravans.

---

[46] A. Wink, 'From the Mediterranean to the Indian Ocean: Medieval History in Geographic Perspective', *Comparative Studies in Society and History* 44 (2002), 416–45, on whom I rely heavily.

Whereas the Mediterranean world is fragmented into a series of neighbouring micro-zones offering different and complementary supplies, each with immediate access to the sea, the Indian Ocean provides a limited series of larger zones, each with sharply different potential and ecology. This provides an excellent base for long-distance trade. But radical difference between deserts and wet zones did not create the same background of local, small-scale connectivity that can be observed in the Mediterranean of the past. Internal connectivity by sea in the different sub-zones cannot be regarded as a common feature of the Indian Ocean. It existed between south-western Arabia and East Africa, and between Oman and India. But nothing similar can be found on either coast of the Red Sea. Whereas climate instability and unpredictability as well as geographical fragmentation are the main characteristics of the Mediterranean world, it could be said that an everlasting extreme climate is a basic feature of the larger part of the Indian Ocean coasts, with the noteworthy exceptions of East Africa, Yemen and of the largest part of India, where the monsoon rains prevail. So management of the ecological milieu is even more a key factor in this area, but not unpredictability as such.

It is fascinating that during antiquity, first under the Ptolemies, then under the Roman Empire, the Greeks of Egypt managed to be the people who played the role of ethnic go-between which had been theirs in the Mediterranean, although this time they were clearly outsiders who were in control of only a small part of the route—its extreme western extremity, which put them in a key position for contact with the Mediterranean Sea.[47] Their technical achievements and above all the capital they could gather were surely key factors in this control, which assured them enormous profits. Later, the Arabs took over this role. At the end of the fifteenth century, it was by force, thanks to the superiority of their guns, that the Portuguese could impose themselves as the 'go-between' people in the commerce between Europe, the East African coast, and India and gain the

---

[47] G. K. Young, *Rome's Eastern Trade: International Commerce and Imperial Policy, 31 BC–AD 305* (London and New York, 2001), 28–36, and 201–12 for the profits.

important profits of this commerce, although they were far from eliminating the local bonds of trade and merchant families of many different origins who traded throughout the area and interacted with local societies.[48]

It seems in short that discontinuity, as opposed to the general continuity of the Mediterranean, was the main ecological feature of the Indian Ocean. In antiquity at least, although enormous profits could be obtained from trade between India and Egypt, although the small states scattered along the coast of Arabia could benefit extensively from this trade, and although local accumulations of profit could be quite important, hostile ecological conditions prevented a general rise of the population, a transformation of the techniques of production, and a cycle of capital of the kind that has been observed in the Mediterranean zone, until modern times. On the contrary, while local and regional connectivity played important roles in the background, the ubiquitous presence of the sea allowed a general lowering in transportations costs that had a key role in the specific Mediterranean development in antiquity. The fact that the Mediterranean world saw the development of the first market economies was due to the specific ecological conditions of this milieu. When a new development of markets occurred from the sixteenth century onward in northern Europe, the specific ecological conditions of the region had not the same weight: the presence of fossil-energy sources is a factor of another kind, and then the new developing market soon managed to free itself from any fortuitous ecological conditions.

To sum up: thanks to the sea, connectivity in the Mediterranean zone greatly accelerated the movement of history. In the first millennium BC, with the unification of the Mediterranean, the concentration of wealth and the movement of ideas reached

[48] K. N. Chaudhuri, *Trade and Civilisation in the Indian Ocean from the Rise of Islam to 1750* (Cambridge, 1985), and *Asia before Europe: Economy and Civilisation in the Indian Ocean from the Rise of Islam to 1750* (Cambridge, 1990); S. Subrahmanyam, *The Political Economy of Commerce: Southern India, 1500–1650* (Cambridge, 1990); D. Lombard and J. Aubin, *Asian Merchants and Businessmen in the Indian Ocean and the China Sea*, new edn. (New Delhi and New York, 2000); 1st edn. (Paris, 1988).

levels and forms that were then completely unknown anywhere else on the globe. But the specific market that emerged at that time was in fact heavily dependent on the ecological milieu: this milieu gave the market its best opportunity, but it also set definite limits on its development.

Angles of Vision

5

The Eastern Mediterranean
in Early Antiquity

Marc Van De Mieroop

1. INTRODUCTION

'Mediterraneanism' involves itself with a region, and as such it
needs to define its subject of study and set its borders. While the
aim of the approach is to be trans-historical—inspired as it is by
Braudel's *longue durée*—it should be obvious that historical
circumstances defined what belonged to the Mediterranean
world at any given point in time. Political and economic conditions determined what regions were in contact with those at
the Mediterranean shores, and these changed over time. While
the Mediterranean might be a timeless and trans-historical
concept, what falls within its reach is not. In his study of the
Mediterranean world in the age of Philip II, Fernand Braudel
could include the Flemish city of Antwerp, but no one would
claim that city to have been a Mediterranean one throughout
its history.

Human agency thus defines the limits of the Mediterranean
world, and the reach of people of that world depended on
historical circumstances. In their book *The Corrupting Sea*,
Horden and Purcell stressed the concepts of micro-region and
interconnectivity. The small zones that make up the Mediterranean world are connected to one another to an extent that
depends on the activities of the humans inhabiting them. The
geographical extent of those connections varies—and therefore
what can be called the Mediterranean world changes. At times
the focus of that world could be outside Europe, in the regions
of Asia and Africa that are often somewhat marginalized in
Mediterranean studies.

As an example of such a situation, I will discuss the Mediterranean in pre-classical times, in a period sometimes called early antiquity.[1] As used here, the term connotes the two millennia of human history that we can study on the basis of the rich textual sources produced by the people of the Ancient Near East. My emphasis lies on those textual sources. While I agree with archaeologists that other material remains provide a rich domain to be explored and used by the historian, such remains by themselves do not allow for as detailed a reconstruction as the textual sources do. This is an important second element in the definition of the Mediterranean world as studied by us: the historian's grasp on certain regions depends on the availability of sources and the degree to which they can be analysed. Even for the sixteenth century AD, Braudel had a lot more data to work with from the western side of the Mediterranean than from the eastern. That was to a great extent due to his lack of familiarity with Ottoman sources, which are in fact abundant, a shortcoming he acknowledged candidly. In other times we just lack the evidence to talk sensibly about a certain region, and our focus is forced onto a better documented part of the world we are studying. That is the case in early antiquity when the western Mediterranean was prehistoric, while the eastern Mediterranean was home to a number of well-documented cultures, including those of Egypt and Mesopotamia. The latter societies are not always regarded as part of the Mediterranean world, and often their histories are written as if the importance of that sea was only marginal, in the basic sense of that term as referring to a border. I would argue, however, that at times the Ancient Near East was the Mediterranean world, or at least the eastern part of it. I will discuss here the era of Near Eastern history that is often referred to as the Late Bronze Age. As archaeological subdivisions have little relevance in historical terms, I do not like to use that term, however, and prefer the temporal designation of the second half of the second millennium BC, admittedly an awkward mouthful.

---

[1] I borrow the term from I. M. Diakonoff, who used it as the title of a collection of papers discussing world civilizations until *c.*1000 BC (*Early Antiquity* (Chicago, 1991)). I employ it as a purely chronological term, outside a Marxist evolutionary model of the development of ancient society.

2. THE STATES OF THE EASTERN
MEDITERRANEAN WORLD

In the centuries from 1500 to 1100 BC the eastern Mediterranean world, including a large landmass that stretched more than 1200 kilometres inland to the east and south, formed a system of states and cultures that tied the whole region together. One of the consequences of the system's existence was that many of the states simultaneously produced a rich written record. This enables the historian to look at them without the bias of one point of view dominating the entire picture, as is often the case. The first part of this paper will be descriptive, introducing these actors. All of them have their individual histories, which have been studied with great detail and care by scholars of various disciplines. I will move here, arbitrarily, from east to west, north to south, but my order is not important. Afterwards, I will try to explain how they came together as one eastern Mediterranean system. I will focus at first on politics as the organizing force, but I hope it will become clear that the unity provided by the political setting extended into many other aspects of life as well. The political system was only part of a greater process of the formation of a Mediterranean world, one that does not overlap in geographical terms with the worlds discussed elsewhere in this volume (see Map 1).

   In the south-west corner of modern-day Iran was located the state of Elam, where the timespan from about 1450 to 1100 BC is identified as the Middle Elamite period in modern scholarship. This was an era during which the state became centralized and powerful enough to get militarily involved in the affairs of its direct neighbors, Babylonia and Assyria. Famous today is the campaign by King Shutruk-Nahhunte who around 1165 raided Babylonia. Because he brought back an enormous amount of booty from all major cities there, most of the famous early Babylonian monuments were excavated in Iran rather than Iraq, such as the stela of Naram-Sin and the law code of Hammurabi. While Elam was only peripheral to the eastern Mediterranean world for a long time, its late military campaigns and involvement in the Mesopotamian region ultimately made it an important actor on the scene.[2]

---

[2] For the history of Elam, see D. T. Potts, *The Archaeology of Elam* (Cambridge, 1999).

Moving west we find Babylonia, which at this time was ruled by its longest-lasting dynasty, that of the Kassites who were in control from 1595 to 1155 BC. This period is often portrayed as one of decline and weakness for the region, but that is a misconception. We find a stable unified state, considered to be equal to the major states of the time, Egypt and Hatti. Internally there was an economic resurgence after a difficult period in the mid-second millennium, and by all accounts culture flourished. Babylonia was not always successful in keeping Assyria and Elam at bay, and it knew its low points, but the Kassite period can be seen as a golden age rather than a dark one.[3]

Its northern neighbour, Assyria, was somewhat of a late comer on the scene. In the early part of the period, up until the mid-fourteenth century, it was a small state centred around the city Assur, which was perhaps not fully independent, but controlled by the Mittani state in northern Syria to be discussed next. But from *c*.1350 on, through a succession of strong military rulers, Assyria asserted its authority throughout the region: it reduced in power and finally annexed the adjoining part of the Mittani state, which allowed it to compete with the great powers of Babylon and Hatti.[4]

Northern Syria at the beginning of the second half of the second millennium was governed by a state called Mittani. Its history is less known than that of its neighbours because the capital city, known from texts to have been Washukanni, has not yet been found. We are certain, however, that Mittani was the major power of western Asia in the fifteenth and early fourteenth centuries—only Egypt equalled it. Its fortunes, however, were determined by its northern and eastern neighbours, Hatti and Assyria. In their expansion into the Syrian plains the Hittites had to confront Mittani, and successfully reduced its power in the second half of the fourteenth century.

---

[3] Kassite Babylonia remains relatively poorly studied. For a survey, see A. Kuhrt, *The Ancient Near East c.3000–330 BC* (London and New York, 1995), 332–48. A recent discussion of many socioeconomic aspects is L. Sassmannshausen, *Beiträge zur Verwaltung und Gesellschaft Babyloniens in der Kassitenzeit, Baghdader Forschungen* 21 (Mainz, 2001).

[4] For surveys of Middle Assyrian history, see A. K. Grayson, 'Mesopotamia, History of (Assyria)', in D. N. Freedman (ed.), *The Anchor Bible Dictionary* (New York, 1992), iv. 737–40, and Kuhrt, *Ancient Near East*, 348–62.

The main beneficiary of this expansion was ultimately Assyria, however, as it managed in the long run to take over all Mittani territory as far west as the Euphrates. By 1250 BC Mittani was no more.[5]

To the north, the central area of Anatolia was the heartland of the Hittite state, called Hatti in contemporary sources. It established control over Anatolia in the early fourteenth century, and extended into northern Syria in the second half of that century. The first opponents in the Syrian theatre were the Mittani, but later the conflict there was with Egypt. Taking advantage of internal Egyptian troubles, the Hittites spread their influence further south with little difficulty. By the time Egypt had gathered itself together and wanted to reassert its interests in western Asia, Hatti was in control of the region as far south as Qadesh. It was near that city in 1274 BC that Ramesses II clashed with the Hittite king Muwatalli, a battle that was lost by the Egyptian king (which did not prevent him from describing it as a major victory in numerous texts and representations). The Hittite focus upon the south left the state exposed on its northern and western borders. The north was the territory of a group called Gasga, seemingly not organized in any kind of state, but a constant military threat.[6]

The western regions of Anatolia present a different picture, although one not easy to draw because of the shortcomings of the documentation. States under an internationally recognized king existed there from early on in this period. The king of Arzawa in south-west Anatolia, for example, was in correspondence with Amenhotep III of Egypt, who sought his daughter's hand in marriage in order to conclude an alliance to put pressure on Hatti. In the latter part of the period an important player on the western scene was the kingdom of Ahhiyawa. The study of this state is complicated by the question of whether or not its name is related to the Achaeans, the Homeric term to designate the Greeks at Troy.[7] If indeed Ahhiyawa and Achaea

[5] See G. Wilhelm, *The Hurrians* (Warminster, 1989) for a history of the Mittani state.

[6] The Hittites have been studied extensively. A recent survey is by T. Bryce, *The Kingdom of the Hittites* (Oxford, 1998).

[7] The question has been vociferously discussed ever since the 1920s with no definite solution in sight. For a short summary, see ibid. 59–63.

were the same, we may have evidence that something resembling the Trojan war had taken place in reality: Greek expansion onto the Anatolian coast could have included long-term sieges of the type described by Homer. The question will not be settled on the basis of linguistic evidence, and its solution depends on further archaeological work which can clarify the nature of Mycenaean presence in western Anatolia. On balance, I believe that the connection between the two can be made, and that the Hittites knew of a political entity in the west that can be related to the Mycenaeans of the Greek mainland and the Aegean islands.

The study of the Aegean region is much more restricted because of the limitations of the textual data. Although writing was in use, with the so-called Linear B texts, the content is of little historical value. The tablets have to be regarded as illustrative of a civilization whose main characteristics are revealed through (other) archaeological remains. In the second half of the second millennium, the Aegean developed from a bipolar order, with differing cultural traditions in Crete and on the Greek mainland, to one where the Mycenaean material culture of the mainland was attested throughout the region. It is possible that there was some type of regional political unification of a nature similar to what we see under the Mittani, for instance. In any case, Mycenae was a crucial part of the trade that flourished throughout the eastern Mediterranean, with goods in exchange between Greece, the Near East, and Egypt.[8]

This last state, Egypt, is the best documented of them all at this time. Archaeological and textual data abound, and we can reconstruct elements of political and social history in great detail. It also was the state that steadily remained for the longest time a crucial player on the international scene. New Kingdom Egypt resurrected itself from the chaos of the so-called Hyksos period as early as the sixteenth century, and stayed strong within and outside its borders almost constantly until about 1200. It extended itself far south into Nubia and annexed it. It kept a constant presence in the Syro-Palestinian area, although the greatest expansion there was reached at an early point and

---

[8] The literature on the Aegean world is enormous, see, for example, O. Dickinson, *The Aegean Bronze Age* (Cambridge, 1994).

Egypt gradually lost territory thereafter. This was the period of the great temple constructions at Luxor and Karnak, of the Valley of the Kings, and of Abu Simbel. In many respects it was one of the greatest periods in Egyptian history.[9]

These were the great states of the region in the second half of the second millennium—not all equally centralized and powerful, but all regional powers. Stuck in the centre of the region was the Syro-Palestinian area, an interstitial zone with several important and well-documented states (for instance, Ugarit on the Syrian coast), but these were all much smaller in size and minor players on the international scene. Their secondary status was maintained by the great powers, because these needed a buffer zone between them. The Syro-Palestinian states had their own rulers, who had to pledge allegiance to the nearby power that was the strongest: Mittani, Hittite, or Egyptian. At home they were kings; in their relations with the regional overlords they were servants. They partook in a system where their proper place was one of obedience to the distant lords, useful in proxy wars and providing tribute on an annual basis.[10]

3. POLITICAL EVOLUTION IN THE SECOND HALF OF THE SECOND MILLENNIUM BC

The remarkable aspect of these states' histories is that they developed, flourished, and then declined, more or less at the same time. The simultaneity of the cycles was not pure coincidence. The proximity of the states and the close interactions between them, as attested in numerous sources, force us to look beyond their individual histories to explain the waxing and waning of their fortunes. A lot of ink has flowed over the question of the collapse of the period, primarily for the Aegean, Anatolian, and Syro-Palestinian regions where the role of foreign invaders has been much debated. The development across the region of a shared social and political organization has not received the same attention, however, and deserves to be

---

[9] The literature on the period is also enormous. For a recent survey, see I. Shaw (ed.), *The Oxford History of Ancient Egypt* (Oxford, 2000).

[10] A good basic survey of many of these states is provided by H. Klengel, *Syria 3000 to 300 B.C. A Handbook of Political History* (Berlin, 1992).

addressed. Ironically a lot has been invested in discovering how the system failed, but not on how it evolved.

In the sixteenth century the entire region had been characterized by political fragmentation: nowhere do we see strong states and as a result the textual documentation is extremely scarce. Only in Egypt do we have a grasp on the situation, but even there our understanding is limited. From the mid-seventeenth century on, the country had been divided into a number of principalities, several of which were considered to be ruled by foreigners, named 'Hyksos' in later Egyptian tradition. Although only one Hyksos dynasty may have had hegemony over the north and a Theban dynasty may have controlled the entire south, it is clear from contemporary and later sources that other petty rulers considered themselves to be kings as well.[11]

This pattern extended everywhere throughout the sixteenth-century eastern Mediterranean world. Competing dynasties ruled small areas. The near-total absence of textual remains indicates that their economy was underdeveloped and their political control weak. The only exception to this may have been in the early Hittite state, where two rulers, Hattusili I and Mursili I, were highly successful militarily and may have unified all of eastern Anatolia. Their ability to roam throughout the entire region, with Mursili reaching Babylon in 1595 BC, shows how weak resistance must have been. The short period of Old Kingdom Hittite strength was abruptly terminated by Mursili's assassination leading to a decline of that state as well. Mesopotamia, Anatolia, and Syria-Palestine thereafter saw a sharp reduction of inhabited zones and an increase of semi-nomadic life. Urban centres became fewer in number, islands in a countryside with less permanent settlement.

The situation of political weakness and economic decline was reversed in the late-sixteenth and fifteenth centuries, when a system of territorial states with more or less equivalent powers developed. Many, if not all, of the states involved, attained a size and coherence never known before in their histories. The best-known examples are Egypt, and Babylonia and Assyria in Mesopotamia. The Mesopotamian states became truly territor-

---

[11] J. Bourriau, 'The Second Intermediate Period (c.1650–1550 BC)', in Shaw (ed.), *Oxford History of Ancient Egypt*, 185–217.

ial states, ruled from one political centre by dynasties that considered themselves to rule a country, not a city. The territories included several cities and their hinterlands, and had a degree of economic integration never seen before. Ideologically, the idea that the city was at the heart of cultural and political life survived, but the political autonomy and economic autarky of cities had disappeared.

In Egypt the situation had always been different. There, a territorial state had developed already by the early third millennium, and the entire Nile valley from the first cataract to the Mediterranean had been unified from about 3000 BC on. Even in the so-called Intermediate periods, the periods of political fragmentation, the situation was very different from what we see in Mesopotamia: provinces, not cities, detached themselves from the capital city. While these provinces had cities in them, the latter never developed into the crucial centres of political, economic, and ideological organization that they were in Mesopotamia. The New Kingdom was something new, however, both because of its geographical extent and its integration of the conquered regions outside the heartland. Geographically, the early New Kingdom extended far beyond anything reached before or afterwards in Egypt's history. By the reign of Amenhotep III in the first half of the fourteenth century, Egypt controlled an area from northern Syria to central Sudan, and its northern and southern borders were more than 2,000 kilometres apart. Throughout the New Kingdom, Nubia was regarded as a part of the Egyptian heartland, its government assigned to a 'viceroy of Kush.' The grasp on the Asiatic territories, on the other hand, was loose, at first at least. Egyptian policy changed in the nineteenth dynasty, however. By the reign of Ramesses II (1279–1213 BC), the geographical extent had decreased in the north, with a much greater level of integration, however. Only Palestine was in Egypt's hands, but the area was more directly controlled than ever before, with an imposition of Egyptian material culture and administration.[12]

---

[12] B. M. Bryan, 'Art, Empire, and the End of the Late Bronze Age', in J. Cooper and G. Schwartz (eds.), *The Study of the Ancient Near East in the 21st Century* (Winona Lake, Minn., 1996), 33–79.

In the other states of the region the changes between the early and the late second millennium are more difficult to ascertain because we are less able to determine the political organization in prior times. The cohesion of the Middle Elamite state and the differences with what preceded it are difficult to evaluate, as is the case for the Aegean world. In the latter the attestation of states in Hittite texts (e.g. Arzawa and Ahhiyawa) and the homogeneity of material culture, may indicate a substantive political change from before. Northern Syria under the Mittani and Anatolia under the Hittites, were certainly politically integrated under one central ruler, even if he effected his rule through a system of viceroys and vassals.

The only exception to this general trend toward larger regional political units was the Syro-Palestinian area: here the basic system of small states centred around a single city continued to exist. Numerous examples are known—Jerusalem, Byblos, Damascus, Ugarit, Aleppo, and others. Qualitatively, we see no difference with the situation in the first part of the second millennium, even if the earlier picture is a lot murkier. Perhaps this exception to the rule underscores how fundamental the changes elsewhere were. The Syro-Palestinian region was interstitial between competing territorial states; first Egypt and Mittani, later Egypt and Hatti with Assyria lurking in the background. It acted as a buffer between these states and as a place where they could interact competitively. The region could not be permitted by the great powers to unify and to develop into a territorial state itself, nor was any of those powers able to firmly integrate the region within its territory. The other surrounding great states were strong enough to prevent that from happening. The qualitative difference between themselves and the Syro-Palestinian rulers was acknowledged in their interactions. Only the rulers of the territorial states could regard each other as equals, while those of the Syro-Palestinian states were of a distinctly lower rank. Thus these small states were forced to pledge allegiance to one or another of the neighbouring overlords, switching that allegiance to the stronger power as needed. They continued to exist as separate political entities, distinct from their suzerains in the great states, and they were prevented from uniting with their fellows by those great states.

Can we explain why such a concurrent development of territorial states took place? It would be shortsighted to look at every
case individually and to try to find the reasons for the changes in
the sociopolitical organization within the histories of each state
by itself. The idea that the simultaneous and parallel developments were accidental is in contrast to the truly international
character of the subsequent era. If we look at the entire region as
a whole, as a system, we can interpret it through an interpret-
ative model called 'Peer Polity Interaction', developed by Colin
Renfrew to explain change and interaction in early states,[13]
units smaller than the ones we encounter in the second half of
the second millennium. He quantified the size of those polities,
which he called Early State Modules, as some 1,500 square
kilometres in extent with a diameter of about 40 kilometres.
The model has been applied to various early states, in the Old
World as well as the New World, in prehistory as well as
history. The benefit for using it in the context discussed here
is that the level of sociopolitical integration of the Early State
Modules is irrelevant.[14] The advantage of this model is that it
urges us to look beyond the borders of the individual polity in
order to explain change, especially when simultaneous increases
in social and economic complexity are visible in several polities
in the same region. The model focuses on early states because
anthropological archaeology has been preoccupied with the
development of pristine states, but we should seek to apply it
to the study of more complex state societies as well. It is far
from unusual in history that similar social and political changes
take place in neighbouring regions. For example, the simultaneous growth of nation-states throughout nineteenth-century
Europe was surely not coincidental. The concept of peer polity
interaction seems thus ideally suited to investigate change in the
Eastern Mediterranean in the second half of the second millennium, because it avoids stressing dominance by one centre and
does not look at the units involved in isolation.

---

[13] C. Renfrew, 'Introduction: Peer Polity Interaction and Socio-political
Change', in C. Renfrew and J. F. Cherry (eds.), *Peer Polity Interaction and
Socio-political Change* (Cambridge, 1986), 1–18.

[14] 'Epilogue and prospect', ibid. 149–58.

4. SOCIAL STRUCTURE

A set of political and social characteristics was shared by all states of the Eastern Mediterranean in the second half of the second millennium, not coincidentally, but because they formed part of the same structure. These characteristics included the political structure, which as described above involved the development in most regions from city-states to territorial states. The similarity in political organization was paralleled in other areas of life as well. All states in the region, even the Syro-Palestinian ones, were made up of strict hierarchical societies in which a small palatial elite dominated the mass of the population. These elites were resident in urban centres, where their conspicuous consumption clearly distinguished them from the rest of the people. The strict social hierarchy and the great divisions in wealth in these societies are perhaps best illustrated by the building projects of this time. They included the construction of luxurious palaces everywhere, often separating the ruling classes from their subjects, such as in the citadels at Mycenae and Hattusa, the Hittite capital. The building of entirely new capital cities was a logical extension of the practice of providing the elite with its own separate residences, and is attested throughout the eastern Mediterranean.

Akhetaten (El-Amarna) in Egypt is a good example of that practice. This city was gigantic in size, contained several palaces and a temple in honour of the king's personal god Aten, as well as living quarters for the population imported both to build the city and to run the king's household and the state. All the official buildings were decorated with reliefs, frescos, and statuary. There is now little of this city left to admire, but its sheer size and the few representations of parts of it[15] show that its building was a massive project. Started in Akhenaten's fifth year and abandoned soon after his death in his seventeenth year, it must have required a colossal effort to build the city in such a short period. Akhetaten was not an exception in New Kingdom Egypt: Ramesses II built his own capital in Per-

---

[15] B. J. Kemp, *Ancient Egypt: Anatomy of a Civilization* (London, 1989), 272.

Ramesse, little known today but praised in antiquity. In other states we find the same practice of building new capitals: Al-Untash-Napirisha in Elam, Dur-Kurigalzu in Babylonia, and Kar-Tukulti-Ninurta in Assyria. The names of these cities all incorporate a specific ruler's name, except for Akhetaten which refers to the king's personal god rather than himself. These were not constructions for the people, but cities entirely built as residences for the king. His ability to construct them, all of them substantial if not gigantic in size, demonstrates the wealth of resources that were available to him. They show a desire to distance the ruler from the people, and reflect the power struggles that went on among the elites. It is likely that in these places an altogether new bureaucracy was created, one of *homines novi* who were fully dependent on the king rather than on familial ties for their social status.

The practice of palace construction and separation from the populace is visible on a different scale in the Syro-Palestinian area. Because of its political dependence on the great powers nearby it was unacceptable for the local rulers there to build strong fortresses, and we see a decline in that respect in comparison to the first half of the second millennium. Yet, they could build themselves extensive palaces, as at Alalakh and Ugarit, for instance. The latter city contained an area with several palaces, the main one of which has been described as one of the largest and most luxurious of the Near East at the time.[16] In such places the dominant powers could secure their control by constructing fortified citadels, as the Hittites did in Emar[17] and Carchemish.[18]

In addition to palaces, temples for the gods favoured by the dynasts were also constructed, and it is clear that the religious elites also benefited from the accumulation of wealth in the hands of the few. One has only to think of the temples of Luxor and Karnak. Not only the living elites enjoyed excessive

---

[16] G. Saadé, *Ougarit. Métropole Cananéenne* (Beirut, 1979), 98–110.

[17] J.-C. Margueron, 'Fondations et refondations au proche-orient au bronze récent', in S. Mazzoni (ed.), *Nuove fondazioni nel vicino oriente antico: realtà e ideologia* (Pisa, 1994), 3–27.

[18] R. Naumann, *Architektur Kleinasiens von ihren Anfängen bis zum Ende der hethitischen Zeit*, 2nd edn. (Tübingen, 1971), 330–2.

wealth, but in certain cultures the dead were lavishly provided with grave goods when buried. Egypt is the best-known example of this practice—remember that Tutankhamun's tomb was merely for a minor ruler—but we also see it in the Aegean world and the Levant. The goods recovered in the shaft tombs at Mycenae and the architecture of the later *tholoi*-tombs all over the Greek mainland show that some individuals commanded great wealth at the expense of the general population. The expenditures reserved for the elites were staggering.

The textual documentation shows the existence of a dual social hierarchy, distinguishing palace dependents from the population in village communities.[19] The palace dependents were not free; they did not own their own land, but if we take movable wealth as an indicator of social status, they were often much better off than the free people. It is in the palace sector, which incorporated temple personnel as well, that we see the greatest degree of social stratification. On the bottom of the hierarchy were serfs working the agricultural estates. Status depended on the services one provided for the palace: the more specialized skills provided a higher status. Thus specialist craftsmen, scribes, cult personnel, and administrators all had their rank and order. For a long time, the military elites topped the hierarchy; specialist charioteers in these societies were highly prized and well-rewarded for their services. In the Syro-Palestinian area they were designated with the term *marjannu* which later became the term for an elite social status in certain societies.[20] The rewards given to palace dependents were issued in rations for the lower levels, payments and the usufruct of fields for the higher ones. As service was expected in return, the use of these fields was granted on an individual basis, not to families; but later in the period military elites tried to make the tenancies heritable and to pay for them in silver rather than services.

[19] I. M. Diakonoff, 'The Structure of Near Eastern Society before the Middle of the 2nd millennium B.C.', *Oikumene* 3 (1982), 7–100; M. Liverani, 'Ras Shamra. Histoire', *Supplément au Dictionnaire de la Bible*, (Paris, 1979), ix. 1333–42.

[20] G. Wilhelm, 'Marijannu', *Reallexikon der Assyriologie* 7 (Berlin and New York, 1987–90), 419–21.

The free people were not entirely outside government control, as they were obliged to pay taxes or provide corvée labour when requested. But they owned their fields, often as communities rather than as individuals, where they scratched a poor living from the soil. The palace provided them with a certain support: in the irrigation societies of Mesopotamia and Egypt they maintained the canal systems. The extent of the free sectors of the various societies is hard to establish and must have varied from state to state. In terms of social stratification its members together with the agricultural palace serfs were at the bottom, seeing much of produce of their labour usurped by those higher up.

It is not my contention that the second half of the second millennium was the only period in ancient Mediterranean history in which we find such uneven distributions of wealth and strict social stratification. That is a characteristic of most societies, ancient, pre-modern and modern. Yet it is unusual that the situation was so similar in numerous places over a large geographical area. Earlier in the history of the region we see such circumstances in isolated places, primarily Egypt and Babylonia. Later there were single centres that commanded the resources of the entire region: the Assyrian, Babylonian, and Persian empires. This was very different from a situation in which neighbouring states were all organized along the same hierarchical lines.

5. WAR AND DIPLOMACY

The conjunction of cultural development in these societies is also visible in their shared ideologies. Certainly there were substantial differences between these peoples' perception of the world, but they shared visions about proper behaviour in social interaction and warfare, about equality and superiority in diplomacy, about the definitions of the civilized and the uncivilized. The participants in the system were aware that they had to adhere to certain standards of conduct in order to fit in. The rulers of the great states saw themselves as peers, and addressed each other as brothers. The rulers of smaller states, those of the Syro-Palestinian area, were inferior, and had to address the great kings as 'lord'. It was probably easy to determine where one belonged in this respect. The king of Ugarit, for instance, was a vassal of the Hittite one, and could not expect to be regarded as a great king. The 'club of the great powers'[21] was select and resistant to change, even when the political reality dictated it: when Assyria tried to translate its military successes into diplomatic equality with Babylonia, Hatti, and Egypt, it was rudely rejected at first until the others realized the legitimacy of its claims.[22]

The interaction between these states was highly competitive, even if they knew that they had to live alongside one another. Competition is a normal aspect of peer polity interaction and can express itself in several ways.[23] The most antagonistic, warfare, was common throughout the region, involving every state. One cannot say that this was a peaceful period, yet also not one that was militarily dominated by one state. Indeed, although we can judge with hindsight that the Hittites seem to have been more successful than the Egyptians in their contest over the Syro-Palestinian area, we cannot proclaim them or any other state at the time to have been the controlling military power. This is a very different situation from that in the first millennium, when we see the Assyrians, for example, dominating the entire region without any true competitors.

Part of the new state expenditures was connected to the introduction of chariotry in all armies. This technological innovation appeared early in the period: we know that Egypt had a fully developed chariotry by the reign of Amenhotep III. Chariotry was something that bound the states of the Eastern Mediterranean together, as it was found in every one of them.[24] In several of the states (Ugarit and Alalakh) the charioteers became

[21] H. Tadmor, 'The Decline of Empires in Western Asia ca. 1200 B.C.E.', in F. M. Cross (ed.), *Symposia Celebrating the Seventy-fifth Anniversary of the Founding of the American Schools of Oriental Research (1900–1975)* (Cambridge, Mass., 1979), 3.

[22] The system has been studied extensively. For a recent analysis, see M. Liverani, *International Relations in the Ancient Near East, 1600–1100 BC* (New York, 2001). The case of Assyria is discussed there on pages 41–2.

[23] Renfrew, 'Introduction', 8–9.

[24] C. Zaccagnini, 'Pferde und Streitwagen in Nuzi, Bemerkungen zur Technologie', *Jahresbericht des Instituts für Vorgeschichte der Universität Frankfurt a. M.* (1977), 28.

the military and political upper class, although they later turned to agrarian interests.[25] While relatively few chariots were used (perhaps only one per one hundred infantry men), they were expensive. Beside the material to build the chariots,[26] each one required two horses for pulling and one or two more reserve animals. In certain places, such as Egypt, horses were rare and had to be imported. Hence the gift of horses featured prominently in the Amarna letters.[27] Other equipment needed to be produced constantly. Chariot horses and some soldiers wore expensive bronze scale armour,[28] although in general protective gear seems to have been limited. In several administrative texts from Nuzi thousands of arrows are mentioned! The procurement of the wood or reed for the shafts, the casting of the copper or bronze for the heads, and the manufacture all must have required a central organization. We have an extensive textual record from Nuzi dealing with the manufacture of weapons, chariots, armour, bows and arrows, etc., and it is thus not far-fetched to claim that a large part of the palace economy in a small state like Arrapkha was devoted to military supply.[29]

Armies also required a lot of manpower. We are not in a position to estimate the sizes of the armies involved in the battles and campaigns we study, as references to numbers of enemies in royal victory statements were probably exaggerated. The Egyptians claimed, for example, that Muwatalli mounted an army of some 47,500 men against Ramesses II in the battle of Qadesh,[30] but we cannot confirm the accuracy of that claim. Yet, for certain states, such as Assyria with a small population in the heartland, the annual levy of troops must have been a heavy imposition. Part of the pressure on the native populations was removed by the use of mercenaries, a habit that seems to have

[25] Wilhelm, *The Hurrians*, 43.

[26] Zaccagnini, 'Pferde und Streitwagen', 28–31.

[27] D. O. Edzard, 'Die Beziehungen Babyloniens und Ägyptens in der mittelbabylonischen Zeit und das Gold', *Journal of the Economic and Social History of the Orient* 3 (1960), 37–55.

[28] Zaccagnini, 'Pferde und Streitwagen', 32–4.

[29] S. Dalley, 'Ancient Mesopotamian Military Organization', in J. M. Sasson (ed.), *Civilizations of the Ancient Near East* (New York, 1995), 417.

[30] R. H. Beal, 'Hittite Military Organization', in Sasson (ed.), *Civilizations*, 547.

become common in the later part of the period. At the battle of Qadesh, for instance, mercenaries were used by both the Hittites and the Egyptians, many of them drawn from the very populations that later contributed to the fall of these states, the Sea Peoples and the Libyans. That these groups could become powerful elements in the societies that recruited them is demonstrated by the case of Egypt, where the 'Chieftains of the Ma', i.e. the Libyan mercenaries, grabbed control over certain territories after the end of the New Kingdom.[31]

Even if we are unable then to quantify the expenditures involved in the military activities of the states of the region, we can suggest that they were not minor and that warfare probably necessitated a concerted economic effort. That focus by itself was partly responsible for the maintenance of the international system of the eastern Mediterranean area, as some of the resources required, ironically perhaps, could only be obtained abroad. Copper and tin had to be imported by many in order to make the bronze weaponry needed by a competitive army, horses were an item of exchange between the kings. Thus warfare not only brought states together in a competitive way, but also forced them to trade.

6. CULTURAL AND MERCANTILE INTERACTIONS

Not all competition between the states of the region was of a military nature, however. Among peer polity interactions Renfrew included what he called competitive emulation, the urge to display greater wealth and power, to outdo the others in exhibiting the fashions of the time. Archaeologists and art historians have spent a lot of energy in tracing how styles of pottery decoration, wall paintings, and so on were passed on from one culture to another in the region of the eastern Mediterranean. They speak of an 'International Style' that merges indigenous and foreign elements in its artistic expression.[32] The

[31] D. O'Connor, 'New Kingdom and Third Intermediate Period, 1552–664 BC', in B. F. Trigger *et al.*, *Ancient Egypt: A Social History* (Cambridge, 1983), 238–9.

[32] M. H. Feldman, 'Luxurious Forms: Redefining a Mediterranean "International Style", 1400–1200 B.C.E.', *Art Bulletin* 84 (2002), 6–29.

interactions between the Aegean and Syria-Palestine and Egypt have especially drawn a lot of attention.[33] For example, wall paintings found at Tell Kabri in Palestine and Tell el-Daba'a in the Egyptian delta shared decorative motives and styles with those excavated in Crete. The focus of attention has been in trying to identify the direction of the borrowing, the source of the style, but it is more important here to realize that the elites of the region shared a lifestyle transcending political borders which distinguished them probably more from their own countrymen than from their counterparts elsewhere. These cultural borrowings were certainly not limited to materials we can recognize in the archaeological record today, but must have included ephemeral things such as clothing, foods, perfumes, drugs, etc.[34]

It may even be possible to include language in this. Just as the European elites in the eighteenth century AD conversed in French, could the eastern Mediterranean ones of the fourteenth century BC not have shown off their knowledge of the Akkadian language? The palace scribes used that language for international correspondence with various levels of competence, but are we not looking at their skill in a too purely utilitarian way? Several examples of Akkadian literature were found amongst the tablets excavated at Hattusa, Emar, Ugarit, and Akhetaten. A fragment of the Epic of Gilgamesh was picked up at Megiddo in Palestine, and it seems certain that the numerous palaces of the region can only continue to yield further evidence that the Akkadian language was not used just for purely practical purposes. We cannot determine who enjoyed reading or listening to these texts; yet their presence suggests that a certain class in these societies thought it useful to study a foreign language and its literature.

---

[33] For example, H. J. Kantor, 'The Aegean and the Orient in the Second Millennium B.C.', *American Journal of Archaeology* 51 (1947), 1–103.

[34] A. and S. Sherratt, 'From Luxuries to Commodities: the Nature of Mediterranean Bronze Age Trading Systems', in N. H. Gale (ed.), *Bronze Age Trade in the Mediterranean* (Jansered, 1991), 351–86. For opium trade from Cyprus to the Levant, see R. S. Merrillees and J. Evans, 'Highs and Lows in the Holy Land: Opium in Biblical Times', *Eretz Israel* 20 (1989), 148–54.

What exactly constituted a fashionable lifestyle must have changed over time and place. It was probably made up by a mixture of local traditions and influences from abroad. The elites of the area must have seen in the 'International Style' a way in which to distinguish themselves from those they considered to be lower classes. We can easily imagine, however, that they also tried to impress the emissaries and visitors of other states by showing off their lifestyle. The gigantic size of many of the buildings constructed at this time, most notably in Egypt but certainly elsewhere as well, must not only have been used to impress the local populations, but foreign visitors as well.

In addition to the competitive character of the interactions between these states, they were also tied together by a great exchange of goods. This has been studied extensively, especially with respect to the Aegean world whose pottery, for instance, can be found all over the Syro-Palestinian coastal area and in Egypt. Similarly, Egyptian and western Asiatic material is found in the Aegean.[35] The exchange of goods took place on several levels in the societies. Kings traded high-value prestige items, such as ivory, gold, and hard woods. They shared the ideology that they did not acquire such items by cheap market-eering, but that they were given to them by colleagues to whom they would return the favour by giving something else valuable. Parallel to this system existed a more basic one in which goods were traded by merchants travelling along the coast or through the countryside. The sea trade is well-attested archaeologically, including by two shipwrecks found off the southern coast of Turkey. Merchants circulated in the eastern half of the Mediterranean in an anticlockwise direction, following the coast. They picked up goods wherever they came ashore along the way, which they acquired by trading-in some of their cargo.

The latter was so eclectic that one cannot assign a country of origin to the merchants. The shipwreck of Uluburun dating to the late fourteenth century, for example, had as its main cargo ten tons of Cypriot copper and one ton of tin of unknown origin, both poured into easily transportable ingots. The ship also

---

[35] See, for example, E. H. Cline, *Sailing the Wine-Dark Sea. International Trade and the Late Bronze Age Aegean* (Oxford, 1994).

contained logs of ebony, which the Egyptians must have obtained in tropical Africa, and cedar logs from Lebanon. Ivory tusks and hippopotamus teeth also came from Egypt, while murex shells, prized for their dye, could have been obtained in various locations in north Africa and the Syrian and Lebanese coast. In addition to these materials the ship held manufactured goods, such as Canaanite jewelry, Cypriot pottery, beads of gold, faience, agate, glass, and so on, all from different sources. There was even a jeweller's hoard on board with scraps of gold, silver, and electrum, a scarab with the name of the Egyptian queen Nefertiti, and cylinder seals from Babylonia, Assyria, and Syria.[36]

7. AN EASTERN MEDITERRANEAN SYSTEM

The extent of the interactions and the shared culture we observe in the region make the eastern Mediterranean of the second half of the second millennium an ideal place for application of the peer polity interaction model. This allows us to see the simultaneous changes in the various states as a result of processes throughout the region. We need not look for a place where developments happened first, nor need we see the diffusion of ideas as the motor behind change. The political culture of the eastern Mediterranean did not originate in one state alone, and was not adapted by others later; it grew up because of the interchange of influences from all participants. We can obviously locate the source of certain elements, such as that the Akkadian language and literature in use derived from Babylonia. But this is not really important. An international system had developed through the input of many who closely interacted with one another. That system was not static once it had been developed, and changed through and because of the actions and developments of individual states. The general characteristics that determined its nature lasted for at least 200 years. The competitive coexistence of this set of equivalent states makes this period unique in ancient history.

[36] C. Pulak and G. F. Bass, 'Uluburun', in E. Meyers (ed.), *The Oxford Encyclopedia of Archaeology in the Near East* (New York and Oxford, 1997), v. 266–8.

My argument here is that we can see a world that is united in many respects. It can be called a Mediterranean system, because this sea acted as one of the connecting arteries in it. Parallel to maritime connections existed networks of movement by river and overland routes, and it is thus senseless to make a division between the regions abutting the sea and those further inland. The region of the Mediterranean extended far to its east. At the same time, this Mediterranean world did not include the regions west of the Greek mainland. Contacts with the western Mediterranean existed during this period, but it was peripheral to the system I have described. Archaeologically, we can determine that the Mycenaeans visited mineral rich regions in the west. But this was a periphery, one that did not participate in the system as an equal partner, and one that cannot be studied by the historian on equal terms as there are no sources beyond the archaeological ones which are often silent on questions we need to ask.

Despite the importance of the Mediterranean Sea as an artery of contact between these states as we observe it today, the inhabitants of the region did not themselves acknowledge this. On the contrary, they saw the sea as a hostile force, a place of chaos and danger. That travel by boat took place regularly is clear from the archaeological record, including the shipwrecks, and textual material attests to it, including at the level of royal correspondence. Egyptian ships seem to have been considered superior—or at least Egyptologists tend to think so[37]—and a letter, most likely from Ramesses II to the Hittite Hattusili III, discusses the sending of such ships to function as models for Hittite carpenters. Ramesses states:

[Look, I did send you] one ship, and a second [one I will send you next year]. Your [carpenters] should draw a plan [on the basis of the ships that I send you]. Let them make a plan [and let them imitate the ship, and my brother] will make the fixtures (?) [artfully. You should tar the boat on the inside and the outside] with pitch [so that no water will] seep in [and cause the ship to sink] in the midst of the sea![38]

[37] e.g., T. Säve-Söderbergh, *The Navy of the Eighteenth Dynasty* (Uppsala, 1946).

[38] E. Edel, *Die ägyptisch-hethitische Korrespondenz aus Boghazköi in babylonischer und hethitischer Sprache* (Opladen, 1994), 186–7, no. 79. The passages in square brackets are restored in the broken text.

The textual material from the Levantine coast, especially the city of Ugarit, has a substantial number of references to seafaring, and some have even suggested that there was a Canaanite 'thalassocracy' in the second half of the second millennium.[39] People from all states along the Mediterranean shore travelled the seas, however. An eleventh-century tale from Egypt[40] describes the voyage of Wen-Amun, a priest of Amun, to Byblos in order to obtain timber. As must have been common practice for centuries, he took passage on a Syrian boat, and there is no indication that this was regarded as unusual. The tale clearly acknowledges the dangers involved in this travel, however, and seems to show the sea as a world with laws of its own. First, Wen-Amun was robbed of the goods he brought with him by one of the crew members in the Philistine harbor of Dor. His demand to the local ruler for restitution was rejected, so he stole it from yet another ship. Later in the story, he was seized by people from Cyprus and barely escaped with his life. Piracy is mentioned in several letters of the second millennium as well, so it was a real danger. On the other hand, we have to keep in mind that people travelling overland were also reported as being attacked, so the dangers may have evened out.[41]

The sea was dangerous, however, and a force that could not be easily controlled. It is a recurrent motif in the literatures of the ancient Near East that chaos was personified by the sea. The so-called Babylonian creation myth describes how the god Marduk brought order to the universe by defeating the sea-goddess Tiamat. In the literature of the Syrian coastal city Ugarit the god Ba'al likewise defeated Yam, 'the Sea', who sometimes is replaced by the god Mot, 'Death'. This topic of Canaanite literature survived into the first millennium Hebrew Bible, where Yahweh replaced Ba'al.[42] There was a distinct fear

[39] J. M. Sasson, 'Canaanite Maritime Involvement in the Second Millennium B.C.', *Journal of the American Oriental Society* 86 (1966), 126–38.

[40] An English translation can be found in M. Lichtheim, *Ancient Egyptian Literature* (Berkeley, 1976), ii. 224–30.

[41] A. Altman, 'Trade between the Aegean and the Levant in the Late Bronze Age: Some Neglected Questions', in M. Heltzer and E. Lipinski (eds.), *Society and Economy in the Eastern Mediterranean (c.1500–1000 B.C.)* (Louvain, 1988), 229–37.

[42] For a convenient recent survey of Near Eastern mythological material where the sea appears as a danger and the scholarly literature, see A. Catastini,

of the sea, which is understandable as the eastern Mediterranean was indeed dangerous to sail. Yet the sea was crucial for the contacts the people at its shores maintained. Such a paradoxical attitude was not unique in antiquity: while the Romans called the Mediterranean *mare nostrum*, they did have a world-view focused on the land and feared the sea.[43] One can rely on the sea without liking it.

The historical situation I described changed drastically by the first millennium, after the so-called Dark Age when we are truly at a loss about most of what took place. From a Near Eastern point of view the Mediterranean became a distant world. The sea was a border that could only be crossed by specialist people living on its coast, the Phoenicians. The Near Eastern states, at first Assyria, then Babylonia and Persia, were landlocked powers, without true equals as neighbours. The Mediterranean Sea was no longer a unifying force, connecting the regions at its eastern shores. The Mediterranean world of the first millennium BC had a much more western orientation and the lands to its east were part of another world. The changes took place due to political, economic, cultural, and techno-logical factors. They were caused by humans, not by nature, and the human as a historical agent has to remain in the centre of our Mediterranean history.

'Il mostro delle acque: reutilizzazioni bibliche della funzione di un mito', *Mediterraneo Antico: Economie, Società, Culture* 4 (2001), 71–89.

[43] O. A. W. Dilke, 'Graeco-Roman Perception of the Mediterranean', in M. Galley and L. Ladjimi Sebai (eds.), *L'Homme méditerranéen et la mer* (Tunis, 1985), 53–9.

6

Ritual Dynamics in the Eastern Mediterranean: Case Studies in Ancient Greece and Asia Minor

Angelos Chaniotis

1. MEDITERRANEAN RITUALS[1]

One of the many monuments the Athenians proudly showed their youth and the visitors to their city was the ship with which Theseus was believed to have sailed to Crete. In the course of the centuries the ship's wooden parts rotted, and the Athenians had to replace them, providing ancient philosophers with an unsolved puzzled: did Theseus' ship remain the same even though its rotten components were continually being replaced?[2] I cannot help thinking about this puzzle when I am confronted with diachronic studies on 'the' Mediterranean. Can the Mediterranean be a somehow distinctive object of historical and cultural study, given the continual change of its living (and therefore, ephemeral) components (human populations and their cultures, animals, and plants)? Or is the Mediterranean as a historical and cultural entity just a construct of the collective imagination of scholars who contribute to journals, books, or conferences that have the name 'Mediterranean' in their title?

[1] The views expressed here stem from the project 'Ritual and Communication in the Greek cities and in Rome', which is part of the interdisciplinary projects 'Ritualdynamik in traditionellen und modernen Gesellschaften' funded by the Ministry of Science of Baden-Württemberg (1999–2000) and 'Ritualdynamik: Soziokulturelle Prozesse in historischer und kulturvergleichender Perspektive' funded by the German Research Council (2002–5); references to my own preliminary studies on relevant subjects are, unfortunately, unavoidable. I have profited greatly from theoretical discussions with my colleagues in this project.
[2] Plu. *Theseus* 23.

The question of the unity of the Mediterranean should be asked not only 'vertically' (with regard to diachronic developments); it must be asked 'horizontally' as well. Can the Mediterranean in its entirety be a meaningful and distinctive object of study in any given period of the antiquity, given the heterogeneity of cultures and environments in this geographical region? And if continuities, convergences, and homogeneities can somehow be detected in a non-anthropogenous framework—for example there *is* such a thing as a Mediterranean climate, we can study Mediterranean seismic activities, and we know from personal observation the Mediterranean karstic landscapes—can we characterize cultural phenomena as 'Mediterranean phenomena'? Is there such a thing as a Mediterranean mentality, a Mediterranean way of life, typical Mediterranean cultic practices or rituals, or even Mediterranean values?[3] These questions sound rhetorical. Most of us would spontaneously deny the existence of *a* Mediterranean culture, *a* Mediterranean religion or *a* Mediterranean way of life, perhaps only making allowances for certain historical periods or certain limited aspects. It is necessary to rethink what is specifically 'Mediterranean' in Mediterranean studies, to distinguish between objects and observation and constructs—but also to ask ourselves if there is any legitimacy for Mediterranean studies other than the natural geographical limits of this closed sea, and if yes, which parameters we should take into consideration.

I have chosen to explore this issue by treating a cultural phenomenon for which geographical factors do not seem to be determinant: rituals. Admittedly, religious responses to space and landscape have often been observed, and P. Horden and N. Purcell have very aptly included in their *Corrupting Sea* a chapter on territories of grace.[4] This chapter deals with a great variety of subjects pertaining to the relation between religion and the physical environment and to geographical parameters, such as the topographical features of cult places (holy waters, high places, woods and groves, natural catastrophes such as bad weather, earthquakes and vulcanic activity), the

---

[3] See e.g. J. G. Peristiany (ed.), *Honour and Shame. The Values of Mediterranean Society* (London, 1965).

[4] *CS* 401–60.

sacralized economy, and the mobility of religious practices. The questions of continuities, survivals, and changes, convergences and divergences naturally occupy an important position in their discussion. Although no claim is made in this book (or has ever been made, at least to the best of my knowledge) that there is a 'Mediterranean' religion or that there is anything specifically Mediterranean in the religions of the ancient Mediterranean, still continuities in worship are detected in certain sites—the 'classical' example being the use of the same sacred space by pagans, Christians and Muslims; also similarities in the religious use of space and landscape practices with a wide geographical distribution in the Mediterranean have been observed. Interestingly, this discussion of continuities, survivals, and similarities in the sacred landscapes of the Mediterranean refers to *cult, religion, worship*, or the *sacred*; it does not to refer to *rituals*. Although rituals are often alluded to by Horden and Purcell, there is hardly any direct reference to the term *ritual* or to individual rituals, and very prudently so, for reasons that will be given in a moment.

2. FROM MEANINGS TO FUNCTIONS

But despite the prudence and caution that should be shown in the treatment of rituals as objects of a comparative or a diachronic study, yet rituals are essential for the understanding of cult, religion, and worship, for the use of sacred space, but also for the cultural profile of a group, in the ancient Mediterranean as in any other region and period. It was with the description of differences in rituals (especially burial customs and the rituals of dining) that many ancient historians (notably Herodotus) established cultural difference and identity between Greeks and barbarians or among the Greek communities.[5] In one of the longest and most detailed ancient treatments of rituals, in Athenaeus' description of the dining rituals of various peoples, the peculiarities of each group are detected through a comparison of the rituals at the dining table.[6] There is an unspoken, but

[5] e.g., F. Hartog, *The Mirror of Herodotus. The Representation of the Other in the Writing of History* (Berkeley and Los Angeles, 1988); R. Bichler, *Herodots Welt* (Berlin, 2000), esp. 48–56, 84–93, 123–31, 151–78.

[6] Athen. 4.148–54d.

relatively widespread view (in Germany in particular), perhaps
influenced by the spirit of Protestantism, that religious beliefs
and doctrines have a supremacy over rituals, that rituals are
meaningless. And yet, scholars still search for the meaning of
rituals no less than some antiquarians did in antiquity.
Agatharchides narrates a very instructive anecdote:[7] 'The Boeotians sacrifice to the gods those eels of the Kopaic Lake which
are of surpassing size, putting wreaths on them, saying prayers
over them, and casting barley-corns on them as on any other
sacrificial victim; and to the foreigner who was utterly puzzled
at the strangeness of this custom and asked the reason, the
Boeotian declared that he knew one answer, and he would
reply that one should observe ancestral customs, and it was
not his business to justify them to other men.' This anecdote
of Agatharchides, rather than confirming the view of those who
regard rituals meaningless, advises us to shift the focus of the
discussion from meaning to functions. The Boeotians continued to sacrifice eels, not because of an original, now forgotten, obscure and entirely insignificant meaning, but because of
the importance attached to the preservation of ancestral traditions for the coherence and identity of a community.

One of the primary functions of rituals, at least in the civic
communities in Greece, was the communication between
humans and other beings within and without human society.[8]
Public religious rituals—sacrifice in particular, and other activities connected with sacrifice (the singing of hymns, ritual
dances, etc.), rituals of purification and rituals of dedication—
are privileged means of communication between mortals and
gods; ritual activities establish the communication between the
living and the dead, in the funerary cult and the cult of heroes; it
is also with rituals—the secret rituals of magic—that men establish a contact with superhuman beings. Public rituals (such as

---

[7] *FGrH* 86 F 5 (from Athen. 7.297d).

[8] e.g. F. Graf, 'Zeichenkonzeption in der Religion der griechischen und
römischen Antike', in R. Posner, K. Robering, and T. A. Sebeok (eds.),
*Semiotik. Ein Handbuch zu den zeichentheoretischen Grundlagen von Natur
und Kultur* (Berlin and New York, 1997), 939–58. Cf. N. Bourque, 'An
Anthropologist's View of Ritual', in E. Bispham and C. Smith (eds.), *Religion
in Archaic and Republican Rome and Italy: Evidence and Experience* (Edinburgh, 2000), 21–2.

oath ceremonies, banquets, processions, and initiatory rituals) play an important part also in the communication between communities, groups and individuals; the performance of rituals expresses symbolically roles, hierarchical structures, and ideals; rituals include or exclude individual persons or whole groups from communal life. Communication is also the aim of all those forms of ritual and ritualized behaviour that accompany the social and political life of the Greeks—the drinking party or the celebration of a victory, the honouring of benefactors or the assembly, the enthronization or the *adventus* of a ruler, or even diplomatic negotiations, as my next anecdote will hopefully demonstrate. In 86 BC Sulla was at war with Athens. After a long siege of their city the Athenians sent a delegation to negotiate with the Roman general. Plutarch reports:[9] 'When they (the envoys) made no demands which could save the city, but talked in lofty strains about Theseus and Eumolpus and the Persian wars, Sulla said to them: 'Be off, my dear sirs, and take these speeches with you; for I was not sent to Athens by the Romans to learn its history, but to subdue its rebels.' This anecdote may present more than the confrontation of Athenian oratory and Roman pragmatism. I think we have here the case of a misused and misunderstood ritual, the function of which would have been the establishment of the basis of communication, but which failed to do so. From the times of Plato's *Menexenus* to Aelius Aristides, the Athenians reminded themselves and others stereotypically and in an almost ritualized way of the same three victories over barbarians: the victory of Theseus over the Amazons, Erechtheus over the Thracians of Eumolpus, and the victory in the Persian Wars.[10] These standardized components of their cultural memory are to be found not only in orations held in festivals (in other words within the framework of a ritual), but also in their diplomatic contacts, e.g. with Sparta.[11] This ritualized use of history as an argument that can be observed in many occasions and in many forms in the history of Greek diplomacy, from the Peloponnesian War to the 'kinship diplomacy' of the

---

[9] Plu. *Sulla* 13.
[10] Plat. *Menex.* 239b–40e; Ael. Arist. *Panath.* 83–7, 92–114.
[11] Xen. *Hell.* 2.2.20; 6.2.6.

Hellenistic and Imperial period, established and facilitated communication among the Greek communities that shared the same cultural memory and values.[12] This diplomatic ritual failed in the case of Sulla, and quite naturally: Sulla himself was a barbarian aggressor, not unlike the Amazons, the Thracians and the Persians that had threatened the freedom of the Athenians in the remote past.

3. RITUALS AND CULTURAL TRANSFER

I have stretched out this communicative function of rituals and ritualized activities because I think it shows why we should include rituals and ritualized behaviour in comparative and diachronic studies of the ancient Mediterranean, despite all the obstacles and methodological problems that confront us. It would be misleading, for instance, to ignore the ritual components in discussions of continuities in the use of sacred space. Two Cretan sanctuaries with the longest record of an uninterrupted use as sacred places, the sanctuary in Simi Viannou and the Idaean Cave, demonsrate that it is exactly the change of the rituals that reveals substantial breaks in the tradition, discontinuities rather than continuities. In Simi Viannou there was a shift in the worship from sacrificial rituals and banquets to the initiatory rituals of ephebes in the historical period.[13] In the Idaean Cave the offering of food items in the Minoan period is replaced by blood sacrifices, the dedication of weapons—again, possibly in connection with military rites of passage—in the early historical period, and the celebration of a cult of death and rebirth.[14] That the continuity of use can be accompanied by

---

[12] See most recently C. P. Jones, *Kinship Diplomacy in the Ancient World* (Cambridge, Mass., 1999).

[13] A. Lebessi and P. M. Muhly, 'Aspects of Minoan Cult: Sacred Enclosures: The Evidence from the Syme Sanctuary (Crete)', *Archäologischer Anzeiger* (1990), 315–36; A. Lebessi, 'Flagellation ou autoflagellation? Données iconographiques pour une tentative d'interpretation', *Bulletin de Correspondance Hellénique* 115 (1991), 103–23; K. Sporn, *Heiligtümer und Kulte Kretas in klassischer und hellenistischer Zeit* (Heidelberg, 2002), 85–9 (with the earlier bibliography).

[14] J. Sakellarakis, 'The Idean Cave: Minoan and Greek Worship', *Kernos* 1 (1988), 207–14; Sporn, *Heiligtümer* 218–23 (with the earlier bibliography).

a radical discontinuity in ritual practices is also demonstrated by the conversion of pagan temples. Scholars often refer to the existence of Christian churches on the ruins of pagan sanctuaries as a case of continuity in the use of sacred space; sometimes it was not the sanctity of the space that invited the Christians to build their places of worship there, but on the contrary its unholiness; not the effort to continue the sacred use of a site, but the effort to expel the pagan demons; the effort to conquer an unholy and impure place and *make* it sacred. As Horden and Purcell put it: 'the "hardware" of locality and physical form, including temple, church or tomb, is in practice infused with changing structures of meaning by ritual and observance.'[15]

Rituals have been and should remain an intrinsic part of comparative studies in the Mediterranean. There is a plethora of comparative studies on rituals that not only contain the name of the Mediterranean in their title, but also address the convergences and divergences in rituals in the ancient Mediterranean.[16] Without claiming the existence of *a* Mediterranean

[15] *CS* 422. For a methodological approach see P. Pakkanen, 'The Relationship between Continuity and Change in Dark Age Greek Religion: A Methodological Study', *Opuscula Atheniensia* 25–6 (2000–1), 71–88.

[16] To give only a few examples from the last decade or so, a conference in Rome was devoted to dedicatory practices in the ancient Mediterranean (G. Bartoloni, G. Colonna and C. Grotanelli (eds.), *Atti del convegno internazionale Anathema. Regime delle offerte e vita dei santuari nel mediterraneo antico, Roma 15–18 Giugno 1989*, in *Scienze dell'antichità* 3–4 (1989–90) (1991)); another conference in Lyon had Mediterranean sacrificial rituals as its subject (R. Étienne and M.-T. Le Dinahet (eds.), *L'Espace sacrificiel dans les civilisations méditerranéennes de l'antiquité: Actes du colloque tenu à la Maison de l'Orient, Lyon, 4–7 juin 1988* (Paris 1991); R. E. DeMaris, has studied the cult of Demeter in Roman Corinth as a 'local development in a Mediterranean religion' ('Demeter in Roman Corinth: Local Development in a Mediterranean Religion', *Numen* 42 (1995) 105–17); D. J. Thompson approached Philadelphus' procession in Alexandria as an expression of 'dynastic power in a Mediterranean context' ('Philadelphus' Procession: Dynastic Power in a Mediterranean Context', in L. Mooren (ed.), *Politics, Administration and Society in the Hellenistic and Roman World: Proceedings of the International Colloquium, Bertinoro 19–24 July 1997* (Louvain, 2000) 365–88); and L. LiDonnici has recently studied 'erotic spells for fever and compulsion in the ancient Mediterranean world' ('Burning for it: Erotic Spells for Fever and Compulsion in the Ancient Mediterranean World', *Greek, Roman, and Byzantine Studies* 39 (1998), 63–98). See also B. Gladigow, 'Mediterrane

religion or of *Mediterranean* rituals, these scholars regard a comparative study of rituals limited to this area as a meaningful task. And there are good reasons for doing so, at least in certain historical periods. The Mediterranean Sea has more often been a facilitator of communication than a barrier, and communication contributes to the wide diffusion not only of flora, fauna, and artefacts, but also of culture. And rituals are an important component of cultural traditions. Ritual transfer is, therefore, neither a rare nor a surprising phenomenon.[17] The mechanisms of the transfer and the factors that contribute—in certain periods—convergences in ritual practices are manifold and have so often been studied that a brief reference to the most common forms would suffice: massive movements of population—invasion, migration, conquest, and of course colonization, with the introduction of the rituals of the mother-city to the colony—were sometimes no more influential than the settlement of small groups of foreigners (especially merchants, garrisons, and exiles: for example, Ptolemaic mercenaries were as important for the diffusion of the cult of Egyptian deities, as the Roman army for the diffusion of many Oriental cults).[18] In addition to this, administrative measures of empires and even diplomatic contacts contributed to the uniformity of ritual practices. One should also underscore the missionary activity of individuals or organized groups. Finally, we should not forget the importance of canonical texts, either orally transmitted or written, for ritual transfer for instance, the uniformity of magical rituals throughout the Mediterranean or the uniformity

Religionsgeschichte, Römische Religionsgeschichte, Europäische Religionsgeschichte: Zur Genese cinse Faktkonzeptes', in *Kykeon: Studies in Honour of H. S. Versnel* (Leiden, etc., 2002), 49–67.

[17] See, e.g. E. R. Gebbard, 'The Gods in Transit: Narratives of Cult Transfer', in A. Y. Collins and M. M. Mitchell (eds.), *Antiquity and Humanity. Essays on Ancient Religion and Philosophy presented to D. Betz on his 70th Birthday* (Tübingen, 2001), 451–76.

[18] M. Launey, *Recherches sur les armées hellénistiques* (réimpression avec addenda et mise à jour en postface par Y. Garlan, Ph. Gauthier, Cl. Orrieux, Paris, 1987), 1026–31; A. Chaniotis, 'Foreign Soldiers—Native Girls? Constructing and Crossing Boundaries in Hellenistic Cities with Foreign Garrisons', in A. Chaniotis and P. Ducrey (eds.), *Army and Power in the Ancient World* (Stuttgart, 2002), 108–9.

of rituals of mystery cults was to a great extent the result of the existence of ritual handbooks.[19]

In what follows, I will not discuss the mechanisms of ritual transfer and uniformity in the Mediterranean, but simply address some problems we are confronted with when we attempt to make rituals a meaningful subject of Mediterranean studies—either diachronically or in particular periods.

4. THE ELUSIVENESS OF RITUALS

Rituals belong to the most elusive phenomena of ancient religious and social behaviour. As widely established, stereotypical activities, followed consistently and (at least in theory) invariably, they are rarely described and hardly ever explained by those who perform them; they are rather described by those who observe them and are astounded at the differences from the rituals of their own culture, or they are described by puzzled antiquarians. Whereas religious activity at a site can be established by various means (e.g. through the existence of a cult building, ex-votos, or dedicatory inscriptions), we often lack any knowledge of the rituals involved; and the cult of a divinity may be practised continually, even though the rituals of the worship change. To give a few examples, there was a decline in the offering of blood sacrifice in the later part of the Imperial period, and instead a preference for the singing of hymns and the offering of libations.[20] Another change we may observe

---

[19] For magical handbooks see F. Graf, *Gottesnähe und Schadenzauber: Die Magie in der griechisch-römischen Antike* (Munich, 1996) 10; M. W. Dickie, 'The Learned Magician and the Collection and Transmission of Magical Lore', in D. R. Jordan, H. Montgomery, and E. Thomassen (eds.), *The World of Ancient Magic: Papers from the First International Samson Eitrem Seminar at the Norwegian Institute at Athens, 4–8 May 1997* (Bergen, 1999), 163–93. An impression of initiatory liturgical books is provided by the so-called 'Mithrasliturgie' in a papyrus in Paris (*Papyri Graecae Magicae* 4 475–824); see R. Merkelbach, *Abrasax III. Ausgewählte Papyri religiösen und magischen, Inhalts* III (Opladen, 1992).

[20] S. Bradbury, 'Julian's Pagan Revival and the Decline of Blood Sacrifice', *Phoenix* 49 (1995), 331–56; see e.g. F. Sokolowski, *Lois Sacrées de l'Asie Mineure* (Paris, 1955), no. 28; A. Rehm, *Didyma* II. *Die Inschriften*, ed. R. Harder (Berlin, 1958), no. 217; R. Merkelbach and J. Stauber, 'Die Orakel des Apollon von Klaros', *Epigraphica Anatolica* 27 (1996), 1–54, nos. 2 (Pergamon), 4 (Hierapolis), and 11 (Sardes or Koloe).

thanks to inscriptions with sacred regulations is a shift from the preoccupation with the ritual purity of the body to a preoccupation with the purity of the mind;[21] the relevant evidence dates from the fourth century BC onwards and is widely diffused in the eastern Mediterranean (in Macedonia and mainland Greece, in Crete and many islands of the Aegean, and many places in Asia Minor). Both changes in rituals occurred in sanctuaries used without any interruption and devoted to the same divinity. All this has been observed thanks to the rather unusual abundance of literary texts and above all of inscriptions (sacred regulations) in the respective periods. Such changes have a social parameter as well. Both aforementioned changes seem to have influenced only part of the worshippers, the intellectual elite and the persons that stood under its influence. Social and intellectual differentiations in the practice of rituals should be taken into consideration, but it is only in exceptional cases that our sources allow us to do so.

Another example of continual use of a sacred place connected with a disruption of ritual practices is provided by the altar of the Jerusalem temple. It was used as an altar for blood sacrifices throughout the Hellenistic period, with no interruption in its use—a wonderful case of continuity in rituals, one might have thought, if we did not have the literary evidence that informs us that for a period of three years and six months during the reign of Antiochus IV the altar was used for the sacrifice of swine;[22] the change of just one component of the ritual of blood sacrifice (the species of the sacrificial animal) provocatively demonstrated a disruption of the ritual tradition. In this particular case we happen to know of this short-term interruption, in others we do not, and it has often been observed that continuity in use of the same space does not necessarily mean its identical use.[23] It is

[21] A. Chaniotis, 'Reinheit des Körpers—Reinheit der Seele in den griechischen Kultgesetzen', in J. Assmann and Th. Sundermeier (eds.), *Schuld, Gewissen und Person* (Gütersloh, 1997), 142–79.

[22] Joseph. *Ant. Jud.* 12.253.

[23] A. Chaniotis, in J. Schäfer (ed.), *Amnisos nach den archäologischen, topographischen, historischen und epigraphischen Zeugnissen des Altertums und der Neuzeit* (Berlin, 1992), 88–96; L. V. Watrous, *The Cave Sanctuary of Zeus at Psychro. A Study of Extra-Urban Sanctuaries in Minoan and Early Iron Age Crete* (Liège, 1996), esp. 106–11; *CS* 404–11.

often this elusiveness of rituals that makes scholars very prudently talk about continuity of cult, but not of continuity of rituals.

But except for interruptions and disruptions that escape our notice, sometimes there are elusive continuities. Rites of passage in particular, long abolished or neglected, have the tendency to emerge in unexpected places and forms (very often as the background of literary narratives—an important subject that cannot be addressed here).[24] The activities of the Athenian ephebes in the Hellenistic period, after the artificial revival of the ephebic institutions but without the institutionalized performance of initiatory rituals, present an interesting case. An honorific decree of 123 BC describes these activities, which included participation in festivals, processions, and athletic competitions, attendance at philosophical schools, military exercises, visits to important historical monuments and sanctuaries, and acquaintance with the borders of Athenian territory; these activities are more or less standardized, since we find references to them in similar decrees. It is in this passage that we find the following report:[25]

and they made an excursion to the border of Attic territory carrying their weapons, acquiring knowledge of the territory and the roads [lacuna] and they visited the sanctuaries in the countryside, offering sacrifices on behalf of the people. When they arrived at the grave at Marathon, they offered a wreath and a sacrifice to those who died in war for freedom; they also came to the sanctuary of Amphiaraus. And there they demonstrated the legitimate possession of the sanctuary which had been occupied by the ancestors in old times. And after they had offered a sacrifice, they returned on the same day to our own territory.

What at first sight seems a harmless excursion, acquires another dimension when we take into consideration the fact that in this period the sanctuary of Amphiaraus was *not* part of the Athenian territory, but belonged to the city of Oropos. The Athenians had lost this territory less than a generation earlier (this was the occasion of the famous embassy of the Athenian philosophers to

---

[24] Cf. J. Ma, 'Black Hunter Variations', *Proceedings of the Cambridge Philological Society* 40 (1994), 49–80.

[25] *IG* II² 1006 lines 65–71.

Rome). The Athenian ephebes marched under arms into foreign territory, reminding their audience with speeches that the
Athenians were the legitimate owners of the sanctuary, and then
withdrew behind the Athenian border. This looks very much
like the survival of an initiatory ritual: separation from urban
life, liminality through visit of the borders of the territory,
exposure to a danger and achievement of an important deed,
and reintegration—return to Athens and acceptance into the
citizen body.

5. ARTIFICIAL REVIVALS

A second problem involved in the study of continuities in
rituals (but also in the study of religious continuities in general)
is the fact that what at first sight seems a survival may well be an
artificial revival. Some time in the fifth century AD, a pagan
priest in Megara, one Helladios, set up an inscription on the
monument of the dead of the Persian Wars, restoring Simoni-
des' epigram (written almost one millennium earlier) and
adding the remark that 'the city offered sacrifices up to this
day'.[26] It would be a big mistake to take this statement as proof
that this ritual had been continually performed in Megara for
ten centuries. A long time after the prohibition of pagan sacrifices, Helladios provocatively defies the laws of the Christian
emperors—a phenomenon to which I will return later. Here, we
are more probably dealing with a revival rather than a survival.

This is more clear in my second example, a Milesian decree of
the mid-first century concerning a banquet which should be
offered by the *prophetes* (the priest of Apollo Didymeus) at
Didyma to the *kosmoi* (probably a board of sacred officials
responsible for some kind of decoration in the sanctuary) and
by the *stephanephoros* to the *molpoi*, the old, respected priestly
board of singers.[27] This decree was brought to the assembly by
Tiberius Claudius Damas, a well-known citizen of Miletus.

---

[26] *IG* VII 53.
[27] P. Herrmann, *Inschriften von Milet*, Part 1 (Berlin, 1997), no.134 (with
the earlier bibliography); F. Sokolowski, *Lois sacrées de l'Asie Mineure* (Paris,
1955), no. 53. For a detailed discussion of the religious context of Damas'
initiative and further examples see A. Chaniotis, 'Negotiating Religion in the
Cities of the Eastern Roman Provinces', *Kernos* 16 (2003), 177–90.

Thanks to numerous inscriptions and coins we know a few things about his personality. He held the office of the *prophetes* for at least two terms and he initiated a coinage with representations of Apollo Didymeus and Artemis Pythie.[28] We are dealing with an individual with a particular interest in the old, revered, but also often destroyed and neglected sanctuary at Didyma. The actual subject of the decree is presented in fewer than six lines: The acting *prophetes* and the *stephanephoros* are obliged 'to organize the banquet of the *kosmoi* and the *molpoi* according to ancestral custom and in accordance with the laws and the decrees which have been previously issued.' Surprisingly enough, this short text is followed by twenty-four lines, devoted to measures preventing future violations of this decree and the punishment of wrongdoers. The responsible magistrates were not allowed to substitute this celebration with a money contribution.[29] Any future decree which did not conform to this decree should be invalid; its initiator would have to pay a fine, in addition to the divine punishment which awaits the impious; and the ritual would have to be performed, nonetheless. This decree is declared to be 'a decree pertaining to piety towards the gods and the Augusti and to the preservation of the city'. Damas was obviously afraid that his decree would be as persistently ignored by future magistrates as all those earlier laws on the same matter which he quotes. His concern must have been justified. Damas himself served as a *prophetes*, voluntarily; in the text which records his first term in this office Damas underscores the fact that 'he performed everything which his predecessors used to perform'. Such statements in honorific inscriptions indicate that some magistrates were less diligent in the fulfilment of their duties. Damas served a second term later, after a year of vacancy in this office;[30] not a single

---

[28] L. Robert, *Monnaies grecques. Types, légendes, magistrats monétaires et géographie* (Geneva and Paris, 1967), 50.

[29] That this occasionally happened, following the demand of the community, is demonstrated by a new inscription from Dag'mara/Karaköy (Tempsianoi?): a priest acceded to the request of the city and provided the money he was supposed to spend for banquets for the construction of an aqueduct (*c*.AD 180–92). See H. Malay, *Researches in Lydia, Mysia and Aiolis* (*TAM*, Ergänzungsband 23) (Vienna, 1999), 115 no. 127.

[30] Rehm, *Didyma*, no. 268.

Milesian had been willing to serve as a *prophetes*—not an unusual situation at Didyma.

Numerous inscriptions document a general unwillingness amongst the citizens to serve as *prophetai* and an even greater unwillingness to perform *all* the traditional rituals. In the long series of more than one hundred inscriptions that record the names of the *prophetai* many texts inform us time and again of the difficulties in finding candidates. One of the *prophetai*, Claudius Chionis, explicitly states that he served both as *archiprytanis* and as *prophetes* in a year in which 'no citizen was willing to accept either office'.[31] We get some information about Damas' second term as a *prophetes* from the above inscription from Didyma. It reports that Damas served voluntarily a second term as a *prophetes*, at the age of 81, and that 'he revived the ancestral customs' and celebrated the banquet in the sanctuary at Didyma twelve days long. Similar references to the rites performed by the *prophetes* appear occasionally in the inscriptions of the *prophetai*. The explicit certification that the particular priest had fulfilled his duties indicate that this was not always the case. And some officials seem to have done more than their predecessors. An anonymous *prophetes*, for example, provided the funds for a banquet for all the citizens for 13 days; he distributed money to women and virgins in a festival; he offered a dinner for the boys who officiated in a celebration; and he distributed money to the members of the council on Apollo's birthday.[32]

These sporadic references to revivals seem to me to reflect failures rather than success. This evidence (and there is much more from other cities) show us how an individual with a vivid interest in ancestral customs revived rituals long forgotten and neglected. The fact that inscriptions which refer to these initiatives survive does not permit the conclusion that the success of these initiatives was lasting. Damas' decree offers an interesting example of a revival which was apparently accepted by the people, but whose success was ephemeral. From his own

[31] Ibid. no. 272. Similar problems are alluded to in nos. 214 B, 215, 236 B III, 241, 243, 244, 252, 269, 270, 277, 278, 279 A, 286, 288, and 289.

[32] Ibid. no. 297. Two other *prophetai* claim that they had revived ancient customs, but their inscriptions are too fragmentary to allow us to see what exactly the object of the revival had been: nos. 289 and 303.

inscriptions we know that at least *he* followed the custom, but otherwise there are only sporadic references to this celebration. When the driving force of a revival was an individual, not the community, the revival often died with its initiator, exactly as certain festivals or cults did not survive the death of their founders. I have discussed this case in such detail, because it seems to me a very characteristic example of how misleading it may be to try to draw conclusions about the continual performance of rituals from isolated pieces of evidence. This example also demonstrates the role of individual personalities and idiosyncrasies for the performance of rituals, a subject to which I return later. Needless to say artificial revivals sometimes are accompanied with changes in meaning. The initiatory ritual of the flagellation in the sanctuary of Artemis Orthia in Sparta (known also from Crete) was revived as a touristic attraction in the imperial period.[33]

6. MISLEADING ANALOGIES: THE DAIDALA OF PLATAIA AND ITS MODERN EXEGETES

A third problem is that sometimes similarities in isolated elements of rituals attested in distant parts of the Mediterranean are regarded as proof of the identity of these rituals, or of an analogy between them. Let us take, for example, the carrying of the wooden image in a procession, the central ritual of the festival of the Daidala.[34] The aetiological myth is narrated by Plutarch and Pausanias:[35] once Hera had quarrelled with Zeus and was hiding. Alalkomenes advised Zeus to deceive Hera, by acting as if he were going to marry another woman. With Alalkomenes' help, Zeus secretly cut down a big and very beautiful oak-tree, gave it the shape of a woman, decorated it as a bride, and called it Daidale. Then they sang the wedding song for her, the nymphs of the river Triton gave her the nuptial bath, and Boiotia provided for flautists and revellers. When all this was

[33] Plu. *Mor.* 239d.

[34] For a more detailed discussion see A. Chaniotis, 'Ritual Dynamics: The Boiotian festival of the Daidala', in *Kykeon: Studies in Honour of H. S. Versnel* (Leiden, 2002), 23–48 (with the earlier bibliography).

[35] Plutarch, *FGrH* 388 F 1 (*peri ton en Plataiais Daidalon*); Pausanias 9.2.7–9.3.3.

almost completed, Hera lost her patience. She came down from Mt. Kithairon, followed by the women of Plataia, and ran full of anger and jealousy to Zeus. But when she realized that the 'bride' was a doll, she reconciled herself with Zeus with joy and laughter and took the role of the bridesmaid. She honoured this wooden image and named the festival Daidala. Nonetheless, she burned the image, although it was not alive, because of her jealousy. Pausanias gives us the most detailed description of the ritual:

In this way they celebrate the festival. Not far from Alalkomenai is a grove of oaks. Here the trunks of the oaks are the largest in Boeotia. To this grove come the Plataians, and lay out portions of boiled flesh. They keep a strict watch on the crows which flock to them, but they are not troubled at all about the other birds. They mark carefully the tree on which a crow settles with the meat he has seized. They cut down the trunk of the tree on which the crow has settled, and make of it the *daidalon*; for this is the name that they give to the wooden image also. This festival the Plataians celebrate by themselves, calling it the Little Daidala, but the Great Daidala, which is celebrated with them by the Boeotians, is a festival held at intervals of fifty-nine years, for that is the period during which, they say, the festival could not be held, as the Plataians were in exile. There are fourteen wooden images ready, having been provided each year at the Little Daidala. Lots are cast for them by the Plataians, Koronaians, Thespians, Thangraians, Chaironeis, Orchomenians, Lebadeis, and Thebans. For at the time when Kassandros, the son of Antipater, rebuilt Thebes, the Thebans wished to be reconciled with the Plataians, to share in the common assembly, and to send a sacrifice to the Daidala. The towns of less account pool their funds for images. Bringing the image to the Asopos, and setting it upon a wagon, they place a bridesmaid also on the wagon. They again cast lots for the position they are to hold in the procession. After this they drive the wagons from the river to the summit of Kithairon. On the peak of the mountain an altar has been prepared, which they make in the following way. They fit together quadrangular pieces of wood, putting them together just as if they were making a stone building, and having raised it to a height they place brushwood upon the altar. The cities with their magistrates sacrifice a cow to Hera and a bull to Zeus, burning on the altar the victims, full of wine and incense, along with the *daidala*. Rich people, as individuals sacrifice what they wish; but the less wealthy sacrifice the smaller cattle; all the victims alike are burned. The fire seizes the altar and the victims as well, and consumes them all together. I know of no blaze that is so high, or seen so far as this (trans. W. H. S. Jones, modified).

From Frazer's times onwards the Daidala of Boeotia have fascinated scholars studying the relation between myth and ritual. Amongst the many studies on the Daidala the most influential approach recognizes the heterogeneity of the details described by Pausanias, but focuses on the construction and burning of the wooden image or images, investing this ritual with a variety of meanings which range from the idea of an annual fire expressing the rejuvenation of nature to the appeasement of a mighty chthonic goddess. This approach associates the Daidala with the spring and mid-summer bonfire festivals of modern Europe (of the Maypole or Johannesfeuer-type), at which a wooden image is brought to the settlement and burned. According to Frazer's interpretation, the Daidala represent the marriage of powers of vegetation; Hera's retirement is a mythical expression for a bad season and the failure of crops.[36] M. P. Nilsson speculated that the image which was burned represented a demon of vegetation that had to go through fire in order to secure the warmth of the sun for everything that lives and grows. Since this fire ritual had the purpose of promoting fertility, it was understood as a wedding; Hera was associated with this festival at a late stage, as the goddess of marriage; the discrepancies in the myths and the rituals reflect the late conflation of two separate festivals, a fire festival and a festival of Hera.[37]

The prominent position of a holocaust offering at two festivals of Artemis, the Laphria and the Elaphebolia, led A. Schachter to the assumption that the burning of the images at the Daidala was also originally dedicated to Artemis and at some later point connected with the cult of Hera.[38] Needless to say, the similarity between the Daidala on the one hand and the Laphria and the Elaphebolia on the other is rather

---

[36] J. G. Frazer, *The Golden Bough: A Study in Magic and Religion.* Part I: *The Magic Art and the Evolution of Kings,* 3rd edn. (London, 1913), ii. 140–1.

[37] M. P. Nilsson, *Griechische Feste von religiöser Bedeutung mit Ausschluss der attischen* (Lund, 1906), 54–5; *Geschichte der griechischen Religion,* 3rd edn. (Munich, 1967), i. 130–1, 431.

[38] A. Schachter, *Cults of Boiotia* (London, 1981), i. 247.

superficial; the burning of slaughtered sacrificial victims at the Daidala cannot be compared with the throwing of living animals on the pyre at the Laphria. In addition to this, I can see no evidence for the assumption that in the holocausts of the Laphria and the Elaphebolia Artemis was conceived as the patroness of childbirth; and of course there is no evidence for the sacrificial burning of wooden images in these festivals of Artemis.

Finally, W. Burkert has attributed the Daidala to a category of myths and rituals the common theme of which is the departure and return of a goddess of fertility—well known from Oriental iconography and myth.[39] Burkert recognized an ancient Greek parallel in a representation on a *pithos* of the ninth century BC found at Knossos. A winged goddess, richly dressed and with a high *polos*, stands on a chariot. She is represented in two different ways in two panels on the two opposite sides of the *pithos*. In the one panel the goddess raises her hands on which two birds are seated. On the other panel the goddess has dropped her arms, her wings are lowered, the birds fly away. The trees in the first representation blossom, the trees on the other side do not. According to Burkert's plausible interpretation, the two panels are connected with a festival of the coming and the departure of the great goddess of fertility; the chariot implies that an image of the goddess was brought into the city. There are indeed obvious analogies to the myths and the ritual of the Daidala: the departure of an (angry) goddess and her return, the carrying of an image on a chariot. But there are also obvious differences: the representation from Knossos is the image of a goddess; the wooden *daidala* were not; the *daidala* were burned; and there is no indication that the image on the Knossian *pithos* is that of a bride.

Another parallel was recognized by Burkert in the report of Firmicus Maternus concerning a festival of Persephone.[40] A tree was cut and was used for the construction of the image of

---

[39] W. Burkert, 'Katagógia-Anagógia and the Goddess of Knossos', in R. Hägg, N. Marinatos, and G. Nordquist (eds.), *Early Greek Cult Practice. Proceedings of the Fifth International Symposium at the Swedish Institute at Athens, 26–29 June 1986* (Stockholm, 1988), 81–7.

[40] *Err. prof. rel.* 27.2.

a maiden, which was then brought to the city; there, it was mourned for forty days; on the evening of the fortieth day, the image was burned. This ritual is supposed to reflect the annual cycle of nature. The joy at the coming of the goddess was followed by the sadness at her departure in the fall. Again, the differences from the Daidala are no less striking than the similarities. Persephone's periodical death finds no analogy in any known cult of Hera; the wooden *daidala* were not brought to the city, they were not mourned, and they were not supposed to represent the periodical death of a virgin. Aelian and Athenaeus have reports of a similar festival at Eryx in Sicily, this time for Aphrodite—the festival Anagogia. It owed its name to the departure of Aphrodite, who was thought to leave for Africa, followed by birds (pigeons). Nine days later a very beautiful pigeon was seen coming from the south, and its coming was celebrated as the festival Katagogia. We observe, however, that in this festival there is no image, no marriage, no pyre. Burkert suggested associating this group of festivals with mankind's primordial fears: threatened by drought, bad harvests, infertility, and bad weather, people from time to time leave the area of agricultural activity and return to the forest, where they used to find food at the stage of hunters and gatherers. The burning of an image may be a survival of the great pyres on peak sanctuaries in Minoan Crete.

Modern research has not only isolated these two important components of the Daidala, the sacred marriage and the fire ritual; it has also pointed out that the burning of the Daidala can be conceived of as a sacrifice, and this is a very important element which is difficult to reconcile with the other two approaches. K. Meuli has assigned the sacrifice of the Daidala to the category of the 'chthonische Vernichtungsopfer', sacrifices offered to chthonic deities whose dangerous power should be appeased;[41] the myth about the quarrel between Hera and Zeus and the goddess' withdrawal can be associated with this interpretation, which, however, fails to explain other components of the ritual in the Imperial period (especially the allusions to a wedding). The fact that the *daidala* cannot be conceived as

---

[41] K. Meuli, 'Griechische Opferbräuche', in *Phyllobolia für Peter von der Mühll zum 60. Geburtstag am 1. August 1945* (Basel, 1946), 209–10.

divine images led E. Loucas-Durie to the assumption that their
burning was the substitute for a human sacrifice, which may
have constituted a central part of the ritual in its early phase.[42]

I have dealt with the Daidala at some length—without mentioning all the interpretations offered so far—because it offers a
characteristic example of the problems we face with similarities
and analogies between rituals, especially when our sources come
from a period in which the performance of the ritual is the result
of amalgamations and syncopations.

7. RITUALS AND THE PHYSICAL ENVIRONMENT

A fourth obstacle in the way of studying rituals in a Mediterranean context is the fact that rituals present an aspect of worship
that seems to be least related to geography, physical environment and landscape. One may raise one's hands in prayer, kneel
before a cult statue, kiss an object of worship, pour a liquid
during an oath ceremony, or take a ritual bath near the banks of
the Nile or in the rocky landscape of Kappadokia—or virtually
anywhere else. No geographical factors seem to be directly in
operation when people perform rites of passage according to the
threefold structure established by van Gennep and modified by
Turner and others, whether they are in ancient Greece, medieval India, or a contemporary student fraternity.

This position which dissociates rituals from geographical
factors and landscapes is related to a widespread attitude in the
study of rituals that reappears in different forms from Frazer's
Golden Bough to Burkert's *Creation of the Sacred*: rituals are
primeval, they are not invented but transmitted—either through
natural processes of acculturation or even biologically—and
adapted to new cultural environments. According to this view,
rituals observed in various cultures should be regarded as mutations or variants of archetypal forms.

It should not therefore be a surprise that the study of rituals
in modern scholarship has primarily been a study of origins.
Even when we have detailed descriptions of rituals from the
Imperial period, such as the description of the Daidala in

---

[42] E. Loucas-Durie, 'Simulacre humain et offrande rituelle', *Kernos* 1 (1988),
151–62.

Boeotia, the question asked is not what the function of the ritual was in the period from which the eye-witness reports come, but how we can reconstruct the ritual's original form and meaning. This is not the place to discuss the ethological background of rituals[43] or how meaningful the discussion of origins may be. Nonetheless, given the Mediterranean context of this volume, it is not inappropriate to emphasize the importance of physical environment, not for the origin of rituals perhaps, but certainly for their evolution and diffusion. Again, Horden and Purcell have presented a strong case for a distinctively Mediterranean sense of place and have shown that place can be a useful instrument of analysis.[44] The most important feature of the Mediterranean, in this respect, is the fragmented topography, a factor that contributes to divergences and divisions between cultural systems, but has in many periods also challenged Mediterranean populations to overcome this fragmentation. The challenge has made the Mediterranean a zone of 'lateral transmission of ideas and practices', including the transmission of rituals.[45] The significance of the physical environment as the setting in which rituals are performed can sometimes, unexpectedly, be observed when an attempt is made to reproduce the physical environment of a particular ritual in a new environment, the transmission not only of the environment, but also of its original setting. The best known example is the reproduction of Nilotic landscapes in sanctuaries of the Egyptian deities outside Egypt;[46] similar phenomena are the construction of artificial caves for the celebration of the Mithraic mysteries or for Dionysiac celebrations (compare the construction of caves in modern India to reproduce the cave of St Mary at Lourdes). One can include here the construction of pools for the worship of the nymphs,[47] and perhaps even peak sanctuaries on eleva-

---

[43] W. Burkert, *Creation of the Sacred: Tracks of Biology in Early Religions* (Cambridge, Mass. and London, 1996); id., 'Fitness oder Opium? Die Fragestellung der Soziologie im Bereich alter Religionen', in F. Stolz (ed.), *Homo naturaliter religiosus. Gehört Religion notwendig zum Mensch-Sein?* (Bern, 1997), 13–38.

[44] *CS* 401–60.   [45] *CS* 404, 407–8.

[46] e.g. R. Saldit-Trappmann, *Tempel der ägyptischen Götter in Griechenland und an der Westküste Kleinasiens* (Leiden, 1970), 1–25.

[47] Cf. *CS* 431. Bakchic caves: Athen. 4.148bc. Cf. the term *androphylakes* ('the guardians of the cave') in an inscription of a Dionysiac association in

tions that do not deserve the designation mountain, but present 'imaginary mountains'.[48] The Samaritans on Delos were so bound to the holy place of their homeland that they designated their association as 'those who sacrifice in the holy sacred Mt. Argarizein' (*aparchomenoi eis hieron hagion Argarizein*).[49] Finally, even if it would be futile to look for rituals originating in the Mediterranean or practised only in the Mediterranean, one can observe certain preferences that to some extent are favoured by the physical environment, for example the prominent part played by processions or the widespread custom of setting up tents, attested in a variety of contexts, from the Hebrew *succah* to the Greek Thesmophoria and from the Ptolemaia of Alexandria to the *skanopageia* of Kos.[50]

8. THE ROLE OF RELIGIOUS IDIOSYNCRASIES

A factor of enormous importance for the evolution of rituals—no matter whether we are dealing with revival or transmission, amalgamation or syncopation, aesthetic or ideological transformation—is the part played by individuals, their idiosyncrasy, personal piety, social position, education, or even political agenda. I have already referred to two men (unfortunately our sources mostly refer to men) whose role was essential for the revival of rituals: the priest Helladios in Megara and the *prophetes* Damas in Miletus. We often hear of persons who on their own initiative introduced cult and rituals from one place at another, for instance the Telemachos who introduced the cult of Asklepios in Athens or Demetrios who founded a sanctuary of the Egyptian deities at Delos.[51] Sometimes we hear of persons

Rome (G. Ricciardelli, 'Mito e performance nelle associazioni dionisiache', in M. Tortorelli Ghedini, A. Storchi Marino, and A. Visconti (eds.), *Tra Orfeo e Pitagora. Origini e incontri di culture nell'antichità. Atti dei seminari napoletani 1996–1998* (Naples, 2000), 274).

[48] For 'imaginary mountains' see R. Buxton, *Imaginary Greece: The Contexts of Mythology* (Cambridge, 1994), 81–96.

[49] R. Goggins, 'Jewish Local Patriotism: The Samaritan Problem', in S. Jones and S. Pearce (eds.), *Jewish Local Patriotism and Self-Identification in the Graeco-Roman Period* (Sheffield, 1998), 75–7.

[50] Thesmophoria: H. S. Versnel, *Inconsistencies in Greek and Roman Religion* (Leiden, 1993), ii. 236 n. 25.

[51] H. Engelmann, *The Delian Aretalogy of Sarapis* (Leiden, 1975).

who revived a neglected ritual, for example Damas who revived the ritual banquet at Didyma, Symmachos of Lyttos who revived the distribution of money to tribal subdivisions in his Cretan city on the occasion of the festivals Welchania and Theodaisia,[52] or Mnasistratos in Andania who gave the sacred books of the mysteries to the city, thus contributing to a reorganization of this cult.[53]

Let us take one of the most interesting cases of ritual transfer, the mysteries of the rural sanctuary at Panóias in northern Portugal.[54] A *lex sacra* informs us that the senator C. Calpurnius Rufinus founded a mystery cult dedicated to Hypsistos Sarapis, to deities of the underworld (*Diis Severis*), and the local gods of the Lapiteae. The texts mention a temple (*templum, aedes*) and various cult facilities constructed on the natural rock (*quadrata, aeternus lacus,* a *gastra*); their function is explained in several texts: *hostiae quae cadunt hic immolantur. Extra intra quadrata contra cremantur. Sanguis laciculis superfunditur* (1), *in quo hostiae voto cremantur* (3), *lacum, qui voto miscetur* (5). From these instructions given to the initiates Alföldy reconstructs the ritual, which included the preparation of sacrificial animals, the offering of their blood to the gods of the underworld, the burning of their intestines, a banquet, and purification. The mystery cult was probably introduced from Perge (cf. the Dorian form *mystaria,* for *mysteria*), Rufinus' place of origin. If we only had the dedicatory formula (Rufinus dedicated to Hypsistos Sarapis), we would naturally have assumed that Rufinus' activity was similar to that of Telemachos in Athens or Demetrios in Delos. The detailed description of the rituals shows that under the guise of mysteries of Sarapis we have an amalgamation of different ritual traditions. Rufinus is not an isolated case. The cult foundation of Alexander, the

---

[52] *I. Cret.* 1. xviii 11 (2nd/3rd century).

[53] F. Sokolowski, *Lois sacrées des cités grecques* (Paris, 1969), no. 65. For the cult see most recently L. Piolot, 'Pausanias et les Mystères d'Andanie: Histoire d'une aporie', in J. Renard (ed.), *Le Péloponnèse. Archéologie et Histoire. Actes de la rencontre internationale de Lorient, 12–15 mai 1998* (Rennes, 1999), 195–228 (with earlier bibliography).

[54] G. Alföldy, 'Inscriciones, sacrificios y misterios: El santuario rupestre de Panóias/Portugal', *Mitteilungen des Deutschen Archäologischen Instituts—Abteilung Madrid* 36 (1995), 252–8: id., 'Die Mysterien von Panóias (Vila Real, Portugal)', ibid. 38 (1997), 176–246.

false prophet, at Abonouteichos is very similar, including the adaptation of heterogeneous elements from the cult of Asclepius, different oracular practices, Neopythagorean observances and doctrines, and the mysteries of Eleusis.[55] And a certain Dionysios who founded a mystery cult and a cult association at Philadelpheia composed a sacred regulation with strict moral and ritual observances not modelled according to a particular mystery cult, but influenced by many different traditions.[56] It is certainly not necessary to underline how difficult it is to grasp the personal religiosity of the individuals that introduced or revived rituals, not to mention the case of persons who performed rituals. How can we ever know how an Epicurean philosopher thought and felt when he served as a priest responsible for the traditional rituals scorned by his fellow philosophers?[57]

9.   THE MANIFOLD CHARACTER OF RITUAL TRANSFER

Ritual transfer means not only the transmission of rituals from one place to another, it implies a far more complex process: the transfer of a ritual from a particular context to another—to

---

[55] See most recently U. Victor, *Lukian von Samosata, Alexander oder Der Lügenprophet* (Leiden, etc., 1997); G. Sfameni Gasparro, 'Alessandro di Abonutico, lo "pseudo-profeta' ovvero come construirsi un'identità religiosa I', *Studi e Materiali di Storia delle Religioni* 62 (1996) (1998), 565–90; ead., 'Alessandro di Abonutico, lo "pseudo-profeta" ovvero come costruirsi un'identità religiosa II', in C. Bonnet and A. Motte (eds.), *Les syncrétismes religieux dans le monde méditerranéen antique. Actes du colloque international en l'honneur de Franz Cumont* (Brussels and Rome, 1999), 275–305; A. Chaniotis, 'Old Wine in a New Skin: Tradition and Innovation in the Cult Foundation of Alexander of Abonouteichos', in E. Dabrowa (ed.), *Tradition and Innovation in the Ancient World* (Krakow, 2002), 67–85. For the influence of magical rituals on Alexander of Abonouteichos, see A. Mastrocinque, 'Alessandro di Abonouteichos e la magia', in *Imago Antiquitatis. Religions et iconographie du monde romain: Mélanges offerts à Robert Turcan* (Paris, 1999), 341–52.

[56] S. C. Barton and G. H. R. Horsley, 'A Hellenistic Cult Group and the New Testament Church', *Jahrbuch für Antike und Christentum* 24 (1981), 7–41.

[57] Rehm, *Didyma*, no. 285. For personal religiosity see F. Graf, 'Bemerkungen zur bürgerlichen Religiosität im Zeitalter des Hellenismus', in M. Wörrle and P. Zanker (eds.), *Stadtbild und Bürgerbild im Hellenismus* (Munich, 1995), 103–14.

a new social context, a new cultic context, a new ideological context. My last examples aim at demonstrating this complexity.

The first concerns the transfer of sacrificial rituals from the cult of the gods to the cult of the dead, the ruler cult, and the appeal to superhuman powers in magic. In all these cases the transfer is accompanied either by reversals or by syncopations. In the case of magic, for instance, the sacrifice takes place in the dark and involves the killing of unusual animals in unusual ways.[58] Analogous reversals can be observed in the *enagismoi* of funerary cult; in the ruler cult, the element of prayer, integral part of the sacrifice, hardly plays any role.[59]

My second example concerns the transfer of a ritual into a new ideological context. Let us take again the ritual of blood sacrifice. Until the late fourth century AD it was a widely attested and accepted practice. It was performed in private and in the community; it did not have a liminal position. Of course things changed after the year 391, when sacrifices were forbidden. The sporadic performance of sacrifices, attested by several inscriptions after this prohibition (e.g. the inscription of the priest Helladios in Megara), acquires a different meaning in the new historical context. It is not just the performance of a custom, but the demonstrative defiance of Christian legislation and observance of ancient customs in a period of religious intolerance.[60] But even before the prohibition, we know from

---

[58] Graf, *Gottesnähe*, 203–4. Cf. now S. I. Johnston, 'Sacrifice in the Greek Magical Papyri', in P. Mirecki and M. Meyer (eds.), *Magic and Ritual in the Ancient World* (Leiden, 2002), 344–58.

[59] S. R. F. Price, *Rituals and Power: The Roman Imperial Cult in Asia Minor* (Cambridge, 1984), 118–21; M. Clauss, *Kaiser und Gott: Herrscherkult im römischen Reich* (Stuttgart and Leipzig, 1999), 413–19. In the East, the only unequivocal reference to a prayer (*euche*) to an emperor is in an inscription at Thyateira (*IGRRP* 4.1273, lines 11–13). More problematic are the references to *euche* in the context of the emperor cult in *SEG* 2.718 and 45.1719. For a discussion see D. Fishwick, 'Votive Offerings to the Emperor?', *ZPE* 80 (1990), 121–30, and A. Chaniotis, 'Der Kaiserkult im Osten des Römischen Reiches im Kontext der zeitgenössischen Ritualpraxis', in H. Cancik and K. Hitzl (eds.), *Die Praxis der Herrscherverehrung in Rom und seinen Provinzen: Akten der Tagung in Blaubeuren vom 4. bis 6. April 2002* (Tübingen, 2003), 3–28.

[60] General survey of the evidence: F. R. Trombley, *Hellenic religion and Christianization, c.370–529* (Leiden, 1993–4). Examples: A. Chaniotis,

the fourth century several cases of late pagans who emphasize in their inscriptions that they have observed the pagan rituals. Not so many people bothered to write epigrams commemorating the fact that they had offered sacrifices before the fourth century AD. In the period of advancing Christianization many did—for example Plutarch, *praeses insularum* during the reign of Julian, who mentions in an epigram on Samos the fact that he had sacrificed in the Idaean Cave,[61] or Vera in Patmos (fourth century), selected by Artemis to be her priestess; as a *hydrophoros* she came to Patmos from Lebedos in order to celebrate a festival which included the sacrifice of a pregnant she-goat.[62] Finally, ritual transfer may imply a radical change in the social context of its performance. It has been observed, for instance that initiatory rituals in early times performed by all the members of a community, survived as rituals of a privileged group (e.g. in Athens the ritual of the *arkteia*).[63]

10. CONTEXTUALIZING MEDITERRANEAN RITUALS

The plethora of 'Mediterranean' studies makes clear how urgent the need to conceptualize the Mediterranean is. This can only work if it goes along with the continual effort to contextualize 'Mediterranean' phenomena. I hope that the case studies presented here have shown the necessity to contextualize rituals and ritual behaviour in the ancient Mediterranean and their survivals in later periods. The title of the book with which the *heros ktistes* of our common subject, Fernand Braudel, inaugurated Mediterranean studies, reminds us that the study of the Mediterranean is the study of historical contexts.

'Zwischen Konfrontation und Interaktion: Christen, Juden und Heiden im spätantiken Aphrodisias', in C. Ackermann and K. E. Müller (eds.), *Patchwork: Dimensionen multikultureller Gesellschaften* (Bielefeld, 2002), 101–2.

[61] *SEG* 1. 405. For the identity of Plutarch see A. Chaniotis, 'Plutarchos, praeses Insularum', *ZPE* 68 (1987), 227–31.

[62] R. Merkelbach and J. Stauber, *Steinepigramme aus dem griechischen Osten* (Stuttgart and Leipzig, 1998), i. 169–70.

[63] On the *arkteia* see recently N. Demand, *Birth, Death, and Motherhood in Classical Greece* (Baltimore, 1994), 107–14, and B. Gentili and F. Perusino (eds.), *Le orse di Brauron: Un rituale di iniziazione femminile nel santuario di Artemide* (Pisa, 2002).

7

The East–West Orientation of Mediterranean Studies and the Meaning of North and South in Antiquity

G. W. Bowersock

Historians of both classical and late antiquity have a natural tendency to view the world they study as fundamentally divided into East and West. The reasons are obvious. Greeks were in the east, Romans in the west. The Roman Empire brought the parts together for some centuries before the successors of Constantine divided it definitively once again. Christianity perpetuated the split between East and West, and papal authority in the West confronts the eastern patriarchs down to this day. This division has taken the Mediterranean Sea as its nodal point, largely for reasons of communication and commerce. If the Greeks reached Marseilles or the Phoenicians Carthage, they got there by sea. The centrality of the Mediterranean for the very different cultures and economies that surrounded it is a major premise of the important first volume of Horden and Purcell's *The Corrupting Sea*.[1] In scholarly literature the West tends to include the northerly regions, such as Gaul, Germany, and Britain, as well as the western Balkans. The eastern Balkan countries, such as Bulgaria and Romania, tend to be incorporated into the eastern Mediterranean orbit, along with Turkey and the Near East. Even North Africa is divided into East and West with Juba's Mauretania counting as a western kingdom despite its Hellenic character, whereas Libya is joined with Egypt as part of the East. This is a distinction enshrined today in the Arabic terms Maghreb and Mashriq.

---

[1] N. Purcell and P. Horden, *The Corrupting Sea* (Oxford, 2000).

Whether this habit of orienting study of the ancient Mediterranean into East and West presupposes a meaningful interpretation of Mediterranean history is questionable. Convenience,
dictated by the use of the Greek and Latin languages and later
by ecclesiastical hierarchy, has probably played a large part in
the persistence of this habit. But it is not inexorably rooted in
the geography and history of the region. Horden and Purcell,
commenting on Bismarck's notorious denial of the concept of
Europe, suggest that North and South might properly tell us
more about the Mediterranean, particularly the romantic obsession of Europeans with lands of the South (*Kennst du das
Land, wo die Zitronen blühn?*, as Goethe said). This obsession
had its own simplistic convenience, whereby southerners,
whether Italian, Greek, or Arab, were all seen to possess the
same engaging characteristics—openness, generosity, hospitality, and, as we ought not to forget, for many Europeans a
relaxed attitude to sexual interests. It looks almost as if the
orientation of east and west persisted among historians and
classical scholars, whereas north and south provided the orientation for travellers and artists of all kinds (including writers).
A scholar, such as Winckelmann, who was also a traveller,
partook of both orientations at the same time.

Edward Gibbon, as historian, traveller, and literary artist of
genius, was another writer who was sensitive to both orientations. So it is scarcely surprising that the problem caught his
attention from the beginning of his work on the Roman Empire.
In the first chapter, commenting on the recruitment of legion-
aries, Gibbon observed with his usual irony that the Romans
had a preference for northerners since they were tougher and
more reliable: 'In all levies, a just preference was given to the
climates of the North over those of the South.' As Horden and
Purcell were alert to notice, Gibbon himself added a handwrit-
ten note on this point in his personal copy of the *Decline and
Fall*, now in the British Museum. This note is generally assumed to have been part of preparation for a seventh volume of
his great work. It is worth quoting in full: 'The distinction of
North and South is real and intelligible; and our pursuit is
terminated on either side by the poles of the Earth. But the
difference of East and West is arbitrary, and shifts round the

globe.'[2] Gibbon's point, which is a good one, depends crucially upon the termination of the two directions in the North and South Poles. The ancients lacked any knowledge of these Poles, and this, I suggest, is why for them the world they inhabited was more naturally arranged from East to West.

There can be little doubt, as already remarked, that the scholarly disposition to employ an east–west orientation derives from antiquity. It inevitably presupposes the Mediterranean, which runs right through the geographical space, although the sea is not always mentioned when the terminal points are invoked. Juvenal, in the famous opening lines of his tenth satire, tells his reader that vanity is to be found everywhere in the wide world: *Omnibus in terris, quae sunt a Gadibus usque / Auroram et Gangen, pauci dinoscere possunt / vera bona . . .*[3] The orientation is memorably and unmistakably east–west (or rather in this instance west–east), from Cadiz to the Ganges. There was nothing at all except the Atlantic Ocean beyond Cadiz, and beyond the Ganges there was nothing that the Romans knew about (or, it may be argued, cared about). In rendering these lines into English verse, Samuel Johnson brilliantly adjusted them for eighteenth-century readers: 'Let Observation, with extensive View, / Survey Mankind from China to Peru.'

Juvenal's orientation is repeated in many ancient texts. It occurs as early as Pindar, who cites Cadiz in a Nemean ode as the place beyond which a traveller cannot go. It is fundamental to Aristotle's account of the inhabited zone of the earth in the second book of his *Meteorologica*, where the pillars of Hercules and India are named.[4] Among Roman writers Seneca and the elder Pliny both anticipated Juvenal's memorable formulation. Solinus, borrowing directly from Pliny, called Cadiz simply *extremus noti orbis terminus.*[5] But Seneca, writing in the preface

---

[2] Patricia B. Craddock (ed.), *The English Essays of Edward Gibbon* (Oxford, 1972), 339 ('Materials for a Seventh Volume') = E. Gibbon, *The Decline and Fall of the Roman Empire*, ed. D. Womersley (London, 1994), app. 2, iii. 1095. Cf. G. Traina, 'Hellenism in the East: Some Historiographical Remarks,' *Electrum* 6 (2002), 15–24, especially 22: 'the opposition East /West is mostly a modern projection.'

[3] Juv. *Sat.* 10. 1–3

[4] Cf. Pind. *Nem.* 4. 69, Aristot. *Meteor.* 2. 362b.   [5] Sol. 23. 12.

to his *Natural Questions*, explictly connected this physical space with the temporal space of a journey by sea: *Quantum enim est, quod ab ultimis litoribus Hispaniae usque ad Indos iacet? Paucissimorum dierum spatium, si navem suus ferat ventus, implebit.*[6] The Budé and Loeb editors both interpret these words as a reference to travel westwards across the Atlantic to India, in the manner of Columbus. But Strabo, like Aristotle, had firmly ruled out such a journey (though admitting it was theoretically possible) on the grounds of the vastness of the Atlantic. Besides, the context of this passage is Seneca's discussion of the constricted world of the ancients, and the expression 'space of very few days' seems to me to make far better sense as a reference to travel from west to east than as rhetorical overstatement. To be sure, this would make Seneca sound as if he were writing after the construction of the Suez Canal, but we may perhaps suppose that Seneca allowed for a little overland travel, such as between Gaza and Elath. In any case, whatever the correct interpretation, the latitudinal *termini* that Seneca names remain the traditional ones.

In general the east–west orientation of the *oikoumenê* seems clearly determined by the possibility of travel across the wide expanse of sea. When the creator of the mosaic map at Madaba chose a vantage point from which to view the cities and topography of Palestine, Trans-Jordan, and Egypt, he positioned himself looking due east from the Mediterranean waters off the Palestinian coast. Similarly the map preserved on the Peutinger Table gives the Mediterranean the central place as its east–west axis. It seems to have been rare for an ancient author to describe the civilized world by longitude, in a straight north–south direction. Aristotle did it in the *Meteorologica* to make his point that the distance between Ethiopia and Lake Maeotis (the Sea of Azov) was less than the distance between the west coast of Spain and India by a ratio of three to five. North–south communications were clearly not determined by sea travel in the same way as east–west communications.

But Plutarch, in the opening of his essay on the failure of the oracles, proposed an interesting and subtle variant of the east–west orientation by combining it with north–south, and

---

[6] Sen. *NQ* 1 praef. 13.

thereby eliminating the centrality of the Mediterranean from the latitudinal axis. After pointedly discarding the traditional view of Delphi as the mid-centre (*omphalos*) of the earth, a point in space that he claimed only the gods can know, he nevertheless went on to introduce two men as coming together at the shrine 'from the opposite ends of the *oikoumenê*.' He thereby implicitly affirmed the centrality of his beloved Delphi. It appears that one of the men had come from Britain and the other from beyond the Red Sea (presumably this is the Arabo-Persian Gulf). Here we have new set of generalized *termini* that extend from the far north-west to the far south-east. In this text Plutarch has artfully transformed the *perata* for the *oikoumenê*. Cadiz has become Britain, and the Ganges has turned into the Indian Ocean. On that diagonal line Delphi can reasonably be put in the middle, while the Mediterranean can be ignored. But, for all that, the arrangement of space is still fundamentally what it was in Pliny, Seneca, and Juvenal.

For the ancients the northern and southern extremities normally had no fixed and familiar boundaries that were comparable to the west coast of Spain or the Ganges, or even Britain and the Arabo-Persian Gulf. The far north and far south were regions of legend and wonder, the homeland of savages. *Ultima Thule* and the travels of Pytheas of Marseilles did not indicate the limit of the *oikoumenê* but rather what lay beyond it. These regions were most frequently defined by the curious peoples who were thought to inhabit them. In antiquity the situation that Gibbon concisely described was exactly reversed. It was not the distinction between North and South that was real and intelligible, but the distinction between East and West. For the Greeks and the Romans Cadiz and the Ganges were the equivalent of Gibbon's two earthly Poles. The North and South Poles were celestial poles in antiquity, as the allusion to the Bear in their terms 'arctic' and 'antarctic' implied, and were used to explain climatic change. Those who believed, like Aristotle and Eratosthenes, that one could reach the east by sailing west or

---

[7] Plut. *De def. orac.* 2, 410a : ἀπὸ τῶν ἐναντίων τῆς οἰκουμένης περάτων ἔτυχον ἄνδρες ἱεροὶ δύο συνδραμόντες εἰς Δελφούς, Δημήτριος μὲν ὁ γραμματικὸς ἐκ Βρεττανίας... Κλεόμβροτος δ' ὁ Λακεδαιμόνιος... πόρρω δὲ τῆς Ἐρυθρᾶς Θαλάττης ἀναπεπλευκώς...

even postulated that there was more than one habitable zone on the earthly globe were nonetheless locked into a latitudinal perspective that was effectively dominated by the Mediterranean, although explained by the excessive cold to the north and heat to the south.

But the savages who inhabited the unbounded extremes of north and south could also be invoked as shorthand for the ancient *oikoumenê* that lay between them. In an important paper published in the *Journal of Jewish Studies* in 1998 David Goldenberg identified a *topos* in rabbinic texts that summarized what Juvenal had called *omnes terrae* by the citation of peoples in the extreme north and extreme south.[8] In connection with the problem of the appearance of the messiah only after the Jews have been subjugated to the rule of 'seventy nations' (comprising the world), God replies, 'If one of you is exiled to Barbaria and one to Sarmatia, it is as if you had all been exiled . . . If one *kuthi* and one *kushi* subjugate you, it is as if all the seventy nations had done so.' The *kuthi* are acknowledged to be an Aramaic rendering of Scythoi, and the *kushi* are the Ethiopians, who live in a territory often identified vaguely as Barbaria. Hence there is a clear geographic division, or what Goldenberg calls a merism, between the Sarmatians or Scythians in the north and the Barbarians or Ethiopians in the south. Between the two regions lies the whole inhabited world (the 'seventy nations'). Goldenberg has conveniently assembled a list of the rabbinic references to the ends of the earth in these terms, and it is compelling testimony to the prevalence of this formulation.

Goldenberg has traced the *topos* directly and convincingly to the Graeco-Roman world where Sarmatians or Scythians are repeatedly contrasted with Barbarians or Ethiopians as representatives of the outermost limits of the world. Goldenberg's discovery allowed him to offer for the first time in modern exegesis a persuasive interpretation of the vexed passage in Paul's *Letter to the Colossians*: 'where there is not Greek and Jew, circumcised and uncircumcised, barbarian, Scythian,

---

[8] David Goldenberg, 'Scythian-Barbarian: The Permutations of a Classical Topos in Jewish and Christian Texts of Late Antiquity,' *Journal of Jewish Studies* 49 (1998), 87–102. Cf. סרמטים/ברבריים and כותי/כושי.

slave, free: but Christ is all and in all'.[9] The mention of barbarian and Scythian has always seemed to sit oddly among obvious pairings of opposites, such as circumcised and uncircumcised, or slave and free. But what we can now assert confidently is that barbarian and Scythian is another clear set of opposites, signifying peoples from the remote south and the remote north. Hence the first letter of barbarian should be capitalized to indicate the people of Barbaria.

Unlike the east–west orientation of the world, this north–south one has fuzzy boundaries that accommodate strange and unfamiliar tribes. In particular the southern regions, Ethiopia and beyond, have long been recognized as uncommonly capacious in Greek and Roman traditions, sometimes including Brahmans of India, gymnosophists, and apparently, in a remarkable passage in Lucan, the Chinese. In imagining a possible Roman conquest of the whole world at the opening of his epic on the Civil War, the poet invokes east and west by sunrise and sunset (*unde venit Titan, et nox ubi sidera condit*), and then south and north by hot and frozen regions, the latter explicitly connected with Scythians (*quaque dies medius flagrantibus aestuat auris, / et qua bruma rigens et nescia vere remitti / astringit Scythicum glaciali frigore pontum*). In a subsequent line the contrast between south and north is evidently repeated by reference to the Chinese and the Araxes (*Sub iuga iam Seres, iam barbarus isset Araxes*).[10]

As quintessential outsiders, the Chinese were simply relegated to the outside in unscientific texts (the elder Pliny knew better), and Ethiopia was the obvious outside territory. In view of seafaring in the Indian Ocean, with its links to the Horn of Africa, it is not surprising that Brahmans or Chinese were often wrapped into the southern extremity of the world rather than the northern one. Pausanias is a witness to the tradition of the Chinese as Ethiopians, and Heliodorus even has them as tributaries of the king in Meroe. But Pausanias also reports another tradition that put the Chinese in the opposite region

---

[9] NT, Col. 3. 11 ...ὅπου οὐκ ἔνι Ἕλλην καὶ Ἰουδαῖος, περιτομὴ καὶ ἀκροβυστία, βάρβαρος, Σκύθης, δοῦλος, ἐλεύθερος, ἀλλὰ πάντα καὶ ἐν πᾶσιν Χριστός.

[10] Luc. *Phars.* 1. 15–19. Cf. *Scythicus Oceanus*, north of the Caspian, in Pliny, *NH* 6. 33, 36, 37, 53.

on the north–south axis, as Scythians consorting with the
Indians.[11] What is consistently striking about the north–south
axis is that there is never any suggestion that the inhabitants
of the ancient world would travel along it from one extremity
to the other. This makes the distinction altogether different
from the east–west axis, where transverse travel was a real
possibility.

The special feature of the north–south *topos* is that the
peoples it names lie beyond, in other words above or below,
the civilized world. Orientation by the concept of above or
below seems to arise from the habit of geographers and travellers, who regularly used such expressions as *hyper, anô, ultra,
superior* and their opposites, in locating territories. This habit
was usually reserved to the north–south axis. It was already
rooted in the ancient geography of Egypt through the designations of Upper and Lower Egypt for the southern (upriver) and
northern (downriver) territories respectively. It can readily be
seen in the Roman administrative system with its upper and
lower provinces, reflecting upriver and downriver situations on
the Rhine and Danube. Although in some cases the use of these
terms coincides with differences in physical elevation there are
many instances where it does not. But overall there is a remarkably consistent pattern that connects the orientation of above or
below, or upper and lower, on an approximately north–south
axis with reference to the sea. The upper Nile and hence Upper
Egypt are more remote from the Mediterranean coast than the
lower Nile and Lower Egypt. Upriver on the Rhine is at a
greater distance from the North Sea than downriver, and in
a south-east direction. Upriver on the Danube is at a greater
distance from the Black Sea, but this time in a north-west
direction. Hence the designations of Upper and Lower Germany, Upper and Lower Pannonia, Upper and Lower
Moesia.

It is inescapable, therefore, that both the relative terms
'above/up' and 'below/down' can designate either 'north' or
'south', depending on the maritime point of reference. We must

---

[11] Paus. 6. 26. 4, 9: Οὗτοι μὲν δὴ τοῦ Αἰθιόπων γένους αὐτοί τέ εἰσιν οἱ Σῆρες . . .
οἱ δὲ αὐτοὺς οὐκ Αἰθίοπας, Σκύθας δὲ ἀναμεμιγμένους Ἰνδοῖς φασὶν εἶναι. Cf.
Heliod. *Aeth.* 10. 25.

not be surprised to find counterintuitive designations. At first blush, it seems odd that northern Egypt should be called Lower, or that Upper Germany should be south of Lower Germany. The division of Britain in the third century produced an even more counterintuitive division. Upper Britain lay in the south, with London at its centre, whereas Lower Britain encompassed Scotland. In this case no great river imposed such an orientation, nor is there the slightest possibility that geographical elevation dictated the names. The determining feature appears to have been the outlying sea, the *Mare Germanicum* or North Sea. The case of the late antique provinces of Upper and Lower Libya is equally instructive since again there is no river into the interior to provide any guidance. In addition both provinces had Mediterranean coastlines. Upper Libya, the territory of the old Pentapolis of Cyrenaica, lay to the west and to the north of Lower Libya. It was thus more remote from the Nile delta, which must therefore have been considered the maritime point of reference.

In terms of the perspective of north–south orientation the Mediterranean is, accordingly, merely one of many seas that can determine geographical nomenclature. The Scythian Ocean, placed north of the Caspian by the elder Pliny, may be an extrapolation from travellers' reports of the Aral Sea. But the Indian Ocean and the Black Sea (itself an offshoot of the Mediterranean) were well known. The ancients had experience of the gulfs of the Indian Ocean—Suez, Aqaba, Arabo-Persian, and they were certainly not inclined to see the Black Sea as an extension of the Mediterranean, at least to judge by the terminology they used. The euphemistic Euxine as well as the bland Pontus sharply distinguished the Black Sea from the inner sea (or *nostrum mare* of the Romans), and the distinction had a very long history subsequently through the colour names used by the Arabs and Turks. For the former the Black Sea was precisely black (*al-baḥr al-aswad*) whereas the Mediterranean was the White Sea (*al-baḥr al-abyaḍ*). The Turks have maintained the same nomenclature with Kara Deniz for the Black Sea and Ak Deniz for the Mediterranean.

The author of the *Periplus of the Red Sea* shows clearly the force of *hyper* in orientation when, for example, he uses the verb *hyperkeitai* to locate the city of Savê in relation to Muza at the south-western corner of the Arabian peninsula.[12] The verb indicates remoteness of three days from the sea in a north-eastern direction. This may seem perfectly obvious in an instance that starts from the coast, but Strabo shows repeatedly that *hyper* can also be used to indicate inland orientations and, specifically, in a southwards direction. When he moves to his discussion of the Nabataean kingdom after his survey of Syria he states that the Nabataeans and Sabaeans were *hyper* the Syrians.[13] If the preposition were construed simply to mean 'beyond' there would be no way of telling whether the Nabataeans lived to the north, east, west, or south. Strabo is too careful a geographer. He is clearly telling us that they were to the south of the Syrians on a north–south axis (which is the only axis appropriate for this preposition in such contexts). They are 'above' in precisely the same way as the Nitriote nome in Egypt is above Momemphis.[14] It lies to the south. Similarly going south from Heliopolis the traveller embarks upon the Nile 'above the Delta', as Strabo puts it.[15] The journey is upriver (*anapleôn*), southwards from the *katô chôra* to the *anô chôra*. In an unusual passage concerning the interior of Ethiopia Strabo's text explicitly glosses his use of *hyper* as meaning 'to the south'.[16] Whether this is his gloss or an interpolator's is open to debate. In any case the Nile flows down all the way into the Mediterranean, which controls the north–south terminology in Ethiopia as well as Egypt. Similarly Plutarch's Delphic visitor from the east is said to have 'sailed up' beyond the Red Sea This can only imply southwards into the Indian Ocean. It is far less obvious what determines the inland orientation for Syria and Trans-Jordan. Strabo's description of the placement of the Nabataeans and Sabaeans is another of those counterintuitive arrangements.

---

[12] *Peripl. Maris Erythr.* 22: ὑπέρκειται δὲ αὐτῆς ἀπὸ τριῶν ἡμερῶν πόλις Σαυή...

[13] Strabo p. 779C (16. 4. 21): Πρῶτοι δ' ὑπὲρ τῆς Συρίας Ναβαταῖοι καὶ Σαβαῖοι τὴν εὐδαίμονα Ἀραβίαν νέμονται.

[14] Strabo p. 803C (16. 4. 23): Ὑπὲρ δὲ Μωμέμφεώς εἰσι δύο νιτρίαι πλεῖστον νίτρον ἔχουσαι καὶ νομὸς Νιτριώτης.

[15] Strabo p. 806C (16. 4. 30): Ἐντεῦθεν δὴ ὁ Νεῖλός ἐστιν ὁ ὑπὲρ τοῦ Δέλτα· τούτου δὴ τὰ μὲν δεξιὰ καλοῦσι Λιβύην ἀναπλέοντι...

[16] Strabo p. 771 (16. 4. 10): Ἔτι δ' ὑπὲρ τούτων ὡς πρὸς μεσημβρίαν οἱ κυναμολγοί...

Yet a striking parallel occurs in the elder Pliny's description of the same region. He says that Hierapolis Bambyce, Beroea-Aleppo, and Chalcis are *infra Palmyrae solitudines*. These well-known places are associated with a region named for the site of Teleda. Both the three cities and the region are north of Palmyra, and so the word 'below' here can only imply north. Consistently Pliny goes on to say that *ultra Palmyram* lay part of the territory of Emesa as well as Elath, which he reasonably observes is about half as far distant from Petra as Damascus is.[17] All these toponymns leave no doubt whatever that the word 'above' here indicates south, just as it did in Strabo's location of the Nabataeans 'above' the Syrians. I suggest that this terminology is as much controlled in these instances by the location of a sea as it is in the case of Egypt or southern Arabia. In this case the sea cannot be either the Gulf of Aqaba or the Arabo-Persian Gulf, either of which would necessarily reverse the terminology as it stands in Strabo and Pliny. Likewise, appeal to the Euphrates or Tigris would have the same result, since both rivers debouch into the Arabo-Persian Gulf.

The Mediterranean is naturally irrelevant for a north–south orientation. As far as I can tell, the maritime point of reference can only be the Black Sea. This inference is confirmed if we look, for example, at Strabo's terminology for Pontic Cappadocia. Here *hyper* pretty clearly designates 'south' once again although now the sense is more apparent because of the immediate proximity of the Black Sea coast at the northern edge of the region. Phanaroea is situated above (south of) Sidene and Themiscyra, for example,[18] and Pontic Comana lies above (south of) Phanaroea.[19] The elder Pliny provides another point of comparison in his description of Latium in Italy as *infra* the Sabines.[20] This time his *infra*, has the opposite sense

---

[17] Pliny, *NH* 5. 89: Infra Palmyrae solitudines Telendena regio est dictaeque iam Hierapolis ac Beroea et Chalcis. Ultra Palmyram quoque ex solitudinibus his aliquid obtinet Hemesa, item Elatium, dimidio proprior Petrae quam Damascus.

[18] Strabo p. 556C (12. 3. 30): Τούτων [i.e. Sidene and Themiscyra] δ' ἡ Φανάροια ὑπέρκειται μέρος ἔχουσα τοῦ Πόντου τὸ κράτιστον.

[19] Strabo p. 557C (12. 3. 32): Ὑπὲρ δὲ Φαναροίας ἐστὶ τὰ Κόμανα τὰ ἐν τῷ Πόντῳ . . .

[20] Plin. *NH* 3. 109: Infra Sabinos Latium est.

of his use of the word with reference to Palmyra. It means 'south' because Latium lay nearer to the sea.

Undoubtedly the north–south axis in antiquity has not yet yielded all its secrets. But if the foregoing argument is valid, there are serious implications for the much-discussed passage in the elder Pliny about the Essene community. Debate over the identification of the inhabitants of Qumran with the Essenes continues, and a central piece in the debate is Pliny's statement that En Gedi lay 'below' the Essenes: *infra hos Engadda*.[21] What I have said here will certainly not close the debate, but it is worth remarking that if Pliny is following the usage that emerges from other parts of his work as well as from Strabo's *Geography*, he ought perhaps to be understood as saying that En Gedi lay to the north of the Essenes. Since that site is in fact located south of Qumran, this interpretation would provide support for those who deny the identification of the Essene community with it.

The ancient inhabited world, situated as it was between extreme cold and extreme heat, looked very different when viewed from east to west and from north to south. It seems evident that it was the Mediterranean that determined the east–west orientation, but not the north–south one. For that axis the Mediterranean was but one of the bodies of water that impinged upon the ancient peoples, and even when it was as close to them as it was in Palestine and Trans-Jordan the north–south axis paid no attention to it. Of course all these peoples had perfectly serviceable words for the four directions of the compass and could use them when they wished. But the instinct to describe space in terms of the relation of one place to another was very strong. Those two great axes of orientation, which we know today as latitude and longitude, provided them with the most comprehensible way to demarcate the civilized *oikoumenê* that they knew.

---

[21] Plin. *NH* 5. 73: Infra hos [i.e. the Essenes] Engada oppidum fuit.

8

Travel Sickness: Medicine and Mobility in the Mediterranean from Antiquity to the Renaissance

Peregrine Horden

1. INTRODUCTION

He was evidently old when he passed away, for his unsurpassed accuracy in material detail indicates an advanced age. That he travelled to many parts of the world can be inferred from his wide knowledge of places. We must also suppose a great abundance of wealth to have been at his disposal, for long journeys call for much expenditure, especially in those times when it was not the case that all seas could be safely sailed or that people could easily visit each other.

Thus the late antique *Life* of Homer by one Proclus (possibly not the famous Platonist).[1] He implicitly contrasts the limited mobility of the Homeric age with the greater ease of maritime communications characteristic of Roman imperial times. He offers us a perception of increasing Mediterranean mobility.

This paper too is about perceptions. In *The Corrupting Sea* Nicholas Purcell and I offered a partial definition of the integrity and distinctiveness of the Mediterranean in terms of the region's fluid communications and the concomitant mobility of its peoples.[2] My aim now is not to defend our definition; it is to revisit it from an unusual angle—that of medicine. What were the connections between personal mobility and health in the ancient and medieval Mediterranean? How is mobility represented in the medical texts?

---

[1] Ch. 8, trans. M. L. West, who kindly directed me to this passage in his Loeb edition of the *Homeric Hymns, Homeric Apocrypha, Lives of Homer* (Cambridge, Mass. and London, 2003).

[2] *CS*, especially chs. II, V, IX.

First, some very wide context within which to locate my particular subject. Mobility and therapy interconnect in a variety of ways in pre-modern times. Doctors itinerate, and not just quacks but Galen and his like.[3] Living holy men and saints perform healing wonders *en route*—and hagiography provides some of our most detailed evidence of medieval Mediterranean mobility and its infrastructure.[4] Dead saints also heal 'on the hoof'—sometimes literally, as their relics are ceremoniously 'translated'.[5] Nor should we forget trade or transfers involving drugs,[6] medical texts, and healing artefacts such as magic bowls.[7] Patients, finally, move in search of therapy—like Aelius Aristides—to healer, to shrine.[8] They also travel to hospitals. They flee epidemics. And their travels bring on new pathologies: travel sickness.[9]

All that is obvious enough. Less well known are the two aspects of the topic on which I want to focus here. 1. Regimen *for* travel: medical advice on how to preserve health while mobile or how to restore it through self-help while away from one's usual healer. 2. Travel *as* regimen, or as therapy. These both counterbalance the familiar theme of the tribulations of Mediterranean movement—for example, the penitential

[3] Hence the need to pin some of them down in cities by offering retainers: V. Nutton, 'Continuity or Rediscovery? The City Physician in Classical Antiquity and Mediaeval Italy', in A.W. Russell (ed.), *The Town and State Physician in Europe from the Middle Ages to the Enlightenment* (Wolfenbüttel, 1981), 9–46.

[4] E. Malamut, *Sur la route des saints byzantins* (Paris, 1993).

[5] M. Heinzelmann, *Translationsberichte und andere Quellen des Reliquienkultes* (Turnhout, 1979); P. Geary, *Furta Sacra* second edn. (Princeton, 1990).

[6] V. Nutton, 'The Drug Trade in Antiquity', *Journal of the Royal Society of Medicine* 78 (1985), 138–46.

[7] F. Maddison and E. Savage-Smith, *Science, Tools and Magic*, i. *Body and Spirit, Mapping the Universe*, The Nasser D. Khalili Collection of Islamic Art 12 (London, 1997), 72–100.

[8] C. A. Behr, *Aelius Aristides and the Sacred Tales* (Amsterdam, 1968); R. Schlesier, 'Menschen und Götter unterwegs: Ritual und Reise in der griechischen Antike', in T. Hölscher (ed.), *Gegenwelten zu den Kulturen Griechenlands und Roms in der Antike* (Munich and Leipzig, 2000), 129–57. For medieval pilgrims see R. C. Finucane, *Miracles and Pilgrims: Popular Beliefs in Medieval England* (London, 1977), ch. 9.

[9] R. Wrigley and G. Revill (eds.), *Pathologies of Travel* (Amsterdam and Atlanta, 2000).

suffering required of the pilgrim or the shipwreck risked by the voyager.[10] They offer a more positive view of personal mobility. They also bring together two poor relations. Migration is the most neglected aspect of pre-modern demography.[11] Regimen—preventive medicine, diet—is the most neglected aspect of pre-modern medicine, mainly, I conjecture, because medical historians are still subconsciously in thrall to the therapeutic, interventionist, bias of modern biomedicine.[12]

2. MOBILITY AND FIXITY

Before I consider those two themes separately, let me next try to generalize about the perceptions of Mediterranean movement that the medical texts offer. I must warn in advance that no big demographic conclusions will emerge. It is not inevitable that mobility should engender a commensurate literature of advice. That is, the medical literature cannot, through any changes in emphasis or quantity, give us a reliable index of changing Mediterranean mobility. Still less is this evidence sufficiently detailed or geographically widespread to permit Mediterranean and non-Mediterranean comparisons—comparisons that might suggest where mobility was greater. What the medical material can do, however, is show how at least some contemporary authors perceived, classified, and evaluated mobility.

In the late fifth to early fourth century BC the author of the Hippocratic *Regimen* (*Peri diaites*) claims (ch. 68) to be writing for the majority of men: those who use ordinary, accessible, food and drink, who exert themselves as much as is essential, who undertake land journeys and sea voyages to collect their

---

[10] D. J. Birch, *Pilgrimage to Rome in the Middle Ages* (Woodbridge, Suffolk, 1998), 3–4, on the 'white martyrdom' of pilgrimage, contrasted, but not too strongly, with the 'red martyrdom' of death. See further C. Stancliffe, 'Red, White and Blue Martyrdom', in D. Whitelock, R. McKitterick, and D. Dumville (eds.), *Ireland in Early Medieval Europe* (Cambridge, 1982), 21–46. For the overrated dangers of Mediterranean sea voyages see *CS*, chs. V.3, X.4, with bibliography.

[11] *CS*, Bibliographical Essay to ch. IX.6.

[12] P. Horden, 'Religion as Medicine: Music in Medieval Hospitals', in P. Biller and J. Ziegler (eds.), *Religion and Medicine in the Middle Ages* (Woodbridge, Suffolk, and Rochester, NY, 2001), 135–53.

livelihood.[13] The claim is perhaps disingenuous. But the image of the small producer who of necessity sometimes has to travel long distances to gather sustenance, and who benefits from the maritime 'connectivity' of the Mediterranean, seems like a condensation of *The Corrupting Sea*.[14] It is exactly the form and degree of mobility that Purcell and I postulated. It contradicts the retrospective account of Mediterranean communications implied by that extract from the *Life of Homer* with which I began. In the early first century AD, Celsus (*De medicina* 1.1) offered a more aristocratic version. The healthy man, his own master, needs no medical attendants to stay healthy. Variety spices his life. He is now in the country, now in the town, and more often 'in agro'; he should sail, hunt, rest sometimes, but more frequently take exercise. He avoids common foods, goes to the baths but avoids athletics, and eats as much as he wants twice a day. In the Hippocratic-Galenic tradition, on which Celsus to some extent draws, the balance between mobility (usually meaning exercise) and rest is central. It is one of the 'non-natural' determinants of health hinted at in the Hippocratic corpus, mentioned unsystematically by Galen, and canonized by medieval Islamic medical writers.[15] Mobility is also figuratively present, in a variety of ways. For example, nautical metaphors abound in Plutarch's short treatise offering 'instructions for health' (*Hygieina paraggelmata*). In the tenth-century Muslim physician Razi, the illness itself is imaged as a journey. 'The patient's strength is like a traveller's provisions. Disease

---

[13] *Oeuvres complètes d'Hippocrate*, ed. and trans. E. Littré, 10 vols. (Paris, 1839–61), vi. 594. For guidance as to other editions see P. Potter, *Short Handbook of Hippocratic Medicine* (Quebec, 1988). Galen will be cited by reference to the standard (but incomplete) edition of C. G. Kühn (hereafter K), *Claudii Galeni: Opera Omnia*, 22 vols. (Leipzig, 1821–33), and to better editions where they exist.

[14] *CS*, chs. III, VI.

[15] L. García-Ballester, 'On the Origin of the "Six Non-Natural Things" in Galen', in G. Harig and J. Harig-Kollesch (eds.), *Galen und das Hellenistische Erbe*, Sudhoffs Archiv Beiheft 32 (Wiesbaden, 1993), 105–15; G. Olson, *Literature as Recreation in the Later Middle Ages* (Ithaca, NY and London, 1982), 40–4, esp. 41 n. 3 for earlier bibliography; H. Mikkeli, *Hygiene in the Early Modern Medical Tradition* (Helsinki, 1999), 9–10 (esp. 10 n. 4 for bibliography), 14–23.

is the highway, and the culmination of the disease his destination'.[16]

Beyond these generalities two contradictory tendencies are evident in the medical literature. On one hand, everyone is mobile. That is, the possibility of considerable movement is mentioned at the outset and presupposed in all the medical advice that follows. In the fourth century AD, the imperial physician Oribasius prefaced the advice on food that begins his massive *Medical Collections* (1.1) with the reminder that, 'on arrival in a foreign country one is obliged to eat something unusual', and one should test the food in advance (as well, other ancient authors recommended, as eating lots of garlic).[17] Movement is also presupposed in the institutional and social obverse of this regimen for the well to do. The late antique hospital, which was developing in Byzantium around the time Oribasius was writing, is a *xenodocheion*. It offers rest, nursing, and, sometimes, medicine—to *xenoi*, strangers: to the rootless poor, those who move to survive because they have no personal support networks.[18] At the extreme, the regimen of the mobile and that of the rooted are represented as almost identical. After all, as far as much dietary advice is concerned, where you are makes little difference. As Anthimus wrote in *De obseruatione ciborum* to Theuderic, a sixth-century king of the Franks: 'let us suppose that someone asks how anyone can take this sort of care [over food] when engaged in military manoeuvres or a long journey. I would say that if a fire can be lit...what has been suggested ought to be possible.'[19] The early medieval European compil-

[16] A. Z. Iskandar, *A Catalogue of Arabic Manuscripts on Medicine and Science in the Wellcome Historical Medical Library* (London, 1967), 4.

[17] Trans. M. Grant, *Dieting for an Emperor* (Leiden, 1997), 26–7, and see also 100.

[18] For the hospital see now P. Brown, *Poverty and Leadership in the Later Roman Empire* (Hanover and London, 2002), 33–44; P. Horden, 'The Earliest Hospitals in Byzantium, Western Europe and Islam', *Journal of Interdisciplinary History*, forthcoming. On networks of support, P. Horden, 'Household Care and Informal Networks: Comparisons and Continuities from Antiquity to the Present', in P. Horden and R. Smith (eds.), *The Locus of Care: Families, Communities, Institutions and the Provision of Welfare since Antiquity* (London and New York, 1998), 21–67.

[19] Anthimus, *De obseruatione ciborum, On the Observance of Foods*, ed. and trans. M. Grant (Totnes, 1996), 48–9.

ation of general medicine known as the *Medicina Plinii* was packaged as advice for travellers who would otherwise be at the mercy of ignorant and expensive quacks.[20] There, it is the perceived need of self-help that slants the text towards mobility. But the ninth-century medical handbook of Ibn al-Jazzar entitled, impartially, *Provisions for the Traveller and Nourishment for the Sedentary*, was addressed to physicians.[21] It was for use in regular consultation, even though its title suggested to Manfred Ullmann that its overt appeal was to 'Jedermann'.[22] In the eleventh century it was translated into Greek by one Constantine of Reggio, as the *Ephodia tou apodemountos*, and, in 1124, into Latin by 'the' Constantine—Constantine the African—as the *Viaticum peregrinantis*.[23] Both these translations obscured its titular appeal to the sedentary, however. It passed into the European medical curriculum of Bologna, Montpellier, and elsewhere as part of the *Articella*.[24] That guidance for travellers could subsume all the basics of medical learning thus in a sense became very widely accepted. What could the implication of the title *Viaticum* have been? That we are all in a literal sense travellers, all mobile at one stage or another? Or that, in some higher sense, we are all on the journey, the pilgrimage, of life?

[20] Prologue, *Plinii Secundi Iunioris qui feruntur de medicina libri tres*, ed. A. Önnerfors, *Corpus Medicorum Latinorum* 3 (Berlin, 1964), 4.

[21] *Ibn al-Jazzar on Sexual Diseases and their Treatment: A Critical Edition of 'Zad al-musafir wa-qut al-hadir, Provisions for the Traveller and Nourishment for the Sedentary, Book 6*, ed. and trans. G. Bos (London and New York, 1997), 8; M. G. Dugat, 'Études sur le traité de médecine d'Abou Djàfar Ah'mad', *Journal Asiatique*, 5th ser., 1 (1853), 287–353. Here and in what follows Arabic is represented in 'open transliteration'.

[22] M. Ullmann, 'Neues zu den diätetischen Schriften des Rufus von Ephesos', *Medizinhistorisches Journal* 9 (1974), 23–40, at 38.

[23] M. F. Wack, *Lovesickness in the Middle Ages: The 'Viaticum' and its Commentaries* (Philadelphia, 1990), ch. 2, for bibliography; C. Burnett and D. Jacquart (eds.), *Constantine the African and 'Ali ibn l-'Abbas al Magusi: The 'Pantegni' and Related Works*, Studies in Ancient Medicine 10 (Leiden, 1996).

[24] On the *articella*, see C. O'Boyle, *The Art of Medicine: Medical Teaching at the University of Paris, 1250–1400* (Leiden, 1998). See also J. Arrizabalaga, 'The Death of a Medieval Text: The *Articella* and the Early Press,' in R. French, J. Arrizabalaga, A. Cunningham, and L. García-Ballester (eds.) *Medicine from the Black Death to the French Disease* (Aldershot, 1998), 185–6, for summary and full bibliography.

The latter reading, perhaps implicit in medieval medicine, was to be made explicit in a Renaissance regimen to which I shall return at the end.

Against all this, on the other hand, are ranged what might be called the medical forces of 'fixity': those who image a static world to us.[25] This is the second of the contradictory tendencies to which I referred. Take the two corpora that came to dominate the medical output of antiquity and that thus moulded the medical learning of both Europe and the Middle East until at least 1700 (if not much later in some places). These are the Hippocratic corpus and the massive output of Galen. In the most significant of the earlier Hippocratic texts such as *Airs, waters, places* or *Epidemics I* and *III*, it is the healer who is on the move. Patients—my earlier quotation from the Hippocratic *Regimen* notwithstanding—are envisaged as closely related to their environments, which change with the seasons but are geographically stable.[26] Patients take exercises, *ponoi*, but they do not 'travel'. When the Hippocratic texts describe the questions that the physician should put to the patient (for example at the beginning of the treatise on *Prognosis* or in *Epidemics* 1.3.10) they do not juxtapose 'where have you been?' with 'where does it hurt?'. (For something approaching an enquiry of that sort we have to wait until Roman times (*c*.100 AD and Rufus of Ephesus, who also composed a regimen for travellers.)[27]

Galen is much the same as his Hippocratic exemplars.[28] In *De sanitate tuenda*, books 2–3, he writes at some length about the different ages of life, about exercise (including the long-distance exercise of riding and hunting) and fatigue.[29] But apart from a few stray asides he has virtually nothing else explicitly

[25] N. Purcell, 'Fixity', in R. Schlesier and U. Zellmann (eds.), *Mobility and Travel in the Mediterranean from Antiquity to the Middle Ages* (Münster, 2004), 73–83.

[26] e.g. *Epidemics*, 1.1–5.

[27] *Rufus von Ephesos, Die Fragen des Arztes an den Kranken*, ed. H. Gärtner, *CMG*, Suppl. 4 (Berlin, 1962).

[28] V. Nutton, 'Galen and the Traveller's Fare', in J. Wilkins, D. Harris, and M. Dobson (eds.), *Food in Antiquity* (Exeter, 1995), 359–70, is far more about Galen's dietetics in general than its title suggests.

[29] R. M. Green, *A Translation of Galen's Hygiene* (Springfield, Ill., 1951); 6.1–452K, *CMG* 5.4.2. For analysis, see G. Wöhrle, *Studien zur Theorie der Antiken Gesundheitslehre, Hermes* Einzelschriften 56 (1990), ch. 7.

directed at those on the move. Presumably he did not want his patients to feel they could do without him. Galen's practice is dedicated to (at the least) the wealthy in their villas, whom he counsels to stay put, avoiding urban insalubrities.[30] Some of his clearest recommendations to a sufferer who has to travel come in his letter of 'Advice for an epileptic boy'. Its sheer specificity perhaps indicates how marginal the topic was to him.[31]

A final point under this heading of 'fixity'. Galen's silence on the matter of travel extends to women, and is exemplary of the whole field of medicine for the mobile. Women should exercise, to the extent of going for a walk or riding in a carriage. But women do not travel. At least, they are not, I think, explicitly addressed, or represented, as travellers. Regimens for women and girls were composed by Rufus of Ephesus, yet, like almost all previous dietary advice directed at women, their purpose is to facilitate a reproductive marriage.[32]

3. TRAVEL AS THERAPY

I have arrived now at the first of my two principal themes, travel as therapy. Exercise (for both men and women) is pain, *ponos*. But travel is torture: Old French *travail* apparently descends, via the hypothetical verb *tripaliare*, from the medieval Latin *tripalium*, three-pronged instrument of torture on which the victim is stretched—an instrument attested in sixth-century Gaul.[33] Why should anyone welcome travel? Aelius Aristides underwent deliberate shipwreck at the prompting of a perverse deity.[34] His was an extreme case. Yet we still tend to think of ancient Mediterranean travel as fearful, whatever may be said about the ease of maritime communications in the region. It is

[30] *De curandi ratione per venae sectionem* 17, 11.299–300K.

[31] O. Temkin, *The Falling Sickness: A History of Epilepsy from the Greeks to the Beginnings of Modern Neurology*, 2nd edn. (Baltimore and London, 1971), 72–3, with Temkin's translation in *Bulletin of the Institute of the History of Medicine* 2 (1934), 179–89, from 11.357–8K.

[32] R. Flemming, *Medicine and the Making of Roman Women* (Oxford, 2000), 221–4, 316–17.

[33] W. von Wartburg, *Französisches Etymologisches Wörterbuch*, vol. 13.1 (Basle, 1966), s.v. **tripaliare*.

[34] *Oration* 48 (= *Sacred Tales* 2), 11–13, trans. C. A. Behr, *P. Aelius Aristides: The Complete Works* 2 (Leiden, 1981), 293–4.

clear, nonetheless, that travel for one's health is no invention of the age of 'grand tourism', or spas and sanatoria. Ebenezer Gilchrist's *The Use of Sea Voyages in Medicine* (London, 1756) may have been the first book of its kind in English. It could, however, have drawn on ancient example.

Not that ancient, though; a chronological change can be detected. This seems to be a Hellenistic and Roman rather than a classical Greek theme. (It may even, as Nicholas Purcell has suggested to me in conversation, have something to do with the Hellenistic vogue for pleasure boating.) Take Celsus (*De medicina* 3.22.8). In cases of true consumption, he says, if the patient is strong enough, then a long sea voyage, with a change of air, is called for—ideally the voyage from Italy to Alexandria. If the patient is not strong enough, he recommends *gestatio* (passive exercise while being transported), in a ship not going very far. If a sea voyage is impossible, the patient should be carried in a litter. (Compare Celsus 1.10 for the same 'fallback' in cases of pestilence.) Pliny asserts in the *Natural History* (31.62 ff.) that Egypt is not chosen for its own sake as the destination of therapeutic voyages but simply because of the time it takes to get there. Yet the young and 'consumptive' Seneca went to Egypt precisely to take the air in the Nile valley (*Letter* 78).[35] And Galen admits that many like him returned from Egypt seemingly cured, only to relapse later through self-indulgence.[36] Mountain air was also highly beneficial to consumptives, as Cassiodorus reminds us in the sixth century (*Variae* 11.10).

Sufferers from other diseases might also be helped by a long journey. Caelius Aurelianus, the fifth-century North African physician, recommends travel, preferably by sea, for more ailments than any other ancient authority—ailments including bladder problems, diseases of the colon, obesity, epilepsy, and elephantiasis. For headaches,

make use of natural waters, dry heat, and long sea voyages [*longa per maria navigatio*]. Voyages on rivers, bays, and lakes are considered

---

[35] M. Griffin, *Seneca* (Oxford, 1976), 43.

[36] *De simplicium medicamentorum temperamentis ac facultatibus* 9.1 (12.191K); L. Friedländer, *Roman Life and Manners under the Early Empire*, trans. A. B. Gough, 4 (London, 1913), 321.

unsuitable, since they cause the head to become moist and cold by reason of the exhalation from the earth; but sea voyages imperceptibly and gradually open the pores, give rise to a burning effect by reason of the saltiness of the sea, and, by working a change, repair the bodily condition.[37]

In the Methodist scheme of things, which Caelius represented, the relative constriction or dilation of the pores, rather than humoral balance, was the key to health. A long journey was a form of relaxation, but primarily in a physiological sense.

There are aspects of therapeutic travel that affront modern notions. For Pliny and others, the rolling and pitching of the boat, and the occasional bouts of seasickness that it brought on, were also beneficial for many ailments. Whether the patient was on horseback or in a carriage or on a boat, the rhythms of the journey were as much part of the cure as the air was. So also were the emotions induced. Among the 'non-natural' determinants of health in late antiquity were the 'passions of the soul', in effect positive emotions.[38] That is what, centuries later, permitted learned physicians to recommend 'wine, women, and song' as preventive measures against bubonic plague and syphilis.[39] In the context of the slightly different form of mobility that is the hunt, Galen explains: in hunting 'with dogs and all other kinds', exertion and pleasure combine. 'The motion of the soul involved is so powerful that many have been released from their disease by the pleasure alone.'[40]

I suggested that travel as regimen is noticeable in Hellenistic medicine but not earlier. Perhaps Hellenistic and Roman times together constitute its apogee. For I do not think we find nearly as much of it in the Middle Ages and later, although Burton would write in *The Anatomy of Melancholy* that 'peregrination

[37] *Chronic diseases* 1.44, ed. and trans. I. E. Drabkin, *Caelius Aurelianus On Acute and Chronic Diseases* (Chicago, 1950), 467.

[38] P. Gil-Sotres, 'Modelo teórico y observación clínica: las pasiones del alma en la psicología médica medieval', in *Comprendre et maîtriser la nature au Moyen Âge: Mélanges d'histoire des sciences offerts à Guy Beaujouan* (Geneva, 1994), 181–204.

[39] P. Horden, 'Musical Solutions', in Horden (ed.), *Music as Medicine: The History of Music Therapy since Antiquity* (Aldershot, 2000), 24.

[40] *Exercise with the Small Ball* 1, trans. P. N. Singer, *Galen, Selected Works* (Oxford, 1997), 299 (5.900K = *Scripta Minora*, ed. J. Marquardt, I. Müller, and G. Helmreich, 1. 93–4).

charmes our senses with such unspeakable and sweet variety',
and would of course urge it on melancholics; and Sydenham
once reportedly cured a patient by sending him on a journey to
see a non-existent physician in Aberdeen.[41] 'Dr Horse', as he
became known, is the commonest recommendation. Sailing is
rare, long sea voyages rarer still. In general, medieval doctors'
regimens and *consilia* have little to offer on the theme of 'gesta-
tion' other than a few brief topoi.[42]

Between antiquity and the Middle Ages, the categories of
personal mobility changed as well. That is a huge theme.
Here, I simply want to stress the value of the medical evidence
as an indicator of the sometimes alien ways in which the varieties of movement in space were conceptualized. Many of the
texts I have been citing, and a number of others (for instance
Book 2 of Galen's *De sanitate tuenda*), discuss different forms
of exercise. And these discussions have obvious implications
for the classification of more extensive movement. In the Hippocratic *Regimen* (chs. 2, 61) *ponoi* are either natural (*kata
phusin*) or violent (*dia bies*). Perhaps to our surprise, natural
exercises are those of sight, hearing, voice, and thought.
Walking partakes of both the natural and the violent. We have
seen different, but equally unfamiliar, taxonomies of movement
in Celsus and Caelius. For those who could not afford to hunt,
Galen recommended playing with a small ball, hardly the obvious alternative.[43] In the medieval learned tradition, physical

[41] *Anatomy of Melancholy*, pt. II, sect. ii, memb. 3, subs. 1, ed. T. C.
Faulkner, N. K. Kiessling, and R. L. Blair 2 (Oxford, 1990), 65.
K. Dewhurst, *Dr. Thomas Sydenham (1624–1689): His Life and Original
Writings* (London, 1966), 53–4 (a story not told until the nineteenth century,
and of other physicians, such as John Abernethy, as well; I am grateful to
Alick Cameron and John Forrester for references).

[42] P. Gil-Sotres, 'The Regimens of Health', in M. D. Grmek (ed.), *Western
Medical Thought from Antiquity to the Middle Ages* (Cambridge, Mass., and
London, 1998), 291–318, at 307; D. P. Lockwood, *Ugo Benzi: Medieval
Philosopher and Physician 1376–1439* (Chicago, 1951), 44–78, for a sample
discussion of *consilia*.

[43] *Exercise with the Small Ball* 2, trans. Singer, 299 (5.900–1K = *Scripta
Minora*, ed. J. Marquardt *et al.*, 1.94). For hunting see R. Lane Fox, 'Ancient
Hunting: From Homer to Polybius,' in J. B. Salmon and G. Shipley (eds.),
Human Landscapes in Classical Antiquity: Environment and Culture (London,
1996), 119–53, esp. 122, 147.

exercise is voluntary movement only; and 'voluntary' is defined in a way that separates the labouring from the leisured classes.

The work of carpenters, farmers, merchants, *et al.*, is not a physical exercise, since we do not observe voluntary movement, speaking properly, but rather forced movement. Moreover, merchants, bourgeois, and their like, walk a great deal, for long periods and over long distances; but here too we are not dealing with a genuine physical exercise. In order to have this one must walk at one's own initiative.

Thus Bernard of Gordon in the fourteenth century.[44] Exercise is for the few, not the many.

4. REGIMEN FOR TRAVELLERS

From travel *as* regimen, and the ways in which travel was understood, I turn to regimen *for* travellers, the second of my two themes. This is a topic on which, as I have indicated, the Hippocratics and Galen have very little to contribute. As the evidence comes down to us, the earliest we meet it is in the fourth century AD. I have referred to Oribasius' *Medical Collections*. The relevant material is not there (at least not in the 25 books that survive out of an original 70) but in one of the two Synopses of it that he later wrote. In the Synopsis addressed to his son Eustathius, he includes short regimens for travellers on foot (*pros tas poreias*) and for seafarers.[45] The context is this: preceding sections on exercise for out-of-sorts 'businessmen' (derived from Galen's *De sanitate tuenda*) and those with a corruption of food in the stomach; succeeding sections on drunkenness and sexual excess. In between the two regimens is some advice taken from Erasistratus (fragment 158)[46] on how to cope with a change of water. A train of thought is just detectable in Oribasius' layout and selection. From stomach problems he moves to 'the easiest way to depart on a journey on foot' (not, I submit, a 'walking-tour' as the passage's new editor-translator has it; that conjures up anachronistic

---

[44] *Regimen sanitatis*, MS. Cues 508, f. 52vb, trans. Gil-Sotres, 'Regimens of Health', 305.

[45] *Synopsis ad Eustathium* 5.31, 33, ed. I. Raeder, *CMG* 6.3 (Leipzig and Berlin, 1926), v. 166–8.

[46] In *Erasistrati fragmenta*, ed. I. Garofalo (Pisa, 1988).

images).[47] This 'easiest way' is 'with bowels emptied...in summer, with a soft band six or seven fingers wide and not more than five yards long wrapping up the loins as far as the flanks'. So now we know how to dress, or at least what underwear to don (to prevent chafing?). We are told about the use of a stick. We learn about what to drink, how to avoid being dried out by the sun, and so forth. As for sea voyages, the great thing is not to resist being sick—an empty stomach again being an advantage—and to counteract the stench of the bilge water.[48]

These are not Oribasius' own prescriptions. He takes them from writers of the fourth century BC who survive, for us, only in fragments (such as these extracts). They are among the numerous casualties of the Galenic near monopoly of subsequent medical learning and copying. Presumably Oribasius turned to these two writers because they were distinctive: because there was nothing like them in his principal source, Galen. The regimen for travellers comes from the works of Diocles of Carystus (fragment 184 van der Eijk), known to the Athenians of his time as 'the younger Hippocrates'.[49] The regimen for seafarers is from his rough contemporary Dieuches (fragment 19).[50] The latter, to judge by what remains of his writing, dealt mainly with food and drink, and also with the use of seawater as a purgative (fragment 18).[51]

Diocles reportedly wrote twenty or so books on a great variety of medical topics. Given his concern for the welfare of travellers, it is ironic that one of the most substantial fragments of his to come down to us (fragment 182) is a detailed daily regimen, from the moment of waking onwards, for the man who has no need to do anything more than sleep, eat, groom himself, walk, and visit the gymnasium. Beyond that, he does not go anywhere. Duties (if any there be) seem to occupy only a tiny

---

[47] P. J. van der Eijk, *Diocles of Carystus, A Collection of the Fragments and Translation with Commentary: Text and Translation* 1 (Leiden, 2000), no. 184, p. 323.

[48] Dieuches, ed. Raeder, *CMG* 6.3, 167–8.

[49] For context, apart from van der Eijk's admirable edition, see Wöhrle, *Studien zur Theorie*, ch. V.3.

[50] In *Mnésithé et Dieuchès*, ed. J. Bertier (Leiden, 1972).

[51] From Oribasius, *Medical Collections* 8.42, ed. Raeder, *CMG* 6.1.1 (Leipzig and Berlin, 1928), 292–3.

portion of his ideal day. Social life, unless in the gymnasium, and, still more, long journeys, are by implication 'off limits'. They must not interfere with the maintenance of health. The chief division, in this fragment, is not between the mobile and the sedentary: it is between the flatulent and the rest of us. I have saved mention of this fragment until now, yet it could well have been offered earlier, as a representation of fixity—and indeed as a depiction of the path to hypochondria, since anything less than healthy perfection in one's day must by definition bring on illness.[52]

Such contributions to regimen are part of the great 'confidence trick' that ancient Greek medicine first worked on the leisured and fastidious elite of the fifth and fourth centuries BC. Greek physicians persuaded this public that diet in the broad sense was a, if not *the*, key to health, its preservation and its restoration. A little like the expensive personal trainers of modern plutocrats, ancient doctors offered the illusion of autonomy to mask the reality of the patient's ultimate dependence on them for advice on every aspect of daily life, and the environment within which it is lived—every aspect from the gravest risk to a rumbling stomach. Regimens for travellers belong in the same expansionist, 'medicalizing', context as those for the different ages of life, from infancy onwards, or treatises on the properties of different foodstuffs: they are the spatial part of a supply-led movement towards extreme specialization in dietetics.[53]

Byzantine regimens have yet to be studied with any thoroughness: the accessible ones seem to vary regimen chronologically—month by month—rather than by degree of mobility or fixity.[54] I can better illustrate the fortunes of such material through the Middle Ages with glances at the Islamic

[52] Oribasius, *Medical Collections* 40, ed. Raeder, *CMG* 6.2.2, iv. 141–6. The fragment was the principal subject of L. Edelstein, 'The Dietetics of Antiquity', reprinted in translation in his *Ancient Medicine* (1967); abbreviated edn. (Baltimore and London, 1987), 303–16.

[53] Cf. Ibid. Wöhrle, *Studien zur Theorie*, 111–16; I. M. Lonie, 'A Structural Pattern in Greek Dietetics and the Early History of Greek Medicine', *Medical History* 21 (1977), 235–60.

[54] A. Delatte (ed.), *Anecdota Atheniensia et alia*: 2. *Texts grecs relatifs à l'histoire des sciences* (Paris, 1939), 455–99; J. L. Idler (ed.), *Physici et medici graeci minores*, 2 vols. (Berlin, 1841–2); repr. (Amsterdam, 1963), i. nos. XXVIII, XXIX, XXXI; ii. no. III.

and Latin European worlds. My underlying questions remain these. Is mobility represented as something special and separable from normal life? To what extent is it emphasized in the texts?

In an eleventh-century Arabic treatise on poisons can be found paragraphs attributed to Rufus of Ephesus about how travellers can protect themselves from reptiles and cold weather. These may have been taken from a fuller, even monographic, treatment of travel regimen that is listed as having been among his compositions. If this work once existed, however, it has left no trace in the Greek manuscript tradition and its influence must remain conjectural.[55] Oribasius was, more likely, the main link between antiquity and the Middle Ages. The fragmentary regimens for walkers and sea-voyagers that he preserved were translated, as part of his *Synopsis*, into Latin, and they were copied by the seventh-century Greek medical encyclopaedist Paul.[56] Thence they passed to the Arabs—or, if not these excerpts in particular, then the idea of including such regimens in more general guides to health preservation.

To take only the biggest names—those that, in translation, were later to dominate the Latin tradition: Ibn Sina (d. 1037) included in his *Canon of Medicine* a few pages for travellers on coping with fatigue and indigestion, extremes of heat and cold, changes of water supply, and seasickness (his advice on the last is simply 'ignore it').[57] If Ibn Sina is the most famous of the 'big names', Razi (d. 925) is the most interesting, and his writings offer the most variegated information. His vast, posthumously published, notebooks, the *Hawi*, give us, in their disorder, some hint of the progress of his reading and thinking on the topic of travel. He (or the students who published his work) placed the section on travel in the context of regimen for the aged and the obese.[58] This section runs through broadly the same topics that

[55] Ullmann, 'Neues', 39.

[56] Paul of Aegina, 1.50, 51, trans. F. Adams, *The Seven Books of Paulus Ægineta* (London, 1849), i. 76–9.

[57] Book I, 3rd fann, 4th talim, 1st jumla, in e.g. O. C. Gruner, *A Treatise on the Canon of Medicine of Avicenna, Incorporating a Translation of the First Book* (London, 1930).

[58] Abu Bakr Muhammas Ibn Zakariyya ar-Razi, *Kitab al-Hawi fi at-tibb* 23 (Hyderabad, 1974), 209–24. I am immensely grateful to Cristina

would later appear in the *Canon*, but displays its sources in Galen, Oribasius, and Muslim scholars. It also adds, in both its title and some of its jottings, a novel though obviously related subject: regimen for the army (where they should pitch camp, how they should protect their animals, etc.). A tidier, less alluring, version of all this was to appear in Razi's *Kitab al-Mansuri*, dedicated to the governor of his native Rayy.[59] Razi, however, affords us the chance to get behind the scenes of his formal treatises and come as close as we can get to the daily practice of a major Islamic physician. His *Kitab al-Tajarib* or *Casebook* contains records of almost 900 cases treated or supervised by him. We might expect the pathologies of travel to figure significantly in it. Not so. One traveller about to depart complains to him of dullness of vision in one eye. Another needs help because he has swallowed some coins while on a journey, presumably to avoid robbery, and cannot excrete them.[60] And that is all. The paucity raises uncomfortable questions about the bearing of regimen on reality, and not just in the Islamic context.

To Europe. Sections on travel are a relatively common feature of general regimen, both Latin and vernacular (though not, I think, in those associated with Salerno or in the Arabic work known in Latin as the *Tacuinum sanitatis*).[61] Most often their contents descend from Ibn Sina (Avicenna in the Latin West) or Razi (Rhazes). But they do so in subject matter—food, drink, weather, fatigue, seasickness—more than in detail: naturally there are local adaptations and individual touches. For example, in the earlier fourteenth century Maynus de Mayneriis says that the rich should prepare for a voyage by mixing sea water with their wine for several days beforehand, while the poor should drink the sea water neat. Both will thereby avoid

Álvarez-Millán for help with this text and for informing me of the contents of the manuscript cited in the next note.

[59] Escorial, Real Biblioteca del Monasterio, Arabic MS 858, fos. 73a–81a.

[60] C. Álvarez-Millán, 'Practice versus Theory: Tenth-Century Case Histories from the Islamic Middle East', *Social History of Medicine* 13 (2000), special issue, *Medical Practice at the End of the First Millennium*, ed. P. Horden and E. Savage-Smith, 298, 301.

[61] Though see Ibn Butlan, *Taqwim al-Sihha, Tacuini sanitatis*, ed. H. Elkhadem (Louvain, 1990), 217, 272. See further C. Thomasset, 'Conseils médicaux pour le voyage en mer au moyen âge', in C. Buchet (ed.), *L'homme, la santé et la mer* (Paris, 1997), 69–87.

seasickness.[62] It is a token gesture towards inclusiveness, reminiscent of the Hippocratic author who claimed to be writing for the great majority; and it goes well beyond the brief references to wine in the Muslim authorities. As well as such additions to the mainstream, there are also chronological developments. The most striking of these is the inclusion in travel regimens, from the close of the fifteenth century on, of measures to reduce the risk of contracting syphilis by avoidance of communal baths and by checking the bed linen wherever one stays.[63]

5. FREE-STANDING REGIMENS

I take the last example from an article of 1911 by the great Karl Sudhoff.[64] Besides publishing some short fifteenth- to sixteenth-century *consilia pro iter agentibus*, this paper has introductory material which remains, in some respects, the most recent synoptic view of its topic in print (despite two invaluable sections in the Catalan edition of Arnald of Villanova, to whom I return).[65] Sudhoff implicitly raises the question of whether the *Reiseregimen* is a distinct genre. We have seen it developing as a predictable presence in larger medical works. I should like to end by sharpening Sudhoff's question into this one: when, and in what circumstances, has travel regimen been the subject of a whole, free-standing, work? When has it been privileged by separate treatment and publication, at greater length than that of the *consilia* or the sections in handbooks and encyclopaedias?

From antiquity the answer is reasonably clear. There is no evidence that Diocles of Carystus wrote a whole book on the subject. Rufus of Ephesus, as we saw, is attested as having done that, but no one else. Who came next? From medieval Islam only two works of this kind are recorded and only one of them survives. The survivor is a strange production. Qusta ibn

---

[62] *Praxis medicinalis*, 2.30 (Lyons, 1586), 43, quoted by P. Gil-Sotres in *Arnaldi de Villanova Opera Medica Omnia*, vol. 10.1, ed. L. García-Ballester and M. R. McVaugh (Barcelona, 1996), 861 n. 112.

[63] K. Sudhoff, 'Ärztliche Regimina für Land- und Seereisen aus dem 15. Jahrhundert', *Archiv für Geschichte der Medizin* 4 (1911), 263–81, at 279–80.

[64] See ibid.

[65] *Arnaldi de Villanova Opera Medica Omnia*, 10.1, 384–94/851–61; 10.2, ed. M. R. McVaugh (Barcelona, 1998), 191–200. But also see Thomasset, 'Conseils médicaux'

Luqa's *Medical Regime for the Pilgrims to Mecca* is the only known medieval work with such a title.[66] Its author (d. *c.*912) wrote it for a secretary of the Caliph in Baghdad around the middle of the ninth century. Qusta was a Christian and so would not have made the hajj himself. Nor could he have been admitted to Mecca. He excuses himself, however, from accompanying his dedicatee on the ground that he must not leave his children. He identifies the need for a regimen as arising from the pilgrim's passing through 'a country where there is no doctor nor any required drug', yet he reassures himself by noting that the secretary will be accompanied 'by a doctor able to obtain whatever is necessary'.[67] He goes through what he takes to be the standard topics that any travel regimen should contain—food, fatigue, diseases caused by different winds, prophylaxis against vermin, etc. He then adds some topics which he thinks are especially necessary for the pilgrim to Mecca: improving contaminated water, quenching one's thirst, dust in the eye, and, lastly, dealing with the worst of Arabian parasites, the metre-long *dracunculus medinensis*, the Medina worm or guinea worm, which some Islamic authors unfortunately confused with a varicose vein.[68] On both kinds of topic, the pilgrim and the 'normal' travel regimen, Qusta is ultimately indebted to the Greek encyclopaedists Oribasius and Paul. He is not deploying local knowledge. One cannot imagine the secretary reading this work in his tent each night so as to anticipate the next day's risks. It seems more like a display of learning designed to impress a powerful patron.

The same is true of the two known medieval European examples of free-standing travel regimens. Pilgrimage remains the occasion of writing, but in Europe it is the armed pilgrimage of crusade. And the patrons are not less than royal. Beyond a short chapter in Vegetius (*Epitoma rei militaris* 3.2), no sus-

---

[66] *Qusta ibn Luqa's Medical Regime for the Pilgrims to Mecca: The Risala fi tadbir safar al-hajj*, ed. and trans. G. Bos (Leiden, 1992). See 5–6 for other writings in Arabic in the genre.

[67] Ibid. 16, 17.

[68] D. Bennett, 'Medical Practice and Manuscripts in Byzantium', *Social History of Medicine*, 13 (2000) (special issue, *Medical Practice at the End of the First Millennium*, ed. P. Horden and E. Savage-Smith), 289–90; M. Ullmann, *Islamic Medicine* (Edinburgh, 1978), 81–3.

tained writing survives from antiquity on the problems of keeping a field army healthy. Thus, when Adam of Cremona wrote a *Regimen iter agentium vel peregrinantium* to guide the Emperor Frederick II as he prepared to set off on his (as it turned out) disastrous expedition to the Holy Land in 1227, he had to turn to Arabic sources in translation.[69] His is indeed one of the earliest Latin works to make extensive use of the *Canon* of Avicenna (Ibn Sina). He does not seem to have had access to the Latin version of Rhazes's military advice. And what he borrowed from Avicenna was almost always the standard stuff of *individual* regimen: the health needs and problems of men *en masse* hardly occurred to him. As a church cantor writing for crusaders, he wanted to include spiritual advice too. This would have been a new departure in regimen, though one based on the inclusion of appropriate emotions among the 'non-natural' determinants of health. But Adam more or less forgot his religious task in the composition; the result is far more conventional than he intended.

A genuinely new departure was achieved by the next writer in this uneven sequence, the great Spanish physician Arnald of Villanova. His *Regimen castra sequentium* or *Regimen Almarie* belongs here because it is a free-standing treatise, albeit a very short one.[70] It is full of sensible, non-generic, advice, not all of it medical: 'When the army must move from one place to another, infantry shod with heavy-soled shoes should precede it by a mile or two, who will search in and around the route to see whether iron caltrops have been sown or scattered there . . . And so that the army may be preserved from epidemic, let pits be dug everywhere outside its lines, like trenches, where animal waste and bodies can be thrown; and when they are half full

[69] Ed. F. Hönger, *Ärztliche Verhaltungsmassregeln auf dem Heerzug ins Heilige Land für Kaiser Friedrich II. geschrieben von Adam v. Cremona (ca.1227)* (Leipzig, 1913). For context see T. C. van Cleve, *The Emperor Frederick II of Hohenstaufen: Immutator Mundi* (Oxford, 1972), 316–17; M. R. McVaugh, 'Medical Knowledge at the Time of Frederick II', *Micrologus* 2 (1994), 12–13; McVaugh, 'Arnald of Villanova's Regimen Almarie (Regimen castra sequentium) and Medieval Military Medicine', *Viator* 23 (1992), 201–13, at 204–5.

[70] Ibid. and *Arnaldi de Villanova Opera Medica Omnia*, ed. McVaugh, 10.2. The quotation following is from para. 2.

cover them with earth.' And so on. It is rather a miscellany. And
that doubtless reflects the circumstances of its composition.
James II of Aragon had launched a crusade into the kingdom
of Granada and was besieging Almería on the Mediterranean
coast. In late 1309 or early 1310 he angrily summoned Arnald
thither to explain the bizarre and undiplomatic statements he
had reportedly been making at the papal court. Arnald seems to
have composed the regimen as a peace offering en route from
Sicily. By the time he arrived the campaign was virtually over,
the Aragonese-Castilian alliance that underlay it having
crumbled.

Ingratiation seems to be the leitmotif of these free-standing
regimens. Failure of some kind also seems to be associated with
all of them. As we have moved from ancient to medieval evidence, I have been suggesting that the confidence trick first
attempted by the early Hippocratics—to the effect that thorough concern for regimen was essential to health—had a very
uneven success rate. The regimens were designed to impress;
and perhaps some did. How far they were actually implemented
is, of course, another matter.

My final exhibit raises the question of purpose and effect in a
slightly different form. We move from the world of crusades
and military regimen into the Renaissance, with its systematic
recovery of ancient dietetics. The pertinent texts of Celsus,
Galen, and Paul are edited anew and commented upon.[71] Specialized treatises reappear, now of course in print: for example,
De arte gymnastica (1569) of Girolamo Mercuriale, so all-
embracing a work as to include gynaecological matters.[72] In
this virtuoso context belongs the *Regimen omnium iter agentium*
(1556) by Guglielmo Gratarolo (1516–68), a scarcely studied
Renaissance physician.[73] In just under 200 pages he considers
all the standard topics for those travelling on horseback, on foot,
by ship, in a carriage, with an elegance and thoroughness that

[71] Mikkeli, *Hygiene in the Early Modern Medical Tradition* 23–32.

[72] V. Nutton, 'Les exercices et la santé: Hieronymus Mercurialis et la
gymnastique médicale', in J. Céard, M.-M. Fontaine, and J. C. Margolin
(eds.), *Le corps à la Renaissance* (Paris, 1990), 295–308.

[73] My knowledge of whom I owe to the kindness of Professor Ian Maclean,
who plans a monograph on him.

befitted his status.[74] The book went through some twelve editions between 1556 and 1670 and was probably the most popular work of its kind in the early modern age. Educated in Padua, Gratarolo had fled to Basle around 1550. He secured a chair there some ten years later. He stressed in his preface the idea that I have seen as implicit in earlier regimens: that we are all travellers on the journey of life. Mobility is standard, not fixity. In his case the emphasis derived especially from contact with the Italian *Spirituali*. A rigorous Calvinist, he yet collected notes on incantations and defended alchemy. He wrote a modern physiognomy, and became famous for a book on repairing memory lapses.[75] The latter might endear him to scholars. Yet he has one further claim to their affection. Besides his regimen for travellers, perhaps inspired by an uncomfortable flight from his native land, he also wrote one in keeping with his profession. This was a regimen (later translated into English) for sedentary *literati*.[76] All others travel. Scholars alone are so immobile as to require special guidance on health.[77]

---

[74] I used *De regimine iter agentium, vel equitum, vel peditum, vel navi, vel curru seu rheda*, 2nd edn. (Strasbourg, 1563).

[75] Englished as *The Castel of Memorie* (London, 1573).

[76] Henrici Rantzouii *De conseruanda valetudine liber . . . Seorsim accessit Guilielmi Grataroli . . . De literatorum, & eorum qui magistratum gerunt, conseruanda valetudine, liber* (Frankfurt, 1591). Englished as *A Direction for the Health of Magistrates and Studentes* (London, 1574).

[77] Acknowledgements: beyond those thanked above, for unstinting advice and references I am grateful to Jim Adams, Sam Barnish, David Bennett, Vivian Nutton, Carole Rawcliffe, Emilie Savage-Smith, Philip van der Eijk, Heinrich von Staden, and Faith Wallis.

9

The Ancient Mediterranean:
The View from the Customs House

Nicholas Purcell[1]

1. ON THE USEFULNESS OF THE HISTORY OF TAXATION

Routine, more-or-less legitimate, organized exactions of materials or labour, or of their symbolic equivalents, are located in a complex conceptual and practical matrix of behaviour and attitudes. This framework includes the purposes, expectations and irregularities of the exactors and the avoidance or hostility of those from whom exactions are made. It varies quantitatively, in levels and in the parameters within which it is possible in a given system to change those levels, in the efficiency of the programme and of its execution. It is obviously qualitatively variable, according to the configuration of what is taxed—human effort, produce, accumulation, artisan skill, exchanges, earnings, inheritances, winnings, windfalls. And it will also depend on the depth of penetration of tax practices, the layout of who is liable at all, and whether differential levying maps

[1] My thanks to William Harris for the invitation to the conference, and especially to Peregrine Horden for delivering the paper in my absence. He has also kindly read this paper in draft, and is of course to be credited as co-author for the arguments that derive from our joint work, *The Corrupting Sea* (Oxford, 2000), without incurring responsibility for anything overstated or inaccurate in the present essay. I am also most grateful to Tony Ñaco for helping me procure Catalan material. This is part of a trio of interrelated investigations arising from *The Corrupting Sea*, and concerned with its possible application to problems of ancient history, alongside 'Colonization and Mediterranean History' in H. Hurst and S. Owen (eds.), *Ancient Colonization: Analogy, Similarity and Difference* (London, forthcoming), and N. Purcell, 'The Boundless Sea of Unlikeness? On Defining the Mediterranean', *Mediterranean Historical Review* 18 (2003), 9–29.

different social groupings within society—or shapes them, brings them into focus, identifies them. While 'exactions' and their regimes may be wholly private, they are also characteristic of the authority systems which we know as states, and it is the public rather than the private end of this spectrum that is examined in this essay. Even at the level of state organization, with all its cultural variety across history, certain distinctively Mediterranean patterns may be discerned.

This cluster of themes may be labelled 'tax morphology', and, involving as it does a cluster of variables of which many are basic ingredients of social organization, economic life, political relations and culture, this is a promising instrument for historical analysis. It should, in particular, lend itself to historical differentiation and comparative perspectives. It should commend itself to the historian of the *longue durée* and of the more recent 'histoire à très large échelle' which Roger Chartier has recently commended.[2] So useful does it appear that it is a real question why it does not take a more regular place among the forms of historical generalization in common use.[3] Apparent dullness must be part of the explanation, combined perhaps with a certain ideological conditioning. It might be thought part of the tax morphology of our own times that our society's grinding resentment or downright disapproval of taxation infiltrates the academic world and impalpably nudges us away from choosing this topic, when we are not so squeamish about torture or genocide. More interestingly, perhaps, the dullness of the discourse deserves to be made an object of reflection. As in many aspects of 'official' business, obscurantism and technical complexity may turn out to be instruments of social control.[4]

---

[2] R. Chartier, 'La conscience de la globalité', *Annales HSS* 56 (2001), 119–23, with Purcell, 'The Boundless Sea'.

[3] Some signs of a more constructive history of taxation have appeared: on direct taxes, see M. Corbier, 'De la razzia au butin, du tribut à l'impôt: aux origines de la fiscalité, prélèvements tributaires et naissance de l'état', in *Genèse de l'Etat* (Rome, 1993), 95–107; T. Ñaco del Hoyo, 'Roman *Realpolitik* in Taxing Sardinian rebels (178–75),' *Athenaeum* 91 (2003), 531–40, for the ad hoc nature of exactions.

[4] This is not to suggest that there are not *real* complexities, especially economic ones, in modern fiscal planning. For the pre-modern world, however—in this case for the world before the late eighteenth century—nothing similar exists.

We need to ask in both these cases what attitudes to the state and what dispositions on the part of its agents are at stake. If it is right to see in the fiscal universe a new opportunity for historical categorization which can map the past in interesting ways, that will need to be established with some care.

This chapter aims to make a preliminary exploration in this area, in the spirit nicely captured by Alain Bresson: 'faire sauter les verroux qui bloquent la réflexion'.[5] I want to suggest that tax morphology as I have briefly outlined it does delineate instructively, since it can be argued that it helps to unite, define, and identify the pre-modern history of the Mediterranean Sea and its coastlands. Those were the goals of *The Corrupting Sea*, which suggested that there were indeed certain possible common denominators which could encourage comparison between Mediterranean history in the periods conventionally known as ancient and medieval, and that—despite the indisputable artificiality and historical contingency of most conceptions of the Mediterranean—there is a coherent, legitimate, distinctive, and interesting subject of historical enquiry for which 'the Mediterranean' is the most convenient label.

The approach was essentially ecological or environmental, and one interesting criticism was the absence of objects of enquiry such as the state from history *of* the Mediterranean— especially by comparison with Braudel's *The Mediterranean and the Mediterranean World in the Age of Philip II*.[6] The implication was that the omission was both damaging and convenient: history can hardly do without such institutions, but had we attempted to say more about them, we should have had much more difficulty in defending the comparability of such very different epochs. In fact it can be argued that the foundations of history *of* the Mediterranean, *Corrupting-Sea*-style, *are* the foundations of major aspects of social and political history too: only the constraints of scale and available time prevented us from expounding this. But we did explore ways in which the 'extraction' of human resources, materials and foodstuffs from

[5] A. Bresson, *La cité marchande* (Bordeaux, 2000), 9.
[6] Further remarks on this discussion will be found in our joint contribution to this volume, P. Horden and N. Purcell, 'Four Years of Corruption' (see below).

the inhabitants of the Mediterranean on the part of the powerful was related to the other factors affecting human choices, and it is naturally in this area that we should seek some of the closest ties between the conditions of production, in a Mediterranean world of high fragmentation and risk but relatively easy redistribution, and the social, political and cultural systems found there. In this chapter, therefore, my aim is to look precisely at an instance of 'tax morphology' to explore how these ties might be presented. By investigating a prominent, and, I want to argue, very individual, aspect of the tax morphology of several different periods of Mediterranean history in widely scattered places, I hope to show—against expectations!—just how interesting and useful differentiation using this tool may actually be; and to suggest how certain basic conditions of human life in the pre-modern Mediterranean do underlie not just the day-to-day realities of life *terre-à-terre*, or the experience of *caboteurs*, but major features of the organization of entire societies. It has rightly been said that 'l'espace insaisissable des économies antiques' is only accessible through the study of social forms.[7]

2. TAXATION AND MOBILITY

State exactions and their morphology are naturally closely adapted to the productive activities which yield the substance which they seek to procure. If those activities are distinctive to a place or time, we may expect tax morphology to follow suit. If the Mediterranean can claim to have a distinctive regime of production, it will be worth looking to see if it has *pari passu* a distinctive set of parameters of extraction.

Mediterranean primary production does have a number of distinctive features, and we shall return to some of them by an indirect route later in this chapter. But one of the characteristics best suited to identifying the Mediterranean as a distinctive object of reflection is provided by the sea itself as the medium and focus of a network of communications which renders the mobility of people and things relatively easy. It is important

---

[7] J. Andreau and A. Schnapp, 'Ettore Lepore, la colonisation et l'écriture de l'histoire ancienne', in E. Lepore, *La Grande Grèce: Aspects et problèmes d'une colonisation ancienne* (Naples, 2000), 7–15 at 8.

neither to forget that this ease of communications is relative, and that the sea remains dangerous and, in pre-modern conditions, extremely capricious; nor to limit this mobility to the sea itself, since it is extended by the waterways of the coastlands and the valleys which lead into the mountains and plains behind them. But it is the sea itself which makes it possible for primary producers to adjust their shortfalls and surpluses through redistribution on a scale and over distances which are hard to parallel elsewhere. As a Hellenistic treatise on political organization puts it, there is a 'transferring or trading' element in the lowest of the three strata of the community, which is concerned with 'the moving abroad of what is in surplus in the city, and that which is in surplus abroad into the city'.[8] These reciprocal movements are part of the productive economy, built into the logic of choices about agrarian strategy, deployment of labour, storage, and processing. And it is in relation to these that we may observe a distinctive Mediterranean morphology of taxation, from the earliest evidence available to us through to the modern period. Michel Gras entitled an essay of 1993 'Pour une Méditerranée des *emporia*'.[9] He was quite right to discern an economic geography characteristic of this sea and its coastlands, and to see it instantiated in the crucial phenomenon of the ancient Greek *emporion*, unjustly neglected for so long. A similar 'Méditerranée des *ellimenia*, une Méditerranée des douanes' awaits our investigation. Similar, not only in the superficial sense that a much-repeated institution patterns the space around it; in both the *emporion* and the regime of taxes on mobility, we are dealing with the structures with which the powerful manage the consequences of the Mediterranean environment. Control of gateways, on whatever scale, takes its place, moreover, in the larger portfolio of environmental opportunities open to communities: it is an aspect of the essentially fissiparous microregional distribution of Mediterranean resources. That 'managing' power has been wielded by prominent individuals in small-scale communities, by regional elites, and by far more complex structures which still ultimately reposed on such foundations. Oppressive levying on interdepend-

---

[8] 'Hippodamos the Pythagorean', Stobaeus 4. 43. 93 Hense (92 Meineke).
[9] In A. Bresson and P. Rouillard (eds.), *L'Emporion* (Paris, 1993), 103–12.

ence can similarly be carried on by aristocracies, such as the Bacchiads, by imperial powers, or even by individuals.[10]

The theme of this paper, then, is levies made on the movement of people and things. This is a subject in which the more minute pursuit of definitions and terminologies has tended to obscure the larger questions, and in what follows, a number of underlying distinctions are elided in the pursuit of the bigger picture. These matters may be studied from an administrative, institutional, fiscal perspective, or from the economic and social angle. Some scholars have chosen one route, usually the former.[11] There is much to be gained from attempting to combine the two, difficult though the exercise may be. In the space of this essay it is not possible to do more than outline the possibilities with reference to one or two items from the rather large dossier of relevant material. Many important instances are referred to only in passing or not at all. A synthesis of what we know from the point of view of Mediterranean history is badly needed.

It should be said at the outset that the English term 'customs' is very ill-suited to the analysis of the complex of practices that make up this tax morphology. While the payment of duty in relation to a particular movement of materials or people does form an important part of what we are considering, it is not easy or useful in most cases to detach it from charges for services connected with the movement (harbourage, escort, provisioning, assistance in the actual movement). The realities of communication in mountainous regions offer an interesting point of comparison. Accompanying travellers and transporting their goods over very difficult terrain generate the possibility of a series of different charges. Against the background of these, the imposition of a more 'abstract' system of tolls may be seen to have developed slowly, with increasing institutional sophistication.[12] In relation to maritime movement too, we shall find

---

[10] Piso's private *teloneion* at Dyrrachium: Cicero, *Prov.Cons.* 5.

[11] Thus, for instance, J. France, *Quadragesima Galliarum: L'organisation douanière des provinces alpestres, gauloises et germaniques de l'Empire romain (1er siècle avant J.-C.—3er siècle après J.-C.)* (Rome, 2001), 9.

[12] D. van Berchem, 'Du portage au péage: Le rôle des cols transalpins dans l'histoire du Valais celtique', *Museum Helveticum* 13 (1956), 67–78. France, *Quadragesima*, 345–6, proposes three types of customs system—lines, circles,

ourselves faced with a dizzying variety of ways of exacting value from those moving and their goods, and a whole gamut of stages of abstraction in the process from simple ad hoc appropriation to sophisticated fiscal systems. The variety of types of movement and kinds of commodity, ranging across the spectra of value, bulk, prestige, and utility, and across the different complex zones of transition from public to private, will also need to be largely overlooked in this account. The diversity of the levying authorities themselves will form an integral part of the argument.

More unsettling still than the terminological clumsiness of modern vocabulary, however, is a conceptual unfamiliarity which deserves to be flagged up at the beginning of the discussion. Strange as it seems to modern fiscalities, the taxation of exports was a crucial element in pre-modern Mediterranean practice. Indeed, it is in this comprehensiveness of the regime of exactions on omnipresent, risk-enduced mobility, that we may seek some of the distinctiveness of the Mediterranean as an object of historical enquiry.

3.　THREE PHASES OF MEDITERRANEAN EVIDENCE

The dossier opens in the early archaic period, when economic transactions and social relations are especially hard to disentangle.[13] The Sidonian silver mixing bowl in the *Iliad* which the Phoenicians gave to Thoas, king of Lemnos, *stesan d'en limenessi* (and set it up in the harbours), may claim to be the first harbour due in western literature.[14] A boustrophedon silver tablet of the mid-sixth century BC from the foundation deposit of the Artemision at Ephesus, which has received attention mainly in the context of the coins in the deposit, is perhaps our earliest fiscal text in Greek, and records in minute detail the deposition in the

and points. The first two are characteristic of a developed sense of fiscal territoriality, and we shall be dealing more in what follows with the less articulated patterns that result from linking sequences of points. Ibid. 309–10, for definitions of *portorium*.

[13] Mycenaean precursors are not inconceivable; for possible earlier instances in the Fertile Crescent and in Egypt, see below.

[14] *Iliad* 23, 741–5; A. M. Andreades, *A History of Greek Public Finance* (Cambridge, Mass., 1933), 21.

Artemision of large sums of bullion derived from the most varied sources, one of which, *to nautikon*, is extremely likely to be a harbour tax.[15] A tempting parallel is the *nauton* from which the honorand of a sixth-century immunity decree from Cyzicus is not to be exempt.[16] Strabo believed that the Bacchiad aristocracy of Corinth had become rich in the early archaic period on the levies they exacted from their (admittedly uniquely well-located) *emporion*, and imagines the Crisaians of the plain below Delphi becoming rich at a very ancient period on the dues on goods coming from Italy and Sicily; and it is *a priori* likely that other elites attempted to do something similar.[17] It is likely, though not demonstrable, that wherever there was an *emporion* some such arrangement was likely: the institutional nature and systematic purposes of the *emporion* even at an early date have rightly been stressed in recent years.[18]

Taxes connected with the seaborne movement of people and materials were in fact, and are still—though things are beginning to change—an insufficiently appreciated fact of Greek history, universal, and extremely important to the communities which levied them.[19] The people of Aeolic Kyme were

[15] E. Schwyzer, *Dialectorum Graecarum Exempla* 707 (= *SGDI* 4 no. 49). For the details, A. Bammer, *Das Artemision von Ephesos: das Weltwunder Ioniens in archaischer und klassischer Zeit* (Mainz 1996); H. Wankel, *Die Inschriften von Ephesos* Ia (*IGSK* 11.1), (Bonn, 1979), 1–5 (no. 1); *LSAG* p. 339, *c*.550. See G. Manganaro, '*SGDI* 4. 4 n. 49 (*DGE* 707) e il bimetallismo monetale di Creso', *Epigraphica* 36 (1974), 57–77. A more interesting discussion: C. Ampolo, 'Greci d'Occidente, Etruschi, Cartaginesi: circolazione di beni e di uomini', in *Magna Grecia, Etruschi, Fenici, Atti del trentatreesimo Convegno di Studi sulla Magna Grecia, Taranto 1993* (Naples, 1996), 223–52.

[16] *SIG*³ 4; M. M. Austin and P. Vidal-Naquet, *Economic and Social History of Ancient Greece* (Berkeley and Los Angeles, 1977), no. 92.

[17] M. Shanks, *Art and the Greek City-state: An Interpretive Archaeology* (Cambridge, 1999), 52–4, discusses Strabo 8. 6. 20, but does not investigate the mechanism by which the Bacchiads might have benefited. Crisa: Strabo 9. 3. 4. We may perhaps see Ephoros behind both passages.

[18] A. Bresson, 'Les Cités grecques et leurs *emporia*', in A. Bresson and P. Rouillard (eds.), *L'Emporion*, 163–226. The mechanics are of course obscure. But it is worth noting that there is no reason to make the exaction of harbour dues subsequent to the introduction of coinage. It is likely that important movements of material even in the fourth century BC remained largely unmonetized.

[19] Andreades, *History*, 297: 'the customs dues were the chief source of income for the Greek states.'

proverbial for being slow on the uptake: 300 years after their foundation they 'gave away' their customs dues, and before that the people had not made use of (*ekarpouto*) this revenue at all, so that people said the Kymaians had not noticed that their city was on the sea.[20] The implication is obvious—any community, however small, as long as it was on the sea, was expected to derive income from customs dues.[21] Scattered later evidence confirms how ubiquitous dues of this kind were. Alponos on the Malic Gulf is hardly a name to conjure with: we hear incidentally of an undated occasion, Classical or Hellenistic, when twenty-five girls climbed the *purgos ellimenion*, the tower of the harbour-due authority, there, to see better during the festival of the Thesmophoria, but it collapsed and they fell into the sea.[22] That the headquarters of the harbour-due exacting authorities should be a *purgos*, even if such an inadequate exemplar of the genre, is to be noted.

But it is from the epigraphic record that the most abundant testimony to the ubiquity of these practices comes. This is not the place even to outline the principal characteristics of this material, which ranges from the stele by which Pharaoh Nectanebo II in the mid-fourth century BC gave the revenues of the customs of Naucratis to the goddess Neith—under whose tutelage lay the Great Green, the Mediterranean—to municipal tariffs from Carales in Sardinia and Anazarbus in Cilicia at the end of Antiquity.[23] We are dealing with an essentially oppor-

---

[20] Strabo 13. 3. 6. When was the foundation, and when and what was the 'giving away' of the dues?

[21] The inscription-rich and densely packed little cities of Crete offer good examples such as *I. Cret.* IV. 186 (customs arrangements between Gortys and Lappa). *I. Cret.* IV. 184, discussed by M. Guarducci, 'Ordinamenti dati da Gortina a Kaudos in una iscrizione inedita di Gortina', *Rivista di Filologia* 8 (1930), 471–82, is also very instructive: the harbour tax of the tiny island of Gaudhos, insignificant in itself but offering a refuge on a dangerous but much-frequented coast, is part of a carefully delineated portfolio of revenues available to the community of *katoikountes* and the city from which they come.

[22] Strabo 1. 3. 20 (unclear how this fits into the context of flood-damage caused by the Spercheios).

[23] Carales: J. Durliat, 'Taxes sur l'entrée des merchandises dans la cité de Carales-Cagliari à l'époque Byzantine (582–602)', *Dumbarton Oaks Papers* 36 (1982), 1–14; Anazarbus: G. Dagron and D. Feissel, *Inscriptions de Cilicie* (Paris, 1987), 170–85, (no.108).

tunistic practice, which was by its nature flexible and variable, and the particularities of the levies recorded in the Elephantine palimpsest suggest that a Mediterranean captain or merchant of the fifth century BC needed to be alert to the same bewildering range of port-specific information that is so eloquently witnessed by the Italian merchant *pratiche* of the later Middle Ages.[24] While there were certain places, such as Rhodes and its *peraia*, or the approaches to the Hellespont, or the Isthmus of Corinth, which were specially well suited to the levying of revenues of this kind, and where large sums might be taken, it is important to repeat that such places were not rare, and that every community with access to the sea participated, as the Aeolic Kymaians so laughably failed to, in this activity.[25] Moreover, it is not appropriate to use the language of determinism about the development of communities in zones favoured in the geography of connectivity. The place did not somehow spontaneously generate the entrepôt: Bacchiad Corinth, post-synoecism Rhodes, Delos after 166 BC were in suitable places, but their response to the advantages was the result of the political choices of elites, inside or outside the community.

The document that sheds most light, however, on how harbour taxation worked in Antiquity is a Roman-period inscription published in 1954, from Caunus in south-western Anatolia, on the borders of Lycia and Caria, in the *peraia* of Rhodes, and indeed, at a vital period in its history, a major mainland

---

[24] C. Ciano, *La Pratica di mercatura datiniana (secolo XIV)* (Milan, 1964), is an excellent example. But note the growing consensus that these documents are not intended to be directly practical, for all their technicality: rather they evoke a world of expertise and broad information, the education of a merchant on the edge of the Renaissance. Thus B. Dini, *Una pratica di mercatura in formazione (1394–1395)* (Florence, 1980), publishing the treatise of Ambrogio de' Rocchi (*c*.1374–96). The Vélissaropoulos principle that differential taxation of different commodities begins only in the Hellenistic period is excessively rigid.

[25] Contra M. I. Finley, *The Ancient Economy* (Berkeley and Los Angeles, 1974), 130, on Rhodes ('the outstanding example of a port-of-call'): 'a significant group [of cities] which by their location were clearing-houses and transfer-points, deriving substantial income from tolls, harbour-dues and dock-charges'. Oropos in Xenon, ap. [Dicaearchus] 8 (*Geographi Graeci Minores* I.101): *pantes telonai, pantes eisin harpages.*

dependency of the Rhodian state.[26] Caunus was a middling port, in a significant location for maritime communications. In Mediterranean terms, it was not very singular. From the original publication on, it has been clear that one of the most important aspects of the document is that it illustrates the absolute normality, even under the universal dominion of Rome, of local taxation by communities of the movement of goods. The document is a benefaction, in which the burden of the payment of the dues for a certain period is taken on by a local euergete. In this golden age of civic benefaction, indeed, the customs house, sometimes in monumental form, took its place in the prestige architecture of the community.[27]

If this topic is at last beginning to attract scholarly attention, however, that may be the result of the discovery of one of the most novel pieces of evidence for ancient economic history to be published for many years, the Elephantine palimpsest. Overwritten with a text of Aramaic wisdom literature of the end of the fifth century BC, a papyrus from Elephantine in Upper Egypt preserves the complete record of the duties paid on the cargoes and crew of all the ships putting in to a harbour of the Egyptian delta, in a year which has a good chance of being

---

[26] Pol. 30. 31. 6, 197–188 BC. Caunus and Stratonicea, 120 talents p.a. for Rhodian state. G. E. Bean, 'Notes and Inscriptions from Caunus', *Journal of Hellenic Studies* 74 (1954), 10–35; H. W. Pleket, 'Notes on a Customs-law from Caunus', *Mnemosyne* 11 (1958), 128–35; L. Robert, 'Limenes', *Hellenica XI-XII* (Paris 1960), 264–6. Early discussions were not able to resolve the many problems of this text, which has therefore had relatively little attention. More recently considerable progress has been made: G. Purpura, 'Il regolamento doganale di Cauno e la lex Rhodia in D. 14. 2. 9', *Annali del Seminario Giuridico della Università di Palermo* 38 (1985), 273–331. See also J. France, 'Les Revenus douaniers des communautés municipales dans le monde romain (république et haut-Empire)', in *Il capitolo delle entrate nelle finanze municipali in occidente ed in oriente: Actes de la Xe rencontre franco-italienne sur l'épigraphie du monde romain, Rome, 27–29 mai 1996* (Rome, 1999), 95–114.

[27] *ILS* 8858 = *OGIS* 525, two slave agents of a second-century contractor for the Asian *portorium* (also an imperial procurator) at Halicarnassus 'rebuilt the customs house and its portico from the foundations and gilded the statue of Aphrodite', cf. *ILS* 1654 (Bibba in Africa, also to Venus (Augusta), in this case a fiscal accounts office rather than customs house in the strict sense, *Ephemeris Epigraphica* 5. 112); *OGIS* 496: the fishing-due *teloneion* at Ephesus and its shrine of Isis.

475 BC.[28] From these duties, we gain a snapshot of the precise composition of the cargoes, the origins of the ships and their captains, and the value of the whole exercise to the Achaemenid state.

The sophistication, complexity and prominence of the administrative machinery attested here gives an insight into Mediterranean trade in the fifth century BC that was wholly unexpected. No comparable record survives until the archives of Genoa in the thirteenth century AD, and there is an intuitive resemblance between the world evoked by the papyrus and the much more familiar images of the late-medieval Mediterranean, as we see it for instance in the vignette of the sexual hazards of commercial seafaring which Boccaccio set around the *dogana* of Palermo.[29] It is impossible not to be reminded of the courtesan Rhodopis in Herodotus' account of the *emporion* Naucratis, which was itself to become a key centre for the fiscal control of Egyptian commerce.[30] The tenor of recent scholarship has been wholly against such intuitions: yet the new document may encourage us to enquire whether that resistance to comparison is well founded.[31] Take the issue of scale, which is sometimes

[28] Most recently, P. Briant and R. Descat, 'Un registre douanier de la satrapie d'Egypte à l'époque achéménide', in N. Grimal and B. Menu (eds.), *Le Commerce en Egypte ancienne* (Cairo, 1998), 59–104.

[29] Boccaccio, *Decameron*, VIII 10: 'Soleva essere, e forse che ancora oggi è, una usanza, in tutte le terre marine che hanno porto, cosi fatta che tutti i mercatanti che in quelle con mercatantie capitano, faccendole scaricare, tutte in un fondaco, il quale in nostri luoghi e chiamato "dogana", tenuta per lo comune o per lo signor della terra, le portano. E quivi, dando a coloro che sopra ciò sono per iscritto tutta la mercatantia e il pregio di quella, è dato per li detti al mercatante un magazzino, nel quale esso la sua mercatantia ripone e serralo con la chiave; e li detti doganieri poi scrivono in sul libro della dogana a ragione del mercatante tutta la sua mercatantia, faccendosi poi del lor diritto pagare al mercatante, o per tutta o per parte della mercatantia che egli della dogana traesse. E da questo libro della dogana assai volte s'informano i sensali e delle qualità e delle quantità delle mercatantie che vi sono, e ancora chi sieno i mercatanti che l'hanno, con li quali poi essi, secondo che lor cade per mano, ragionano di cambi, di baratti e di vendite e d'altri spacci. La quale usanza, sì come in molti altri luoghi, era in Palermo in Cicilia.'

[30] Herodotus 2. 134–5. Boccaccio would not have shared Herodotus' bafflement as to why major Mediterranean *entrepôts* were good places to find *epaphroditoi hetairai*.

[31] See however J. Rougé, 'Prêt et société maritimes dans le monde romain', *Memoirs of the American Academy in Rome* 34 (1980), 291–303, for

thought to be a decisive differentiator: in the papyrus 42 ships are registered during the year, which does not seem very many, for all the richness of their cargoes. Figures from the *strazzetto*, the tax exclusively on transit goods, at Genoa in 1445, however, rather similarly refer to 70 voyages made by 52 Genoese and 12 foreign boats.[32]

Or take the case of a prosperous port in the south-west of England, Exeter, where the customs records are unusually well preserved.[33] Over a period of 55 years at the end of the fourteenth century, 641 arrivals of 302 individual ships (half based in Devon) with dutiable cargoes were recorded (a considerably smaller number per annum than the anonymous port of the Canopic mouth in 475 BC). Imports were overwhelmingly more important than exports; a rough breakdown by yield of the commodities taxed is manufactured goods 6%, raw materials 7%, materials for the textile industry 10%, foodstuffs 24% (including some notable imports of cereals, as the period in question covers some notable years of dearth in local cereals), and wine 53%. The goods were already in the possession of, or would be bought by, the civic elite, who intended to retail them at a profit; the duties provided 8–9% of the city's revenue. This was no Antwerp; but it was fairly typical of the ports of the narrow seas at this period. Much of the detail is perfectly plausible for an archaic Aeolic Kyme, a Roman Caunus, or a Byzantine Carales. The way in which immunities were made available to certain shipowners to articulate a network of mutual cooperation within networks of more or less privileged ports is very suggestive of Mediterranean practice. But two things are quite un-Mediterranean—the asymmetry of export and import, so alien to the banal economic viewpoint of ancient observers like 'Hippodamos'; and the density of the network. There was a

---

resemblances to the Middle Ages in the Roman western Mediterranean, especially Arles.

[32] P. Gourdin, 'Présence génoise en Mediterranée et en Europe au milieu du XVe siècle: L'implantation des hommes d'affaires d'après un registre douanière de 1445', in M. Balard and A. Ducellier (eds.), *Coloniser au Moyen âge* (Paris, 1995), 14–35.

[33] For what follows, see M. Kowaleski, *The Local Customs Accounts of the Port of Exeter, 1266–1321* (Exeter, 1993).

mere handful of ports of this size in the entire south-west of Britain; Caunus was one of dozens.[34]

But it is to the western Mediterranean that I wish to turn for more detailed comparison of ancient and medieval. The late antique tariffs of Anazarbus and Carales resemble in detail and in spirit a body of material from six hundred years later that has recently been interestingly displayed by Silvia Orvietani Busch.[35] Her work compares two Mediterranean coastlines in the twelfth century—the Catalan litoral from Roussillon to the mouth of the Ebro, and the Tuscan shore on both sides of the mouth of the Arno. The evidence for the ports of Catalonia in this period is particularly rich, and includes quite detailed regulations for the customs dues of ports such as Collioure at the end of the Pyrenees, Barcelona itself, for which a particularly detailed regulation or *lleuda* survives, and the little port of Tamarit, further to the south.[36] What is especially important about the material and this analysis of it is that it does not concern a single port, understood necessarily in isolation, or as part of a duet with a partner on the other side of the sea, as one finds in the contemporary trading treaties between the Italian republics and the principalities of the Maghreb, interesting as they are.[37] Here we have evidence for the working of an entire *façade maritime*, in which the warp of long-distance coastwise *cabotage* and the weft of the exchanges between ports and their

---

[34] For an overview of the system, N. S. B. Gras, *The Early English Customs System: A Documentary Study of the Institutional and Economic History of the Customs from the Thirteenth to the Sixteenth Century* (Cambridge, Mass., 1918).

[35] S. Orvietani Busch, *Medieval Mediterranean Ports: The Catalan and Tuscan Coasts, 1100 to 1235* (Leiden, 2001).

[36] For Barcelona, J. Sobrequés i Callicó, and S. Riera i Viader, 'La lleuda de Barcelona del segle XII', *Estudis universitaris catalans* 26 (1984), 329–46. David Abulafia adduces further eloquent examples from the same coastline. Abulafia, 'Industrial Products: The Middle Ages', in *Prodotti e tecniche d'Oltremare nelle economie europee, secc. XIII–XVIII. XXIX Settimana dell'Istituto internazionale di storia economica 'F. Datini'* (Florence 1998), 333–58; repr. in *Mediterranean Encounters, Economic, Religious, Political, 1100–1550* (Aldershot 2000), v. 347 (*lezde* of Collioure and Perpignan); 348 (of Tortosa).

[37] For these see the extraordinary compilation of J. M. J. L. Mas Latrie, *Traités de paix et de commerce et documents divers concernant les relations des chrétiens avec les Arabes de l'Afrique septentrionale au moyen âge* (Paris, 1866).

hinterlands may both be discerned, and their connections plotted. Above all, what we see here is the piecemeal welding
together of a complex system out of the opportunities for taxation of a policy on the part of the rulers of this coastland, the
Counts of Barcelona.

Texts of this kind come from both sides of the religious
divide.[38] Indeed, the most remarkable is a document concerning—once again—the ports of the Nile delta, in the reign of
Saladin, towards the end of the twelfth century, the *Minhaj* of
al-Makhzumi, edited, translated and luculently interpreted 25
years ago by Claude Cahen.[39] The regulations for the ports of
Tinnis, Damietta, and Alexandria are set out at a period when a
new phase of change in fiscal institutions in the Mediterranean
of the later Middle Ages was only beginning, and they are
remarkably redolent, as Cahen observed, of Byzantine and ancient practice.[40] So much so, one may remark, that it is startling
to find a distinction between large and small ships being observed for which Cahen could find no medieval parallel but
which now evokes in the most vivid way the practice attested
in these same waters in the fifth century BC in the Elephantine
palimpsest.[41] It is no part of a comparativist vision to pursue
continuities, but this coincidence reminds us forcibly that bureaucracies are palimpsestic too, and the most insignificant foi-
bles of administrators may outlast ideologies and sceptres.

From the comparative perspective too we may be unsur-
prised to find that the Fatimid state was not remotely interested

---

[38] Anecdote of the civet merchant at Oran; R. Brunschvig (ed.), *Deux récits
de voyage inédits en Afrique du nord au XV siècle* (Publications de l'Institut
d'études orientales de la Faculté des lettres d'Alger, VII) (Paris, 1936), 130–3.

[39] C. Cahen, 'Douanes et commerce dans les ports méditerranéens de
l'Égypte médiévale d'après le Minhadj d'al-Makhzumi', *Journal of the Economic and Social History of the Orient* 7 (1965), 217–34.

[40] Ibid. 220: 'nous sommes en une période et une région où l'élaboration
des institutions et usages qui caractériseront le commerce Méditerranéen de la
fin du Moyen Age n'a pas encore détruit entièrement les traditions qui
peuvent, par l'intermédiaire de Byzance, remonter jusqu'à l'Antiquité.' The
document also mentions in passing the refuge ports of Rosetta and Nastaru.
Backward-looking elements include the presence of traders from Sardinia
(p. 235) and Gabala (North Syria); and we note the 'piggy-back' presence of
lower value trade in ships conveying higher value goods (pp. 233–4).

[41] Ibid. 234–5.

in promoting exports, and that it was concerned in its administration of trade only with the supply of strategically significant
materials and the revenues that it could raise at harbours.[42]
Even at Genoa, from which the richest late-medieval customs
records survive, there is no hint of the least protectionist intention in the management of harbour taxes before the fifteenth
century.[43] The same is naturally true of the Counts of Barcelona
in their manipulation of the privileges of different communities
against the background of the normal regime of customs exactions in their harbours: the development of naval capabilities, in
the age of the conquest of the Balearics, and the intrusions of
Christian states southward across the Ebro, and their immediate fiscal advantage, were prominent in their planning. But
what they can be seen most clearly to be doing is building the
edifice of their regional power on the interplay of advantages,
privileges, and opportunities in a fragmented and interconnected world. Another socioeconomic phenomenon which is
strongly promoted by customs institutions, which displays distinctively Mediterranean characteristics, and which is illustrated by comparable material from both ancient and medieval
periods, is therefore an essentially economic diplomacy.

The latter returns us to the theme proposed at the beginning
of the paper: the ways in which the study of the Mediterranean
environmental infrastructure supports and shapes the social
and political structures of the history of Mediterranean communities, small and—especially—large.

4. MANAGING INTERDEPENDENCE: THE NATURE OF THE NETWORK

The material so far presented reveals a cellular world of separate
productive communities interlinked by intricate webs of normal
exchange—an interdependence so usual and basic that it
required no encouragement, could be regarded as a rhythm

---

[42] Ibid. 264–5: 'le souci majeure du gouvernement égyptien est de se
procurer un certain nombre de denrées indispensables à son économie ou à
sa puissance; secondairement il cherche aussi à effectuer de fructueuses opér-
ations fiscales, mais il a tendance à considérer que toute marchandise emportée
par les étrangers appauvrit le pays auquel elle est prise.'

[43] J. Day, *Les douanes de Gênes, 1376–1377* (Paris, 1963), p. xi.

of nature to be exploited to the advantage of local accumu-
lators.[44] We have seen that such creative management of the
resource of taxable redistribution is already to be found in the
communities of the archaic Aegean. The *polis* was constrained
to have a fiscal identity by the realities of the Mediterranean
environment. The resource of redistribution encourages more
general thinking about solutions to the problems of risk outside
the immediate landscape. Why should we not extend our portfolio of resources to include springs, forests, pastures—or arable
lands and labour—in neighbouring microregions? The *polis*—
among many other things—was an institution accommodated to
being part of a large set of other places like it, to being the frame
within which rough equipollence was precariously shored up, to
policing balance in the mutual demands made within a constrained environment by competing producers under the
shadow of risk.

This constant renegotiation of autonomy had much more
famous consequences for Greek history; but it also took the
form of the invention of expedients for regulating the economic
competition and interaction of communities within a network.
It is important to recognize that the customs regime (*sensu lato*)
of a community was a crucial locus for the negotiation of dependence or freedom. Even in a world of notionally equal cities,
asymmetric privileges in this domain mapped out a hierarchy in
exquisitely delicate penmanship. Where a hegemony existed,
either of a dominant city, or of a kingdom or league, which
might dictate elements in the customs regime, the pattern of
immunities and liabilities enunciated propositions about the
relations of power in more explicit terms. Take Rome's treaty
with Ambracia, of 187 BC, in which it was declared that the
citizens of this important and potentially prosperous community 'might exact indirect taxes on the movement by land and
sea of commercial goods, provided that Roman citizens and
Latins should be exempted from them'.[45] Twenty years later,

---

[44] B. D. Shaw, 'Challenging Braudel: A New Vision of the Mediterranean',
JRA 14 (2001), 419–53, at 424, uses the happy metaphor of valence to describe
this interdependence.
[45] Livy 38. 44. 4: 'ut . . . portoria quae vellent terra marique caperent dum
eorum immunes Romani ac socii nominis Latini essent.'

the Delian *ateleia* and the discomfiture of Rhodes are the most famous example of this form of behaviour.[46]

Just as political autonomy was always relative, zealously pursued because it was so vulnerable, so economic autarky was a dream in a world in which interdependence was essential. It is clear, therefore, that customs and harbour dues were essentially a levy upon interdependence. *Autarkeia*, if it could be achieved, would have the result of diminishing them to nothing. It is therefore consistent of Plato and Aristotle to promote both an autarkic vision of the polis and a *vision anti-prosodique* (the eloquent term is Raymond Descat's).[47] That said, we can distinguish at least two ethical themes in the wish to tax interdependence. One is the sumptuary—that it is better to control levels of consumption by moving towards autarky. The less obvious one is the view that our harbours—and by extension our producers and consumers—constitute a resource belonging to us which outsiders should not be permitted to benefit from without payment.[48]

This reasoning appears in the link which was sometimes made between *ellimenia*, taxes on seaborne redistribution, and *epinomia*, pasturage taxes.[49] In the latter, the uncultivated hillsides of the territory are made available either to citizens or to outsiders who will benefit from the animals that have been

---

[46] Polybius 30. 31.

[47] A. Bresson, 'Aristote et le commerce extérieur', *Revue des Études Anciennes* 89 (1987), 217–38; repr. in *La cité marchande* (Bordeaux, 2000), 109–30; cf. L. Judson, 'Aristotle on fair exchange', *Oxford Studies in Ancient Philosophy* 15 (1997), 147–75 , also C. Pébarthe, 'Fiscalité, empire athénien, et écriture: retour sur les causes de la guerre de Péloponnèse', *ZPE* 129 (2000), 47–76, at 71 on *Pol.* 7 1327a, with A. Descat, 'La cité grecque et les échanges: Un retour à Hasebroek', in J. Andreau, P. Briant, and A. Descat, (eds.), *Les échanges dans l'antiquité: Le rôle de l'état. Entretiens d'archéologie et d'histoire* (Saint-Bertrand-des-Comminges, 1994), 11–30, at 18, criticism of the *vision prosodique*.

[48] J. France, 'Les revenus douaniers', 95–114, at 95, for the autarkic spirit in city-based customs regimes.

[49] Pasturage taxes as parallel for *ellimenia*: J. H. Thiel, 'Zu altgriechischen Gebühren', *Klio* 20 (1926), 54–67 is one of the key items of bibliography, but Pleket, 'Notes', was right to take him to task and might well have gone further. Papadakis, *Archaiologikon Deltion* (1923), 192: Acraephia grants Kallon *epinomia* for 50 goats/sheep. Kallon is probably an Acraephian. Cf. Thiel on Eubulus of Orchomenos.

grazed there. The comparison between harbours and pastures has appeared odd to scholars attempting to impose modern taxonomies of taxation on the ancient world, but makes considerable sense when the problems of survival in the Mediterranean environment are considered as a whole.[50] This was a world in which risk in essentially fragmented landscapes is countered above all through the myriad forms of interdependence that connectivity makes possible. Pastoralism, with its frequent requirement of mobility, is an essential element in Mediterranean agrosystems, and it is quite natural that levies on it should be juxtaposed in the fiscal *mentalité* with those on the seaborne redistribution which is taxed in harbours. The analogy also reminds us that for all the crucial importance of normal redistribution by sea, the interdependence of Mediterranean communities involved their terrestrial neighbours too. The assets of a microregion included not only harbours, but mountain passes and land routeways.[51]

The spotlight of the Greek evidence thus illuminates a remarkable world of maritime interconnectedness, made up of hundreds of local clusters of consumers and producers, each netted with the others, near and far, by exchanges through their outlets to the sea, occasionally built-harbours, more often sheltered coves or convenient beaches. That spotlight shines because of a group of cultural attitudes—the ethical concerns with economic issues of the community and its leaders, the sometimes diffident but always potent orientation of early Greek culture toward the sea, that intensity of community self-definition through the interplay of individuality and imitation which we think of as characteristic of the early history of the *polis*. The spotlight appears for what it is in a text such as the delineation of the key subjects for deliberation in Book 1 of Aristotle's

[50] L. Nixon and S. R. F. Price, 'The size and resources of Greek cities', in O. Murray and S. R. F. Price (eds.), *The Greek City from Homer to Alexander* (Oxford, 1990), 166, called for more investigation of the economic relationship between *poleis*, instead of a preoccupation with *autarkeia*, and used harbour taxes to show that such relationships were important.

[51] A striking individual case has recently been examined in a straggly ancient village on the pass between Pisidia and Pamphylia, where a gate—a literal gateway—for customs duties obstructed the Via Sebaste, beside a Roman milestone, still preserved in situ, and a couple of hero shrines: *Journal of Hellenic Studies Archaeological Reports* 45 (1999), 173.

Rhetoric, where imports and exports hold their own alongside other revenue, war and peace, defence, and legislation.[52]

Within the world so delineated, it may be easier to make sense of the problem of ancient states' *politique douanière*. On the one hand, ancient communities saw the intricate play of taxes on mobility as part of *oikonomia*, within which they were very alert to the opportunities and the pitfalls, just as they were in other sections of the struggle for survival in a risky environment. On the other, their priorities were wholly different from those of modern states. The epigraphic and papyrus evidence for revenue extraction from maritime redistribution exhibits what Julie Vélissaropoulos called 'l'indifférence envers le commerce en tant que tel'.[53] The most important proposition is simple and unexpected: it is indeed a central element of the tax morphology that we are looking at that exports were taxed too.[54] Taxing what you need to survive and what you produce in exchange for it, even at such a low rate, has rightly been seen as essentially oppressive, especially in a world in which, in Guiraud's words, 'states produced little of what they needed and consumed little of what they produced'; but it is characteristically Mediterranean in its tendency to regard all movement of goods and people as an undifferentiated, generalized phenomenon.[55]

The Caunus law spectacularly confirms this point. This was a regulation of a more-or-less independent city. Although it seems, even in post-*Ancient Economy* days, counterintuitive, the Caunians were happy enough about taxing their own citizens, until the benefaction which was the subject of the particular inscription; and they had no compunction at all about taxing their own exports.[56] Neither is there any trace of awareness that a city like Caunus, which does not have an unusually large, varied, or fertile territory, is bound to depend for its

[52] Aristotle, *Rhet.* 1. 4. 7. cf. 11.

[53] J.Vélissaropoulos, *Les nauclères grecs: Recherches sur les institutions maritimes en Grèce et dans l'Orient hellénisé* (Geneva, 1980), 231.

[54] See for instance Eupolis, *Autolycus*, the *ellimenion* which you have to pay before you go. Cahen, 'Douanes', emphasizes this in a medieval context.

[55] Andreades, *History*, 141. P. Guiraud, *La main-d'oeuvre industrielle dans l'ancienne Grèce* (Paris, 1900), 72.

[56] A payment of 60,000 *denarii* yielding 7,200 in interest was sufficient for the relief commemorated.

survival at least at some times, on what is imported through the harbour. But it was not the primary purpose of the law to tax trade, let alone to foster a commercial policy. Customs dues in general concerned the regime of imports and exports to each city community, and they took the ideal of self-sufficiency as their basic principle.

In the Greek and Roman city, then, we see a very developed response to Mediterranean conditions. Despite the difficulties of the evidence, the density of the interconnections, the mesh of the net, and the critical mass of the connectivity, all appear plainly. But the underlying logic of the exactions, and the network which they trace, is not unique to the ancient city, since it is plainly apparent in the medieval examples which we have noted. It remains to explore certain contexts in which these systems have been developed on a much larger and more integrated scale, and to investigate how those too relate to the question of the distinctiveness of Mediterranean history.

5. PROGRESSIVE REGRESSION?

The minimalist view that harbour taxes are another reason for playing down the overall significance of ancient commerce has been prominent in their discussion: 'one should not underestimate the ubiquitous harbour taxes', and so on.[57] 'The whole tax structure was regressive, and became increasingly so as the years went on', it was claimed.[58] Progressive regressiveness— something of a *reductio ad absurdum* of the teleological view of history! The alternative view is that the vigour of ancient redistribution was such that it made light of burdens of this kind, which demonstrate the buoyancy of ancient trade rather than explaining its weakness. In fact, the deleterious effect of customs barriers is a venerable historical commonplace which is no longer current in the historiography of post-Classical periods. Thus, on the middle and upper Rhine, where until Napoleon there were 39 toll stations, mainly between Mainz and Cologne, these can be exonerated from responsibility for the decline in

---

[57] Finley, *Ancient Economy*, 175; 159, cf. 164.
[58] Ibid. 165.

the economic fortunes of the waterway.[59] More generally, it is nearly twenty years since Braudel formulated a similar point about early modern economies in general.[60] We may also observe that one of the most interesting data derived from the Caunus inscription is the revelation that local customs dues did not greatly affect the *caboteur*.[61] The trader did not usually pay duty on goods in transit. Even unsold goods that he had clearly intended to sell were usually not liable, if his stay was a relatively short one. This principle, which finds close parallels in commercial treaties of the Middle Ages, mitigates the problem of how the normal commercial activity of ancient time, the *basso continuo* of *cabotage*, of coastwise tramping trade, in small boats with mixed cargoes hopping from one anchorage to the next, survived both the notorious unpredictability of route in Mediterranean navigation, and the propensity of every harbour, however small, to charge customs dues.[62] There is clear

[59] T. Scott, *Regional Identity and Economic Change: The Upper Rhine, 1450–1600* (Oxford, 1997), 293–5, following U. Dirlmeier, 'Mittelaltliche Zoll- und Stapelrechte als Handelhemnisse', in H. Pohl (ed.), *Die Auswirkungen von Zöllen und anderen Handelshemnissen auf Wirtschaft und Gesellschaft vom Mittelalter bis zum Gegenwart (Vierteljahrschrift für Sozial- und Wirtschaftsgeschichte* Suppl. 80) (Stuttgart, 1987), 19–39.

[60] Braudel, *Civilization and Capitalism*, 289–90.

[61] The phrase is *paragogimon phortion*. The issue discussed by Cicero, *Att.* 2. 16. 4, the *portorium circumvectionis* in Asia, may be related. His researches found no reason why this duty should be payable—which would not necessarily prevent him from pleading the cause of the *publicani*. It looks as if the latter had opportunistically attempted, perhaps in some specific context, to impose this extra duty, damaging, as Cicero perceives, to both *negotiatores* and the Graeci of the whole province. E. M. Harris, 'Notes on the New Grain-tax law', *ZPE* 128 (1999), 269–72, postulates that we are dealing here with a diagoge or transit tax, a specially interesting instance of harbour dues. For the distinction between *exagoge* (import–export tax) and *diagoge*, Vélissaropoulos, *Les nauclères*, 205–31.

[62] In recent papers, David Abulafia has presented a number of cases which demonstrate how essential the notably complex world of *cabotage* is to our understanding of high commerce in the later Middle Ages. D. Abulafia, 'Industrial Products'; and above all id., 'L'economia mercantile nel Mediterraneo occidentale (1390 *ca*—1460 *ca*): Commercio locale e a lunga distanza nell'età di Lorenzo il Magnifico', *Schola Salernitana* 2 (1997), 21–41: repr. in *Mediterranean Encounters* (Aldershot, 2000). He also makes clear how important it is to study the exchanges of smaller centres: id., 'East and West: Comments on the Commerce of the City of Ancona in the Middle Ages', in

testimony of smuggling, and no doubt taxes on mobility were unpopular, and both evaded and avoided; but the fact remains that, like piracy, they attest a world of high intensity redistribution rather than diagnosing the causes of its absence.

It is not easy to say whether most traders paid more on average as fiscal systems became larger and more complex with the increasing cultural and political integration of the Mediterranean coastlands from the Classical Greek to the Roman Imperial period, the theme to which we now briefly turn. But, even if that were the case, few would say that this period exhibits any signs of exchange suffering from increasing burdens.

6.   ATHENS AND ROME: MEDITERRANEAN AND OTHER HEGEMONIES

Intensification of production can be achieved by managing redistribution better, which may involve an increase in institutional complexity, even a move in the direction of bureaucracy; but it may also involve the pursuit of wider networks with which to engage, and better terms on which to engage with them. These intensifications might be pursued by single producers or by groups; but developing them was also one of the possible functions of the collective institutions of the *polis*. Institutional inventiveness combined with what one might call 'fiscal superfetation' as an opportunistic intensification, in a case which is becoming clearer with the steady publication of new inscriptions: the island of Thasos.[63]

The legislators of Thasos were clearly concerned with an economic portfolio which comprised their city, their island, its *peraia*, their interactions with their independent neighbours,

---

M. P. Ghezzo, (ed.), *Atti e memorie della società Dalmata di storia patria 26. Città e sistema adriatico alla fine del Medioevo. Bilancio degli studi e prospettive di ricerca* (Venice, 1997), 49–66; repr. in *Mediterranean Encounters* (Aldershot, 2000), 50.

[63] *IG* XII, Suppl. 345 (the late fifth-century *karpologoi*) (very fragmentary, but clearly commercial), with D. C. Gofas, 'Les carpologues de Thasos', *Bulletin de Correspondance Hellénique* 93 (1969), 337–70; *SEG* 18, 347 (the boustrophedon law, *c*.480 BC).; *IG* XII, Suppl. 347, with F. Salviat, 'Le vin de Thasos: amphores, vin et sources écrites', in Y. Garlan and J.-Y. Empereur (eds.), *Recherches sur les amphores grecs* (*Bulletin de Correspondance Hellénique*, Suppl. 13) (Paris 1986), 145–96.

and indeed in one remarkable statement, all seafaring within their zone of the northern Aegean. This is a typically complex hinterland, partly maritime. Customs regulations are all too often studied in isolation, in relation to a single port. But the whole point about them, as our post-Classical examples have shown, is that they are a subtle instrument for shaping interactions between harbours, and so creating networks. Through advantages won in the formation of such webs of reciprocal support regulating the taxation of movement becomes an extremely flexible and sophisticated way for extending the environmental catchment of the community.

There is a much more substantial testimony to this aspect of Classical Greek community behaviour, which shows us the next level up of extending the networks shaped by control of movement of people and things. Thasos has been widely cited as parallel and to an extent precursor of the maritime hegemony of the Athenians. In the desperate crisis of 413 BC, when they were fully engaged in Sicily, and with the Spartan occupation of Dekeleia seriously incommoding them at home, the Athenians radically altered the central structure of their imperial revenues. Abolishing, at a stroke, the *phoros*, the exactions which we usually call 'tribute', and which had been the distinctive fiscal feature of their dominion, they replaced it with a demand for monies levied by member states of the alliance on the goods that passed through their territories by sea.

Thucydides, who is our only source for the measure, states simply that:

as a result [sc. of the effort of taking on another commitment the size of the war against Sparta in Sicily, as well as hanging on for 17 years in the war at home] combined with the considerable damage which was being done at that time from Dekeleia, and with their other expenses rising, the Athenians became financially incapacitated, and at this time imposed on their subjects a tax of one twentieth on goods moved by sea instead of the *phoros*, taking the view that more money would be raised for them in this way. For their expenses were not like they had been before, but had increased greatly, as the war had grown, and their revenues had disappeared.[64]

There are many problems connected with this remarkable passage which must be passed over here. One important con-

---

[64] Thucydides 7. 28. 4.

clusion, however, is that the Athenians knew that there was no member-state, however small, which did not have the machinery and the ambition to collect at least some monies in this way by 413 BC. The bulk of their tribute too had derived from numerous small contributions from tiny states.[65] It is also a very valuable acquisition that the Athenians felt themselves capable of calculating approximate figures involved, for some 200 separate communities. It is also apparent that they cannot have thought that this measure would bring them less revenue than had the *phoros*, which suggests high levels of taxable commerce in the late fifth-century Aegean.[66] It also seems likely to indicate the relative indifference of traders to burdens of this kind. Consider two propositions: 'The Athenians, perceiving that the levying of tribute was costly and unpopular, resolved instead to rest their future fortunes on the appropriation of the monies which were extorted from ailing traders whose livelihoods were already on the line because of intervention of this sort'; and 'the Athenians, looking for a relatively painless and guaranteed throughput of funds resolved to tax the dynamism inherent in the circulation of goods on which all ancient states depended.' I know which I find more plausible.

The Aristotelian *Athenian Constitution* makes a famous statement of the nature of Athenian power: Athens could maintain (*trephesthai*—that is feed, sustain) 20,000 people on its fiscal base.[67] There follows a long list of those maintained at public expense. The money came from *phoroi*, naturally; but also from

---

[65] Nixon and Price, 'The Size'. L. Kallet-Marx, *Money, Expense, and Naval Power in Thucydides' History 1–5.24* (Berkeley, 1993), 8, also stresses small contributors, and recognizes the different logic of their relationship with the imperial power.

[66] It is therefore generally agreed that the yield of the empire's harbour taxes must be approximately equal to the attested size of the tribute over the immediately previous years. A simple multiplication sum should give the historian a datum fit to conjure with: the notional value of all goods moving in the Athenian *arche* outside the Piraeus and the other ports of Attica.

[67] *Ath.Pol.* 24. 3, with P. J. Rhodes, *Commentary*, more cautious than Pébarthe, 'Fiscalité', at 48, with n. 17. What is meant by *trephesthai*? Not 'bénéficier' (Pébarthe, 49). 1 talent sufficed for 20 citizens p.a. at this rate: L. Foxhall and H. Forbes, '*Sitometreia*: The Role of Grain as a Staple Food in Classical Antiquity', *Chiron* 12 (1982), 41–90. The yield of Piraeus would have 'maintained' 720 citizens.

tele, which certainly includes the revenues from harbours. The text is most valuable as a glimpse of a way of thinking about money and power: *prosodoi* make possible high population. There was a clear link between communications and *euandria*. Such arithmetic was a commonly practised form of rhetoric about Athenian finance and policy, and *tele* are central to it. Passages like this do much to illuminate the nature of thalassocracy—a concept much used but more seldom anatomized.

The most important point, however, for this argument, is the powerful sense that this episode gives us of the normality, regularity, ubiquity, and importance of the practice of taxing seaborne redistribution—and that we are in the presence not simply of some contingent fiscal practices, but of a veritable tax morphology. The Athenian expedient of 413 BC displays on a large scale the place of the fiscal control of mobility in contemporary thought about interdependence. The widespread later conformity to a standard two per cent due also suggests that local practices in this regard had already started to converge— an example of those maritime social and cultural forms which display curiously widespread similarities in other periods of Mediterranean history.[68] By the Hellenistic period, many of these practices and precedents were encapsulated in that body of principles which we usually call the Rhodian Sea Law, a third-century BC body of norms and regulations and statements of general practice for seafaring in the Eastern Mediterranean. It is likely that we have substantial quotations from this material in the Caunus inscription, which cites a *demosionikos nomos*, a 'public contract law'.

Conquest (that is, incorporation into a power structure), it still needs to be said, does not mean annexation, and no one in antiquity expected it to: 'la possession d'une terre à la suite d'une guerre n'entraînait pas nécessairement une occupation mais plutôt une administration de celle-ci destiné à tirer des revenus.'[69] In particular, as should always have been clear from a proper understanding of Thucydides, Athenian imperial

---

[68] H. Francotte, *Les finances des cités grecques* (Liège, 1909), 12, notes the curious uniformity of the 2% tax across different communities.

[69] C. Pébarthe, 'Thasos, l'Empire d'Athènes et les emporia de Thrace', *ZPE* 126 (1999), 121–54, at 133.

power in the fifth century was presented and perceived as a fiscal entity, to which indirect taxation was a matter of the highest importance.[70] We need only cite the Athenian willingness to take over from the Thasians the fruits of their interests in the Thasian *peraia*,[71] and their interest in taking control of certain specially favoured locations for seaborne transit and the extortion of tolls there, the classic instances of this being naturally the Hellespont and Bosporus.[72] The reform of the tribute in 413 BC should have occasioned no surprise. Thalassocracy entailed control of all the things that the sea meant to those who were united by it, and dependent on it. Customs dues are intrinsic to regional as well as to local power.

At the same time, although it embraced the whole Aegean, the Athenian hegemony was still, like the medieval powers we have noted briefly, ruling through its disposition of a diverse portfolio of resources, comprising hundreds of individual localities, each with its own specialities, resources, perennial problems, and distinctive patterns of production, and—crucially— through its control of their interdependence and its modalities. In other words, the nature of this dominion was very markedly shaped by the underlying realities of distinctively Mediterranean existence.

The same opportunism in the dealing out or sequestering of the yields from local resources, productive or redistributive, is clearly apparent in the imperial fiscal politics of Republican Rome, whether we look at the notorious example of Rhodes in the second century or at the management of the Attalid system of customs dues in Asia as we now understand it from the *Monumentum Ephesenum*. And the central significance of duties of this kind to perceptions of Roman power is easy to

---

[70] Pébarthe, 'Fiscalité', 147–9. For Thucydides and fiscality, Kallet-Marx, *Money, Expense*; also lately L. J. Samons, *Empire of the Owl: Athenian Imperial Finance* (Stuttgart, 2000).

[71] This much Pébarthe has certainly shown, e.g. 'Thasos', 140, etc., with his discussion of *nemesthai*. But he did need to prove it at length—which rather shows up his 'ce qui était rappelons-le le but de la guerre, comme Thucydide l'écrivait clairement' (p. 142)!

[72] Demosthenes 34; for Alcibiades in the Bosporus: Polybius 4. 44, Xen. *Hell*. 1. 1. 22, Diod. Sic. 13. 64. 2.

attest—from Cicero's recognition, for instance, that Rome's imperial hegemony was hated for its arrogant display of power and for the economic advantage that it drew from it through the system of *portoria*: the insignia of our magistrates are hated, our name is bitter in their mouths, our taxes and duties—like death.[73] The yield of interdependence continued, the Mediterranean environment being what it was, to be one of the most important and flexible pieces in the game of economic diplomacy.

Some have seen an important transition from civic autarky to imperial fiscality in the early Roman empire.[74] This should not, however, be envisaged as a part of a grand narrative of the erosion of local power by larger hegemony. Rather, local fiscal self-determination in the ancient world was always in tension with the demands, more or less urgent, more or less imperative, of a wider frame. The fiscal was one of the most important domains on which the unifying, ordering, controlling forces of supra-regional integrative hegemony might operate. Within that operation, it was normal for pluralism—the patchwork fiscality which we observed in the Classical Greek Mediterranean—to subsist.[75] Rather than building grand administrative structures or conceiving of novel fiscal schemata, the Romans continued, albeit on a larger scale than ever before, to adapt the rhythms and opportunities that they found, granting the enjoyment of the fruits of harbour dues to certain cities, even handing out major new opportunities, as when Marius donated to Massalia the right to tax movements on his new canal at the mouth of the Rhône, but reserving for the ruling power the yield of major nodes in the network of movements of goods and people.[76] So France has been able to show that in Gaul it was

---

[73] Cicero, *Flacc.* 19: 'odio sunt nostrae secures, nomen acerbitati, scriptura, decumae, portorium morti'.

[74] France, *Quadragesima* 11–12, for Gaul.

[75] S. Mrozek, 'Le fonctionnement des fondations dans les provinces occidentales et l'économie de crédit à l'époque du Haut-Empire romain', *Latomus* 59 (2000), 327–45, argues interestingly for a microregional distribution of credit trust in the empire, reflected in the incidence of foundations. This fiscal patchwork is recognizably the same texture as the one I am trying to evoke here.

[76] *Fossae Marianae* toll: Strabo 4. 18; Plutarch, *Marius* 15. 4.

the age-old routeways that formed the basis of Augustus' system for taxing trade, and that there was no attempt to put into place either a province-wide customs system, or, in all probability, a general frontier tariff at the edge of the Roman empire.[77] At the symbolic heart of the empire, Rome maintained its separate status on the fiscal map by operating a custom barrier around its own urban periphery. This is usually taken to be a levy on inbound goods, but given the concerns of the emperors with the provisioning of the city, it is worth considering the possibility that it was aimed at merchants who had bought goods from the huge stocks shipped in to Rome for resale elsewhere in Italy or still further afield. In that case the singularity of Rome's economic geography would be effectively displayed.[78]

Certainly the advantages to any community of drawing its own revenues from this source were never forgotten, even at the height of centralization and Roman imperial order, and in the fourth century of our era the right to do so was restored in many cities. Rome's system, as the epigraphic dossier grows, seems ever less systematic—and ever more Mediterranean!

7.   THE EDGES OF THE SYSTEM: CONCLUSION

There is, then, a spectrum of power derived from controlling the resources of the network of redistribution through taxation. The higher positions on that spectrum may derive from the extent and comprehensiveness of the control, from the size of the network and the efficiency of the institutions of exaction. But they may also derive from certain specially significant gateways: the Hellespont or the Rhône valley, the harbours of Piraeus, Smyrna, or Byzantium, the Alpine passes or the Isthmus of Suez, the desert routeways or the Vardar corridor, the Strait of Messina or the Cilician Gates. But a share for a

---

[77] France, *Quadragesima*, 347, no repeated payments; 450 for the main conclusion, the E–W barrier line; 266 for taxes on main axes.

[78] R. E. A. Palmer, 'Customs on Market Goods Imported into the City of Rome', *Memoirs of the American Academy in Rome* 36 (1980), 217–34, gives a rather complicated account of these duties, about which unfortunately little can be said with certainty.

Mediterranean community in the control of such access points was only the biggest prize in a sequence which started with the only sheltered beach on the most unpromising island, and it is vital to acknowledge the whole sequence if we are to understand any part of it. Some of these gateways are interior to a recognizably Mediterranean world: but an interesting and important group—major transition points such as Palmyra, Pelusium, or Zarai, or the zone from the Pyrenees to the Alpine passes which was the object of the Roman tax of the *Quadragesima Galliarum*—derived their significance from their role in mediating the world of Mediterranean production and consumption to the ecologically distinct regions which abut the Mediterranean to north, east, and south.[79] In this sense, the whole Mediterranean region functions on the largest of scales like the microregions of which it is composed, offering its surpluses in return for those of its neighbours; neighbours which can however, through this logic, be seen as essentially different from the Mediterranean world.[80]

This difference is apparent in the tax morphology which we are discussing. No one can deny that the states of west and south Asia beyond the Mediterranean or those of northern Europe in the Middle Ages, taxed mobility. But there is a difference in the place of this exaction in the fiscal scheme and in the economic history of the regions, a difference which the Greeks already recognized in making a schematic distinction between *polis*-economies and 'satrapal' ones. In the well-known economic taxonomy of pseudo-Aristotle, there are four types of fiscal system: royal, satrapal, city, and individual. In the satrapal there are six kinds of revenue, in order of importance, from land, the tithe; from materials, gold, silver, and bronze; from trade; from overland trade and market dues; on pasturage, called *epikarpia* or tithe; and on persons.[81] In the city there

---

[79] Customs duties and the boundary of the Mediterranean: the *arabarchia*, with *IGRR* 1, 1183, the Coptos tariff of AD 90. France, *Quadragesima*.

[80] For the ways in which the highly complex and variable edge of the Mediterranean region promotes its inherent fragmentation and interdependency, see Purcell, 'The Boundless Sea'.

[81] Pseudo-Aristotle, *Oec.* 1426 a. On the satrapal mode of taxation, Andreades, *History of Greek Public Finance*. See also some extremely helpful pages by C. Nicolet, *Tributum: Recherches sur la fiscalité directe sous la*

are three, also in order of importance, from individuals in the territory, from trade and *diagogai*, and from *enkuklia*.

We have already suggested that these fiscal *polis*-institutions are in fact in a broader sense Mediterranean ones, and not to be regarded as distinctive to Hellenism, though it remains an intriguing thought that the Greeks should base an economic theory of the difference between free cities and tribute-exacting despotisms in part on a fiscal criterion deriving from the environment. It may further be supposed that, beyond the Mediterranean, taxing mobility takes rather different forms which are to be predicated of many systems other than the Achaemenid one which the Greeks knew best. In fact, there is some evidence that the Persian state adapted its exactions to the Mediterranean world. The arrangements for taxing redistribution at the Canopic mouth of the Nile seem to owe more to the Egyptian, Saïte, practice, than they do to Achaemenid precedent.[82] When faced with ruling coastlands, the Persian empire adapted to the distinctive opportunities offered by the *parathalassia*.[83] The extension under the Roman Republic and empire of a regime of *portoria* to non-Mediterranean zones could be seen as the imitation of the continental imperial behaviour of earlier powers combined with the development of institutions built out of local networks of redistribution taxation by kingdoms such as Pergamon.[84]

république romaine (Bonn, 1976), 8–11. For the possibility that the thought involved derives ultimately from Ephoros, L. Cracco Ruggini, 'Eforo nello Pseudo-Aristotele, *Oec.* II', *Athenaeum* 53 (1966), 199–236. See also O. Murray, 'Ho archaios dasmos', *Historia* 15 (1966), 142–56.

[82] Briant and Descat, 'Un registre'; nothing resembling customs dues is to be found in the survey of the west-Asian antecedents of Achaemenid practice by C. Zaccagnini, 'Prehistory of the Achaemenid tributary system', in *Le Tribut dans l'Empire Perse* (Paris, 1989), 193–215. Cf. also G. Posener, *Les Douanes de la Méditerranée dans l'Egypte Saïte* (Paris, 1947).

[83] See H. T. Wallinga, 'Persian Tribute and Delian Tribute', in *Le Tribut dans l'Empire Perse* (Paris, 1989), 173–81, for the portfolios of different exactions in Persian coastlands and in the Athenian empire.

[84] J. De Laet, *Portorium: Etude sur l'organisation douanière chez les romains, surtout à l'époque du haut-empire* (Bruges, 1949), is still basic; the link with Hellenistic practice is shown by the new Ephesus regulation of the *portoria* of Asia: H. Engelmann and D. Knibbe, 'Das Zollgesetz der Provinz Asia: Eine neue Inschrift aus Ephesos', *Epigraphica Anatolica* 14 (1989), 1–206 (= *SEG* 39, 1180); for imperial *portoria* see further France, *Quadragesima*, 205–27.

But my principal provisional conclusion is of course that tax morphology maps a historical congruity within the Mediterranean that stretches from the late Bronze Age to the Renaissance, and which—again—seems to distinguish a Mediterranean historical object from its neighbours. The explanation lies in the durability of a distinctive set of economic and social relations deriving from the opportunities offered by high connectivity in a fragmented, risky environment: in durability of a set of relations—but not, let us be clear, in immemorial continuities. The resemblances which we can trace in the morphology of levies on interdependence are based on the regeneration and recreation of fluid and responsive patterns of behaviour.[85] The opportunism of the people who produced for redistribution, those who moved what they produced, those who taxed what was moved, and those who built their power on the proceeds of those taxes, was founded on a highly developed capacity for adaptation. Bewildering change in the patterns of population, production, consumption, and hegemony, are not mere accidental hindrances to making sense of Mediterranean history, but part of its distinctiveness.[86]

The study of this tax morphology, bridging the gap, as I have argued it must, between the microregional foundations and the organization of social and political systems on even a very large scale, would, among other things, begin to offer a way of using an economic anthropology alongside other aspects of anthropology in the pursuit of a distinctively Mediterranean history. It would also invite us to consider other structural comparanda across the longer term in Mediterranean history—overseas settlements, trading communities, allotment of land, and so on. Indeed, the morphology of the exaction of indirect taxes is likely to be one of the fields in which networks and phases of overseas settlement have individual characteristics.[87] And none of these can be understood without reference to the sea.

---

[85] Cahen, 'Douanes', 226, on change; on the other hand, for the establishment of regular rhythms, Briant and Descat, 'Un registre', 73.

[86] The 'differences that resemble each other': Horden and Purcell, *CS* 52 and ch.III.

[87] This point is developed further in Purcell, 'Colonization and Mediterranean History'.

'Customs houses', says Boccaccio, in the passage quoted above, are found 'in all the marine lands which have a harbour': *terre marine*, a beautiful oxymoron which in two words holds one of the keys to the individuality of history *of* the Mediterranean—not so much the body of water that is located in the middle of the lands, but the cluster of lands whose history has been uniquely adapted to the life of the sea.

The Archaeology of Knowledge

10

Travel and Experience in the Mediterranean of Louis XV

Christopher Drew Armstrong

1. INTRODUCTION

Travel in Enlightenment culture was seen as differing essentially from travel in earlier periods.[1] Circumscribed by extensive commercial and diplomatic networks, travel took place within an administrative framework that facilitated the gathering of knowledge around the world.[2] Transformed by the development of new navigational technologies—specifically the invention of the marine chronometer and mathematically rigorous cartography—the relationship between the traveller and the environment could be plotted with an unprecedented degree of certainty. While knowledge of the world remained fragmentary, it was possible nonetheless to fully apprehend the extent of missing geographic information and to imagine a future state when a complete understanding of the earth's geography would be realized through the efforts of scientific travellers. As Georges-Louis Leclerc, comte de Buffon, noted with cautious optimism in 1749: 'L'astronomie & l'art de la navigation sont portés à un si haut point de perfection, qu'on peut raisonnablement espérer d'avoir un jour une connoissance exacte de la surface entière du globe.'[3] Throughout the eighteenth century,

[1] See B. M. Stafford, *Voyage into Substance. Art, Science, Nature, and the Illustrated Travel Account, 1760–1840* (Cambridge, Mass., 1984); J. Stagl, *A History of Curiosity: The Theory of Travel 1550–1800* (Chur, 1995).

[2] On the French consular network in the eighteenth century, see A. Mézin, *Les Consuls de France au siècle des Lumières (1715–1792)* (Paris, 1997).

[3] Georges-Louis Leclerc, comte de Buffon, *Histoire naturelle, général et particulière* (Paris, 1749), i. 225.

the apparatus of commercial administrations and the impact of new scientific techniques were nowhere more apparent than in representations of the Mediterranean Sea.

This chapter examines the emergence in the mid-eighteenth century of a new model for conceptualizing the properties of cognition based on the concept of the scientific traveller-observer or *voyageur-philosophe*, in contrast to the more dominant but static *camera obscura* model of visual perception.[4] In the Mediterranean Sea, the idea of travel as a dynamic form of perception emerges against the backdrop of cartographic missions coordinated by the French Ministry of Maritime Affairs and in the context of private, proto-archaeological missions to the Levant. The ground-breaking work of the French architect Julien-David Leroy on the ruins of Greece (1758; 2nd edn. 1770) and the British scholar Robert Wood on the poetry of Homer (1767; 2nd edn. 1769) are two important examples of a radical reinterpretation of antiquity based on the model of the *voyageur-philosophe*, emphasizing the subjectivity of judgement and the primacy of individual points of view in analysis and representation.

2. CONSTRUCTING THE SCIENTIFIC TRAVELLER-OBSERVER

Following the creation of the Royal Society in 1660 and the Académie Royale des Sciences in 1666, the need for a new form of specialized, itinerant researcher or traveller-observer rapidly emerged as an essential component of these institutions. Before the invention of such categories as the archaeologist and the scientific explorer in the nineteenth century, the combined activities of travel and research encompassed a more disparate range of objectives and practitioners. Variations in the competence and scrupulousness with which travel accounts were produced undermined the principal objective of scientific enquiry,

---

[4] See J. Crary, *Techniques of the Observer* (Cambridge, Mass., 1990), 25–66. The idea of the *voyageur-philosophe* might be contrasted with the idea of the 'romantic traveller' of the nineteenth century. See R. Cardinal, 'Romantic Travel', in R. Porter (ed.), *Rewriting the Self: Histories from the Renaissance to the Present* (London and New York, 1997), 135–55.

the ability of the sedentary scholar to judge the veracity of data gathered by travellers.

The heightened significance of travel as a form of scientific research required that travellers be properly instructed in contemporary techniques of information gathering. To this end, a set of nine instructions drawn up by the astronomer and mathematician Lawrence Rooke (1622–62) were published in the *Philosophical Transactions* of the Royal Society in 1666.[5] Rooke was interested exclusively in phenomena with direct applications to navigation and cartography, necessitating that the scientific traveller-observer sound depths, describe coasts, and record tides. Instruments were to be used (a clock, a magnetic compass), the method was to be described and the latitude and longitude of observations were to be recorded. Unlike the Humanist traveller of the Renaissance, the scientific traveller-observer of the Enlightenment was to be accountable and nothing was to be taken on authority.

A distinct set of instructions by Robert Boyle (1627–1691) appeared in the *Philosophical Transactions* a few months after those by Rooke, in which the author established a much wider field of enquiry, encompassing all manner of phenomena both natural and human.[6] Boyle's 'General Heads of a Natural History of a Country, Great or Small' was but a précis of a more extensive set of instructions that were a *summa* of the Royal Society's general objectives: 'to study Nature rather than Books, and from Observations, made of the Phænomena and Effects she presents, to compose such a History of Her, as may hereafter serve to build a Solid and Useful Philosophy upon'.[7] Like Rooke, Boyle insisted that the traveller-observer first determine the longitude and latitude of the places visited, in order that all other data could be plugged into a universal, mathematically rigorous system.

The instructions of the Royal Society were a model that remained useful well into the eighteenth century and were reprinted in a number of important collections of travel literature. Rooke's nine 'Directions' were published in full as part of

[5] *Philosophical Transactions* no. 8 (8 Jan. 1665/6), 141.
[6] Ibid., no. 11 (2 April 1666), 186–9.
[7] Ibid., no. 8 (8 Jan. 1665/6), 141.

the 'Introductory Discourse' of each edition of Churchill's popular *Collection of Voyages and Travels*.[8] To these were added lists of instruments that would permit the traveller-observer to quantify phenomena and to verify the work of his predecessors:

Every Traveller ought to carry about him several sorts of Measures, to take the Dimensions of such things as require it; a Watch by which, and the Pace he travels, he may give some guess at the distance of Places, or rather at the length of the computed Leagues, or Miles; a Prospective-glass, or rather a great one and a less, to take views of Objects at greater and less distances; a small Sea-Compass or Needle, to observe the situation of Places, and a parcel of the best maps to make curious Remarks of their exactness, and note down where they are faulty.[9]

In the decades following the publication of Rooke's and Boyle's instructions, a number of British traveller-observers operating in the Mediterranean eagerly sought to demonstrate their participation in the new scientific project. Francis Vernon (1637?–77), a member of the Royal Society who visited the Dalmatian Coast, Greece, and the Levant in 1675–7, was careful to record astronomical measurements of latitude at eight sites on the Greek mainland and to dispatch his findings to the secretary of the Royal Society, Henry Oldenburg.[10] At the same time, the botanist George Wheler (1650–1723), travelling through Greece and the Aegean with the French physician and antiquary Jacob Spon (1647–85), was highly attentive to the geography of Attica, spending considerable time surveying the terrain and publishing an important 'Map of Achaia' in his *Journey into Greece* (1682, French trans. 1689). The map was based on Vernon's latitudes supplemented by Wheler's own observations, made with a 'Mariner's Needle, from several

---

[8] *Collection of Voyages and Travels* (London, 1704), i. pp. lxxiii–lxxvi; (2nd edn., 1732), pp. lxix–lxxi; (3rd edn., 1744), pp. lxix–lxxii.

[9] Ibid. (1704), i. lxxv–lxxvi.

[10] 'Mr. Francis Vernon's letter, written to the publisher Januar. 10th 167^5/$_6$, giving a short account of some observations in his travels from Venice through Istria, Dalmatia, Greece, and the Archipelago to Smyrna, where this letter was written', *Philosophical Transactions* no. 124 (24 April 1676), 582. Athens: 38°; Corinth: 38° 14′; Sparta: 37° 10′; Coron: 37° 02′; Patras: 38° 40′; Delphos: 38° 50′; Thebes: 38° 22′; Chalcis: 38° 31′.

stations on divers Mountains and eminent places of that Country'.[11] Earlier observations made by the mathematician and astronomer John Greaves (1602–52) at Constantinople and Rhodes had already begun to erode confidence in ancient geographic texts and specifically the latitudes of sites provided by Ptolemy. The case of Rhodes was particularly troubling, since, as Greaves pointed out: 'it may be presumed, that, having been the Mother, and Nurse of so many Eminent Mathematicians, and having long flourished in Navigation, by the direction of these, and by the vicinity of the Phœnicians, they could not be ignorant of the precise Latitude of their Country, and that from them *Ptolemy* might receive a true Information.'[12] Based on his own measurement of the latitude of Rhodes (37° 50'), Greaves was forced to conclude that the Hellenistic geographer erred by almost two degrees in his estimate (36°).

The utility of this kind of work and the merit of the instructions published by the Royal Society were self-evident. Boyle's 'General Heads' were translated into French and expanded by the publisher Jean-Frédéric Bernard as an 'Essai d'instructions pour Voyager utilement', included in his *Recueil de Voyages au Nord* (1715–27).[13] Bernard claimed that the 'science de voyager' required such a broad range of knowledge that no one individual could hope to encompass all relevant disciplines. Among these, he included natural history, astronomy, geography, hydrography, philosophy, and commerce. He criticized most published travel accounts for their contradictions and lack of precision. His collection of voyages was intended to correct these faults and the list of instructions was supplied to guide the 'voyageur curieux, & philosophe' in making reliable observations. His first demand

[11] G. Wheler, *A Journey into Greece* (London, 1682), preface.

[12] 'An account of the Latitude of Constantinople, and Rhodes, written by the Learned Mr. John Greaves, sometime Professor of Astronomy in the University of Oxford, and directed to the most Reverend James Usher, Archbishop of Armagh', *Philosophical Transactions* no.178 (December 1685), 1298.

[13] *Recueil de Voiages au Nord, Contenant divers Mémoires très utiles au Commerce & à la Navigation* (Amsterdam, 1715), i. 1–102. A modified version of this text was published as a 'Dissertation Contenant des Instructions pour voyager utilement' included in the first volume of the 1725–38 edition and is signed 'J. F. B.' *Recueil de Voyages au Nord* (Amsterdam, 1731), i. pp. xliii–cxliv.

was that the traveller observe the latitudes and longitudes of places visited. In addition to the apparatus described by Boyle, Bernard recommends that measurements of temperature be made with a portable thermometer. If phenomena could not be quantified, sensory impressions were to be carefully recorded without embellishment. The fundamental geographic and climactic features of a region were to be established preliminary to defining the character, rituals, and behaviour of any human populations that might be encountered.

For Bernard, the Mediterranean, its islands and adjacent territories represented a particularly complex terrain that offered limitless potential for discovery. The remains of antiquity and the customs of modern nations were both deemed worthy of interest. Those travellers who had previously investigated Greece, Turkey, Egypt, and the Levant were generally regarded as ignorant and unreliable: comparisons of accounts made by different travellers demonstrated the degree to which evidence could be falsified. This was particularly true of illustrations, which purported to represent truth but were often in fact fabrications. He was perhaps thinking of the publications of Spon and Wheler, notorious for their crude and inaccurate renderings of ancient monuments. Bernard was wary of all information that had not been verified or corroborated by several travellers: by the medium of collections of voyages such as his *Recueil* and a multiplicity of others published in Britain and France throughout the eighteenth century, the reader was empowered to compare observations made by different travellers in the same territories and thereby to root out error and falsification.

A better means of verifying information collected by travellers was to centralize the analysis of this material in state institutions. Unlike the traveller-observer defined by the Royal Society who was left entirely to his own devices, the activities of traveller-observers connected to the French administration were tied to a larger framework of state-sponsored research, and their work fed directly into a number of on-going projects coordinated by a variety of closely integrated Paris-based government agencies.[14] The voyages of official French traveller-

[14] N. Broc, *La Géographie des philosophes: Géographes et voyageurs français au XVIIIe siècle* (Paris, 1975), 16–25.

observers were carefully planned by members of the Académie des Sciences, the Jardin du Roi, the Observatoire, and the Bibliothèque du Roi. They exploited the resources of the French consular network, used the most sophisticated instruments and techniques for their work and contributed to such monumental enterprises as the enlargement of the royal collections and the scientific re-mapping of the world by members of the Paris academies.[15] The merit of this system was underlined by Voltaire who proclaimed that the first voyages coordinated by the Académie des Sciences were among the most significant contributions to the progress of scientific research in the seventeenth century.[16] Through the efforts of the traveller-observer and the sedentary *géographe* (i.e. cartographer), the mathematically correct relationships of geographic and cultural features were increasingly refined. The scientific re-mapping of the world coordinated by the French government was perhaps one of the most striking and ambitious projects of the Enlightenment and is frequently encountered as a metaphor for scientific progress.

Imposing a uniform structure on the Mediterranean Sea was one of the core projects of the French Ministry of Maritime Affairs (Ministère de la Marine) from Colbert's administration to the Revolution.[17] During that period, France became the dominant commercial power in the Mediterranean, a position that was complemented by continual efforts to rectify representations of the geography of that sea. These efforts were essential for the safety of navigation, were coordinated by the cartographic bureau of the Ministry of Maritime Affairs (the Dépôt des Cartes, Plans et Journaux de la Marine) and were executed with cooperation from members of the Académie des Sciences and Académie des Inscriptions et Belles-Lettres. The

---

[15] See J. W. Olmsted, 'The Académie Royale des Sciences and the Origin of the First French Scientific Expeditions, 1662–1671' (Ph. D. thesis, Cornell University, 1944).

[16] Voltaire, *Le Siècle de Louis XIV* (London, 1752), 329.

[17] See P. Masson, *Histoire du commerce français dans le Levant au XVIIe siècle* (Paris, 1896); id., *Histoire des établissements et du commerce français dans l'Afrique barbaresque (1560–1793) (Algérie, Tunisie, Tripolitaine, Maroc)* (Paris, 1903); id., *Histoire du commerce français dans le Levant au XVIIIe siècle* (Paris, 1911).

Mediterranean of Louis XV may be bracketed by two techno-
logical innovations that transformed the practice of cartography, the first being the development by the Bolognese
astronomer Gian Domenico Cassini (1625–1712) in the 1680s
of tables of the eclipses of the moons of Jupiter, which were
used to determine longitude relative to a fixed meridian; the
second being the application in the late eighteenth century of
marine chronometers to the same problem of fixing a traveller's
location relative to an arbitrary point of reference. During the
period between these two developments, the extraordinary pro-
liferation of systematic astronomical observation within academic bodies throughout Europe and the publication of
increasingly precise observations of celestial phenomena
resulted in an unprecedented potential for the verification of
astronomical and geographical data. The Académie des Sciences, occupying a dominant position within the academic universe of the Enlightenment, and the highly centralized
administration of French external commerce were, between
1669 and 1749, linked directly through the person of the Secretary of State for Maritime Affairs.[18] The result was an un-
paralleled system for the coordination of geographic
information that transformed representations of the world and
the practice of cartography, nowhere more dramatically than in
the Mediterranean Sea.

3. THE MEDITERRANEAN SEA
AND ENLIGHTENMENT SCIENCE

French dictionary and encyclopedia definitions of 'Mer Méditerranée' give little sense of the radical transformation of representations of that body of water in the course of the eighteenth
century or of the immense significance of the adjacent territories—particularly those under Ottoman control—to French
commerce. In the article 'Mer Méditerranée' published in the
1768 edition of La Martinière's *Grand dictionnaire géographique*, the Mediterranean is understood primarily as a collection
of smaller seas, gulfs and bays, defined by a number of peninsulas and large islands:

[18] See M. Vergé-Franceschi, *La Marine française au XVIIIe siècle* (Paris,
1996).

La Mer Méditerranée, grande mer entre l'Europe, l'Asie & l'Afrique. Son nom signifie qu'elle est au milieu des terres. Elle est séparée de l'Ocean par le détroit de Gibraltar, de la mer Rouge par l'isthme de Suez, & de la Propontide par le détroit des Dardanelles. Elle contient plusieurs grands golfes. Les principaux sont le golfe de Lyon, le golfe Adriatique, l'Archipel, & le golfe de Barbarie. Elle contient trois grandes presqu'isles, savoir, l'Italie, la Gréce & la Natolie. Ses principales isles sont,

Sicile, Sardaigne, Corse, Majorque, Minorque, Malte, Corfou, Céphalonie, Zante, Candie.

Et cette multitude d'isles qui sont comprises dans la partie de cette mer, nommée l'Archipel. Nous avons sur cette mer le Portulan de la Méditerranée par Michelot, & la carte marine de cette mer par Berthelot.[19]

La Martinière's definition differs little from one published in Moréri's *Grand dictionnaire historique* in 1698. The maps by Michelot and Berthelot referred to by La Martinière were each first published in Marseilles, in 1689 and 1693 respectively. Michelot's map was reissued as late as 1756[20] and François Berthelot's crude, four-sheet map served as the standard chart used by French navigators through the first half of the eighteenth century.[21] A clear indication that already by 1700, these maps were known to be defective was implied by the author of the article 'Mer Méditerranée' in the *Encyclopédie* who added to the basic geographic definition the following details:

La meilleure carte de la *Méditerranée* que nous ayons, a été donnée par M. Guillaume de Lisle. Cette *mer* si connue de tout tems par les nations les plus savantes, toujours couverte de leurs vaisseaux, traversée de tous les sens possibles par une infinité de navigateurs, s'est trouvée n'avoir que 860 lieues d'occident en orient, au lieu de 1160

[19] Bruzen de La Martinière, *Le Grand Dictionnaire géographique, historique et critique* (Paris, 1768), iv. 212. L. Moreri, *Le Grand dictionaire historique* (Amsterdam, 1698), iii. 497.

[20] 'La Mediterranée en 2 feuilles aprés Michelot dediée à Son Altesse Serenissime M. le Comte de Clermont...par Le Rouge ing. Geographe...1756', Bibliothèque nationale de France (Paris) [henceforth BNF] Cartes et Plans, portfeuille 64, pièce 21.

[21] 'Nouvelle Carte de la mer Méditerrannée présentée a Messieurs les Maire, Eschevins, et Deputez du Commerce de la Ville de Marseille, par leur très humble serviteur François Berthelot...1693', BNF, Cartes et Plans, Ge. D 13557 (1–4).

qu'on lui donnoit; & c'est ce que M. de Lisle a rectifié par des observations astronomiques. Cependant non content de ces observations astronomiques, dont on vouloit se défier, il entreprit, pour ne laisser aucun doute, de mesurer toute cette *mer* en détail & par parties, sans employer ces observations, mais seulement les portulans & les journaux des pilotes, tant des routes faites de cap en cap, en suivant les terres, que de celles qui traversoient d'un bout à l'autre; & tout cela évalué avec toutes les précautions nécessaires, réduit & mis ensemble, s'est accordé à donner à la *Méditerranée* la même étendue que les observations astronomiques dont on vouloit se défier.[22]

The above information was taken directly from the *éloge* of Guillaume Delisle (1675–1726) written by the Secrétaire Perpétuel of the Académie des Sciences, Bernard le Bouvier de Fontenelle (1657–1757). A student of Cassini, member of the Académie des Sciences, and professor of geography to Louis XV (he was appointed Géographe du Roi on 24 August 1718), Delisle's reformed version of the geography of the Mediterranean appeared in a globe and series of maps produced in 1699–1700. For Fontenelle, Delisle's work was of epochal significance: 'L'ouverture du siécle present se fit donc à l'égard de la Geographie par une Terre presque nouvelle que M. Delisle presenta.'[23] The transformation of the shape and size of the Mediterranean Sea was the most breath-taking feature of Delisle's research. He continued to work on the problem of rectifying the coasts of the Mediterranean, drawing attention to the gross errors that underlay most representations of that sea in a paper presented to the Académie des Sciences in 1714.[24] His work was illustrated with a map of Italy and Greece in which he superimposed his own representation of the coasts

---

[22] *Encyclopédie* (Denis Diderot and Jean de La Rond d'Alembert (eds.), *Encyclopédie, ou Dictionnaire raisonné des sciences, des arts et des métiers* (Neufchatel, 1765), x. 366.

[23] Bernard le Bouvier de Fontenelle, *Eloges des académiciens* (The Hague, 1740), ii. 284.

[24] In what follows *HAS = Histoire de l'Académie royale des sciences. Avec les mémoires de mathématiques et de physique... tirés des registres de cette académie (1699–1790)*, 92 vols. (Paris, 1702–97). Each volume comprises two separately paginated parts, referred to as Hist. and Mém., respectively. G. Delisle, 'Sur les Mesures Geographiques des Anciens', *HAS*, 1714, Hist. 80–3; 'Justification des mesures des anciens en matiere de geographie', *HAS*, 1714, Mém. 175–85.

based on recent astronomical observations and careful study of the works of ancient geographers, over the standard representation of the same features used by the best modern mapmakers ('les meilleurs Géographes modernes'), in order to demonstrate the pressing need for more systematic research (Fig. 10.1).

Fig. 10.1. Corrected map of Italy and Greece, from Guillaume Delisle, 'Justification des mesures des anciens en matiere de geographie', *HAS*, 1714, Mém. pl. 8. (Courtesy of the Thomas Fisher Rare Book Library, University of Toronto.)

Despite Fontenelle's rhetoric, Delisle could not claim sole credit for the shrinking of the Mediterranean Sea: the first significant attempt to correct representations of its coasts based on astronomical observations of longitude was carried out by the Provençal scholar Nicolas-Claude Fabri de Peiresc (1580–1637). In 1635, he coordinated observations of a lunar eclipse made by a number of travellers stationed at different points around the Mediterranean, and thereby determined that the length of the sea was around 200 leagues shorter than was commonly believed.[25] Due to the complexity of the operations involved in such an enterprise, Delisle's work was evidently impossible without the backing and resources of the French administration. Delisle himself never travelled, and he based his work on the researches of a number of engineers working for the Royal Navy and astronomers connected to the Académie des Sciences. Beginning in 1678, Colbert sponsored a number of cartographic missions in the Mediterranean as part of his larger agenda of encouraging maritime commerce and protecting French navigation. According to Colbert, the best way to assure the glory of the king and the prosperity of France was to obtain control of the Mediterranean Sea, admonishing his son and successor Jean-Baptiste, marquis de Seignelay (1651–90) to do everything in his power to further this enterprise.[26]

Following on work by members of the Académie des Sciences to rectify the coasts of France in the 1670s and 80s, the first rigorous observations of the longitude of sites in the Levant by an operative of the French administration were made by the astronomer Jean-Mathieu de Chazelles (1657–1710). Like Delisle, Chazelles received his astronomical training from Cassini at the Paris observatory. In 1685, he was appointed professor of hydrography in Marseilles and participated in cartographic campaigns in the Mediterranean between 1686 and 1688 sponsored by Seignelay. In 1693, Seignelay's successor, Louis Phélypeaux, comte de Pontchartrain (1643–1727) appointed Chazelles to travel to Egypt, Greece, Syria, and

[25] H. Brown, *Scientific Organizations in Seventeenth-Century France (1620–1680)* (New York, 1934), 4–5; Broc, *La Géographie*, 17.

[26] P. Clément, *L'Italie en 1671: Relation d'un Voyage du marquis de Seignelay.* (Paris, 1867), 38. Seignelay served as Secrétaire d'Etat à la Maison du Roi, chargé de la Marine from 1683–90.

Turkey to gather data for the production of the second volume of the *Neptune français*, the official compilation of maps used by French navigators.[27] Upon returning from this mission, Chazelles was appointed to the Académie des Sciences (1695). In 1701, he read a paper to the academy proposing the complete rectification of the geography of the Mediterranean but died before he could realize this enormous undertaking.[28]

A new impetus for correcting representations of the Mediterranean arose in the early 1730s during the administration of Louis Phélypeaux's grandson, Jean-Frédéric, comte de Maurepas (1701–81), who served as Secretary of State for Maritime Affairs from 1723 to 1749. Like his predecessors, Maurepas served concurrently as Secretary of State for the King's Household (Maison du Roi) and was thus simultaneously responsible for all royal collections and scientific bodies in Paris as well as an extensive network of consulates scattered around the world. Although he was no 'savant', Maurepas was regarded as an enlightened facilitator who used his position to further all forms of scientific research during his twenty-six-year administration. The famous scientific missions sent by Maurepas to South America and the Arctic Circle in the 1730s to determine the shape of the earth have eclipsed a multitude of other projects undertaken during his administration, notably expeditions to Egypt, the Levant, Mesopotamia, and Persia that were directly connected to the extension of French commerce and to the expansion of the collections of the Bibliothèque du Roi and the Jardin du Roi. All these missions contributed directly to the principal scientific project of Maurepas' administration, the rectification of nautical charts:

Les déterminations astronomiques de plusieurs points, qui n'étoient connus auparavant que par des estimes, l'exactitude des instrumens qui se perfectionnent sans cesse, la découverte de nouveaux instrumens & de méthodes nouvelles, la multiplication même des observations qui se corrigent & se réforment mutuellement, toutes ces causes exigent dans les Cartes marines des fréquens changemens & des corrections perpétuelles. M. de Maurepas ordonna un grand nombre

---

[27] Fontenelle, *Eloges* I, 213–27.
[28] 'Sur un projet d'un nouveau portulan pour la Méditerranée', *HAS*, 1701, Hist. 119–21.

de Cartes nouvelles, envoya des Officiers examiner des côtes peu connues, & déterminer des positions importantes, mais qui restoient encore incertaines; il mit plus d'activité & de suite dans le travail habituel de la correction des Cartes & du recueil des Observations.[29]

Observations made in the course of official French military tours of the eastern Mediterranean and North African coasts throughout the 1730s and 1740s demonstrate that correcting the errors of Berthelot's map of the Mediterranean was a constant effort. The necessity of concentrating resources on the re-mapping of the Mediterranean Sea was made evident in a manuscript map presented to Maurepas in January 1735 by the Premier Ingénieur Géographe or chief cartographer of the Dépôt des Cartes, Plans et Journaux de la Marine, Jacques-Nicolas Bellin (1703– 72)[30] (Fig. 10.2). A printed map based on this work appeared in 1737; a detailed chart of the Aegean Sea was published the following year.[31] The work was intended as a tool for French navigators, but its impact was felt in Britain as well. In 1738, the London-based publisher Robert Sayer issued: 'An New Map, or Chart of the Mediterranean Sea made from the draughts of the Pilots of Marseilles and Corrected by the best astronomical Observations by Order of the Comte de Maurepas.'[32] A multiplicity of efforts to improve and correct this map were made by French navigators and pilots in the 1740s.

The last major French initiative to systematically re-map the Mediterranean in the eighteenth century was proposed by Joseph-Bernard, marquis de Chabert (1724–1805) and read to the Académie des Sciences during a public assembly on 25 April

---

[29] Marie Jean Antoine Caritat, marquis de Condorcet, 'Eloge de M. le Comte de Maurepas', *HAS*, 1782, Hist. 21–2.

[30] 'Projet d'une Carte reduite de la Méditerrannée assujetie aux Observations Astronomiques les plus certains Comparée avec la carte du Sr. Berthelot hydrographe du Roy, le 15 Jan 1735.' BNF, Cartes et Plans, portefeuille 64, pièce 12. On Bellin, see J.-M. Garant, 'Jacques-Nicolas Bellin (1703–1772): cartographe, hydrographe, ingénieur du ministère de la Marine, sa vie, son œuvre, sa valeur historique' (MA thesis, Université de Montréal, 1973).

[31] 'Carte Reduite de la Mer Mediterranée pour servir aux Vaisseaux du Roy Dressée au Depost des Cartes et Plans de la Marine Par Ordre de M. Le Comte de Maurepas 1737', BNF, Cartes et Plans, portefeuille 64, pièce 13. The publication of these maps was announced in the *Mercure de France* (December 1737), 2653–4; (May 1738), 957.

[32] BNF, Cartes et Plans, portefeuille 64, pièce 15.

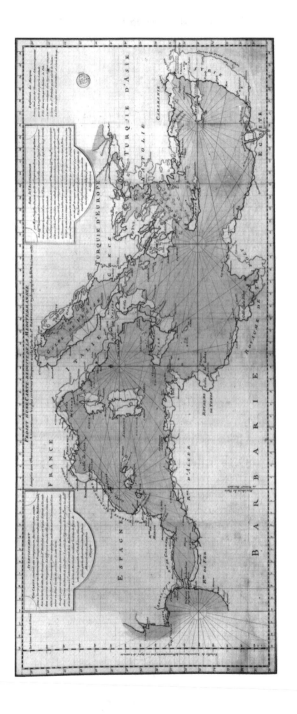

Fig. 10.2. 'Projet d'une Carte reduite de la Méditerrannée assujetie aux Observations Astronomiques les plus certains Comparée avec la carte du Sr. Berthelot hydrographe du Roy, le 15 Jan 1735'. Paris, Bibliothèque Nationale de France, Cartes et Plans, portefeuille 64, pièce 12. (Permission of the Bibliothèque Nationale de France.)

1759. After several years of work, he would contend that: 'Quoique la Méditerranée ait été le théâtre des premières navigateurs, elle n'en étoit pas pour cella mieux connue; on peut dire même que cette partie de l'Hydrographie étoit demeurée jusqu'a nos jours la plus imparfaite de toutes & celle qui avoit le plus besoins d'être rectifiée.'[33]

According to Chabert, only the work of Chazelles was significant; all attempts by mariners to survey the Mediterranean were regarded as deficient and inaccurate since their observations were made on board ships with defective equipment and not from stable points of reference on land with the best astronomical instruments. The methods of the *caboteur* or coastal pilot who was guided by memory and the visual impressions of coasts were to be replaced by the scientific principles employed by the *navigateur*, based on the more difficult but invariable laws of astronomy. Subjective, individual experience was to be replaced with uniform principles of observation guided by the most advanced technology. The complexity of the operations demanded the most sophisticated methods. Chabert concluded: 'je ne dissimule point que la rectification des cartes de la Méditerranée ne soit une entreprise des plus étendues & des plus délicates.'[34]

As a young officer in the French Navy, Chabert was involved in a number of campaigns in the 1740s during which he collected astronomical and geographic data for correcting maps of Acadia and Newfoundland. During the intervals between his trans-Atlantic voyages, he received a special dispensation from the Comte de Maurepas to study astronomy and surveying in Paris. His first work on the Mediterranean was part of a cam-

---

[33] 'Hydrographie. Sur la rectification des cartes marines de la Méditerranée', *HAS*, 1766, Hist. 123–7.

[34] Joseph-Bernard, marquis de Chabert, 'Projet d'observations astronomiques et hydrographiques pour parvenir à former pour la Mer Méditerranée une suite de cartes exactes', *HAS*, 1759, Mém. 484–94. Chabert became a member of the academy on 25 September 1758.

paign to chart the coasts of Spain in 1753, during which time he determined the longitude of Cartagena. In 1757–8 he was at work on Cyprus. These operations were interrupted by the Seven Years War but were resumed in 1764 and 1766 when Chabert undertook two further campaigns to determine the longitude of sites in Sicily and the North African coast. His method required that he establish temporary observatories on land and that his instruments be protected from the elements by a tent. After establishing local time with a pendulum clock and determining the precise north–south orientation of a given site, he spent between six and twenty-four hours observing the course of the moon and noting the exact time that it passed in front of individual stars. Returning to Paris, Chabert compared his work with observations of the same phenomena made by astronomers in such diverse sites as Vienna and Stockholm, and was thus able to establish the longitudes of the points he visited. This method was supplemented by more rudimentary, labour-intensive surveys of coasts based on the principles of triangulation.

In a paper presented to the Académie des Sciences in 1766, Chabert forecast the transformation of cartography that would occur subsequent to the application of reliable spring-driven marine chronometers to the determination of longitude: 'Nous serons toujours forcés de nous contenter d'un très-petit nombre de déterminations jusqu'au temps où l'exécution des horloges marines nous fournira des moyens prompts & sûrs de multiplier les observations de longitude à terre ainsi qu'à la mer.'[35] Such chronometers were in fact being tested by British and French scientists at the time Chabert presented his research to the Académie des Sciences, and in 1771 he wrote to the Contrôleur Général Joseph-Marie Terray (1715–78) requesting a chronometer for his work mapping the Aegean Sea.[36] Chabert

---

[35] J.-B. de Chabert, 'Mémoire sur l'état actuel de l'entreprise pour la rectification des Cartes marines de la Méditerranée', *HAS*, 1766, Mém. 384–94. Chabert's work was supported throughout the 1760s by Etienne-François, duc de Choiseul (1719–75) and his cousin César-Gabriel, duc de Choiseul-Praslin (1712–85) who served as Secretaries of State for Maritime Affairs from 1760–6 and from 1766–70 respectively.

[36] Chabert to Sartine (July 1775) (Archives Nationales (Paris), Marine G 97, dossier 1, fol. 31). During the public assembly of the Académie des Sciences on Easter 1783, Chabert read a 'Mémoire sur l'usage des Horloges marines, relativement à la Navigation, & sur-tout à la géographie', *HAS*, 1783, Mém. 49–66.

renewed his request in 1775 in order to continue his work, commenting that: 'On peut même dire que sans le secours de l'horloge marine, on ne scauroit parvenir à faire de bonnes cartes de l'archipel à cause que cette partie de la Mediterranée renferme dans un espace fort resserré, une multitude de points terrestres dont les positions respectives sont également importante à determiner avec précision et dont le terrein et les habitans présentent presque toujours des difficultés insurmontables à faire des operations geometriques à terre.'[37]

Due to the difficulties of apprehending the precise configuration of the Mediterranean throughout the Enlightenment, it is hardly surprising that conceptualizing the sea as an environmental unit was limited to a relatively superficial understanding of the most obvious features of its geography. In the 'Histoire et théorie de la terre' that served as a preface to his monumental *Histoire naturelle*, Buffon (1707–88) described the Mediterranean as a sea distinguished from the Atlantic and Indian oceans by the fact that the water level was lower and that currents flowed from west to east through the Strait of Gibraltar. These features Buffon took to be proof: 'que la mer Méditerranée n'est point un golfe ancient de l'Océan, mais qu'elle a été formée par une irruption des eaux produite par quelques causes accidentelles.'[38] Buffon realized that the islands and coasts, which created the impression described in contemporary encyclopedias of a sea composed of smaller seas, belied a greater underlying topographical unity that would have been apparent in a prehistoric age before the Strait of Gibraltar were breached: '... les eaux ont couvert toutes les bases terres dont nous n'apercevons aujourd'hui que les éminences & les sommets dans l'Italie & dans les îles de Sicile, de Malte, de Corse, de Sardaigne, de Chypre, de Rhodes & de l'Archipel.'[39] While Buffon was capable of articulating a dynamic theory of the earth to account for evidence of its continual transformation, his own experience of the geographic features he described was limited to a single, brief voyage to Rome in 1732. As the director

---

[37] Chabert to Terray, 20 March 1771 (Archives Nationales, Marine G 97, dossier 1, fol. 19). Chabert was using Ferdinand Berthoud's chronometer no. 3 in the Aegean in the summer of 1771. Terray served as Secretary of State for Maritime Affairs from 24 Dec. 1770 to 10 April 1771.

[38] Buffon, *Histoire naturelle* (1749), i. 99–100.   [39] Ibid. 100.

of the Jardin du Roi from 1739, Buffon based his ideas on material collected by 'travellers of the best credit' and relied on French consuls to supply him with specimens.

4. THE *VOYAGE PHILOSOPHIQUE* IN THE AEGEAN SEA

Throughout the reign of Louis XV, it is clear that while continual efforts were being made to give a precise, mathematical definition to the Mediterranean coasts, the method of achieving this goal was split between the age-old practice of empirical navigation and modern principles of astronomical navigation. Given the difficulty of determining one's position with mathematical rigour throughout the eighteenth century and the many types of information important for science that could not be quantified, the useful data gathered by the scientific traveller-observer could not be confined merely to what was susceptible to measurement. This realization seems to have motivated the development of a distinct form of scientific traveller designated by the term *voyageur-philosophe*.

The concept of the *voyageur-philosophe* was first defined in the context of the Académie des Sciences by Fontenelle in his *éloge* of the botanist Joseph Pitton de Tournefort (1656–1708); it was based on the combination of a disposition for strenuous movement, a systematic approach to the study of natural phenomena, an encyclopedic breadth of interests, and, most important, a special kind of ocular judgement uncontaminated by bias or 'system'. Fontenelle summarized his assessment of Tournefort's abilities by concluding that: 'Avec toutes les qualitez qu'il avoit, on peut juger aisement combien il étoit propre à être un excellent Voyageur, car j'entends par ce terme, non ceux qui voyagent simplement, mais ceux en qui se trouve & une curiosité fort étendue, qui est assez rare, & un certain don de bien voir, plus rare encore. Les Philosophes ne courent gueres le monde, & ceux qui le courent ne sont ordinairement gueres Philosophes, & par-là un voyage de Philosophe est extremement précieux.'[40] Neither Chazelles nor Chabert was ever described as a *voyageur-philosophe*. They were regarded as

---

[40] Fontenelle, 'Eloge de M. de Tournefort', *HAS*, 1708, Hist. 151–2.

astronomers or *géomètres* whose personae disappeared behind the precision of their measurements, whose method required a stationary point of reference and whose findings were largely unaffected by the specificity of local environments.

Fontenelle based his judgement of Tournefort's ability to 'see well' on his *voyage philosophique* through the Aegean and the Black Sea between 1700 and 1702. This was an official mission sponsored by the Secretary of State for Maritime Affairs Jérôme de Pontchartrain (1674–1747) and was closely related to the commercial and military interests of French navigation. In his description of the islands of the Aegean, Tournefort consistently followed a set of instructions similar to those composed by Boyle. The clearest sign that he was participating in the new science, however, occurred first on 7 September 1700 when, like Wheler in Attica some twenty-five years earlier, Tournefort set up a surveying station on Mount Zia on Naxos and began to list the position of surrounding islands relative to himself.[41] The same procedure was carried out a number of times on other islands suggesting that, although he could not establish longitudes, a geometric framework based on triangulation provided an underlying, mathematical certainty for his more subjective observations.

The combined activities of displacement and 'seeing well' that were integral to the definition of the *voyage philosophique* were subsequently transformed into a dynamic method of perceiving the relationship between the observer and the environment. The *voyageur-philosophe* was aware that changing points of view resulted in the accumulation of sense impressions and a more complete understanding of complex spatial phenomena than could be obtained from the single, stationary point of reference that was the basis of the *camera obscura* model of vision. In the context of Mediterranean travels, the idea of the *voyage philosophique*—in which the experiences of the traveller were essential to the accumulation of knowledge—became the basis for a distinctively Enlightenment approach to reinterpreting elements of classical antiquity, notably the poetry of Homer and the architecture of Greece.

While Homer had been imagined around 1700 to be either the epitome of sophistication or barbarism—depending how one

[41] J. Pitton de Tournefort, *Relation d'un voyage du Levant* i (Paris, 1717), 224.

aligned oneself in relation to the *Querelle des Anciens et Modernes*—the Greek poet was always imagined enthroned on Chios scribbling away in his study. The idea that his work was that of an illiterate and what's more, an itinerant bard roaming around the coast of Turkey was apparently first advanced by Robert Wood (1717?–71) in *A Comparative View of the Antient and Present State of the Troade: To Which is Prefixed an Essay on the Original Genius of Homer* (1767)[42] (Fig. 10.3). Wood toured Greece and the Near East extensively in the 1740s. His most innovative ideas were the result of layering his own travel experiences over Homer's descriptions, something that had never been done by any serious scholar. None of those engaged in the *Querelle des Anciens et Modernes* had ever visited Greece.

For Wood, Homer was 'a traveller of curiosity and observation'.[43] He realized that the entire narrative framework of the *Iliad* and the *Odyssey* depended on Homer's experience of the geography of the Aegean Sea. Wood concluded that Homer saw Greece entirely from the Turkish coast and that his descriptions of landscapes can only be reconciled with an 'Ionian point of view'.[44] Significantly, Wood criticized the failure of modern translators, notably Alexander Pope, to understand Homer's point of view. For Wood, the text was not merely a linear narrative but a map of experience. He imagined Homer pointing out landscape features around his audience and connecting his subject to the spot where the recital took place. The relationship between the human and divine planes described in the *Iliad* only made sense if one triangulated the geographical features described by Homer: 'If we form to ourselves a just idea of the respective situation, distance, and perspective, of Olympus, Ida and the Grecian Camp, we shall find Homer's celestial geography so happily connected with his Map of Troy, that the scene is shifted from one to the other naturally.'[45] For Wood, the *Iliad* and the *Odyssey* were as much about the actions of Gods and heroes as the experience of landscape, experiences based on navigation as the principal means of displacement (Fig. 10.4).

---

[42] The edition of 1767 was limited to seven copies.

[43] R. Wood, *An Essay on the Original Genius and Writings of Homer: With a comparative view of the Ancient and Present State of the Troade* (London, 1775), 34.   [44] Ibid. 21.   [45] Ibid. 132.

Fig. 10.3. 'A Head of Homer. From the Collection of Lyde Browne Esq' (J. B. Cipriani, d.; Engrav'd by J. Basire), from Robert Wood, *An Essay on the Original Genius and Writings of Homer* (London, 1775). (Courtesy of the Thomas Fisher Rare Book Library, University of Toronto.)

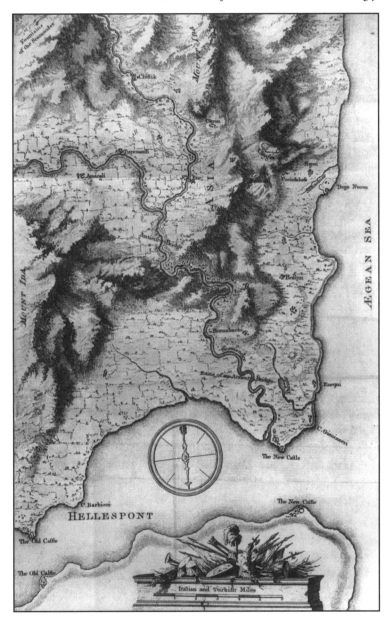

Fig. 10.4. 'View of Ancient Troas together with the Scamander and Mount Ida, as taken anno MDCCL' (Borra delin; Major Sc), from Robert Wood, *An Essay on the Original Genius and Writings of Homer* (London, 1775). (Courtesy of the Thomas Fisher Rare Book Library, University of Toronto.)

Simultaneous to Wood's work on Homer, the little-known remains of Greek architecture were being revealed in the publications of both French and British travellers. By the standard of Roman architecture that had been the touchstone of classical taste since the Renaissance, the Doric monuments of Greece and southern Italy were impossible to inscribe into the classical canon because they lacked the finesse and, most important, the proportions that characterized the Roman orders. At the same time that Wood subjected Homer to analysis based on principles of scientific observation and navigation, a similar operation was carried out on Greek architecture by the French traveller and architect Julien-David Leroy (1724–1803). Leroy rejected proportion as a criterion of aesthetic judgement and established a new, dynamic relationship between the monument and the observer in order to overcome Renaissance barriers to understanding the full range of ancient architectural forms.

An admirer of Wood's 1753 publication on the Roman ruins at Palmyra, Leroy was uniquely equipped for his 1754–5 voyage to Greece. Trained as an architect, he also benefited from a complete immersion in the most advanced concepts in modern science and technology at home. His brothers Jean-Baptiste (1720–1800) and Charles (1726–79) both wrote for the *Encyclopédie* and were members of the Académie des Sciences and the Royal Society. In 1769 and 1773, his brother Pierre Leroy (1717–85) won prizes offered by the Académie des Sciences for the invention of a reliable marine chronometer. The Leroy family was closely connected with several of the leading French scientists and travellers who had worked for the Ministry of Maritime Affairs.[46]

One of the aims of Leroy's voyage to Greece was cartographic. He not only attempted to situate the ruins of Athens

[46] On Leroy, see D. Wiebenson, *Sources of Greek Revival Architecture* (London, 1969); A. Braham, *The Architecture of the French Enlightenment* (Berkeley and Los Angeles, 1980), 64–6; B. Bergdoll, *Léon Vaudoyer: Historicism in the Age of Industry* (Cambridge, Mass., 1994), 12–18; id., *European Architecture 1750–1890* (Oxford, 2000), 16–32; C. D. Armstrong, 'Progress in the Age of Navigation: The *Voyage-Philosophique* of Julien-David Leroy' (Ph. D. thesis, Columbia University, 2003); id., 'De la théorie des proportions à l'expérience des sensations: l'*Essai sur la Théorie de l'Architecture* de Julien-David Le Roy, 1770', *Annales du Centre Ledoux* 5 (2003) (forthcoming); Julien-David Leroy, *The Ruins of the Most Beautiful Monuments of Greece* (trans. D. Britt) with an introduction by R. Middleton (Santa Monica, Calif., (2004)).

based on the testimony of Pausanias, but also surveyed the ports of the city and of the plain of Sparta (Fig. 10.5). Most significantly, Leroy rejected the conventional understanding of the architectural spectator as an immobile observer who perceived beauty through the passive absorption of proportional relationships, proposing instead that the perception of architecture, like the impression of a landscape, was the product of the displacement of an observer in an environment of forms.

In the first edition of *Les Ruines des plus beaux monuments de la Grèce* (1758), Leroy demonstrated that the visual experience of architecture from different points of view was the only basis for aesthetic judgement. Describing the profiles and sculpture of the Parthenon entablature, he commented that: 'On voit ce superbe édifice de fort loin, par quelque chemin que l'on arrive à cette ville par terre, & on l'apperçoit dès l'entrée du golphe d'Engia. Si sa grandeur & la blancheur du marbre dont il est construit impriment, dès qu'on le découvre, un sentiment d'admiration, l'élégance de ses proportions, & la beauté des bas-reliefs dont il est orné, ne satisfont pas moins, quand on le considere de près'[47] (Fig. 10.6).

In the second edition of *Les Ruines* (1770), Leroy turned the experience of architecture into a *voyage philosophique*, proposing that the impression of beauty resulted from changing visual impressions produced by the motion of an observer. Sequences of evenly spaced, freestanding columns such as those that surrounded Greek temples were a particularly effective means of producing rich spatial experiences, vivified by the constantly changing play of light and shadow on mouldings and surfaces. The proportions, dimensions and details of the orders were consequently displaced from their pre-eminent position as the constituent elements of architecture (Fig. 10.7).

The intellectual frame of reference for Leroy's method contrasts dramatically with that of his British contemporaries James Stuart (1713–88) and Nicholas Revett (1720–1804), whose assessment of the same monuments in their *Antiquities of Athens* (1762–1816) was predicated on the idea that precise measurement and the testimony of ancient texts were the only valid means of understanding the ruins of ancient architecture. The

---

[47] J.-D. Leroy, *Les Ruines des plus beaux monuments de la Grèce* (Paris, 1758), part I, 9.

Fig. 10.5. 'Plan de la Plaine d'Athenes, et de quelques lieux qui l'environnent' (Littret de Montigny, sculpt.), from Julien-David Leroy, *Les Ruines des plus beaux monuments de la Grèce* (Paris, 1758), part 1, pl. 9. (Courtesy of the Bibliothèque Municipale de Marseille.)

Fig. 10.6. Detail of capitals and entablature of the Parthenon (Pierre Patte, sculpt.), from Julien-David Leroy, *Les Ruines des plus beaux monuments de la Grèce* (Paris, 1758), part 2, pl. 9. (Courtesy of the Bibliothèque Municipale de Marseille.)

Fig. 10.7. 'Vue du Temple de Minerve Suniade' (Philippe Le Bas, sculpt.), from Julien-David Leroy, *Les Ruines des plus beaux monuments de la Grèce* (Paris, 1758), part 1, pl. 15. (Courtesy of the Bibliothèque Municipale de Marseille.)

distance that separates the *Antiquities of Athens* and *Les Ruines des plus beaux monuments de la Grèce* may be understood as the product of two distinct models of travel-based research, the one first defined in the instructions for travellers published in the *Philosophical Transactions* of the Royal Society, the other conceptualized by Fontenelle in the Académie des Sciences. The former places value only on those findings that can be verified by measurement and can be defined independently of the observer's subjectivity; the latter places the observer and his experience at the very centre of the scientific enterprise. The value of measurement was precisely the issue that bitterly divided Stuart and Leroy, the former emphasizing the many errors in *Les Ruines*, the latter claiming that there was more to architectural experience than recording the dimensions of the orders.

5. CONCLUSION: CHABERT AND CHOISEUL-GOUFFIER

In 1776, the Marquis de Chabert commanded the *Atalante* through the Aegean on his continuing mission to produce a mathematically rigorous representation of the Mediterranean Sea. He was accompanied by the young Gabriel-Florent-Auguste, Comte de Choiseul-Gouffier (1752–1817), who subsequently published his important *Voyage pittoresque de la Grèce* (vol. I, 1782; vol. II, part 1, 1809; vol. II, part 2, 1822) based on the experience. Identified as a *voyageur-philosophe* in his official *éloge* delivered at the Institut de France, Choiseul-Gouffier's book was a model of contemporary travel literature.[48] As he remarked in the first chapter: 'Je vais tâcher de faire voyager le Lecteur avec moi, de lui faire voir tout ce que j'ai vû, de le placer dans l'endroit où j'étois moi-même lorsque je faisois chaque dessin.'[49] He attempted to communicate something of the impressions made on the senses ('sensations') (Fig. 10.8) as well as precise factual information (Fig. 10.9);

[48] B.-J. Dacier, 'Notice historique sur la vie et les ouvrages de M. le comte de Choiseul-Gouffier', *Histoire et mémoires de l'Institut royale de France, Académie des Inscriptions et Belles-Lettres* VII (Paris, 1824), Hist. 175–6. See also L. Pingaud, *Choiseul-Gouffier: La France en Orient sous Louis XVI* (Paris, 1887); D. Constantine, *Early Greek Travellers and the Hellenic Ideal* (Cambridge, 1984), 173–82; O. Augustinos, *French Odysseys: Greece in French Travel Literature from the Renaissance to the Romantic Era* (Baltimore and London, 1994), 157–73.

[49] Choiseul-Gouffier, *Voyage Pittoresque de la Grèce* (Paris, 1782), i. 2.

Fig. 10.8. 'Ruines du Temple de Mars' [at Halicarnassus] (Dessiné par J. B. Hilair; Gravé à l'eau forte par Marillier et terminé au burin par Dambrun), from Choiseul-Gouffier, *Voyage Pittoresque de la Grèce*, i (Paris, 1782), pl. 99. (Courtesy of the Thomas Fisher Rare Book Library, University

Fig. 10.9. 'Détails de ce monument' [Temple of Mars at Hali-carnassus] (Dessiné et Mesuré par Foucherot; Gravé par Sell-ier), from Choiseul-Gouffier, *Voyage Pittoresque de la Grèce*, i (Paris, 1782), pl. 101. (Courtesy of the Thomas Fisher Rare Book Library, University of Toronto.)

Fig. 10.10. 'Carte détaillée de la route de l'Auteur depuis le Méandre jusqu'au Golfe d'Adramyhtti' (Rédigée sur les Lieux par le Cte de Choiseul Gouffier; Gravé par J. Perrier; Ecrit par L. J. Beaublé), from Choiseul-Gouffier, *Voyage Pittoresque de la Grèce*, i (Paris, 1782), pl. 117. (Courtesy of the Thomas Fisher Rare Book Library, University of Toronto.)

he was interested in both contemplating the 'tableaux' made on the mind and, like Chabert, in determining the mathematical relationship of sites in order to correct: 'quelques erreurs de géographie' (Fig. 10.10). Choiseul-Gouffier's conception of the published travel account was to communicate simultaneously to his reader's imagination and reason, demonstrating that experience was the product of changing points of view and changing states of mind. The centrality of motion to the experience of travel was captured by his description of sailing through the Aegean Sea: 'Je ne puis encore, même plusieurs années après, me retracer sans émotion mes courses sur cette Mer semée d'îles, dont les tableaux délicieux varient sans cesse pour le Navigateur.'[50]

[50] Choiseul-Gouffier, *Voyage Pittoresque de la Grèce* (Paris, 1782), i. p. i.

11

The Mirage of Greek Continuity: On the Uses and Abuses of Analogy in Some Travel Narratives from the Seventeenth to the Eighteenth Century

Suzanne Saïd

P. Walcot's influential book *Greek Peasants, Ancient and Modern* (1970) best illustrates the mirage of Greek continuity and the persistence of 'an uncritically survivalist argument'.[1] His 'ancient peasants' include not only 'Hesiod and his fellow Boeotians'[2] and 'early Greek peasant society',[3] but also Greek society in the classical period, since Walcot, following a suggestion of the sociologist A. W. Gouldner,[4] argues that the set of values of the early Greeks were identical to those held by fifth and fourth century Athenians, supporting his claim with a series of random quotations from Xenophon's *Oeconomicus* and from Greek tragedy.[5] As for his 'modern Greeks', they come from the mountain villages studied by contemporary ethnographers such as Friedl (Vasilika), Campbell (the Sarakatsani), and Peristiany (the Pitsilloi), as well as from the Aegean islands described in a report written in 1886 by the 'folklorist-traveller' Theodore Bent.[6] According to Walcot,

---

[1] M. Herzfeld, *Anthropology through the Looking-glass: Critical Ethnography in the Margins of Europe* (Cambridge, 1987), 57.

[2] P. Walcot, *Greek Peasants Ancient and Modern: A Comparison of Social and Moral Values* (Manchester, 1970), 119.

[3] Ibid. 27–8.

[4] A. W. Gouldner, *Enter Plato: Classical Greece and the Origins of Social Theory* (London, 1967), 76.

[5] Walcot, *Greek Peasants* 74–5.

[6] E. Friedl, *Vassilika: a Village in Modern Greece* (New York, 1962); J. K. Campbell, *Honour, Family and Patronage : A Study of Institutions and Moral*

these two groups share strikingly similar customs : the coffee-house of a Greek village is presented as 'the modern equivalent of the *lesche*', and the travelling craftsmen of modern Greece 'function in exactly the same way as Homer's *demioergoi*'.[7] More generally, modern peasants' attitudes towards labour, honour, and shame carry us back to Hesiod's *Works and Days* and are to be explained as a survival from classical antiquity.[8] In short, these modern Greeks, miraculously spared by the course of history and uncontaminated by the encroachments of modern civilization, have been transformed into living aboriginal ancestors. One is reminded of the Braudelian definition of the Mediterranean as 'a collection of museums of man ... a human milieu which the most spectacular invasions have shown themselves incapable of biting into deeply'.[9]

1. THE FIRST WAVE

Long before modern classicists and ethnographers, such analogies were drawn not only by Frederick Douglas, in his *Essay on certains points of resemblance between the ancient and modern Greeks* (1813), but also by earlier French, English, and German travellers who from Pierre Belon (1553) to William Eton (1798) happened to visit Athens, the islands, and what they called the 'Morea' (the Peloponnese) and the 'Levant' (Asia Minor).[10]

Values in a Greek Mountain Community (Oxford, 1964); J. G. Peristiany, 'Honour and Shame in a Cypriot Highland Village', in J. G. Peristiany (ed.), *Honour and Shame: the Values of Mediterranean Society* (London, 1965), 173–90. And see T. J. Bent, 'On Insular Greek Customs', *Journal of the Royal Anthropological Institute* 15 (1886), 391–403, with Herzfeld, *Anthropology*, 73.

[7] Walcot, *Greek Peasants*, 27, 28.

[8] Ibid. 25–44, 57–76.

[9] F. Braudel, *La Méditerranée et le monde méditerranéen à l'époque de Philippe II* (Paris, 1949), 298 (not included in the revised edition, nor therefore in the English translation).

[10] On early travellers in Greece see D. Constantine, *Early Greek Travellers and the Hellenic Ideal* (Cambridge, 1984); H. Angelomatis-Tsougarakis, *The Eve of the Revival: British Travellers' Perceptions of Early Nineteenth-Century Greece* (London, 1990); R. Eisner, *Travelers to an Antique Land: The History and Literature of Travel to Greece* (Ann Arbor, 1991); O. Augustinos, *French Odysseys : Greece in French Travel literature from the Renaissance to the Romantic Era* (Baltimore, 1994). For a checklist of travel narratives see the end of this article.

Scholars, merchants, ambassadors, or 'Grand tourists', they all shared a common educational background, namely the history and literature of ancient Rome and Greece, and they were mostly looking for illustrations of antiquity. Like James Stuart and Nicholas Revett, they went to Athens because 'it deservedly claims the attention and excites the curiosity... whether we reflect on the figure it makes in history on account of the excellent men it has produced in every art..., or whether we consider the antiquities which are said to be still remaining there' (Stuart-Revett (ed.) (1825–30), i. I 13a). But they also, as I hope to demonstrate, had something to say about the modern inhabitants of that antique land.

Any attempt to find positive analogies between ancient and modern Greeks is foreign to the majority of seventeenth-century travellers. They usually tend to enforce the thesis of a 'Hellenism fallen from grace' and a Greece populated by 'wretched orientals'.[11] When they point out continuities between ancient and modern Greeks, they usually rely on the disparaging portrait of the Greeks inherited from the Romans as well as from Christian authors such as Paul,[12] a portrait mirrored by the derogatory sense of 'Greek' in sixteenth-century English :

first the word 'Greek' generally preceded by an epithet like 'gay', 'mad' or 'merry' became an ordinary conversational expression meaning a person of loose and lively habits, a boon companion, a fast liver.... The second common meaning of the word 'Greek'... was based upon the opinion of Greek wickedness, rather than of Greek dissoluteness. A 'greek' meant what we should call a 'twister', that is, a sharper, a cheat, a crook.[13]

But in the *Voyage d'Italie, de Dalmatie de Grèce et du Levant* of Jacob Spon (1678) and *The Journey into Greece* of his fellow English traveller Georges Wheler (1682), as well as in the two fictitious narratives of Guillet de Saint Georges, *Athènes ancienne et nouvelle* (1675) and *Lacédémone ancienne et nouvelle*

---

[11] Herzfeld, *Anthropology*, 49.

[12] See T. Spencer, *Fair Greece, Sad Relics : Literary Philhellenism from Shakespeare to Byron* (New York, 1973), 32–5.

[13] Ibid. 35, 37.

(1676), one may find a new emphasis on a positive, if imperfect, continuity as well as an attempt to account for it.

What has been labelled the 'romantic tradition about the Mediterranean'[14] or 'Mediterraneanism', that is to say the systematic search for survivals of ancient Greeks among the moderns, together with the repertoire of images and commonplaces, always positive, sometimes nearly idolatrous, only became dominant later, with eighteenth-century travellers. Prime exhibits are Lady Montagu's letters from her husband's Turkish embassy, Robert Wood's comparative view of the ancient and present state of the Troad appended to his *Essay on the Original Genius of Homer* (1767), Pierre Augustin Guys' *Voyage littéraire de la Grèce ou lettre sur les Grecs anciens et modernes, avec un parallèle de leurs moeurs* (1771), Baron Johann Hermann von Riedesel's *Remarques d'un voyageur moderne au Levant* (1773, repr. 1802), Richard Chandler's *Travels in Asia Minor* (1775) and *in Greece* (1776), and Comte Choiseul-Gouffier's *Voyage pittoresque en Grèce* (vol. 1, 1782). Among these travellers, Guys is exceptional. While all the others originated in Northern Europe, he was a *marseillais* who was quite aware of the similarities between modern and ancient Greeks, but also between Marseillians and Athenians; he was therefore able to replace the usual contrast between 'them' and 'us' by a first person plural (in letter VIII, which is devoted in part to the 'National character of the Greeks') (Guys (1771), i. 108–10).

From Pierre Belon's *Les Observations de plusieurs singularités et choses mémorables trouvées en Grèce, Asie, Judée* (1553) to the Marquis de Nointel (1670–80) and even Joseph Pitton de Tournefort, *Relation d'un voyage du Levant fait par ordre du Roi* (1717), the main emphasis is indeed on 'the deformation of that once worthy realm' (Lithgow (1632), ii. 71–2), the degeneration of modern Greeks: '[their] knowledge is converted . . . into affected ignorance (for they have no schools of learning amongst them)' and '[their] liberty into contented slavery, having lost their minds with their empire' (Sandys (1610), 77).

Pierre Belon, lured by the glory that was Greece and full of reverence for 'the authors of all beneficial knowlege and

---

[14] *CS* 28.

discipline that we revere today', is struck by the 'amazing state of ignorance' of modern Greeks and shocked by their language which is 'a corrupted idiom of the ancient language' (Belon (1553), 4). More than a hundred years after, another traveller, Aaron Hill, will use the same derogatory terms to criticize 'a much corrupted dialect [which] differs so extremely from the ancient Greek, . . . that they hardly make a shift to understand one word in ten when strangers speak it' (Hill (1709), 202).

Pierre Gilles, in his *Antiquities of Constantinople* (1561), complains about their 'natural aversion for anything that is valuable in antiquity' (p. 21). William Biddulph also contrasts the ancient splendour of a city that was 'the mother and nurse of all liberal arts and sciences' and its present status: 'but now there is nothing but atheism and barbarism, for it is governed by Turks and inhabited by ignorant Greeks' (Biddulph (1609), 10). Similarly, Sir Anthony Sherley, in his account of his journey to Cyprus and Paphos, writes (1613): 'we found no shew of splendor, no habitation of men in a fashion . . . but rather Slaves to cruel Masters or prisoners shut up in diverse prisons' (p. 6).

They also point to the moral debasement of a people from whom 'all civility has been rooted out' (Sandys' dedication), echo the contempt of the Turks for those who 'have lost their liberty and kingdom basely and cowardly, making small or no resistance against the Turks conquest' (Moryson (1597), 496), or denounce the corruption of modern Greeks: 'subtle and deceitful' (Biddulph (1609), 79), 'great dissemblers' (Lithgow (1632), ii. 64), they have been assimilated by their conquerors and are even worse than the Turks : 'Pour leurs coutumes et leurs facons de vivre, elle sont à peu près celles des Turcs, mais ils sont plus méchants. Les Grecs sont avares, perfides et traitres, grands pédérastes, vindicatifs jusqu'au dernier point, du reste fort superstitieux et grands hypocrites' (Thévenot (1655), 158–9).

These laments will still be heard long afterwards: when Gibbon in his *Decline and Fall of the Roman Empire* portrays the Athenians who 'walk with supine indifference among the glorious ruins of Antiquity' and laments 'the debasement of their character', which is 'such that they are incapable of admiring the genius of their predecessors' (Gibbon (1776–88), vi. 486), he is merely repeating George Sandys's 'supine recklessness' (Sandys (1610), 80).

When these travellers, whose perception of the ancient Greeks is mostly influenced by the negative portrait to be found in Latin literature, discover some cultural continuity between ancient and modern Greeks, it is usually for the worse. In John Covel's *Early Voyages and Travels in the Levant* (1670–6), the sentence 'Greeks are Greeks still' is glossed in the following way: 'for falseness and treachery they still deserve Iphigenia's character of them in Euripides, trust them and hang them' (p. 133). According to Duloir, Greeks have only retained 'the worst qualities of their ancestors: namely deceit, perfidy and vanity' (Duloir (1654), 166).

There were, however, some rare attempts to establish some kind of a more positive continuity. Belon (1553, 5, 6) finds that 'the common people . . . whether from the islands or from the mainland, retain something of their antiquity' such as their funeral customs : 'the ancient manner of the pagans to mourn their dead is still practised at the present time in the country of Greece'. Sandys wonders if coffee is not after all 'that black broth which was in use among the Lacedemonians' (Sandys (1610), 66). J. P. Babin (1674) goes further and finds among the Greeks some remains of their past virtues: 'Ils ne tiennent pas seulement cette curiosité par héritage de leurs ancêtres, mais encore une grande estime d'eux-mêmes nonobstant leur servitude, leur misère et leur pauvreté sous la domination Turquesque. . . . Dans Athènes il se rencontre encore des personnes courageuses et remarquables par leur vertu' (pp. 208–9).

With his *Athènes ancienne et nouvelle* and *Lacédémone ancienne et nouvelle*, Guillet de Saint Georges purported to give, under the name of his brother, 'the most faithful and succinct description both of [the] past fortune and present condition' (p. 126) of the two major powers of Classical Greece. Of course, the brother was an invention and Guillet never left France. However, his travel narratives, precisely because they are fictitious, deserve much attention from anyone interested in stereotypes, since, in order to be convincing, they have to stick to verisimilitude and present a picture of the 'modern' Greeks which fulfils the expectations of the audience. His portrayal of the Maniots clearly show how contradictory these expectations were: 'Some will have them brutish perfidious and naturally addicted to robbery; others consider them as the true posterity and the remainder of the magnanimous Greeks who prefered their liberty to their lives' (pp. 28–9). Side by side we find the despicable modern Greek and the true heir of the Spartans who died at the Thermopylae—a tension which often reappears later. One can also find the corruption theme, a corruption explained by Greek contact with other peoples :

The Greek that is vulgarly spoken among the Maniots is the most corrupt of all other; for having a constant trade by reason of the commodities which they take by piracy and trafficking one day with one nation and another day with the other, they are much accustomed to the language which they call the Franck. (p. 32)

He emphasizes the negative continuity: 'I found by their vanity in those descriptions [of their piratical activities] that they were true Greeks and had learned from their ancestors the art of advertising and embellishing their exploits' (pp. 32–3).

On the other hand Guillet praises the Athenians who 'maintain the hospitality that was so honourable in their ancestors' (p. 149). Reviving the prejudices of the Atticists under the Roman Empire, he still finds that 'the language at Athens is the most pure and incorrupt of all the cities in Greece. It is nowhere spoken or understood in its primitive purity but at Athens' (p. 149). Perhaps because this is after all an imposture, he dares to give the floor to an Athenian who questions the usual commonplaces about degenerate Greece:

Our nation is not degenerate: are they not our soldiers who are fighting your armies and overrunning your provinces? And you cannot deny that the Ottoman forces consist principally of persons forced or stolen from us. (p. 232)

2. SPON AND WHELER AND THEIR SUCCESSORS

The narrative of Jacob Spon, who introduces himself first and foremost as an antiquarian: 'C'est seulement l'amour de l'antiquité qui m'a fait entreprendre ce voyage' (Préface), as well as the *Journal* of his companion, George Wheler, offer a more complex view of the relations between ancient and modern Greeks.

There are indeed many traces of the traditional—and completely negative—portrayal of modern Greeks. Their ignorance

is still stressed: 'dans un pays où il n'y a guère que des ignor-
ants, il ne faut pas être beaucoup savant pour y faire quelque
bruit' (Spon (1678), i. 116; see also i. 159, 271; ii. 49, 63,
139). Similarly their lack of taste: the most beautiful convent
of Greece would be considered as 'fort médiocre dans nos
quartiers' (ii. 59). In his disparaging description of Athens
Spon piles up negatives: 'Athènes n'est plus qu'un grand
et pauvre hopital qui contient autant de miserables qu'on
y voit de chrétiens sous la domination des Turcs...on n'y
voit plus...on ne remarque plus...On ne voit aucun fonde-
ment...on ne sait... on ignore...' (ii. 236). Like him, his
companion, George Wheler points some negative continuities: 'yet this old humour of jealousy still continues' (Wheler
(1682), 349).

Nonetheless Spon and Wheler often acknowledge the survival of positive characteristics such as freedom and cleverness
among the Athenians. They are among the first to explain
the modern Athenians by reference to their climate as well
as their ancestors. Spon quotes an Athenian who told him:
'Voyez vous', dit-il, 'nous avons toujours été brouillons,
mais vous savez que nous n'avons jamais pu soufrir ceux qui
prenaient de l'autorité sur nous...l'air du pays porte à cela,
et c'est en partie l'héritage de nos ancêtres'(ii. 135). Wheler
admits that 'their bad Fortune hath not been able to take
from them what they have by nature, that is, much natural
subtlety, or wit, of which the serenity and goodness of the air
they enjoy may be a great natural cause'(p. 347). Relying on
traditional Athenian hospitality, they expected to be welcomed
and were not disappointed: 'nous nous imaginâmes même d'être
entrés dans un pays plus poli que ceux où nous avions passé;
et en effet nous ne rencontrions ni berger ni laboureur qui
ne nous dit que nous étions les très bienvenus...' (Spon
(1678), ii. 75).

Eighteenth-century Hellenism is characterized by a growing
interest in modern Greece. R. Chandler (1776) suggests that
'the traveler who is versed in antiquity may be agreeably and
universally employed in studying the people of Athens' (p. 145),
and Riedesel (1767) is commended by his English translator for
giving 'a very good idea of the modern state' of the countries he
visited. As they look below the surface, travellers like Lord

Charlemont (1749), Riedesel (1767) and Eaton (1798) begin to find fascinating survivals of ancient Greece:

If any person more skilled than I can pretend to be in the manners of the ancient Greeks and with more opportunity than I have had of cultivating their successors would take pain of travelling through Greece with a view to this curious investigation, he would find his troubles most rewarded by the most striking proofs that the modern Greeks, however superficially changed by the sad influence of their present situation and depressed by ages of misery, still retain the great characteristical marks of that glorious people. (Charlemont (1749), 119).

Riedesel is thrilled to discover among the monuments of Athens 'des traces du génie et de la grandeur d'âme de ses anciens habitants' (Riedesel (1767), 119). Eaton (1798, 334) also notices with astonishment that the Greeks 'have retained . . . much energy of character'.

Yet commonplaces about the vices of the Greeks ancient as well as modern, as well as the complaints over their degradation, are still to be found, sometimes in the same texts.

First, the persistence of the same vices culled from Greek and Latin literature and exemplified by their history from the Classical period to the last Byzantine emperor: repeating some ancient clichés about the Lesbians, Richard Pococke says that 'their women have no better character for their chastity nor men for their sobriety than in former times' (Pococke (1743), 21). Alexander Drummond also criticizes the Greek ladies who have 'inherited the libertinism of their ancestors' (1754, 269). Tournefort (1717, i. 282), who assimilates all the ancient Greeks to the Athenians of Aristophanes' *Wasps*, claims that they are 'naturellement chicaneurs'. R. Chandler (1776, 127), taking for granted the portrayal of the Athenians by the Corinthians in Thucydides 1. 70, finds that modern Athenians are similar to their ancestors : 'their disposition as anciently is unquiet; their repose disturbed by factious intrigues and private animosities'. Relying openly on Thucydides, Guys (1772, i. 25) generalizes: 'I have found them, I confess, such as they are represented by ancient historians, Thucydides in particular; artful, vain, flexible, inconstant, avaricious, lovers of novelty, and not very scrupulous observers of their oaths'. Envy, competition, and what Charlemont called 'the spirit of party' (1749, 113), which played a central role in the history of ancient Greece. are still alive among the modern Greeks, according to Riedesel:

Tous les Grecs s'envient mutuellement et aiment mieux être assujettis aux Turcs que de voir prospérer leurs voisins; semblables en cela aux anciens Grecs qu'on a vu appeler dans leur pays tantôt les Perses, tantôt les Gaulois, et enfin les Romains pour affaiblir leurs voisins.... Il paraît que cette nation avec ce caractère inquiet est destinée à se gouverner par de petites républiques comme anciennement ou à porter le joug du despotisme comme aujourd'hui. (Riedesel (1772), 324–5)

He also echoes the disparaging Roman cliché of the perfidious Greek, and exposes the faithlessness of their modern descendants: 'les anciens proverbes, *nulla fides Graiis, garrula gens Graium*, se vérifient encore' (p. 326).

James Porter, constructing a portrait of the ancient Greeks from two different periods, the Peloponnesian War and the Byzantine Empire, foists their combined defects on their descendants, but by adding that the modern Greeks only reproduce these defects in miniature, he manages to combine the themes of degradation and corruption:

The modern Greeks are a near image and resemblance of the ancient. Too crafty and subtle, too intriguing, vain, vindictive either to support and maintain the interest, reputation, and glory of a republic or to share with, and submit to Government under a monarch of their own; their busy spirit seems exactly formed and adjusted to live no where tranquil but under a foreign subjection.... whoever could live among the Greeks and observe their refined intrigues... would see *a true portrait in miniature* of the worst Peloponnesian Republics and a most striking resemblance of their abominable practices under their own emperors from Constantine to the last of the Paleologus's. (Porter (1768), ii. 110–12)

Second, complaints about Greek degradation go on and on. According to Charlemont (1749, 114), the Athenians, who 'are accounted by far the most ingenious people of Greece, endowed by nature with the most active mind and the most subtle... wit..., from want of education to give them their proper direction and from a sad dereliction and perversion,... have *degenerated* into low cunning and knavery'. A. Drummond sees 'mean dejection, wretchedness, or deceit' everywhere (1754, 121). Chandler says more or less the same: 'the native quickness of apprehension which characterized the Athenians... not being duly cultivated...has *degenerated* into cunning' (1776, 126–7). Before them, Tournefort mourned over a 'decadence' (1717, i. 76) which was the consequence of ignorance and slavery. Another French traveller, J. B. Lechevalier, lays stress on 'le contraste frappant...entre les beaux siècles de ce peuple immortel et le triste tableau qu'il présente', a truth illustrated later by the laziness of the modern Corfiots as opposed to their industrious ancestors, the mythical Phaeacians (1802, 31). Usually western travellers explain this degeneration by the Turkish conquest. For Riedesel the crucial factor is the adulteration of the 'pure' Greek blood: 'il parait que les Vénitiens et les Turcs ont dénaturé ce beau sang' (1771, 250). Others accuse political institutions and the 'tyranny' of the Turks. Charles Perry denounces 'the great oppressions they [the Greeks] groan under from their cruel, inexorable Tyrant, the Turk' (1743, 23). Charlemont (1749, 119) makes slavery responsible for the 'want of education' of the Greeks. Drummond also portrays 'a conquered people...exposed to...cruelty and extortion...familiarized to oppression, which hath likewise disposed them for villainy' (1754, 121). But there are also some attempts to date this decadence back to Byzantium. According to James Porter (1768, ii. 123), 'whatever arts and sciences, whatever virtues might have been found in ancient times among the Greek Republicans seem to have been obscured or totally lost under their emperors'. Choiseul-Gouffier (1782, p. vii) also believes that Greek culture collapsed under Byzantine influence:

Plaire à leurs maitres, ce fut le seul but de ces sujets ; ils y employèrent tous les talents que leur avait prodigués la nature...dès lors leur caractère fut un mélange de ruse, de bassesse, de férocité et de superstition; leur esprit, dégénérant en subtilité, porta la métaphysique dans les disputes religieuszes et cet entêtement scholastique mêlé aux fureurs du fanatisme...plongea la Grèce dans le dernier degré d'avilissement et fit de de son histoire un tissu de crimes et de perfidies. C'est dans cet excès de dégradation qu'était tombé l'empire à l'époque de la prise de Constantinople.

This moral degeneration may be paralleled in many other ways. The famous wine of Chios 'seems to have degenerated' (Charlemont (1749), 43), and Greek women are no longer 'ces sublimes beautés qu'on trouve sur les bas reliefs' (Riedesel (1771), 250). Most of all, travellers note that modern Greek is no longer 'pure'. This 'daughter of ancient Greek' has lost its subtlety, precision, and beauty. According to Riedesel, the Turks, who, together with the Venetians have polluted Greek blood, bear the major reponsibility for this decline: they have sullied and adulterated Greek grammar: 'la langue grecque vulgaire est fille de l'ancienne, mais elle a perdu sa finesse, sa précision et sa beauté... sa construction est calquée sur celle de la langue turque' (Riedesel (1771), 334).

But at the same time some distanced themselves from these disparaging and exaggeratedly negative comments : 'nous avons exagéré les funestes effets de leur cruelle situation' (Choiseul-Gouffier (1782), ii. 126). Besides, most of those who air these complaints do not come to the same conclusion as their predecessors. Instead of asserting that the virtues of ancient Greeks have vanished and that 'the present Greeks have not a trace of them remaining'—this is still the conclusion reached by James Porter (1768, ii. 123)—they eagerly search for relics. True, the ancient Greek character is 'altered', but it is not totally 'obliterated', still the characteristic marks remain' (Charlemont (1749), 119–20). True, the Greek nation 'is now pretty much estranged to all those splendid virtues and accomplishments ... yet Nature still manifests herself in their favour ... yet they manifest a great deal of cunning subtility and dexterity in all parts of life', according to Charles Perry, author of an important book on the Levant (Perry (1743), 23). Their language is 'disfigured in appearance, yet preserving all the depths, richness and harmony of the ancient Greek' (Guys (1772), i. 115). There are still 'some sparks from the sacred fire that fly out' and some 'glow of the ancient spirit' (Guys (1772), ii. 28). In the same way Choiseul-Gouffier speaks of 'un feu sacré qui s'est affaibli, mais n'est pas éteint' (1782, ii. 125).

Similes are even more significant. The same striking comparison of modern Greece with an old man appears independently in Guys' *Voyage littéraire de la Grèce* and Riedesel's *Remarques d'un voyageur moderne au Levant*. But it is used in two opposite ways. Guys emphasizes the continuity between ancient and modern Greece: '[his] very wrinkles of caducity will never be disfigured to the point of making [the old man] unrecognizable' (Guys (1772), ii. 189–90), whereas Riedesel chooses to stress decrepitude: 'la Grèce moderne, si on la compare à l'ancienne, ressemble à un vieillard qui après avoir été un héros dans sa jeunesse est tombé en enfance par la décrépitude de l'âge' (Riedesel (1774/1802), 319).

Some archaeological metaphors significantly turn modern Greeks into living monuments of the past and assimilate them to ruins, parts of broken statues or obliterated coins, providing a clear demonstration that the perception of modern Greeks was to a large extent conditioned by the interest in classical antiquity and its physical remains. Reconciling ethnography with their primary antiquarian interest, the traveller becomes epigraphist, numismatist, art historian. Tournefort is epigraphical: 'I looked at the brain of these poor Greeks as I would at living inscriptions, which serve to conserve us the names cited by Theophrastus and Dioscorides' (1717, 87–8). Guys is numismatic:

Look at me as an antiquarian who instead of neglecting a copper coin ... because it is unpolished and badly preserved takes the trouble to wash it, to clean it carefully and finally discovers the characters that were believed to be entirely effaced ... I have all the satisfactions of the antiquarian when, by observing the modern Greeks step by step and comparing them to the ancient, all of whose signs I have, I recognize the one I am looking for (1772, ii. 14).

Similarly Choiseul-Gouffier:

aussi cherchais-je, au milieu de la dégradation que j'avais sous les yeux, à démêler quelques traits héréditaires du caractère des Grecs comme j'eusse cherché l'empreinte d'une médaille antique sous la rouille qui la couvre et qui la dévore. (1782, p.v)

Guys is the art historian: 'you must already perceive a great conformity between the ancient and modern Greeks: like those mutilated statues still to be found, where all admire the attitudes, the drapery ... ' (1772, i. 26). Likewise Riedesel:

Il est vrai qu'on découvre encore ces traits originaux et caractéristiques qui donnent la ressemblance déjà à l'esquisse d'un portrait. Mais ce sont des traits si obscurs, si mal prononcés, si dénaturés même qu'il faut aujourd'hui chercher à y suppléer le mieux qu'on peut; semblable en cela à l'antiquaire qui, pour expliquer un ancien bas relief, est obliger d'y supposer les parties que la main du temps a détruites. (1773, 321)

Far from being innocuous, all these metaphors are fraught with consequences. If the remains of the ancient Greek character are museum pieces, they have to be sheltered from corrupting influences and eventually restored. Accordingly, European travellers harshly criticize any acculturation or admixture of foreign blood which would 'pollute' even more the precious remains of pure hellenicity. In particular Riedesel condemns 'l'affectation servile que les Grecs mettent à imiter les usages et les costumes Turcs' (1773, 335), in the layout of their houses, in their furniture or in their food (ibid. 326–7).

Therefore it is the duty of the traveller to search for these precious remains, collect them, and underline the continuity between past and present by the use of the ethnographic present and by adverbs such as 'still', 'yet' or 'as formerly'. Travel narratives of the eighteenth century are all full of attempts to discover points of resemblance between the ancient and modern Greeks.

Modern Greeks were supposed to retain the physical appearance of their ancestors. James Dallaway (1797, 6) finds a 'marked resemblance between those of heroes which have been transmitted to us and the peasant or the mariner' he meets in the streets. In walking through a market, William Eton (1798, 334) dreams that he is able, while looking around, to 'put together from different faces . . . the heads of Apollo and the finest ancient statues'.

Travellers also paid particular attention to costume and discovered many common elements between ancient and modern Greece. The letters of Guys and Riedesel are especially interesting, for one may see the arbitrariness of comparisons created with the aid of dubious (to say the least) reconstructions of ancient Greek costume from highly heterogeneous elements, including not only Greek but also Roman works of art. Riedesel relies on a Greek (?) bas relief he has seen in Italy to conclude that on the island of Naxos men wear the same hats as in antiquity: 'les hommes portent de grands chapeaux de paille suspendus à la nuque par un cordon, comme on le voit à une figure du beau bas-relief qui se trouve à la maison de campagne du cardinal Alexandre Albani représentant Amphion et Zethos. *Il paraît que cet usage s'est conservé depuis ce temps là* ' (Riedesel 1773, 260). The modern costume of the women is said to be much similar to the ancient 'tel que nous le représentent les statues antiques et les peintures d'*Herculanum*' (p. 328).

Guys' analogies between the toilet of modern and ancient
Greek women (1772, i. 69) also depend on a highly hypothetical
reconstruction of ancient costume and a collage of many heterogeneous texts: the head-band comes from Plutarch's *Life of
Phocion*, from two Latin texts concerning Greek characters
(Terence's *Andria* and Ovid's letter of Sappho to Phaon),
and from a declamation of John Chrysostom against the women
of his time (i. 79–83); the fan, from Anacreon, Pausanias' description of a marble tomb, the *False Eunuch* of Terence, and
Claudian; the veil, from Nonnos and Valerius Maximus (i. 85–6).

It was also commonly accepted that the Greeks still retain
some resemblance to the character of their ancestors. Their
hospitality is praised by Guys: 'hospitality is another excellent
quality in which the Greeks are never deficient' (1772, i. 285).
Together with tact, it is perceived by Riedesel (1744/1802, 327),
as a relic of ancient times: 'quelques vertus, telles que l'hospitalité et la discrétion, se sont maintenues des anciens temps'.
Choiseul-Gouffier also acknowledges that the inhabitants of
Sigaeum 'conservent quelques traces des moeurs de leurs ancêtres et surtout l'hospitalité envers les étrangers' (1782, 365).

Moreover, some distinctive characteristics of the different
cities are supposed to survive. According to Tournefort (1718,
159), the inhabitants of Paros who were famed for their wisdom
in antiquity (the Milesians are said to have chosen one of them
'to put their city into a form of government') are still chosen as
arbitrators by the Greeks of the neighbouring islands. 'The
Thebans of this day, as formerly, are accounted by their neighbours though brave and honest the least sprightly among the
Greeks' (Charlemont (1749/1984), 149). Above all, the Maniots,
who are said to be the true heirs of the Spartans and 'have always
preserved their liberty' (Pococke 1743, i. 178), serve as an illustration of this continuity. According to Lord Sandwich (1799,
31), '[these] descendants of the ancient Lacedemonians ... still
preserve their love of liberty so great a degree, as never to have
debased themselves under the yoke of the Turkish empire'. This
reappears in Riedesel: 'les habitants actuels du mont Taygète,
connus sous le nom de Mainottes soutiennent leur liberté avec
fermeté et courage contre la puissance ottomane ... leur pays ...
paraît avoir été constamment la véritable patrie de la liberté'
(1774/1802, 223–5). Choiseul-Gouffier (1782, p. ix) is even

more enthusiastic: 'robustes, sobres, invincibles, libres comme au temps de Lycurgue, ils défendent avec succès contres les Turcs cette liberté qu'ils ont maintenue contre tous les efforts de la puissance romaine', a panegyric followed by a narrative of the battle waged by a handful of Maniots againt 40,000 Turks which is obviously modelled on Thermopylae. Morritt (1794, 194, 203), who was not deterred from visiting this impenetrable area, was charmed by the hospitality and goodness of its inhabitants and praises a people who 'retain the spirits and character of Grecians more than we had ever seen and their customs and language are transmitted with greater purity'.

Eighteenth-century travellers, like nineteenth-century ethnographers such as Bent are delighted to notice 'endless parallels to antiquity' in the daily life of modern Greeks, 'in their method of catching fish, in their planting of crops, in their medical and religious lore' (Bent 1886, 401). As Aristophanes would say, in travel narratives Greek men and even more Greek women do everything 'as before', ὥσπερ καὶ πρὸ τοῦ (*Eccl.* 221): baths,[15] embroidery,[16] signatures,[17] salutations,[18] funeral customs,[19] the refusal to talk about women,[20] but also the shape of the boats,[21] methods of cultivating the grapes and making wine[22] are the same. Long before Walcot (1970, 27), Riedesel drew his readers' attention to the analogy between the

[15] Guys, ii. 243: 'The custom of bathing so frequent among the ancient Greeks is no less so among the moderns.'

[16] Ibid. 46: 'embroidery is the constant employment of the Greek women... this is a picture of the industrious wife painted after nature by Virgil... I have a living portrait of the same kind constantly before my eyes.'

[17] Ibid. 80: 'they add the name of their father to their own, which is "an ancient custom attested by Pausanias".'

[18] Guys, i, 65: 'The Greek ladies, according to the custom of the ancient, present the hands to be kissed by their daughters, their slaves and other persons who are their inferiors.'

[19] Riedesel, 327: 'leur manière de porter le deuil et de témoigner leur affliction est également celle des anciens Grecs.'

[20] Ibid. 323: 'la même discrétion des anciens sur le comte des femmes règne encore parmi eux. Ils n'en parlent jamais ni en bien ni en mal.'

[21] Guys, ii, 12: 'the monoxylon (boat) "built exactly upon the model of the ancient Greeks".'

[22] Ibid. 15: 'Their method of cultivating the grape is as ancient as the crane which they make use to draw it off which we find nowhere so well described as in the works of Oppian.'

coffee-house and the Hesiodic *lesche*: 'ils [the Greeks] sont encore dans l'usage de passer leur temps à ne rien faire et à jaser aux bazars et aux cafés comme leurs ancêtres le faisaient dans la lesché' (p. 326). Guys is particularly fond of these parallelisms, but he is also the only one to openly acknowledge that some of them may be forced: 'perhaps too much attached to my plan, I appear to you as if some of the resemblances between ancient and modern Greece were forced and strained to gratify my own predilections' (Guys 1772, ii. 13).

Two parallels are particularly interesting, because they seem to betray the permanence of well-established commonplaces, the emphasis on dances and the remarks on religion.

Lady Mary Wortley Montagu (1717/1965 i. 303) finds girls dancing in the same manner 'that Diana is sung to have danced on the Eurotas'. Similarly, when seeing in the villages of Chios 'the men and women dancing together in the same manner in the public squares', Pococke (1743–5, i. 11) remarks that 'it seems to be a custom continued from the ancient Greeks among whom dancing was looked on as a great perfection'. Porter (1768, ii. 132) also emphasizes the continuity between the dances of the ancient and the modern Greeks: 'they still use the ancient dance led by one person...They also have the manly martial Pyrrhic dance and those most obscene, infamous love-dances'. Riedesel, who piles up quotations from Homer, Sophocles, and Pollux to illustrate the ancient 'Cnossian dances', is even more positive: 'la danse des Grecs modernes est le trait de ressemblance le plus frappant qu'ils aient avec leurs ancêtres. En voyant danser la romeca, je me suis cru transporté dans les champs gnossiens' (Riedesel (1774/1802), 329). Chandler (1776, 141) does not doubt that some of the dances of modern Greeks are 'of remote antiquity'. Choiseul-Gouffier (1782, 68) is struck by the surprising conformity of the *romeca* with ancient Greek dances. I wonder if this repeated emphasis on Greek dances in eighteenth-century travel narratives is not to be explained by its being in keeping with the long accepted cliché of the 'merry Greeks'.

As for religion, eighteenth-century travellers, in agreement with the spirit of the Enlightment, far from contrasting the Christian Greeks with their heathen ancestors often find analogies between them. Tournefort (1718, 88) is among the first to posit a continuity between Orthodoxy and ancient paganism: 'the multiplicity of chapels may be a relick of the ancient custom that prevailed in Greece of raising little temples to their false gods'. Riedesel (1774/1802, 262) witnessed in Paros a religious ceremony that reminded him of 'les anciens mystères de Cérès à Fleusis'. Chandler (1776, 144), followed later by Douglas (1813, 61), draws a parallel between the cult of the Saints and pagan polytheism: 'the old Athenian had a multitude of deities, but relied chiefly on Minerva, the modern has a similar troop, headed by his favourite Panagia'.

In order to explain these similarities, real or imaginary, eighteenth-century travellers usually assumed direct continuities between the present and the past, even when they were aware of other possibilities. So, when Charlemont wonders whether in Athens women's reserve comes 'from an imitation of the Turks or from a more perfect retention of ancient manners' (1749/ 1984, 126), he is, as he says, rather inclined to believe the survivalist argument. In the same way, Guys (1772, 92–3) attributes the wearing of the veil by Greek ladies not, like Montesquieu, to an attempt to protect them from the concupiscence of the Turks, but 'to no other cause than the custom they have so long practised'. Chandler is perhaps the best representative of systematic survivalism, when he says that Athens 'after it was abandoned by the Goths continued, it is likely, for ages to preserve the race of its remaining inhabitants unchanged and uniform in language and manners' (1776, 123).

In order to explain this phenomenon, some assumed that the Greeks, though paradoxically characterized, like Thucydides' Athenians, by their love of novelty, also felt an innate attachment to the past and a healthy resistance to fashion and change:

This people, flighty as they are and lovers of novelty . . . have notwithstanding always resisted the absurd caprice and inconstancy of fashion, which so eminently prevailed with us. (Guys (1772), i. 135–6).

They

tread undeviatingly in the footsteps of their forefathers; while we exert our utmost ingenuity to recede as far as possible from the usages . . . of our ancestors, as if we sought to contrast them with the present times. . . . Inattentive, as the people of the Levant are, to what passes in the world, they insensibly follow the customes of their forefathers. (ii. 32)

Others emphasized the importance of physical, political, or cultural isolation. Physical isolation for the Maniots who live 'among those inaccessible mountains which are the ancient Mount Taygetus' (Pococke 1743–5, i. 178), 'sous l'abri des rochers qui repoussent les vices' (Choiseul-Gouffier (1782), p. viii), and were therefore able to escape the taint of intermarriages (Morritt (1794/1985), 194–5), but also for the inhabitants of the Ionian islands who 'preserve more of the Grecian manners and character than much of the region more properly included in that denomination' (Douglas (1813), 10), their blood being even more 'pure' than the Maniots' according to Douglas (1813, 43). The political isolation of those who live 'loin du siège de l'empire' (Choiseul-Gouffier (1782), p. ix), that is, in the countryside, in the islands or even in Athens, results in their being 'plus originaux, plus vrais et moins corrompus par les Mahométans' (Riedesel (1774/1802), 319). The cultural isolation of the common people is such that they 'refine but little and are ever tenacious of the traditions handed down to them by their forefathers and are so much attached to their customs, that they bear with them the force of so many laws' (Guys (1772), i. 146).

Readers of *The Spirit of the Laws* may also, like Charlemont (1749/1984, 112, 119), 'subscribe to the opinion and fundamental maxim laid down by the Great Montesquieu that "physical causes never cease to operate and to produce their effects, notwithstanding the total subversion of every moral cause"'. Given that Greece 'has not lost the gifts of nature, why then should its inhabitants not retain their native genius?' Guys voices the same opinion in lyrical terms: 'the same sun which formerly enlivened this country continues to shine with undiminished splendour ... the pureness of the air, the softness of the climate, the serenity of the day inspire ideas superior to any thing, but the objects to be met within this country. Every woman I meet conveys to my imagination a Venus from the chisel of a Praxiteles or the pencil of an Apelles' (1772, iii. 21). But the validity of these explanations is also questioned or seriously qualified. Tournefort, for one, compared the Greeks 'who are unmerciful talkers' and the Turks who 'pride themselves on sincerity and modesty more than on eloquence' (1718, i. 156), and concluded that 'though those two nations are born under one climate, their tempers are more different than if they lived very remote from each other, which can be imputed only to their different education'. Riedesel agreed that the harshness of the climate and the cold East and North winds may have contributed to producing 'ce génie guerrier, cette austérité, ce stoicisme ... que nous admirons si justement chez les anciens Spartiates' as well as 'l'esprit d'indépendance' of the modern Maniots (1772: 223), but he does not see any link between the fertile imagination of Athenian artists and the climate of Athens:

ce qui me surprend, c'est de trouver dans une contrée où domine le vent impétueux du Nord cette imagination féconde et brillante qui étonne dans leurs anciens poètes, ce génie créateur qu'on admirait dans les chefs d'oeuvre des Phidias, des Praxitèles ... dont le goût, la délicatesse et la sensibilité me paraissent s'accorder si peu avec un ciel sujet à des changements de température aussi subits que ceux qu'on éprouve à Athènes. ... (Riedesel (1772), 363).

3. THE ROMANTIC SENSIBILITY

The romantic imagination of some eighteenth-century travellers led them to believe it was possible that the past was in fact alive in a country where 'many of the customs, and much of the dress then in fashion [are] yet retained' (Montagu 1717/1965, i. 381). In her letters from Turkey, Montagu was the first to give voice to this new sensibility. Her letter to Alexander Pope describing a picnic among Greek peasants on the banks of the Hebrus, 'a place where truth for once furnishes all the ideas of pastoral', is most remarkable:

I have often seen them and their children sitting on the banks of the river and playing a rural intrument perfectly answering the description of the ancient fistula ... the young lads generally divert themselves with making garlands for their favourite lambs. ... It is not that they ever read romances, but these are the ancient amusements here, as natural to them as cudgel-playing and football to our British swains ... they are most of them Greeks. ... I no longer look upon Theocritus as a romantic writer; he has only given a plain image of the way of life amongst the peasants of his country, which before oppression had reduced them to want were I suppose all employed at the better sort of them are now'. (Montagu (1717/1965), i. 332–3).

This description, which surprisingly transforms Theocritus into a 'realist' artist and an accurate reporter of everyday life, and lumps memories from his *Idylls* together with obvious reminiscences of Longus' *Daphnis and Chloe*, reverses the relationship between ancient texts and contemporary reality:[23]

Those early travellers primarily interested in archaeological remains used the ancient authors, especially Strabo and Pausanias, to elucidate the sites and the buildings. But it is rather a different process, almost a reversal, when a traveller—Lady Montagu being one of the first—applies what is there to be seen, particularly in climate, topography and manners, to the ancient texts, to Homer and Theocritus, to elucidate and enjoy them all the more.

It is also a transformation of the way of looking at modern Greeks: they are promoted from their former status of vestiges to that of living museums.

Other travellers shared this Romantic illusion. So, Choiseul-Gouffier discovers 'une *vive* image de ces moeurs antiques' (Choiseul-Gouffier (1782), ii. 97). Arriving at Siphnos and finding the inhabitants assembled under a kind of portico and asking questions , he writes:

Je me crus transporté aux beaux jours de la Grèce: ces portiques, cette assemblée populaire, ces vieillards qu'on écoutait avec un silence respectueux, leurs figures, leurs habillements, leur langage, tout me rappelait Athènes, ou Corinthe , et ces places publiques où un peuple avide de nouvelles environnait les étrangers et les voyageurs. L'empressement avec lequel on m'offrit l'hospitalité vint bientôt fortifier cette illusion. (i. 14).

The same experience is repeated in Tinos, when he sees old women knitting and telling stories, while young girls are singing: 'je crus alors pour la première fois que les tableaux délicieux que nous offrent les auteurs Grecs etaient moins l'ouvrage de leur imagination qu'une *fidèle imitation de la nature*' (i. 44). In Adrianople, looking at women picking roses, he writes:

les grâces décentes de ces moissonneuses, leurs vêtements, les longues tresses de leurs chevelures et ces voiles qu'elles se plaisent à livrer au vent qui les soutient en voûte sur leur tête, *tout retrace les scènes décrites par Théocrite et Virgile*: il n'est pas une de ces beautés dont

---

[23] Constantine, *Early Greek Travellers*, 149.

vous ne croyiez avoir déjà vu l'image sur quelques bas-reliefs ou sur une pierre antique. (ii. 173–4).

Lechevalier happens to meet in the Laurion 'un jeune berger chausé de cothurnes et exactement vêtu à la manière des anciens Grecs' (1802, 118).

Guys, who was first disappointed at not finding any more 'those celebrated artists whose race is extinct or those paintings or statues which have been destroyed or carried away', is amply compensated by the contemplation of their very original, 'the striking scenes before [him that] might have served as models for the painters, sculptors and poets of ancient Greece . . . the *living* pictures, the *animated* statues which industry and talents must copy with success' (ii., 112, 113). Watching Greek women occupied with embroidery, he sees 'a *living* portrait' of the industrious wife painted after nature by Virgil' (ii. 46); touring the country, he becomes acquainted with 'the shepherds and pipers of Theocritus' (ii. 166).

In modern Greece, travellers are not only transported to ancient Greece. They come into contact with a primeval world characterized by the simplicity of its manners and identified with pure nature—as opposed to the refined modes of modern life. Greeks, according to Guys, 'have to this day preserved the simplicity of the manners and customs of the earliest periods' (i. 46). Choiseul-Gouffier, discovering in Ios a world where 'tout rappelle la simplicité des premiers âges' (1782, 20) would readily have agreed.

Modern Greece becomes a world cut off from history, and a place where time stands still, since it is inaccessible to the civilization and the changes it brings with it. But as modern Greece becomes representative of the primitive, it loses something of its particular appeal. The Greeks are assimilated to these oriental peoples who, as Choiseul-Gouffier says,[24] have not lost the manners described in the most ancient annals of the world, that is Homer but also the Bible. It becomes part of that Levant where Riedesel wanted to go to escape the curse of civilization, and to find 'un pays où l'habillement, les moeurs

---

[24] Choiseul-Gouffier, ii, 104: 'Les peuples d'Orient n'ont donc perdu presque aucun des usages décrits dans les plus anciennes annales du monde, dans les livres saints ou dans les chants d'Homère.'

et usages, la religion, le système d'Etat ne fussent autant sujet que chez nous à des variations continuelles... lequel enfin, ayant moins de lois et moins de connaissances que nous n'en avons fût plus *original* et dont les habitants fussent *plus près de la nature*' (1774/1802, 219). Like the Greeks for Guys, the Bedouin tribes become for Wood, 'a perpetual and inexhaustible store of the *aboriginal* modes and customs of *primeval* life.... *inaccessible to the varieties and fluctuations* which conquest, commerce, arts or agriculture introduce in other places' (p. 136). Likewise, Choiseul-Gouffier begins to look to a more distant Orient to find truly primitive simplicity: 'c'est sous les tentes de ces nomades riches de leurs nombraux troupeaux et heureux de leur indépendance qu'on retrouve les habitudes patriarchales' (1782, 101). In short, the Greeks have become only one among several possible exotic stereotypes of the 'other'.

4. CONCLUSION

It is time to draw some conclusions from this study of the analogies between ancient and modern Greeks, a study which does not pretend to exhaust the topic (I acknowledge that the outbreak of the War of Independence would have been a more logical *terminus ante quem*). I have tried to bring out three aspects. First, the importance of stereotypes inherited from Classical literature, Latin as well as Greek, and their influence for better and for worse on the idea—or better, ideas—of ancient Greece, which was not 'a monolithic thing', but had 'many facets'.[25] Second, the way in which the perception of modern Greeks was completely conditioned by constant comparison with their ancestors. It is rare to find a traveller who attempts to give it up, even momentarily, and acknowledges, like Choiseul-Gouffier, that 'la mémoire de leur gloire passée nous a rendus trop exigeants, et dès lors injustes' (1782, ii. 126). Thirdly, the variety of travellers' conclusions and their arbitrariness. The first ones were usually content to contrast idealized ancient Greeks with debased modern ones, a contrast parallel to their disappointment at finding only 'sad relics' of the glory that was Greece. Then, together with a better

[25] Constantine, *Early Greek Travellers*, 2.

appreciation of the physical remains of ancient Greece, there is an attempt to take a closer look at the modern Greeks and to unearth, from beneath the surface of Turkish corruption, some traces of the virtues of their ancestors. Finally, while pretending to throw some light upon classical authors by careful observation of the manners of the present day, romantic travellers succeeded in fact in accomodating reality to their dreams. They achieved the kind of completion of their quest[26] by creating for themselves and for their readers carefully edited portraits of modern Greece that transformed the present into the living image of the past. An examination of these arbitrary, if not totally imaginary, constructs constitutes a necessary preamble for modern anthropologists as well as for the historians who attempt to use investigations of contemporary societies to generate hypotheses about past societies—if they want to evade the dangers of circularity.

CHECK-LIST OF TRAVEL NARRATIVES

Babin (1674/1854): le père Jacque Paul Babin, *Relation de l'état présent de la ville d'Athènes* (Lyon, 1674, repr. by Laborde in his *Athènes* (Paris, 1854)).

Belon (1553): Pierre Belon, *Les observations de plusieurs singularités et choses mémorables trouvées en Grèce, Asie, Judée* (Paris).

Biddulph (1609): William Biddulph, *The travels of certaine Englishmen into Africa, Asia, Troy, Bythinia* (London).

Chandler (1775): Richard Chandler, *Travels in Asia Minor* (Oxford).

—— (1776): Richard Chandler, *Travels in Greece* (Oxford).

Charlemont (1749/1984): Lord Charlemont, *The travels of Lord Charlemont in Greece and Turkey* (London, 1749, ed. W. Stanford and E. J. Finopoulos (London, 1984)).

Chishull (1747): Edmund Chishull, *Travels in Turkey and back to England* (London).

Choiseul-Gouffier (1782): Comte M. G. A. F. Choiseul-Gouffier, *Voyage pittoresque de la Grèce* (Paris).

Covel (1676/1893): John Covel, Extracts from his diary in *Early Voyages and Travels in the Levant* (ed. J. T. Bent, Hakluyt Society 87, London, 1893).

---

[26] On travel as 'pilgrimage' and as 'quest for a transcendental vision' see J. Elsner's and J. P. Rubiès's introduction to their edited book *Voyages and Visions: Towards a Cultural History of Travel* (London, 1999).

Dallaway (1797): James Dallaway, *Constantinople Ancient and Modern with Excursions to the shores and islands of the Archipelago and to the Troad* (London).

Douglas (1813): F. S. N. Douglas, *Essay on certains points of resemblance between the ancient and modern Greeks* (London).

Duloir (1654): *Les Voyages du Sieur Duloir* (Paris).

Drummond (1754): Alexander Drummond, *Travels through different Cities of Germany, Italy, Greece and several parts of Asia as far as the Banks of the Euphrates; In a Series of Letters containing an Account of what is most remarkable in their present State, As well as in their Monuments of Antiquity* (London, 1754).

Eton (1798): William Eton, *Survey of the Turkish Empire* (London).

Gilles (1561/1988): P. Gilles, *The Antiquities of Constantinople* (New York, 1988).

Guillet (1675): Georges Guillet de Saint George, *Athènes ancienne et nouvelle et l'estat présent de l'empire des Turcs contenant la vie du sultan Mahomet IV* (Paris, 1675, trans. as *An Account of a Late Voyage to Athens* (London, 1676)).

——(1676): *Lacedemone ancienne et nouvelle où l'on voit les moeurs et les coutumes des Grecs modernes, des mahométans et des Juifs du pays* (Paris).

Guys 1772: (Pierre Augustin Guys), *Voyage littéraire de la Grèce ou lettre sur les Grecs anciens et modernes, avec un parallèle de leurs moeurs* (Paris, 1771, transl. as *A Sentimental Journey through Greece* (London, 1772)).

Hill (1709): Aaron Hill, *A full Account of the Present State of the Ottoman Empire* (London).

Lechevalier (1802): J. B. Lechevalier, *Voyage de la Troade fait dans les années 1785 et 1786 par J. B. Lechevalier* (Paris).

Leroy (1758): Julien David Leroy, *Les ruines des plus beaux monuments de Grèce* (Paris, 1758, trans. as *The Ruins of Athens* (London, 1759)).

Lithgow (1632/1906): William Lithgow, *The Totall Discourse of the Rare Adventures and painful peregrinations of William Lithgow* (London, 1632, repr. Glasgow, 1906).

Montagu (1717/1965): Lady Mary Wortley Montagu, *The Complete Letters of Lady Mary Wortley Montagu* (ed. R. Halsband, Oxford, 1965).

Morritt (1794/1985): J. B. S. Morritt, *A Grand Tour* (ed. G. E. Marindin, London, 1914, repr. 1985).

Moryson (1597/1903): *Unpublished Chapters of Fynes Moryson's Itinerary, being a survey of the condition of Europe at the end of the 16th century, with an introduction and an account of Fynes Moryson's career*, by Charles Hugues (London, 1903).

Nointel/Vandal (1900): A. Vandal, *L'Odyssée d'un ambassadeur: Les voyages du marquis de Nointel (1670–1680)* (Paris).

Perry (1743): Charles Perry, *A View of the Levant ; particularly of Constantinople, Syria, Egypt and Greece* (London).

Pococke (1743–5): Richard Pococke, *A description of the East*, 2 vols. (London).

Porter (1768): James Porter, *Observations on the Religion, Law, government and manners of the Turks*, 2 vols. (London).

Riedesel (1771–1802): Johann Hermann van Riedesel, *Reise durch Sicilien und Grossgriechenland* (Zurich, 1771) and *Bemerkungen auf einer Reise nach der Levante* (Leipzig, 1774), trans. as *Voyages en Sicile et dans la Grande Grèce* (Lausanne, 1773) and *Remarques d'un voyageur moderne au Levant* (Amsterdam and Stuttgart, 1773), the translation reissued together (Paris, 1802).

Sandwich (1799): The Earl of Sandwich, *A voyage performed by the late Earl of Sandwich round the Mediterranean in the years 1738 and 1739 written by himself* (London).

Sandys (1610/1973): George Sandys, *A Relation of a Journey begun An. Dom. 1610* (London, 1610, repr. Amsterdam, 1973).

Sherley (1613): Sir Anthony Sherley, *His relation of his travels* (London).

Spon (1678): Jacob Spon, *Voyage d'Italie, de Dalmatie, de Grèce et du Levant* (Lyon).

Stuart-Revett (1762–1816): James Stuart and Nicholas Revett, *The Antiquities of Athens, Measured and Delineated*, 4 vols. (London, 1762–1816; new edn., London, 1825–1830; repr. New York, 1968).

Thévenot (1665): Jean de Thévenot, *Relation d'un voyage fait au Levant* (Paris).

Tournefort (1718): Joseph Pitton de Tournefort, *Relation d'un voyage du Levant fait par ordre du Roi* (Paris, 1717, trans. as *A Voyage into the Levant* (London, 1718)).

Wheler (1682): Sir George Wheler, *A Journey into Greece* (London).

Wood (1769/1971): R. Wood, *An Essay on the Original Genius and Writings of Homer, With a Comparative View of the Ancient and Present State of the Troade* (London, 1769, repr. New York, 1971).

12

Mediterranean Reception in the Americas

Francisco Marshall

The Ancient Mediterranean experience and its transmission throughout the ages has been the main theme of the Western tradition for centuries, helping to shape such a wide set of cultural contexts that we could hardly list them all. Perhaps the best way to perceive the range of Mediterranean influence would be to indicate the non-Mediterranean contexts, in the Orient, Southern Africa, Asia, Oceania, or in the Americas. There are many places outside the Mediterranean that have been exposed to Mediterranean cultural radiation, and developed strong historical and imaginary links, relating places as distant as Brazil, New Zealand, and Denmark to that most powerful cradle of historical meanings. Therefore, to illustrate the outpouring of Mediterranean waters and codes throughout the world, and particularly within the social context in which I live—in Brazil—I will mention two of the most telling circumstances of reception of the Mediterranean experience, presenting key cases that illuminate the whole functioning of a powerful machine of meaning-production. This will take place, firstly, through the illustration of the colonization of collective imageries and, secondly, through a demonstration of the working of an inventive method of palaeographical and epigraphical study, carefully developed to tighten the bonds between the ancient Mediterranean and Brazil, a case which has had wide reverberations from the first decades of the twentieth century until to-day.

Avoiding the automatic identification of the Mediterranean experience with the Western or classical traditions, we may consider that Mediterranean materials are mixed with many other contextual cultural references, which are preserved as genetic information, ready to act as a force shaping history even when the information is stored in recessive genes. This cultural information, however, is transmitted not only through genealogical chains, relating to the ancestry of places, names, institutions, and behaviour; but also through historical lineages and continuities, including the macrohistory of peoples and nations, as well as the microhistory of individuals, villages, and landscapes. There are also cases of constructed filiations: cases where we perceive the driving force of a wish for *méditer-ranéité*, an option for a root, model, or source localized in that central reserve of meanings, the Mediterranean. As these wishes are strong enough to drive larger ideological projects, with their cultural, scientific and political consequences, the imaginary genealogies gain the status of another course of tradition.

When, therefore, I talk about Mediterranean reception, I am focusing on the study of the established connections between different historical contexts, somehow approached by the movement of a modern perception. In this study of the transmission of classical and Mediterranean culture, I will stress the role of the receiver in the making of tradition, and the semiological features involved in these transactions of meanings. In the study of contexts and procedures of reception, we will have to omit the question of whether there was a serious historical affiliation, for what really matters is perceiving the great set of intentions that have presided over the movements towards the Mediterranean tradition, and the ways these movements drove forward the presence of Mediterranean references, shaping pragmatic and long-term social projects, with their corresponding institutions and iconographies. As a two-way path, this process shows a flux of meaning, connecting past and present, local and distant, intentional and casual, connecting also history and fiction, science and fantasy.

Considering the role of the interpreter in the cooperative act of reading permits us to understand the conditions in which images from the past can acquire new life, assuming active functions in the present, within modern fabrics of sense and meaning. As the different trends in the theory of reception have exhaustively shown,[1] the act of reading is much more than an

---

[1] Cf. R. C. Holub, *Reception Theory: A Critical Introduction* (New York, 1984). Cf. also Umberto Eco, *Lector in Fabula: la cooperazione interpretativa*

individual experience or a psychological process; in fact, we know the reader only when he ceases to be a reader, and expresses his own reading, through a publication, commentary, speech, political doctrine, programme of action, aesthetic construct, or some other form of actual historical response. Beyond the reader, we see the agent, and around the agent, contexts and traditions. So, more than a particular person, we have to consider the individual or collective agency of meaning, and the movement of historical intentions in which one context provokes an interchange between the present and the past, in which current and past norms and values,[2] and also goals and intentions intermingle. What matters is what share of the past is selected by the present reader, which images, texts, and concepts are collected, which branch of tradition is handled, which plots and narratives are referred to, how they are read, who listens, who publishes, what is the social reaction to the reader's propositions, that is, the dissemination of the processed contents produced by the act of reading.

In all fields of knowledge and circumstances of social life, we have to deal with a large set of transmitted materials belonging to the ancient and classical traditions, which are mostly expressed in the categories of texts and icons, as well as in organized spaces. Among the most efficient vehicles of tradition, we could point out myths, imageries, and writings; narratives, concepts, genres, and authorships; architecture, icons, and conceptual forms; legal codes, techniques, and pathologies; institutions, ideologies, and mentalities. The ways in which the tradition is transmitted can help us to understand the extended social consequences of the diffusion of Mediterraneanism. The present study aims to assist both in the understanding of the shaping of Brazil as a nation, as well as in the decoding of some relevant core meanings that persist within the potency and magnitude of the Mediterranean tradition.

---

nei testi narrativi (Milan, 1979), and the landmark works of H. R. Jauss, *Rezeptionsästhetik* (Munich, 1975), and W. Iser, *Der Akt des Lesens* (Munich, 1976).

[2] J. Mukarovsky, *Structure, Sign, and Function: Selected Essays* (Yale Russian and East European Studies, 14) (New Haven, 1977).

1. THE AMAZON

The history of Mediterranean reception should begin outside the Mediterranean, in places and epochs where the presence of the Mediterranean was felt as something strong, indicating the active presence of historical messages belonging to that sea and the surrounding civilizations. In the Americas, the imprint of this tradition started and developed during the period of colonization, when institutions, legal codes, writings, schools, myths, religious patterns, perspectives, and artistic and architectural styles, were imported by the Europeans. Yet despite the clarity of the historical record, diffusionists, pre-Columbian archaeologists, and some historians have succeeded in inventing a kind of argument about when Mediterranean cultural information first reached America. The subject has also been a preferred topic of ethnological fantasy ever since the fifteenth century, blending ingenuous curiosity, homocosmic imagination, and a kind of mysticism of origins.

Notwithstanding the permanent scepticism of the academic mainstream, which refuses to recognize any possibility of Phoenician travels outside the Mediterranean, there is something like a *Guinness Book of Records* challenge that impels people to claim that ancient sailors reached ever more remote places in North and South America, Southern Africa, and even the Far East and Oceania. It is not a surprise, therefore, to encounter a note concerning an altar to the god Baal in New Zealand, supposedly built around the sixth century BC by, of course, a tribe of Phoenicians lost and detached from the expedition of circumnavigation of Africa sent by Nekau in the seventh century, as one home page maintains with the very predictable help of inscriptions, old and current myths, drawings, and secret archaeological sites.[3] Phoenician origins have also been claimed for the Rig Vedas and the whole of Hindu culture,[4] as well as for the Scots, Britons and Anglo-Saxons.[5]

[3] http://www.zealand.org.nz/history.htm [on 09/10/2002].

[4] Rajeswar Gupta, *The Rig Veda: A History Showing how the Phoenicians had their Earliest Home in India*, trans. into English from Bengali (Chittagong, 1904).

[5] L. A. Waddell, *The Phoenician Origin of Britons, Scots and Anglo-Saxons Discovered by Phoenician and Sumerian Inscriptions in Britain, by Pre-Roman British Coins and a Mass of New History* (London, 1931).

All these stories of Phoenician, Hebrew, or Greek presence in the Americas, as well as worldwide outside the Mediterranean, can be fitted into a wider collection of imaginary ethnography, a collection, that is, of the imaginary links between the Mediterranean and other spaces in different continents. If we focus on the activities of the first explorers, we may talk about the mimetic projection of traditional references belonging to the old Mediterranean heritage, used as means of recognizing and domesticating strange territories outside the known world; if we look at colonial and post-colonial mentalities, we can recognize recurrent behaviour that expresses the wish of many different elites to be linked to the purest source of civilization. Both constitute monumental historical cases of Mediterranean reception, establishing wider contextual projects of reading, and perpetuating the representations of the ancient Mediterranean world that are always manipulated in such projects. These readings spread images, concepts, vocabularies, and institutions that, true or false, begin to constitute threads running through history, driving cultural traditions forward.

In modern times, the root of this process lies in the adventures of the early explorers after the fifteenth century, when many imaginary veins and arteries established the exchange of blood between Europe and the strange spaces of America. Imbued with myths and traditional knowledge,[6] the explorers brought the names and identities of their own geography to the new lands, founding the first colonies as a sort of projected imaginary topology, using onomastic devices that were destined to have a long future. There have been various studies of the fantastic geography of the Renaissance.[7] One of the best studies of the early shaping of Mediterranean imagery in America is the classic *Visão do Paraíso* (*Vision of Paradise*), a masterpiece of Brazilian historiography, published by Sérgio Buarque de Hollanda in 1959.[8] In this fine, erudite book, the author presents a broad and accurate panorama of letters, reports, maps, treatises,

---

[6] V. J. Flint, *The Imaginative Landscape of Christopher Columbus* (Princeton, 1992).

[7] Cf. S. Greenblatt, *Marvellous Possessions* (Oxford, 1991); Miguel Rojas Mix, *América Imaginária* (Barcelona, 1992); Serge Gruzinsky, *La guerra de las Imágines* (Mexico City, 1994).

[8] S. Buarque de Hollanda, *Visão do Paraíso* (São Paulo, 2000 (1959)).

and a study of the mentalities of the explorers of early America, especially in Brazil. He shows how much the literary convention of Eden-like subjects, tinged by classical reminiscences (the myth of the Golden Age, the Garden of the Hesperides), decisively affected the descriptions of the New World, planting ancient myths in 'new' soil. Some 500 years after that initial drama, many of those myths have flourished greatly and grown in many directions.

As an example of these procedures of migrating imaginaries, we can pick out the many notices about the American Amazons, whose precise location, whether in the Caribbean, in the Yucatan, in Chile or Patagonia, or on some island or other, was disputed among the first Spanish explorers in the first decades of the sixteenth century. Even before they realized they were not in the East Indies,[9] they started trying classical and mediaeval keys in order to understand the new landscape, helping to shape numerous fantastic reports of extraordinary animals and human beings, and challenging the stories of Odysseus among the Phaeacians. That is the kind of thing we can read in the report of the Dominican Friar Gaspar de Carvajal,[10] the chronicler of the expedition of Francisco de Orellana, who in 1541 departed from Quito, Ecuador, and explored the whole extent of the Amazon, all the way to the Atlantic Ocean.

After passing through infernally hot weather and surviving the insects, Indians, and exotic flora and fauna, they reported having met with the actual tribe of warrior women on three occasions—hence the river's naming. The first reports of wild women appeared when they joined the river and a certain *cacique*, Aparia, let them know that those women downstream possessed a splendid treasure of yellow metal (like all the stories of the early explorers, this one is a mixture of extreme cupidity and fiery fantasy). Later, after crossing what appears to have been the Rio Madeira, Orellana finally found them and attacked them in a violent fight, in which the women showed themselves to be much braver and stronger than all their male fellow-Indians, whom they even clubbed to death as they tried to

---

[9] After the Magellan expedition (1519–21).

[10] Cf. Buarque de Hollanda and J. H. Parry, *The Discovery of South America* (New York, 1979), 262–72.

flee. Completely surprised by their audacity, the Dominican describes them as white and as having strong limbs, large stature, and long hair tied up on the top of the head. They were all naked, except for covering their genitalia, and were each as valuable in combat as ten or twelve men. They were peerless archers, and it was said later they used to cut off the right breast just to become stronger in the fighting arm.[11] The Spaniards had to kill all of them, so that they could control the remaining men. Later, as soon as they had made camp, the chief explorer Orellana questioned a recently captured Indian, using instant polyglot skills that would have surprised even Apollonius of Tyana. The Indian told him what he wished to know about the warrior women and their golden treasures. They belonged to a powerful tribe, exercising control over many other tribes in the region: they lived in stone houses, with doors, windows, and corridors, instead of in straw huts; there were no men in their city; and they killed every newborn boy, allowing only the girls to live. Above all, the Indian assured Orellana that they possessed an enormous treasure in gold, and that their houses, called 'sun houses', were all plated in gold, contained golden tableware and were decorated with coloured parrot feathers, which were a sign of richness, as valuable as gold.[12]

With the same acuteness with which Buarque de Hollanda related Tacitus and his reports of the voyage of Odysseus on the Rhine to the description of the Florida of Ponce de León by Pedro Mártir D'Anghiera,[13] he brings out the presence of geographical information from Strabo, Arrian, and Diodorus Siculus in the writings of Friar Carvajal and his fellow cartographers and chroniclers. If we dig a little deeper, we can certainly find some traces of Homer in these texts. The myth of the Amazons 'came directly from Antiquity to install itself in America'.[14]

---

[11] Buarque de Hollanda, *Visão do Paraíso*, 35.

[12] Cf. also the letters of Oviedo in 1543, in Eugenio Asensio, *La carta de Oviedo al Cardenal Bembo sobre la navegación del Amazonas* (Miscelanea Americana, Madrid, 1951), i. 111, quoted in Mix, *América*, 72 n. 42.

[13] Tacitus leaves to the reader the choice of believing or not: 'People say those things, and I narrate them to you', the same formula used by D'Anghiera: 'those things are reported, and I narrate them to you' (Buarque de Hollanda, *Visão do Paraíso*, 28 and 40 n. 26).

[14] Mix, *América*, 70.

This imagery persisted for many centuries, and, for that reason, we can find explorers of the seventeenth and eighteenth centuries still looking for the warrior women and their gold in the so-called Amazon forest, even when Spaniards are not involved, as in De Bry's *Portrait of America* (1596) or in Walter Raleigh's *Voyages* (1601). The approach to American origins was usually based on 'an uncritical acceptance of the comparative ethnological technique of determining origins and a tendency to accept trans-Atlantic migrations',[15] and the tradition of Gregorio Garcia,[16] which was predominant until the early eighteenth century, mixed deductive and exegetical ethnology, Christian theology, and classical literature and mythology. Such thinking did not hesitate to locate the Amazons, the lost tribes of Israel, Phoenician settlements, and so on, in America.[17] There was, however, a dissenting cartography, which located the Amazons not in America, but in the north-east of the Venerean Republic represented in Johann Andreas Schnebelin's *Accurata Utopiae Tabula* (Nuremberg, 1716 (?)),[18] within the heart of his cartography of Paradise, a geographical portrait of vices and virtues. Despite that dispute, the honour of hosting them in modern times has been granted to Brazil, and so we keep them in our territory, forever trying to escape from burnings and the incursions of anthropologists, zoologists, and film-makers.

2. BERNARDO RAMOS: MYTH AND EPIGRAPHY

The Amazon is among the most potent and lively pieces of land in the planet. In its impressive majesty, the trees there grow to

[15] L. E. Huddleston, *Origins of the American Indians: European Concepts, 1492–1729* (Austin, 1967).

[16] Gregorio García, *El origen de los Indios de el Nuevo Mundo e Indias occidentales* (Valencia, 1607; repr. Madrid, 1729, and México City, 1981).

[17] 'Perhaps [the exercises of Santa Ursula] inspired the interest of Columbus as much as the stories of the Amazons had clearly done', Flint, *Imaginative Landscape*, 99.

[18] Cf. cartography (Homann, *c.*1748) in http://www.kfunigraz.ac.at/ub/sosa/karten/[on 28/09/2002]. Cities in the 'state of Amazonia' in Schnebelin's *Republica Venerea*: Blauefenster, der Camer Forst, Camerau, Cratzau, Flohdot, Flohjacht, Hastrecht, Herrinhausen, Kantlberg, Rauffinbart, Schlagenmann, Schelmschlag, Unternbanck, Wiederbellingen, Xantippa.

tens of metres, likewise the snakes and even more so the myths, which are fertilized by heavy rains, intense heat, and the imaginations of scholars and explorers. Our next instance of Mediterranean reception in the New World comes to light in the very heart of the Amazon, from the extravagant work of a numismatist and palaeographer named Bernardo de Azevedo da Silva Ramos, the son of a rich family in Manaus who devoted himself seriously to ancient studies, learning several ancient languages and later spending long sojourns in Greece, Syria, and Egypt. He studied archaeology, epigraphy, and history, and put together a personal collection of around 12,000 coins. The catalogue of his ancient coins was published in four volumes, in 1900, under the auspices of the Accademia dei Lincei and with the help of his correspondents at the Royal Universities of Genoa and Rome, who wrote the preface and co-published three of the four volumes.[19] He had a high reputation and held some important international positions.[20]

After being recognized as a serious numismatist and geographer, he dedicated himself to solving one of the greatest challenges of pre-Columbian history and archaeology, trying to find a meaning in the various drawings that have been found on many pre-Columbian sites in America. Despite all the oddity of his propositions, they were constructed and reproduced with the formal appearance of good scientific practice, and were buttressed by much evidence and semantic analysis, as well as by extensive bibliographical references. They were accepted

---

[19] Bernardo de Azevedo da Silva Ramos, *Catálogo da Coleção Numismática* (Rome, 1900), 4 vols. (preface and revision by Professor Dr. Vincenzo Grossi, 'Libero Docente di etnologia nella R. Universitá di Genova', and Professor Dante Vaglieri, 'Libero Docente di antichità romana e di epigrafia latina nella R. Universitá di Roma').

[20] The list of titles and honorary fellowships beneath his photograph taken before the presentation of the book includes: honorary fellow of the Historical and Geographical Institute of São Paulo (IHGSP), correspondent of the Geographical Society of Rio de Janeiro, the Ceará Institute, and the International Society of Academic History in France; President of Honor of the Geographical and Historical Institute of the Amazon; former vice-president of the international jury of group and class in the Universal and International Fair of Brussels of 1910; honorary member of the Académie Latine des Sciences, Arts and Belles Lettres de la France, etc.

and admired in many contemporary circles,[21] but both volumes end with long compilations of the author's struggles to sell his theories and his fortune in the media and within the circles of power.

In the presentation of his *Inscripções e Tradições da América Prehistórica,*[22] Ramos makes much of his erudition, going back to the work of Pietro del Vale in 1621.[23] He takes his time to stress how much the early epigraphists had been misunderstood by their contemporaries, despite or because of their avant-garde spirit. There were people ready to call him the Champollion of the Amazon, but he was not fated to be recognized as such.

His own analytical tools were derived from the methods of the numismatist and the epigraphist: he assumed the recurrent use of many abbreviations, acronyms, and contractions in the texts or 'texts' he was working with. He established his own code of signals, drawing up tables containing several epigraphical variants of each sign in Greek, Hebrew, and Phoenician scripts. The variants cover not only what we usually recognize as letters, but also many figurative representations that were supposedly related to ancient writings (Fig. 12.1). As the migrations had taken place by the early Iron Age, Ramos

---

[21] He is still found persuasive in the History Department of Wake Forest University, North Carolina. See the website on Algonquins, Egyptians, and Uto-Aztecs at http://www.wfu.edu/~cyclone/titv.htm [on 21/07/2001], which I quote verbatim: 'Carthaginians reached South America. Old Greek top-onyms which Henriette Mertz recovered in Brazil, mostly on the Amazon—Phedra, Hipolito, Thetys, Olimpias, Ateleia, numerous places ending opolis or apolis, Solimoes, Ares, etc. (not to mention Cumana; an Aphrodite sanctuary made Comana on Mt. Eryx, Sicily, the Las Vegas of Ptolemaic/Roman times) could date Greek Archaic to Middle Ages, but Greek names in rhebuses and other inscriptions Bernardo de Azevedo da Silva Ramos discovered and deciphered along the Amazon system by 1929, coupled with non-Brazilian bull and hippopotamus designs, plus funerary terms like thanatos, indicate late-ancient African Greek in plantation cemeteries worked by Greek war-prisoner slaves or Greek-speaking Mediterranean-Roman subjects.' And so on.

[22] Ramos, *Inscripções e tradições da América préhistórica* (Rio de Janeiro, 1929 and 1939), 2 vols.

[23] On deciphering cuneiform and on Assyriology, the main works he drew on were Thomaz Hyde, De Caylus, Pietro Del Vale, Kaempfer, Von Bruyn, Niebuhr, Münter, Grotefend, and Burnouf and Lassen, as well as Westegaard, Hincks and de Saulcy, Oppert and Hincks, Fox, Talbot, and Rawlinson.

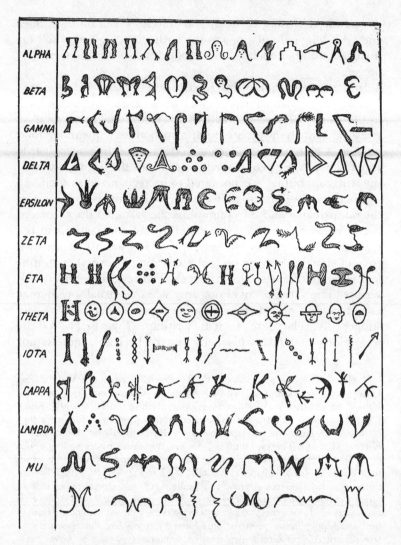

Fig. 12.1. The primitive and figurative variants of Greek script according to Bernardo Ramos.

considered that the American inscriptions followed a different path of evolution, preserving, however, the essential traits and meanings of the original scripts. He supposed that many drawings and works of cave art were, in fact, stylized representations of ancient letters and writings, his favourite objects of analysis being Marajoara ceramics (Fig. 12.2).[24] The 'deciphering' of these signs led to the identification of Greek, Hebrew, and Phoenician names and writings.

The fourth step (up into the stratosphere) was to compare the resulting names and sentences, discovered in encoded Indian inscriptions, with their corresponding references in Greek, Punic, and Hebrew inscriptions, and also the Bible and classical Greek literature. As an example, we can study how he read the inscriptions on a large rock found in Rio Urubu, on the Amazon, which he transliterated, translated, and interpreted as a set of votive formulas dedicated to Zeus (Figs. 12.3 and 12.4). His two volumes contain hundreds of such cases.

Aiming to clarify the history of the first Mediterranean presence in Brazil, supposedly in the early Iron Age, Ramos brought in many names of Egyptian, Greek, Hebrew, and Phoenician gods, patriarchs, tribal leaders, heroes, priests, temples, and shrines. The Amazonian and American materials, taken as a collection of cryptographic writings, were unveiled in direct accordance with what the author-reader had found in his own experience with ancient materials, within the Mediterranean. He did not, on the other hand, find any trace of native American Indian myths or names, any vestige of the linguistic families of American Indians, or even any name not belonging to the Mediterranean repertoire.

Ramos admitted that there was no case of continuity between the older colonization from the Mediterranean and the post-Renaissance occupation, but attempted to persuade his readers that the history of civilization in Brazil was longer than they had realized. The Indians discovered by the early explorers were not wild barbarians, cannibals, and savage warriors, but the

---

[24] The Marajoara is a style of ceramics typical of the Aruans, who belonged to the linguistic group *Arwaq* (*Aruaque*), inhabitants of the Ilha de Marajó (Northern Brazil). It is considered typical of pre- (and post-)Columbian art in Brazil.

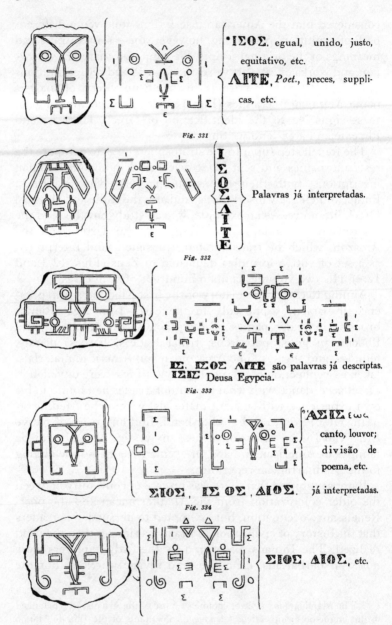

Fig. 12.2. Marajoara ceramics yield Greek.

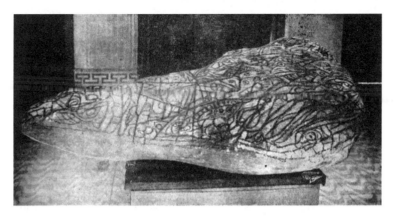

Fig. 12.3. A 'Greek inscription' from the Amazon.

remnants of earlier occupations of the land and hence part of the same tree as modern European civilization. His work of interpretation extended to thousands of cases, embracing stone and cave inscriptions, bas-relief engravings, cave-paintings and different styles of ceramics, all of them bearing meanings that led directly to Mediterranean epigraphy. He included many other places in South and Central America besides Brazil, and even some North American sites such as Grave Creek.

Up to a point, his intellectual ancestry is clear. His reading was deeply rooted in a tradition of diffusionist studies typical of the second half of the nineteenth century,[25] especially the later

[25] Cf. George Jones, *The History of Ancient America, Anterior to the Time of Columbus, proving the identity of the aborigines with the Tyrians and Israelites: And the introduction of Christianity into the Western hemisphere* (London and New York, 1843); A. C. A. Zestermann, *Memoir on the European Colonization of America* (London, 1851); Enrique Onffroy de Thoron, *Amérique équatoriale, son histoire pittoresque et politique, sa géographie et richesses naturelles, son état présent et son avenir* (Paris, 1866); P. Gaffarel, *Étude sur les rapports de l'Amerique et de l'ancien continent avant Christophe Colomb* (Paris, 1869); C. S. Clermont-Ganneau, *L'Imagerie phenicienne et la mythologie iconologique chez les Grecs* (Paris, 1880); F. Bovet, *Egypt, Palestine, and Phoenicia* (London, 1882); L. Netto, *Lettre à Monsieur Ernest Renan à propos de l'inscription phénicienne apocryphe soumise en 1872 à l'Institut historique, géographique et ethnographique du Brésil* (Rio de Janeiro, 1885); V. Grossi, *La questione dei cosidetti 'precursori' di Colombo in America. Conferenza tenuta alla sede della Società geografica di Rio de Janeiro a la sera delli 19 settembre 1891* (Torino,

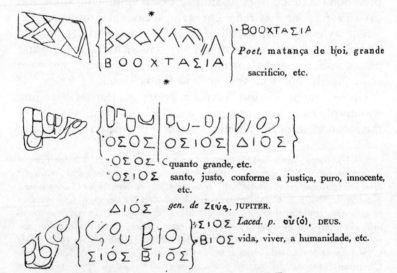

BΟ | B O | *ΒΙΟΤΟΣΧΟΙΙΟΣ *Poet.* quem pre-
| I T | side a existencia.
ΟΧ | O X | R. R. Βιοτος, σχοπέω..
| Σ ΟΙΙΟΣ | Para simplificar a interpretação, passamos a destacar os periodos.

ΣΟΟΣ, são e salvo, etc.
ΔΙΟΣ, *gen. de* Ζεύς,
ΒΙΟΣ JUPITER a humanidade, etc.

ΣΟΟϜ ΔΙΟΣ ΒΙΟΣ

RESUMO:

*ΒΙΟΤΟΣΧΟΙΙΟΣ∻ΣΟΟΣ ΔΙΟΣ ΒΙΟΣ

QUEM PRESIDE A EXISTENCIA DA HUMANIDADE SÃ E SALVA É JUPITER

*ΒΟΟΧΤΑΣΙΑ
ΒΟΟΧΤΑΣΙΑ
Poet, matança de b'oi, grande sacrificio, etc.

ΟΣΟΣ | ΟΣΙΟΣ | ΔΙΟΣ

ΟΣΟΣ ᶜquanto grande, etc.
ΟΣΙΟΣ santo, justo, conforme a justiça, puro, innocente, etc.
ΔΙΟΣ *gen. de* Ζεύς, JUPITER.
∻ΣΙΟΣ *Laced. p.* οὖ(ό), DEUS.
ΒΙΟΣ vida, viver, a humanidade, etc.

ΣΙΟΣ ΒΙΟΣ

ΟΣΟΣ ΟΣΙΟΣ ΔΙΟΣ +ΣΙΟΣ ΒΙΟΣ

QUANTO GRANDE, SANTO E JUSTO É JUPITER, DEUS DA HUMANIDADE

Fig. 12.4. The same markings interpreted by Bernardo Ramos.

work of Enrique Onffroy De Thoron.[26] He of course anticipated some of the work produced some 50 years later by Cyrus
Gordon[27] and the modern diffusionists.[28]

This amazing work cannot properly be seen as a merely
individual eccentricity, for Ramos's work over many decades
took place against an academic background that supported such
discourse and even favoured his interpretations. Furthermore,
his books have a perfectly academic form, and were published
by the National Press, receiving a great acclaim in Rio de
Janeiro and beyond, as well as in his home town Manaus. In
his fight to have the work published, during the twenties, he
presented the material to two presidents of the Republic of the
United States of Brazil, in Rio de Janeiro,[29] as well as to many
senators, journalists, and scientific members of geographical
societies. But he faced the open resistance of another diffusionist, Alberto Childe,[30] the scholar in the Museu Nacional in Rio
de Janeiro who had to approve the text before the government
would allow it to be printed. So, after all the struggle, and its
final posthumous publication, the book became a cultural landmark of a collective dream of the early Mediterranean origin of
an American people, and was, and is, used as a key reference by

1892); Gabriel Marcel, *Sur quelques documents peu connus relatifs a la décou-
verte de l'Amérique* (Paris, 1893); Candido Costa, *As duas Americas*, (2nd edn.
(Lisbon, 1900); Thomas Crawford Johnston, *Did the Phoenicians Discover
America?* (London, 1913).

[26] Cf. E. Onffroy De Thoron, *Les Phéniciens à l'Isle d'Haiti et sur le
Continent Americain: Les Vaisseaux d'Hiram et de Salomon au Fleuve des
Amazones (Ophir, Tarschich, Parvaim)* (Louvain, 1889). De Thoron visited
Manaus in 1876, and Bernardo Ramos was later considered his successor.

[27] C. H. Gordon, *Before Columbus: Links between the Old World and An-
cient America* (New York, 1971). Cf. also Joseph Corey Ayoob, *Ancient
Inscriptions in the New World: Or were the Phoenicians the First to Discover
America?* (Pittsburgh, 1951).

[28] Cf. E. R. Fingerhut, *Explorers of pre-Columbian America? The Diffusion-
ist-Inventionist Controversy* (Claremont, Calif., 1994). Other relatively recent
diffusionist outpourings: Eduardo de Habich, *Los fenicios en la historia del
Perú* (Lima, 1972); J. Yaser, *Fenicios y árabes en el génesis americano* (Córdoba,
Argentina, 1992).

[29] To Epitacio Pessoa in 1922, and to Arthur Bernardes in 1926.

[30] Childe became the chief conservator of the Museu Nacional in 1922; this
was the name the Russian Egyptologist Dmitri Vonizin adopted after migrating to Brazil.

the current sympathizers of the cause—not a few of whom still exist.[31]

Nowadays the most famous place in the Phoenician cartography in Brazil is the Pedra da Gávea, in Rio de Janeiro, where there is a supposed Phoenician inscription. Most probably fake or false, the writing is mysterious enough to bring many curious people, especially tourists, to the place, a very scenic spot. The myth of Phoenician origins is a living force in Brazil, and there is little space for scientific contradiction. A whole literature on the topic grows at its own pace, and it does not matter if the supposed Phoenician inscriptions have been demonstrated to be the remains of Masonic dramatizations or just natural rock formations. The same happens in the cases in Piauí and Paraíba (north-north-eastern states of Brazil), where the signature of the Austrian ancient historian Ludwig Schwennhagen provided the necessary support to confirm that there were ruins of Phoenician cities, in a place later called Sete Cidades, a National Park in Piauí which is much visited.[32]

By the time of Bernardo Ramos, the state of Amazonas was experiencing a great wave of development, the so called Rubber Cycle, with the rise of newly enriched elites eager for their own distinction. These men were ready to give up, or to enhance, their own local and Portuguese colonial identity and build a new image of themselves, based on the best icons of civilization coming from the North. The consequence of that was a cycle of neoclassicism, with its most vehement expression in architecture, sustained by a project full of ideological meaning. The greatest example is the magnificent building of the Teatro de Manaus, a great Opera House built in 1896, where in the first decades of the twentieth century the greatest Mediterranean

---

[31] The text would say: 'Tyro, Phoenicia, Badezir, first-born of Jethbaal', as Ramos 'transliterated' and 'translated' it (*Inscrições e tradições*, i. 436). There are variants.

[32] L. Schwennhagen, *Fenícios no Brasil: antiga história do Brasil, de 1100 a.C. a 1500 d.C.: tratado histórico* (Rio de Janeiro, 1976). The researches and articles of Schwennhagen date from the 1920s and 1930s. Cf. also C. Gordon, 'The Cannanite Text from Brazil', *Orientalia* 37 (1968), 425–36, and the response of F. M. Cross Jr., 'The Phoenician Inscription from Brazil: A Nineteenth-Century Forgery?', *Orientalia* 37 (1968), 437–60, followed by C. Gordon, 'Reply to Professor Cross', *Orientalia* 37 (1968), 461–3, and by F. M. Cross Jr., 'Phoenicians in Brazil?', *Biblical Archaeology Review* (Jan./Feb. 1979), 36–43.

singers, such as Enrico Caruso and Beniamino Gigli, sang for the local magnates.

This trend to neoclassicism in the North was the expression of one of the main cultural facts in the first decades in Brazil, driven by the prosperity of new economic elites, but also by strong ideologies brought in by the positivist doctrine of Auguste Comte, which enjoyed a great success and inspired many political movements, including our early Republic. In this doctrine, a place was reserved for classical references, with the consequent growth of an iconography supporting our close contact with the Mediterranean, its gods, leading figures and symbolic traditions. Beneath the grandeur of columns and the classical orders are the ideas of discipline, authority, and the solemn glory of the State. The preferred classical texts were above all Caesar and Cicero, who could inspire the notions of civic devotion and discipline, so much aspired to by our oligarchic leaders. One side-effect of this trend was the great prestige of Fustel de Coulanges, whose *Ancient City* became so popular that it is still a stunning presence in every used bookstore and a recurrent plague among undergraduate students. The great role that work assigned to the *paterfamilias* well suited our paternalist leaders, the fathers of the newborn Republic, later called República Velha, the first stage of Brazilian republican tradition.

3. EPILOGUE

It is true that there was a wave of neoclassical architecture and ideology in many parts of the world at the end of nineteenth and the beginning of the twentieth centuries. In some cases, arts and architecture can work well as self-referential traditions, reproducing their own rules and canons as a closed system. In this case, however, the aesthetic project was intimately connected to the whole ideological project of the local elites, who wished to show both their own greatness and their close contacts with the mainstream tradition that linked our distant city to the very root of western civilization, within the Mediterranean. Furthermore, at many times, classical studies have been a useful device for the elites in South America, helping to demonstrate their distinctiveness and to provide it with recognizable monuments. The wish to be Mediterranean reinforces the very colonial and post-colonial need to validate social existence in something that surpasses the displaced reality of peripheral spaces. A major consequence of this movement was the importation of a whole set of classical icons to enrich the image of the city. After all, if Poseidon could enjoy the company of the Aithiopes, it is not strange that Athena, Hermes, Atlas, Pericles, nymphs, heroes, and gods can feel at home in such distant corners as Porto Alegre, New York, and many other cities worldwide, both distant from and close to the Mediterranean.

We still have to touch, at least very briefly, on two other Mediterranean traditions that have had a considerable effect on American historical realities. Admittedly, if we were to follow the inventory of the Mediterranean heritage organized by Fernand Braudel and Georges Duby,[33] we could include almost anything in the list, from monotheistic religion to the family. This kind of study, indeed, always risks falling into flat generalities, proving everything and nothing at the same time. Nevertheless, I think we could consider the recurrence of *the myth of the hero*, as a narrative tool adopted by (and to) the national heroes, and as a continuing ideology perpetuating one of the oldest and most enduring structured cultural codes—a myth which is for that reason marked with the unequivocal sign of the Mediterranean basin. Though there have been efforts on the part of nationalistic literature to build anti-hero figures as a means of denying an alien tradition,[34] the pattern corresponds to a very important element in South American imagery, and it is frequently used in demagoguery and mass-media communication. There is in fact a project in train that aims to apply the understanding of the myth of the hero to the study of current ideologies, especially those associated with leadership and political demagogy.[35]

---

[33] F. Braudel (ed.), *La Mediterranée: Les Hommes et L'Héritage* (Paris, 1978).

[34] In Brazil, there is 'Macunaíma, the hero with no character', the anthropophagus, a modernist icon created by Mário de Andrade in 1928, using hero myths of the *taulipang* and the *arecuná*, aiming to deconstruct the model of the hero.

[35] Cf. the project 'The Myth of the Hero and the Figurations of Power', by Francisco Murari Pires (USP), in http://www.fflch.usp.br/dh/heros/. This

Not so distant from this, we find a whole discipline that has built a wide collective imagery in the twentieth century, as well as a new guild with its patterns of truth and authority, and with its images of nature and society: *Oedipus and Freudian psychoanalysis*.[36] This is probably the most striking reappearance of Greek myth, or at least its names and general plots, in contemporary culture, a presence that reintroduces images of the family, names and places of Greece and the eastern Mediterranean, as well as a bond of solidarity between myth, science, and society. More than the analytical patterns of social and structural anthropology, psychoanalysis was a major academic and social trend in Latin America in the twentieth century, especially in Brazil and Argentina, driving the culture back into the ancient landscapes of myth, and thus forcing another movement of reading. The trajectories of reading, however, dressing up Viennese types in Theban clothing and names, were marked by a complex mirroring of images and references that almost put to death the original Mediterranean DNA, previously expressed in the myths of Greek heroes. As a result of this movement, we can perceive that this was a remarkable vehicle for Mediterranean codes, mixing ancient and contemporary identities, wishes, and patterns.

As a source of meaning, the Mediterranean is ready to provide the images and proofs requested by any kind of social project. In every case, a transaction of information and intentions starts a dance of historical information, in which no historian or humanist can ever control the consequences, which are inscribed on a larger social landscape, within the world of life. If we seriously consider the consistency of these collective imageries of the Mediterranean as cultural references of our modern and contemporary cultures, we can perhaps often raise, with absolutely different responses, the central question of this book: what is the Mediterranean?

project investigates the recurrent pattern of the myth of the hero, as well as its social consequences in modern contexts.

[36] Cf. Francisco Marshall, 'Édipo Tirano, Édipo Freud', in *Filosofia Política*, Série III, n. 1, *Filosofia e Literatura: o trágico* (Rio de Janeiro, 2001), 141–52.

13

Alphabet Soup in the Mediterranean Basin: The Emergence of the Mediterranean Serial

Susan E. Alcock

1. INTRODUCTION

Figure 13.1 captures, in graphic form, an arresting phenomenon.[1] In a nutshell, the past two decades or so have witnessed the emergence of a number of academic journals which deal, to a greater or lesser extent, with the historical Mediterranean. The sample is admittedly a small one; the circulation of many rather limited; the life-span of a few regrettably brief. Nonetheless, the pattern is clear enough to invite review and contextualization, and to encourage some thought about the nature, and purpose, of these 'Mediterranean serials'.[2]

First, the nature of the sample should be clarified: what precisely is meant by the term 'Mediterranean serial'? To keep things manageably straightforward, I have applied two very simple but fairly ruthless filters. First, my principal emphasis lies with journals that deal with the history, archaeology, art, or

---

[1] I would like to thank John F. Cherry, co-editor of the *Journal of Mediterranean Archaeology*, for first drawing my attention to the phenomenon and for his subsequent advice, as well as William Harris for his kind invitation to participate in this project. I have attempted to be as comprehensive as possible in my coverage of these journals, although some relevant material remained inaccessible, despite the efforts of Mary E. Alcock and of the library staff at the Center for Advanced Study in the Behavioral Sciences in Stanford, Calif. For other comparative discussions of these periodicals, see P. S. Wells, review of *Mediterranean Archaeology* and *Journal of Mediterranean Archaeology*, *Antiquity* 65 (1991), 1006–1007, and *CS* 543.

[2] Figure 13.1 includes all the 'Mediterranean serials' listed in Table 13.1, with the exception of those explicitly dealing with contemporary conditions: *Mediterranean Quarterly*, *Mediterranean Politics*, and the *Mediterranean Journal of Human Rights*.

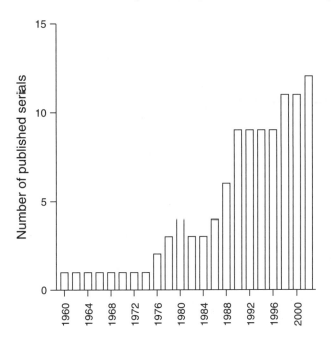

Fig. 13.1. Number of 'Mediterranean serials', 1960–2002

literature of the Mediterranean region over time, and not with, say, its ecology and environment, or with contemporary politics. Second, to be included in this study, a journal must have the word 'Mediterranean' in its title, and moreover in the forepart of its title; cases where it appears, after a colon, in a normally longer and more descriptive subtitle have not been counted. Obviously, such a filter excludes numerous periodicals which, to some degree, cover the ancient, medieval, or early modern Mediterranean.[3] Nevertheless, there is something, I would

---

[3] Examples that do not 'fit' for the first reason would include, for example, *Central Mediterranean Naturalist* (1979–83) or *Mediterranean Language Review* (1983–); for the second, *Boreas: Uppsala Studies in Ancient Mediterranean and Near Eastern Civilizations* (1970–) or *Caeculus: Papers on Mediterranean Archaeology* (1992–). Serial monograph publications, such as *Studies in Mediterranean Archaeology* (*SIMA*; Lund, 1962–), *Studies in Mediterranean Archaeology Pocketbooks* (*SIMA-PB*; Göteborg, 1974–), *Monographs in Mediterranean Archaeology* (*MMA*; Sheffield, 1995–) or *Studies in Eastern Mediterranean Archaeology* (Turnhout, 1997–) are also not considered in this analysis.

argue, in a name. The journals that remain are those that specifically ally and align themselves with the Mediterranean as an entity; they claim something with the label they choose. Totting these up, we are left with some dozen or so cases, and a veritable alphabet soup of acronyms: *JMA, JMAA, JMS, MA, MAA, MHR, MPO, MS* (twice), and so on (see Table 13.1).[4] Rather than trudging through these serials one by one, in survey fashion, this discussion will call them to the bar, as it were, to define and defend their choice of title and of territory, by posing a series of questions to the entire set:

- When do these periodicals appear?
- Who stands behind them and where are they located? In what languages do they publish?
- What face do they show the world? What is on the cover?
- How do they explain their mission? What is their agenda?
- What do they mean by 'Mediterranean'?
- Are they successful?

In the end, we will see what—beyond the obvious—emerges as characteristic of a 'Mediterranean serial', and we can reflect on the utility, and the possible future, of that categorization.

2. CHRONOLOGICAL PATTERNING

As Figure 13.1 has already signalled, the birth of these journals is, on the whole, a relatively recent development. Progenitors include *Méditerranée* and *Peuples Méditerranéens/Mediterranean Peoples* (launched in 1960 and 1977 respectively), although it is worth noting that the first of these appears more geographical in scope, the other more ethnographic, than is the primary focus of attention here. One version of *Mediterranean Studies*, launched in 1978 under the joint auspices of the Faculty of Arts and of Economic and Social Sciences at the University of Malta,

---

[4] Website addresses provided in Table 13.1 were valid as of November 2002. The final category ('WorldCat Citations') is derived from an on-line OCLC FirstSearch of WorldCat for each serial, reporting the number of 'Libraries that Own Item' there recorded. WorldCat claims to be the 'world's largest bibliographic database' (http://www.oclc.org/worldcat/). While its coverage is not comprehensive, and quite biased towards North American holdings, it nonetheless can offer one proxy measure of a journal's level of circulation.

TABLE 13.1. *List of 'Mediterranean serials' considered in the text*

Abbreviation	Journal title	Institution/Place of publication/Website address	Dates of Publication	WorldCat Citations
JMA	*Journal of Mediterranean Archaeology*	Sheffield: Continuum Journals www.continuumjournals.com/ journals/ index.asp?jref = 13	1988–	81
MHR	*Mediterranean Historical Review*	London: Frank Cass www.frankcass.com/jnls/ mhr.htm	1986–	78
MeditArch	*Mediterranean Archaeology: The Australian and New Zealand Journal for the Archaeology of the Mediterranean World*	Sydney: Department of Archaeology, University of Sydney; www.arts.usyd.edu.au/ departs/ archaeol/meditarch/	1988–	55
JMS	*Journal of Mediterranean Studies: History, Culture and Society in the Mediterranean World*	Msida, Malta: Mediterranean Institute, University of Malta	1991–	45
SM	*Scripta Mediterranea: Bulletin of the Society for Mediterranean Studies*	Mississauga, On.: Benben Publications; www.utoronto.ca/ cims/files/jourcurr. htm	1980–	29
MS	*Mediterranean Studies*	Valletta, Malta: Midsea Books	1978–1980	17
BMA	*Bulletin of Mediterranean Archaeology*	Cincinnati, Ohio: Institute for Mediterranean Art and Archaeology	1975/76– 1977/78	16

Continued

TABLE 13.1. *Continues*

Abbreviation	Journal title	Institution/Place of publication/Website address	Dates of Publication	WorldCat Citations
JMAA	*Journal of Mediterranean Anthropology and Archaeology*	Xanthi, Greece: Anthropological Museum of the International Demokritos Foundation	1981; 1990–1	14
PAM	*Polish Archaeology in the Mediterranean*	Warsaw: Warsaw University Press	1989–	13
MA	*Mediterraneo Antico: Economie, società, culture*	Pisa/Rome: Istitute Editoriali e Poligrafici Internazionali www.libraweb.net/dettagli/ MEDITERRANEO%20 ANTICO.htm	1998–	11
MS	*Mediterranean Studies: The Journal of the Mediterranean Studies Association*	Aldershot, UK; Brookfield, VT: Ashgate Publishing Co. www.mediterraneanstudies. org/ms/medstud.html	1989–	10
MAA	*Mediterranean Archaeology and Archaeometry*	Rhodes, Greece: Department of Mediterranean Studies, University of the Aegean www.rhodes.aegean.gr/ maa_journal/	2001–	2

MPO	*Mediterranean Prehistory Online*	Italy: Abaco-Mac srl.; www.med.abaco-mac.it/	1998–	–

Related journals

	Peuples Méditerranéens/ Mediterranean Peoples	Paris: Éditions Anthropos	1977–	58
	Méditerranée	Aix-Marseille: Université d'Aix-Marseille, etc.	1960–	50
	Mediterranean Quarterly: A Journal of Global Affairs	Washington: Duke University Press; muse.jhu.edu/journals/med/	1990–	186
	Mediterranean Politics	London: Frank Cass www.frankcass.com/jnls/mp.htm	1994+	28
	Mediterranean Journal of Human Rights	Padova: CEDAM home.um.edu.mt/laws/test/mjhr/mjhr.html	1997–	4

seems to have survived only a year or two. A *Bulletin of Mediterranean Archaeology* (at its close, based in Cincinnati) also appeared in the mid-1970s, but again had a very short life. The *Journal of Mediterranean Anthropology and Archaeology* appeared only in 1981, then resurfaced (briefly) a decade later. The real burst of activity began in the 1980s (especially the later 1980s) with, for example, the *Journal of Mediterranean Archaeology* and *Mediterranean Archaeology* both first appearing in 1988: an *annus mirabilis* that also witnessed the successful launch of the *Journal of Roman Archaeology* (*JRA*), an event of significance to this inquiry, as shall be seen. Additions continue right up to the present day, the most recent—*Mediterranean Archaeology & Archaeometry*—launched in 2001. Although many have subsequently undergone editorial changes, or transfers in publisher, the majority of these undertakings have endured to the present. It would be intriguing to compare this record with the survival rate of academic periodicals overall.

How to explain this 'boom', however modest? In part, no doubt, it simply participates in the decided increase of academic journal numbers, in the humanities and elsewhere, over this same time span (Figure 13.2).[5] This is not the place fully to consider political and economic factors behind the development, but the overall trajectory is clear. The years after World War II witnessed the beginning of this upsurge (seen in both book and periodical production), with phenomena from the G. I. Bill to the baby boom generating growth in the number of institutions of higher education and in the number of students attending them.[6] Expansion in the academic publishing industry has steadily accompanied that trend, an evolution

[5] Numbers for the year 2000 represent the average number of titles, 1997–2001. Data are drawn from N. B. Brown and J. Phillips, 'Price Indexes for 1981: U.S. Periodicals and Serial Services', *Library Journal* 106/13 (1981), 1387–93; K. H. Carpenter and A. W. Alexander, 'Price Index for U.S. Periodicals', *Library Journal* 116/7 (1991), 52–9; and K. Born and L. Van Orsdel, 'Searching for Serials Utopia', *Library Journal* 126/7 (2001), 53–8. I would like to thank Beau D. Case, Field Librarian in the Department of Classical Studies and the Kelsey Museum of Archaeology, University of Michigan, for his assistance and his advice on matters of journal production and financing.

[6] A. T. Hamlin, *The University Library in the United States: Its Origins and Development* (Philadelphia, 1981), 68–83.

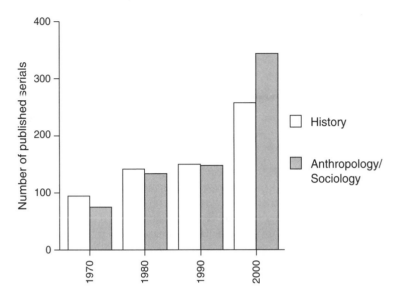

Fig. 13.2. Number of US periodicals, in history and in anthropology/sociology, 1970–2000.

fostered as well by expectations of scholarly productivity in the assessment of promotion, tenure, and salaries.

Our particular pattern, however, should not be lost in global trends. Why the Mediterranean? And why then? In some ways, the development may even appear counterintuitive—at least if we follow Horden and Purcell's arguments about the 'deflation' of Mediterranean studies in the wake of Fernand Braudel's *La Méditerranée et le monde méditerranéen à l'époque de Philippe II*, especially its second revised edition (1966). In *The Corrupting Sea*, they note a subsequent lack of major synthetic works—at least until their own hefty contribution. To paraphrase their argument (in a section entitled 'The End of the Mediterranean'),[7] a pervasive sense of 'been there, done that' long discouraged other attempts at overarching regional narratives. On the other hand, Horden and Purcell acknowledge how Braudel's monumental, and passionate, argument for the 'unity and

---

[7] *CS* 39–43.

coherence of the Mediterranean region' for once and all made a case which others could cite, and build on, with impunity:[8]

It is not only to its author that *The Mediterranean* has seemed the last word. When an eminent economic historian of Antiquity wishes to sum up the Mediterranean environment, whom else should he cite but Socrates—and Braudel...? Whom else, again, when archaeologists seek justification for concerted survey projects in the region and intellectual frameworks within which to locate their discussion of evolving settlement patterns...?

Mediterranean serials too were inspired by, and relied upon, Braudel in justifying their endeavours, as noted below; there exists the strong impression of a torch being passed. Yet the chronology here is also sadly ironic: Braudel died in 1985, as did Shlomo Goitein, author of *A Mediterranean Society: The Jewish Communities of the Arab World as Portrayed in the Documents of the Cairo Geniza* (1967–93)—at just about the time Mediterranean serials started to appear in earnest. With Rostovtzeff and Pirenne, these two form half of Horden and Purcell's quartet of Mediterranean heroes, 'Four Men in a Boat'.[9] The very first issue of the *Mediterranean Historical Review*, for example, carried an appreciation of the latter ('Shlomo Dov Goitein, 1900–1985: A Mediterranean Scholar'); its frontispiece read: 'Fernand Braudel 1902–1985'.

3.   WHERE, WHO, AND IN WHOSE LANGUAGE?

In tracing the homes of these journals (both editorial and press, the two—increasingly—need not be identical), we can start from the farthest peripheries (see Table 13.1). To begin in the western hemisphere, serials based in North America are relatively few in number. *Mediterranean Studies: The Journal of the Mediterranean Studies Association* is supported by a small consortium of American universities (principally their programmes in Medieval and Renaissance Studies) and now co-published in the United States and the United Kingdom; *Scripta Mediterranea* is published by the Canadian Institute for Mediterranean Studies, with editors currently located at the University of

---

[8] *CS* 40.   [9] *CS* 31–9.

Toronto. These two journals, with a strongly literary bent to their articles, form something of a subset within the broader sample. The other side of the world is represented by the University of Sydney's *Mediterranean Archaeology: The Australian and New Zealand Journal for the Archaeology of the Mediterranean World*. Publishers located in the United Kingdom are responsible—apart from the aforementioned *Mediterranean Studies*—for the *Journal of Mediterranean Archaeology* (one of whose editors is in Scotland, the other in the United States) and the *Mediterranean Historical Review* (with an all-Israeli editorial team).

A sub-sample of the journals are produced somewhere 'in' the Mediterranean itself. The University of Malta has been especially active, with that early *Mediterranean Studies* and the more recent *Journal of Mediterranean Studies: History, Culture and Society in the Mediterranean World*. Institutions in Greece have produced the *Journal of Mediterranean Anthropology and Archaeology* and now also *Mediterranean Archaeology & Archaeometry*. Italy appears to offer only one relevant print publication, *Mediterraneo Antico: Economie, società, culture*. One possible harbinger for the future production of periodicals, both in terms of medium and of multi-institutional framework, is represented by the recently launched *Mediterranean Prehistory Online*, an electronic journal funded under the aegis of the European Commission and cyber-supported by institutions in Italy, France, Spain, Portugal, Greece, and Israel. Finally, it is worth noting that—wherever based—almost all of these journals are graced with editorial advisory committees of impressively international flavour.

The language of the Mediterranean in this context is, by and large, English—one demonstration of an increasing, if not always comfortable, acquiescence in the use of English as a scholarly *lingua franca*. Some variety does, however, remain in the picture. *Peuples Méditerranéens/Mediterranean Peoples* and *Scripta Mediterranea* are expressly bilingual in French and English (including on their front covers), though the latter publishes overwhelmingly in English; *Mediterranean Prehistory Online* at least partially presents itself in English and Italian; *Mediterraneo Antico* foregrounds Italian scholarship. In other cases, contributions in European languages (French, German,

Spanish, and Italian) are welcomed, but almost invariably appear in the minority. The *Journal of Mediterranean Anthropology and Archaeology* is represented in library listings as 'in English, some French and German'; *Mediterranean Archaeology* explicitly accepts submissions in English, French, German, and Italian, but only some five per cent of its articles (to date) are not composed in English. Yet other journals are, by policy, English-only, such as the *Journal of Mediterranean Archaeology* or the US-based version of *Mediterranean Studies*.

Not surprisingly, the location of editors and of press appears directly to affect the stand taken on this issue. Maltese publications, for example, tend on the whole to be more catholic. The *Journal of Mediterranean Studies* has published occasionally in Maltese itself; the short-lived *Mediterranean Studies* printed article summaries in French and Arabic—the latter a practice that the *Journal of Mediterranean Studies* hopes to revive (see below). Arabic-language contributions or abstracts, it should be noted, are otherwise almost completely lacking in these Mediterranean journals. Abstracts in Greek are provided in the most recent arrival, *Mediterranean Archaeology & Archaeometry* from the University of the Aegean on Rhodes. This very self-consciously international journal will, however, only take articles in English, and in good English at that, as pointed out in the 'Notes and Instructions for Contributors' promulgated on its website: 'Manuscripts must be written in English, and should be checked by a native speaker for spelling and grammar if possible.' Mediterranean serials, at least in this particular dimension, seem rather to demand connectivity than to celebrate local cultural difference.

4. A GOOD COVER

What face do these journals show to the world? How do they represent 'the Mediterranean'? Some periodicals don't even try: *Mediterranean Studies* (from the United States) and the *Journal of Mediterranean Studies* employ a chaste plain dark blue cover, the *Journal of Mediterranean Anthropology and Archaeology* presented itself in simple light blue. *Mediterranean Archaeology* fronts a purple shell on a white background; the shell is clearly metonymic for the products of the sea, while the purple could be said to lend an authoritative touch. In contrast to these simplicities stands the cover of *Mediterranean Archaeology & Archaeometry*, where a palimpsest of images—time-worn columns, a pyramid, the Sphinx, an apparently magnified view of a scientific specimen (a petrographic thin section perhaps?), and the subtle tracings of a map—are combined within a single, busy collage. For its part, *Mediterranean Prehistory Online* superimposes a steatopygous figure atop a stone axe and a pot. The more frequent response to the challenge of selecting an appropriate image, however, is to give primacy to some form of map. 'Old' maps are clearly preferred: representations that summon up the Mediterranean, the notion of human construction of that world, and a sense of the passage of time—all without inviting debate on the tensions of present-day borders, not to mention the vexed question of just how to delimit the 'Mediterranean' itself geographically. *Scripta Mediterranea* and *Mediterraneo Antico* thus boast medieval or early modern depictions, while the *Mediterranean Historical Review* chose an even older, classically derived mapping, with Europa and Asia (both inscribed) encircling the unnamed inland sea. A predictable blue background was later replaced by a green one.

Probably the most radical design makeover, and the most ambitious cover, belongs to the *Journal of Mediterranean Archaeology*. This journal too originally started with a map—a rudimentary, unlabelled outline drawing of the Mediterranean (on an orange background), with a small man-in-boat motif added to one side. The little boat remains in the redesign, but the journal's ambit is now expressed by a vivid satellite image from NASA, described by the editors as 'a very attractive, intriguing and symbolically appropriate image'.[10] This totalizing view of the sea and of its hinterland forcibly seizes upon the notion of the entire Mediterranean as focus, even as its precise boundaries are left ambiguous. For those who might quibble that such a perspective ignores the actuality of past human experience of the Mediterranean (this is a view, needless to say, that would never have been seen in Antiquity), one could either point to the little man in the boat or say—'It's only a cover'.

---

[10] A. B. Knapp and J. F. Cherry, 'Editorial Comment', *Journal of Mediterranean Archaeology* 7 (1994), 3.

5. MISSION AND AGENDA

At the heart of this investigation lies the question: how do the editors responsible explain their mission, or reveal their agenda? Just why was the Mediterranean found good to think with? Perhaps not surprisingly, little uniformity emerges in answer, but some simple trends can be discerned.

First, there are some periodicals which seem to have felt little or no compulsion (or compunction) to justify their selected title and compass. They merely assert it. One example is *Mediterranean Studies: The Journal of the Mediterranean Studies Association*, whose most informative introductory rubric states: '*Mediterranean Studies* is an interdisciplinary annual devoted to the study of the Mediterranean region from the beginnings to the present... Topics concerning any aspect of the history, literature, politics, arts, geography, or any subject focused on the Mediterranean region in any period of history are appropriate.'[11] Similarly, the *Journal of Mediterranean Anthropology and Archaeology* simply announced, on its inside front cover, what it would publish: 'papers on a wide range of topics relating to the Anthropology and Archaeology of the Mediterranean area, including the latest results of research in biogenetics, classical archaeology, palaeodemography, palaeoecology, the palaeoenvironment, palaeopathology, palaeopopulation genetics, prehistoric archaeology as well as interdisciplinary studies...'. Nor does *Scripta Mediterranea* adumbrate its mission beyond stating, for example on its website, 'the journal publishes articles studying all aspects of Mediterranean culture and civilization, past and present, with a special interest in interdisciplinary and cross-cultural investigation'. Finally, the first issue of *Mediterraneo Antico* leapt directly into substantive articles, though its website offers a more general background (to be further discussed below) for the journal's ambitions.

Other journals, by contrast, are more forthrightly self-conscious and argumentative about what they are trying to achieve. Four cases will be highlighted here, one of strongly historical character (*Mediterranean Historical Review*), two with a principally archaeological focus (*Mediterranean Archaeology:*

---

[11] http://www.asu.edu/clas/acmrs/medstud.html.

*The Australian and New Zealand Journal for the Archaeology of
the Mediterranean World*; *Journal of Mediterranean Archaeology*), and one with a truly interdisciplinary nature (*Journal
of Mediterranean Studies: History, Culture and Society in the
Mediterranean World*). Perhaps not coincidentally, at least
judging by the number of library holdings recorded in World-
Cat, these are the most widely circulating periodicals in our
sample (see Table 13.1).

Fernand Braudel is a very present force in the early years of
the *Mediterranean Historical Review* (*MHR*); apart from articles revolving around him in volumes 1 and 2, the Preface and
Foreword to volume 1 (1986) both regret his recent death and
adopt his view of the region's 'structural unity and coherence ... and hence the comparable nature of its problems'. Braudel's construction of the Mediterranean almost allowed *MHR*
to begin *in medias res*:[12]

The first number of a new historical journal is almost invariably
prefaced by the assertion of a credo. Essentially this Review is the
result of a conviction that the Mediterranean region is a legitimate
subject of historical research and debate requiring little, if any, de-
fense; it is inspired by a penchant for the landscape—physical and
human—of the Mediterranean world.

The Foreword's self-justification, however, moved well beyond
that affectionate 'penchant'. While identifying an academic
shift in emphasis away from the Mediterranean, owing to a
combination of Eurocentrism and Third World 'fascination',
editorial conviction of a continued widespread interest in the
region's history stimulated the enterprise. Within its established disciplinary framework, *MHR* insists upon an openness
to contributions (here in the form of conference proceedings,
articles, book reviews, and a 'testimonia' section) derived from
all parts of the Mediterranean, in all historical periods. The
journal emerges as highly successful in this aspiration, with
periods from protohistory to the modern represented (albeit
with a frequent emphasis on the medieval and early modern
epochs), including the often missing Islamic history of the
sea.

---

[12] S. Ben-Ami, 'Foreword', *Mediterranean Historical Review* 1 (1986), 5.

What particularly distinguishes the journal, however, is its constant emphasis on *interaction*: on 'contacts, relations, and influences within the Mediterranean context...'; it seeks to be 'a forum for those dealing with the mutual influences between the region and the outside world'.[13] Issues of ethnic and cultural contact are returned to repeatedly and fruitfully (for example in volume 4.1: 'Latins and Greeks in the Eastern Mediterranean after 1204'; or volume 11.2: 'Intercultural Contacts in the Medieval Mediterranean'; or volume 15.1: 'Seafaring and the Jews'). These topics echo not only the breadth of Braudel, but the research of Goitein on Jewish-Arab contact, and on medieval trade and exchange. Such an orientation—towards the problems and potential of cross-cultural contact and the shared existence of diverse peoples—may also reflect debates at work in the home base of the chief editorial panel, all of whom are located either at Tel Aviv University, Haifa University, or Hebrew University in Israel.

The impact of the present day, and of a political agenda, announces itself more overtly when one turns to the Sydney-based *Mediterranean Archaeology*. Its official statement of purpose (published in the first issue on the page listing the journal's various editorial, advisory, and managerial committees) reads thus:

Mediterranean Archaeology (abbreviated *Meditarch*) is published annually. One of its main objectives is to provide a forum for archaeologists in Australia and New Zealand whose research and fieldwork focus on the Mediterranean region. At the same time it responds to the need for an international journal that treats the Mediterranean region as an entity.

If one reviews the journal's contents, it could be argued that the first of these goals is more clearly achieved than the second. Antipodean scholarship dominates its pages, as do pieces engaged with museum collections in Australia or New Zealand, together with work carried out in the Mediterranean under the aegis of Australian teams. A local 'angle' to the journal is also revealed in its frequent dedications to major figures in the field, with volume 1 dedicated to A. W. McNicoll, volume 2 (and

---

[13] S. Ben-Ami, 'Foreword', *Mediterranean Historical Review* 1 (1986), 6, and see the journal's website.

volume 8, on the occasion of his death) to the journal's initial
patron, A. D. Trendall, and volumes 9–10 to Peter Connor—all
luminaries of Mediterranean archaeology down under.

In a speech made at the journal's official launch, and published in *Meditarch* 2 (1989), its editor delivered a revealing
programmatic statement;[14]

The extraordinary development of Mediterranean archaeology in
Australia after the Second War, and in particular in the last 20
years, can be understood as part of the country's rapid and radical
transformation from a rural British colony at the periphery of the
world to an independent, increasingly industrialized nation with a
growing awareness of its position in the Pacific and of its unique,
multicultural character.…

He went on to present a general survey of these developments,
in terms of fieldwork and museum initiatives, concluding:[15]

In short, by 1987, it was clear that the time had come for the creation
of an Australian and New Zealand journal of Mediterranean archaeology…At a meeting held in the War Memorial Gallery at the
University of Sydney in April 1987…it was agreed that there could
hardly be a more auspicious year to start such a venture than 1988: the
year of the Australian bicentenary, the year in which the Department
of Archaeology in Sydney was celebrating its fortieth anniversary.

There are things to commend in this journal, not least the fact
that it networks a community of scholars living at some distance
from other 'Mediterranean centres'; it makes known holdings in
unfamiliar Australian and New Zealand museums; it periodically emphasizes, in salutary fashion, teaching and teaching with
artefact collections. On the other hand, the journal's customar-
ily parochial alignment can lead to marginalization, nor does it
particularly seek to question established disciplinary confines.
Even more problematic, as the approving mention of the
Australian bicentenary suggests, *Mediterranean Archaeology*
presents itself as an oddly colonialist enterprise: the Mediterranean is used to validate and celebrate development and success
on the other side of the world. The effort is indicated by the

[14] J.-P. Descoeudres, 'Preface: Australian and New Zealand Contributions
to the Archaeology of the Mediterranean World—A Preliminary Sketch',
Mediterranean Archaeology 2 (1989), 3.
[15] Ibid. 8.

subtitle: *The Australian and New Zealand Journal for the Archaeology of the Mediterranean World*. This 'nationalist' flavour should not, of course, be taken as unique to *Meditarch*; the title of *Polish Archaeology in the Mediterranean* makes one of its principal ambitions eminently clear.

The first issue of the *Journal of Mediterranean Archaeology* appeared in the same year, 1988, as that of *Meditarch*. Since that time, its core mission has never altered. To cite its website manifesto:

JMA ... publishes material that deals with, amongst others, the social, politico-economic and ideological aspects of local or regional production and development, and of social interaction and change in the Mediterranean. We also encourage contributions dealing with contemporary approaches to gender, agency, identity and landscape, and we welcome material that covers both the theoretical implications and methodological assumptions that can be extrapolated from the relevant archaeological data. In terms of its temporal scope, *JMA* welcomes manuscripts from any period of Mediterranean prehistory and history ...

This represents by far the firmest attempt at defining a Mediterranean serial's scope. Yet—beyond an invocation of Braudel and his influence (as with *MHR*)—little time is spent arguing just why the region represents such a vital, valid focus for attention.[16] Far more central to *JMA*'s initial editorial statement were claims for the journal's potential role as mediator: as a bridge over the so-called 'Great Divide' between anthropology and Old World (or 'Classical') archaeology, and as a means to connect and communicate work in that region to a wider archaeological community. The emphasis on 'contemporary approaches to gender, agency, identity and landscape', and on articles dealing with 'theoretical implications and methodological assumptions', is very revealing in this regard. In this formulation, the Mediterranean is featured as a medium through which to challenge standard disciplinary assumptions and boundaries, not least through a regular 'Discussion and Debate' component to the journal.

---

[16] A. B. Knapp, 'Editorial Statement', *Journal of Mediterranean Archaeology* 1 (1988), 3–10.

JMA may be the most editorially vocal of our sample, with periodic public updates on perceived progress towards these goals. What continually stamps these editorial statements, however, is a deep-seated anxiety over the journal's actual diversity of representation. A systematic review in 1994 of all *JMA* articles published six years into the journal's life noted several positive achievements, but also acknowledged: 'At the same time, we note some gaps that need filling, and some biases in need of correction, if *JMA* is to achieve its mission of being a journal of use and importance to all sorts of archaeologists with Mediterranean interests.' The journal, it would seem, tends powerfully to attract submissions from certain quarters (notably prehistory in the Aegean and eastern Mediterranean— the fields of the two co-editors) to an editorially dismaying degree:[17]

... we have so far published nothing (since nothing has been submitted to us) from the African shores of the Mediterranean, other than Egypt... We would gladly welcome the opportunity to include more articles dealing with the Roman, Byzantine, Islamic, Ottoman, Medieval and Early Modern archaeology of the Mediterranean world. Certainly, the editors wish to counter emphatically any impression that *JMA* is a journal aimed primarily at archaeologists with interests in the pre- and protohistory of the eastern Mediterranean.

Improvements have been charted since that appeal, but not to the total satisfaction of the editors: 'And so—somewhat wearily—we would remind all potential contributors of this journal's editorial goals, unchanged since its first issue.... '[18] We will return below to the reasons why those Mediterranean serials principally concerned with archaeological research may face especial difficulties representing the Mediterranean in all facets.

Anxiety about the politics of representation is also evident in the most recent of these four serials to appear—the *Journal of Mediterranean Studies: History, Culture and Society in the Mediterranean World,* a fully interdisciplinary venture launched in 1991 from the Mediterranean Institute of the University of Malta. That journal's first editorial foreword possessed more than a tinge of romance to it:

[17] Knapp and Cherry, 'Editorial Comment', 3.
[18] Ibid. 12 (1999), 5.

A Journal that deals with the Mediterranean may require something more personal which will strike a sympathetic chord among its readers. Here I think the invocation of literature and poetry rather than academic discourse may be more apt, although there is a risk that this approach may mystify even more what many would claim is already a mystified area.

The journal was also likened to 'that well-loved Mediterranean institution, the coffee shop'; its articles and special issues are to be 'arranged as a kind of *mezes* or *antipasto*, which we hope will be filling, exciting and full of different flavours'.[19] Certainly, *JMS* ranges by design far more widely, in both disciplines and periods represented, than the other three examples here considered.

The overall tenor of the journal's aims, however, is very far from a self-involved regional romanticization. Those responsible for *JMS* not only decline to accept the 'unity' of the Mediterranean as self-evident, but amply appreciate the concept's potential manipulation 'for strategic and political ends'. The journal therefore 'aims to encourage interchange among scholars working *in* the area and scholars *from* the area and to stimulate a debate on specific topics, which tackle the complexity of the Mediterranean from different theoretical perspectives'.[20] Such an emphasis on dialogue, particularly on dialogue between academics 'based in North American and North European Universities and in Mediterranean ones', forms part of the boilerplate in the journal's call for papers. In 1999, a reorganized editorial team reiterated that commitment, and took active steps to foster it (for example, with the encouragement of 'Discussion Sections').

In that reorganization, however, the nature of the dialogue was re-examined and expanded: 'The Journal should be a forum for academic collaboration and scholarly dialogue between the North African, Middle Eastern and European parts of the Mediterranean Region'. From the beginning of the journal's existence, gaps in pan-regional coverage were apparent, with the very first editorial apologizing for a lack of papers on

---

[19] P. Sant Cassia, 'Editorial Foreword', *Journal of Mediterranean Studies: History, Culture and Society in the Mediterranean World* 1 (1991), pp. v–vi.
[20] Ibid. p. v.

North Africa. In 1999, the new editorial working group sketched out a hope to publish Arabic abstracts of papers, and to plan 'Special Sections' on the Arabic-speaking world, while admitting: 'Accumulating the resources for these ventures, may take time'.[21]

6. COVERING THE MEDITERRANEAN

As this brief review of the four journals would suggest, while the Mediterranean is normally taken to mean the sum of all its parts and periods, representative coverage of the region is no easy task. *Meditarch* and *JMA*, and to a lesser extent *MHR* and the pre-modern elements of *JMS*, all share a bias towards the eastern Mediterranean; they reveal a tendency to feature contributions on Greece, the Levant, and the Aegean, or on Italy, far more often than, say, pieces on Spain, or southern France, or (certainly) North Africa. The Islamic Mediterranean has been habitually under-represented. The overall situation is explicitly recognized as a problem by *JMA* and *JMS*; *MHR* appears (rightly) more comfortable with its achievement, while *Meditarch* does not seem overly worried by such issues.

To return to our wider sample of periodicals, some, but not all, exhibit similar trajectories. *Mediterranean Studies* (the US version) has maintained a strong Iberian and western Mediterranean presence (if anything, the east is under-represented); *Scripta Mediterranea* can boast a number of publications in Islamic studies. Other journals simply do not aspire to 'full coverage' objectives. The website of *Mediterraneo Antico*, for example, sets itself more decided chronological limits: '*Mediterraneo Antico, Economie, Società, Culture* si propone come luogo e strumento di riflessione critica su uno spazio materiale e umano che ha visto realizzarsi, nella koiné greca ed ellenistico-romana, la propria unità culturale, sociale e poi anche politica.' The journal highlights, as a principal theme to explore, the integration (and possibly repressive integration) of Mediterranean cultures in this particular, Graeco-Roman epoch, as well as the birth of mass religious movements and the transformation

[21] Editorial Working Group, 'Foreword', *Journal of Mediterranean Studies: History, Culture and Society in the Mediterranean World* 9 (1999), 148.

of society in the Late Antique period. The rise of Islam is seen to terminate this particular brand of Mediterranean unity, and thus to lie outside the sphere of the journal.

It might be thought that labelling oneself 'Mediterranean' would send out a sufficiently open invitation to ensure any possible desired variety of contributions. What the relative breadth (or lack thereof) of these various periodicals actually suggests, however, is that a title can only go so far, before numerous other powerful factors intervene. Just the more obvious of filters would include who the editors are, where they are based, who they know, who their students know, the perceived status of the journal, its circulation figures and accessibility, what languages it accepts. Disciplinary differences too stand out as crucial. It is intriguing, for example, that the *Mediterranean Historical Review* apparently overcomes many of the chronological and cultural blockages encountered by the equally ambitious, but more materially oriented, *Journal of Mediterranean Archaeology*. The strength of existing and competing journals, not least the *Journal of Roman Archaeology*, the exact contemporary of *JMA* and *Meditarch*, is one factor here; Roman-period articles—material of vast significance to the archaeological study of the Mediterranean as a whole—now largely gravitate to *JRA*. Flagship periodicals, such as the *American Journal of Archaeology*, also muddy the waters by providing longer established and accepted havens for publication in Classical archaeology. The very rubric 'Mediterranean archaeology' encompasses, of course, a diversity of sub-disciplines: 'Classical' versus 'Egyptian' versus 'European prehistoric' versus 'North African' versus 'Biblical' versus 'Near Eastern', to name a few. That no single periodical has been able to provide a framework—known to, respected by, and published in by all these separate interests—should not perhaps surprise.

As might be suspected from what has already been said, another critical issue is the frequent gulf between representations of the pagan or Judaeo-Christian Mediterranean and the Islamic Mediterranean. Responding to the editorial unease expressed in the *Journal of Mediterranean Studies*, its volume 11 (2001) published UNESCO conference proceedings directly addressing current concerns within Arabic nations: migration, activism, gender stereotypes, and relationships with non-Arab populations. This volume's preface, written in the aftermath of 11 September 2001, despairingly pleaded yet again for the forms of dialogue sought by that journal. But the author also went on to draw an explicit link between the Mediterranean and broader predicaments: 'As a global microcosm, the Mediterranean manifests paradigmatically the interaction of Christendom, Islam and Judaism with all the trappings of the social dilemmas and stereotype delimitations we are witnessing worldwide.'[22]

Growing dichotomies in the modern Mediterranean, arising especially since the end of the Cold War, have been closely observed in many quarters—not least in a parallel sequence of other 'new' serials: for example, *Mediterranean Quarterly* (1990–), *Mediterranean Politics* (1994–), and the *Mediterranean Journal of Human Rights* (1997–). These journals chronicle such present-day traumas of the Mediterranean as the sea's plainly accelerating 'north/south' divide (rich/poor; western/non-western; Christian/Islamic) and its increasing characterization as a region of economic inequality, demographic imbalance and migration, youth frustration, and environmental loss.[23]

This apparently promising breeding ground for a 'clash of civilizations' could seem very distant from the quiet world of our Mediterranean serials. But there exist more points of connection than might at first appear. As this review has suggested, modern agendas undeniably inflect the character and coverage of a journal, sometimes overtly, sometimes not. Conversely, historical study of the Mediterranean—that 'global microcosm' of contact and interaction—may have something, and even something heartening, to offer at this juncture. The Mediterranean has long existed, after all, as a communicative mixture of religions and cultures and languages, as a scene of cultural transmission, as a crossroads. This fact has been recognized by political leaders and analysts of the region, who see in the area's historical diversity some hope—if often only a faint

[22] A. Spiteri, 'Preface', *Journal of Mediterranean Studies: History, Culture and Society in the Mediterranean World* 11 (2001), 2.
[23] See, for example, D. K. Xenakis and D. N. Chryssochoou, *The Emerging Euro-Mediterranean System* (Manchester and New York, 2001), with bibliography.

one—for the possibility of future dialogue and mutual understanding.[24] It remains to be seen how Mediterranean serials
may respond in future to this new, and ever more pressing,
agenda.

The success of 'Mediterranean serials' is, of course, most ob-
jectively gauged by their circulation, as assessed by proxy in
Table 13.1. Apart from such bottom-line measures, however,
their individual virtues clearly lie in the eye (and the needs) of
the beholder. Each of these journals has, at one time or another,
for one user or another, published valuable contributions, often
in interesting and provocative juxtapositions. It is true that, to
employ Horden and Purcell's terminology, these journals deal
more with disparate issues 'in the Mediterranean', than with
encompassing studies 'of the Mediterranean',[25] but that need
not be an unfortunate thing. Mediterranean serials allow and
encourage the study of geographical, cultural, and intellectual
barriers—their causes, consequences and resolutions—in the
past. Whether currently utilized to the full or not, they also
provide one viable form of interface, a framework for connection and dialogue across such barriers in the present.

---

[24] 'Some have pointed to a modern "clash of civilisations" as inevitable. We
who live at the crossroads disagree—indeed, we are living proof that different
cultures and different faiths can co-exist in peace': quoted from His All
Holiness Bartholomew I, Archbishop of Constantinople—New Rome and
Ecumenical Patriarch; cited in Xenakis and Chryssochoou, p. vi; see also
p. 28; M. Lister, *The European Union and the South: Relations with Developing
Countries* (London, 1997), 72.

[25] *CS* 2–3, 9.

Last Words

14

Egypt and the Concept of the Mediterranean

Roger S. Bagnall

These remarks began as a response to a pair of papers in the Columbia colloquium, those of Herzfeld and Armstrong, and they retain that character even as they take up ideas raised in other papers in this volume and reflect on the place of Egypt in *The Corrupting Sea* itself. Those two original papers have in common that they step back from the Mediterranean itself to those who create and represent it as a category, a concept, or a political fact. Although in neither case were scholars and teachers the group under consideration, it is evident that we ourselves are engaged in just this work of creation and representation. A number of other papers printed as chapters in this volume do raise related issues of inclusion and exclusion in the constituting of the Mediterranean as a subject of academic study and public perception, and already as I listened to them it became obvious to me that collectively they bore on an issue of perennial concern to me as an historian of Hellenistic and Roman Egypt, namely, the place of that society in the contemporary Mediterranean world. It was, however, equally striking how slight a place in the conversation of the colloquium Egypt occupied, and this near-omission only reinforced that concern over Egypt's place in the larger Mediterranean conversation. This invisibility takes on an additional irony when one considers that if one thinks of a work other than Braudel's before Horden and Purcell for which the Mediterranean was the programmatic theme, it is unavoidably Goitein's great work, *A Mediterranean Society*. That study, as Abulafia's chapter points out, centres on a community in Egypt.

The colloquium thus embodied in a sense the ambivalence that Horden and Purcell's view of the Mediterranean exhibits towards Egypt. Although they never, as far as I have seen, do a straightforward report card for the land of the Nile, it is not difficult to do an assessment. Of their two great tests for inclusion in their Mediterranean, Egypt fails that of fragmentation outright. Although it is not without variation, there are no major barriers to movement and no radical distinctions of environment within the valley of the Nile.[1] Indeed, it is precisely the twin characteristics of spatial unity and enclosure within a kind of environmental box that historians tend to point to as formative elements in the political geography of pharaonic Egypt.[2] For this reason it lacks the variation in crop yields, as Horden and Purcell note (*CS* 152: the lowest interannual variability). Although it had the wetlands of the Delta to help reduce the risk of crop failure (*CS* 188), they were hardly needed (nor, in case of a major failure of the Nile, sufficient) for that purpose.

Egypt does much better in connectivity, with the Nile never far from any settlement (cf. *CS* 140), although most of the country is distant from the central sea. The extensive traffic on the river, from nome to nome, could reasonably be seen as playing the part played by maritime cabotage in Horden and Purcell's Mediterranean. One might argue about Egypt's contribution to their emphasis on rural rather than urban economies. This is an area in which Egypt changed dramatically during the course of a millennium under Greek and Roman rule, particularly the latter, going from a land characterized by its villages to one of the most urbanized provinces of the Roman Empire.

Overall, Egypt's fit into the Horden and Purcell definition is thus fairly weak. Then again, the Mediterranean is, they say (p. 45), a fuzzy set. Egypt is part of the fuzzy edges. That fact perhaps accounts for the marginal role Egypt plays in the book, although it does not fully explain the fact that medieval Egypt—the Egypt of the Geniza documents—plays a far more important role than Hellenistic and Roman Egypt. Indeed, it is striking that the otherwise omnivorous bibliography of the book

---

[1] The degree of fragmentation emphasized by Horden and Purcell (*CS* 78) as making the Mediterranean distinctive is precisely what Egypt lacks.

[2] For a summary view of this 'caging effect,' see J. G. Manning, 'Irrigation et état en Égypte antique,' *Annales HSS* 57 (2002), 611–23 at 613.

has relatively little on Egypt from Alexander to the coming of the Arabs. Despite the authors' disclaimer of any apology 'for omission or *Tendenz*', the reader is entitled to ask why ancient Egypt is so much less a part of the Mediterranean than medieval.[3] It is hard to avoid the thought that Goitein's magisterial and convenient synthesis, rather than any qualities in Egypt itself, deserves the responsibility.

But first we will turn back to the political dimension of conceptualizing the Mediterranean. This could hardly be better exemplified than by Christopher Drew Armstrong's chapter, where the Mediterranean is shown to be brought into existence both as cartographic concept and representation and as theatre of economic and political influence by the will of successive French ministers, not only ahead of other nations in recognizing the possibilities but creating realities that other nations would then have to deal with. When travellers transform, as Armstrong describes it, the experience of travel from a means of collecting and exchanging into a dynamic model of visual perception, they are framing a usable Mediterranean.

Similarly, but from a very different vantage point, Herzfeld points to the ways in which a supposed toolkit of Mediterranean characteristics can be used as part of rhetorical strategies aimed at defining one's own position in an advantageous fashion and at putting others in their (inferior) place. He shows that the political dimensions of this sort of action extend from the use of such concepts inside societies of the Mediterranean to the academic study of the societies in question and are there rooted in the self-interest of the academics who delineate differences or form alliances with the help of conceptions of what is or is not Mediterranean. The most obvious difference, one might say, is that his examples of Mediterranean stereotyping in Greece and Italy embody negative qualities, however differently they may be used in different national or regional contexts. In scholarship, by contrast, 'Mediterranean' has nothing but good resonances, those that have led to the little bandwagon of journal titles featuring the region that Susan Alcock's paper analyses.

---

[3] This is not just a matter of bibliography, but of substance—for example, the failure (*CS* 211) to recognize the enduring importance of sesame oil in Egypt.

In a number of settings, to be sure, 'Mediterranean' is little more than our imposition of a proxy for another term—perhaps 'Greek' or 'Roman' or 'Byzantine,' in some academic contexts, the 'in the Mediterranean' rather than 'of the Mediterranean' in Horden and Purcell's taxonomy.

It is impossible to comment adequately on the academic political dimension of the Mediterranean concept without at least some disclosure of interests, for those interests exist as much in our academic politics as in the discourse of the Mediterranean societies that Herzfeld discusses. I come to this topic from a particular perspective and background: on the one hand, a training in Greek and Roman history in an era when that field was not much interested in examining the personal or conceptual baggage brought by the historian to the task at hand; on the other, and perhaps more importantly for our purposes, a career-long focus on Egypt, a country that has, as we have already seen from the most cursory of looks at *The Corrupting Sea*, always occupied a rather peculiar position from the point of view of the Mediterranean, particularly in the central periods of Greek and Roman history. It is, however, precisely the combination of these two things that leads me to find a number of the chapters in this volume so suggestive. They require some reflections about both Antiquity and contemporary academe.

Most Classical historians have found it difficult to think of Egypt as being part of their subject at all. I shall never forget being asked, when a graduate student at the American School of Classical Studies in Athens, what business I had being there when I was working on the Ptolemaic empire. The simple and non-confrontational answer, of course (which, believe it or not, was the one I chose), was that the Ptolemaic empire had included parts of Greece (particularly the Aegean islands) and Asia Minor, and that Ptolemy II's troops operated in Attica in the 260s BC. But the larger and more ideological one was that I thought of Ptolemaic Egypt and its dependencies as part of the larger Greek world of the Hellenistic period. This was a viewpoint I had absorbed at a Yale still strongly coloured by the tradition of Michael Rostovtzeff. My questioner thought otherwise, and lest anyone think that he represented some lunatic fringe, I observe that he subsequently occupied one of the most elevated academic positions in the American School in Athens itself. Ptolemaic history did not and does not count as Greek history to many minds. The obvious alternative to treating Ptolemaic history as Greek history would be to think of it as part of the history of Egypt—as, of course, it is to a large extent. There are two problems with locating it only in Egyptology. For one, Egyptology, in contrast to—or perhaps all too much like—the classical view, tends to think of the Hellenistic and Roman periods of Egyptian history as alien ground, too Mediterranean, post-pharaonic. Perhaps more importantly from the point of view of academic interest, because there are (despite very wide and strong public interest) few departments of Egyptology in North America and comparatively far more teaching Classics and Greek and Roman history, it is in my interests and those of people like me to see Egypt as part of the Mediterranean world run by the Greeks and Romans. And indeed, almost everyone in this country who does the sort of thing I do is housed in Classics, History, or both, and there are probably more people interested in Roman Egypt in Religion departments than in Egyptology or Near Eastern Studies.

Near Eastern Studies, for that matter, has never seemed like a plausible alternative, either. Egyptology is located in Near Eastern departments in some universities, but Egypt's relationship with the idea of the Near East is almost as difficult as its connection to the Mediterranean. (It is, incidentally, striking that a volume on the early Roman East edited by Susan Alcock omits Egypt entirely.[4]) The absence of Arabic from journals about the Mediterranean, to which Alcock has called attention (along with the underrepresentation of Islamic topics) fits well with the interests of a disciplinary organization of the sort I have described. Ignorance of Arabic is of course utterly dysfunctional for any kind of fieldwork, and it is no accident that American scholars trained in a classical tradition have played a minor role in archaeological fieldwork in Egypt, especially since the Second World War. The most famous American papyrologist of the twentieth century, Herbert Youtie, famously never

---

[4] S. E. Alcock (ed.), *The Early Roman Empire in the East*, Oxbow Monograph 95 (Oxford, 1997).

visited Egypt. The actual country is thus left to the Egyptologists and Arabists.

Now there is some connection between ancient realities and modern academic politics. Egypt was, and depicted itself as, a rather ethnocentric civilization, with relatively poor communications by sea to the north, a difficult corridor to the south, and deserts elsewhere. (However much Abulafia's metaphorical use of deserts as seas may be of use elsewhere, the Egyptian deserts certainly do not function in that kind of spatially mediating fashion.) It was not actually as isolated as that description would suggest, but its own self-representation is neither African, nor Asian, nor Mediterranean. Nor has Egyptology ever been at home with these fields, not really even, as I have remarked, with Near Eastern Studies. And yet at least from the middle of the second millennium BC Egypt was in fact deeply engaged beyond its borders, as Marc Van De Mieroop's chapter in this volume describes, and in the first millennium it was seriatim under the domination of powers from Africa south of the first cataract, from Asia, and finally from the Aegean. Moreover, at least as early as the same period, and probably earlier, there was a substantial flow of outsiders settling in Egypt and becoming part of the Egyptian population; dozens of languages were spoken. Picking an academic home for a diachronic Egyptology, in other words, means choosing one region against the others, not a question of fact but one of preference. The political value of an African instead of Mediterranean or Near Eastern Egypt has not escaped notice in recent decades.[5]

As I have suggested, geographical realities have some role in Egypt's ambiguous connection to the Mediterranean. And yet, as Van De Mieroop points out, the Near East formed a political unit in the late second millennium BC, one in which the Mediterranean was one, but only one, of the sources of internal communication. He suggests that this unity came to an end at the end of the second millennium, with the Mediterranean

---

[5] See the judicious review by Stanley M. Burstein, 'A Contested History: Egypt, Greece and Afrocentrism', in S. M. Burstein, R. MacMullen, K. A. Raaflaub, and A. M. Ward, *Current Issues and the Study of Ancient History*, Publications of the Association of Ancient Historians 7 (Claremont, Calif., 2002) 9–30.

looking more westward and no longer serving as a unifier for the Near East. Perhaps this was true for a time, but it seems to me that the description he gives of the second millennium could equally well apply to the Persian empire. Certainly it fits later periods. The confrontation of Hellenistic monarchies took place in an important sense around the eastern Mediterranean, with some westward entanglements that grew gradually more imperative as Rome became a central actor; but that eastern Mediterranean world reached far into the Asian continent, with Seleucid power extending deep into what had been the Persian central provinces.[6] Compared to many of these regions, as I have observed, Egypt had a distinct advantage in connectivity, for the Nile brought almost all of its populated hinterland into relatively swift and inexpensive contact with the sea. In the economic sense of Alain Bresson's discussion, Egypt should be the most Mediterranean of countries.

Even in modern Egyptian politics, Mediterranean or not Mediterranean has not been an easy question. For Nasser, there seemed to be advantages in emphasizing pan-Arabism; for others, pointing to Egyptian's historic engagement in the Mediterranean was a means of suggesting that the Arab world was not the natural source of Egyptian identity or contemporary political alliances. Matters are thus practically inverted from the usage that Herzfeld describes in Italy or Greece. Instead of the Mediterranean's serving as a code to explain or justify negative behavioural stereotypes, it has at times served in Egypt the reverse purpose, that of criticizing corruption, nepotism, unreliability, imprecision, and other undesirable stereotyped behaviours as *not* being Mediterranean. In this context, 'Mediterranean' perhaps is the plausible substitute for 'European'. In any event, the often marginal place not only of Greek and Roman studies but of investigation of the millennium from Alexander to Amr in Egypt's universities, and the subsuming of Greek and Roman Egypt under Pharaonic in the Egyptian government's administrative structures for archaeology, show how difficult affirming a Mediterranean identity has been in

---

[6] In this instance, it should be noted, the term 'upper' (*ano*) for the satrapies east of Babylonia certainly cannot depend on the north–south axis that Bowersock postulates.

post-independence Egypt. The national narrative skips from
Pharaonic to Islamic Egypt.[7] As Herzfeld says, 'the history of
even the most distant Mediterranean pasts is always already
politicized.'

Everywhere we turn, then, we find that Egypt's relationship
to the idea of the Mediterranean is fraught with interests, and
there are more that could be mentioned. Whether this means
that there is nothing but interests, politics, and representation,
however, is not so clear, and this is where I would say that I do
not think that the question as posed by Herzfeld is the *only*
Mediterranean question on which it is worth spending energy.

In the end, I am not sure that the heuristic power that he
grants the category and its utility as an analytic tool about which
he is more reserved are really such different things. I shall
briefly give two examples in which the two seem to me to
meet. The question of whether Egypt is to be considered a
real and ordinary part of the Graeco-Roman world—its normality or exceptionality—has long been a staple of debate in my
field, even the stated focus of international congresses. The last
third of a century has driven scholarly consensus sharply in the
direction of Egypt's 'normality' and away from its exoticization.
There are undoubtedly several reasons for this trend, but one at
least is independent of the desires and interests of papyrologists
and their friends: the discovery of documents similar to the
papyri of Egypt in contexts as distant from one another as
southern Jordan (Petra) and northern England (Vindolanda).
These have shown that much once regarded as exceptional in
Egypt, be it in law, language, documentation practices, economy, or administration, is in fact paralleled elsewhere. This
convergence seems to me more marked in the Roman period
than in the Hellenistic. Our evidence for the Hellenistic period,
however, is not so abundant as later, and even in the Hellenistic
period I am prepared to argue that such essential social technologies as the uses of written documents and archives were
essentially common across broad expanses.

---

[7] This is perhaps changing in interesting ways. An Egyptian friend in
Byzantine history reported a prolonged—and to an outsider's eye, curious—
territorial confrontation with a colleague in Graeco-Roman Egypt over which
of them was entitled to teach late Antique Egypt.

One use of a concept of the Mediterranean, then, might be to look at the degree to which Egypt was or was not converging with it—to see that land's participation as something changing over time. At the least, this can help us escape the grip of the sort of unhistorical thinking that has produced any number of variations on *Égypte éternelle.* In fact, however, I think the reality is still more complicated. Part of Egypt's typicality, I believe, is that every other part of the basin was also, like Egypt, becoming less exceptional and more convergent during the same period, that extending from the fourth century BC down to the fourth AD, much as had been the case in the imperial world of what Van De Mieroop calls Early Antiquity.

A second such inquiry is to ask if the category Egypt always makes sense. Were Thebes and the western oases Mediterranean in the same degree that Memphis was? Are we just swallowing too easily the unitary concept of Egypt promulgated by the early kings in their own political self-interest and accepted so readily and uncritically by scholars until quite recently? Can the Mediterranean thus serve as a device to criticize assumptions internal to the study of Egypt, such as the desirability of political unification? I am not sure that the answer is positive; one could as well think that the reverse might happen. But Armstrong's depiction of the dynasty of the families of Colbert and de Maurepas in the ministry of maritime affairs strikes me as relevant here. It is only a moderate exaggeration, I would suggest, to say that France is as much, and as little, a Mediterranean country as Egypt is. If we were to fix our gaze on Egypt in the reign of Ptolemy II, that most thalassocratic of Hellenistic kings, it would not seem less Mediterranean-oriented than Colbertian France. In both cases, conscious choices to focus attention and resources on the Mediterranean were made. These regimes have often been compared in other respects, such as economic *dirigisme*, as well, something that commands less assent now than sixty years ago. For both, in any case, the Mediterranean was a choice made in pursuit of goals. In this sense, perhaps my ingrained desire to remain anchored in a historical study *not* limited to the analysis of interests and representations connects in such settings with Michael Herzfeld's desired agenda.

15

Four Years of Corruption:
A Response to Critics

Peregrine Horden and Nicholas Purcell

'A second instalment will . . . allow us an opportunity to respond to criticisms of the first, in the interests of the debate that we should like to promote.' When we wrote those words, in the Introduction to *The Corrupting Sea* (p. 4), the second instalment that we had in mind was volume 2 of the project, now provisionally entitled *Liquid Continents* (*LC*). Since that volume is still 'in progress', however, we are grateful for the opportunity to offer here some interim discussion of reactions to *CS*, mainly as expressed in the more substantial reviews, but also, occasionally, as conveyed at symposia and in private correspondence and conversation.[1] We have tried to resist the temptation to engage simply in tit-for-tat rejoinder. This is, rather, a contribution to what we hope will be a continuing debate, and it covers only a selection of what strike us as the main issues. The notion of the 'essentially contested concept', invoked in the final paragraph of *CS* (p. 523), may be old-fashioned philosophy, but shows no sign of losing its applicability to Mediterranean studies.

1. *QUID EIS CUM PELAGO?*
THE RESPONSE BY DISCIPLINE

Before we continue the 'contest' we should first like to look at it from the outside and ask, not how, but where *CS* has been

---

[1] We consider only some of the reviews that we have come across, cited hereafter by author's name: D. Abulafia, *Times Literary Supplement* 14 April 2000, 9–10; G. Astill, *Landscape History* 23 (2001), 100–1; A. D'Hautcourt, *Revue Belge de Philologie et d'Histoire* 79 (2001), 219–23; H. Driessen, *American Anthropologist* 103 (2001), 528–31; E. Fentress and J. Fentress, 'The Hole

received. It is striking that the three longest reviews that we have kindly been accorded (Shaw, Fentress and Fentress, Squatriti) should have come respectively from an ancient historian, a duo comprising a social anthropologist and an archaeologist, and an early medievalist—that is, from representatives of disciplines that each, in some form, however fiercely debated, already 'have' a Mediterranean as a unit of study. Elsewhere— among scholars of other historical periods or other disciplines— we have not succeeded in making the Mediterranean so contested. Nor, so far as we know, have we provoked, in print, any sustained argument that the Mediterranean region has been too divided for our kind of synoptic treatment; that it is not really, at any worthwhile level, a single field of investigation. In this limited sense, we have preached to the converted.

The amount of evidence that we adduced from the ancient world, coupled with ancient historians' obviously explicable habituation to Mediterranean-wide horizons, naturally led us to expect interest from classicists, though hardly on the ample scale of Brent Shaw's essay, to which we return throughout what follows.[2]

The generous acceptance of our work by Mediterranean anthropologists as well has been especially pleasing to two historians who have no more than armchair acquaintance with fieldwork. Michael Herzfeld, the ethnographer with whom we are in most extensive debate in the anthropological chapters of

in the Doughnut', *Past and Present* 173 (2001), 203–19; T. F. Glick, *Speculum* 77 (2002), 555–7; R. Hodges, *International History Review* 23 (2001), 377–9; J. G. Keenan, 'The Mediterranean before Modernity', *Classical Bulletin* 76 (2000), 81–94; R. Laurence, 'The *longue durée* of the Mediterranean', *Classical Review* 51 (2001), 99–102; A. Molho, *Journal of World History* 13 (2002), 486–92; G. Parker, 'The Mediterranean and the Mediterranean World of Horden and Purcell', and P. van Dommelen, 'Writing Ancient Mediterranean Landscapes', *Journal of Mediterranean Archaeology* 13 (2000), 226–30 and 230–6; E. Peters, 'Quid nobis cum pelago? The New Thalassology and the Economic History of Europe', *Journal of Interdisciplinary History* 34 (2003), 49–61; B. D. Shaw, 'Challenging Braudel: A New Vision of the Mediterranean', *Journal of Roman Archaeology* 14 (2001), 419–53; P. Squatriti, 'Review Article: Mohammed, the Early Medieval Mediterranean, and Charlemagne', *Early Medieval Europe* 11 (2002), 263–79.

[2] See also Keenan, Laurence, and van Dommelen. One classicist, D'Hautcourt, even credits us with a sense of humour (p. 219).

CS, finds (in his contribution to the present volume) 'surprising common ground in our divergent positions'. Elizabeth and James Fentress note (p. 209) that the anthropological chapters seem 'anomalous in the context of the rest of the book', and they comment (p. 218) that a Mediterranean anthropology without kinship, marriage, inheritance, or social structure is 'like archaeology without pots' (some of those topics will reappear in *LC*; others did not lend themselves to the chapters' particular purposes). But otherwise the Fentresses seem to accept even more of our conclusions than does Herzfeld. Henk Driessen finds an 'affinity with anthropology' in our emphasis on the smaller scale of 'definite places' and sees our discussion of honour in chapter XII as 'a useful starting point for further research'.[3]

The early medievalists have a Mediterranean, but it remains different from ours. For both our critics and us, of course, Pirenne continues to determine the paradigm for debate. His classic *Mohammed and Charlemagne* still provides a useful framework within which to discuss the transition from the late Roman to the early medieval economy; i.e. from a *Mediterranean* world to a *north-western* European one. As Paolo Squatriti notes at the start of his review, Pirenne's stature and clarity of thought, coupled with post-modern scholarship's concern to trace intellectual forebears, and the amount of new archaeology for this period, all keep the late antique and early medieval Mediterranean very much alive in academic discussion. Yet Squatriti devotes surprisingly little of his review to the specifically early medieval sections of chapter V of *CS*, and much more to general issues. 'Change clearly did take place in the Mediterranean, even in its more stable eastern end, during "the Pirenne period"' (*CS* 271)—which we had never denied, characterizing the period as one of dramatic abatement. We are credited with a 'nice reading of the few available documents' (ibid.). But we also downplay 'decades of archaeological research', even though the low-level connectivity that we were

---

[3] He also, surprisingly, misreads us on some minor matters: we do not adopt Rappaport's model of human ecology—rather the reverse; and our comment that anthropology must be fully historical if it is to shed light on the *longue durée* is taken out of context and treated as a general dictum (Driessen 529, 530; *CS* 47, 473).

trying to detect is scarcely revealed by what little of this research illuminates the dark seventh-to eighth-century core of
the Pirenne period.[4] Finally, the supposed tendency of pirates
of the period to raid inland riverine settlements, rather than to
behave as Barbary corsairs on the open sea, is taken as undermining our use of piracy as an index of connectivity (wrongly, as
more recent and more detailed and recent research has shown).[5]
And that is all, even in the longest review by an early medievalist. Our interpretation of the evidence for continued Mediterranean 'connectivity' in the early Middle Ages is ignored
altogether by Richard Hodges, the reviewer from whom we
had expected some sharp dissent because we disagree with his
rightly influential refashioning of 'the Pirenne thesis'.[6] Edward
Peters, a 'high' medievalist, does embrace the early Middle
Ages in his review, but he still does not have much space for it
because he reviews *CS* alongside Michael McCormick's vast
and impressive *Origins of the European Economy: Communications and Commerce AD 300–900*. It is a strange and irritating
coincidence that this important work should come out so soon
after *CS* that no debate could take place between McCormick
and ourselves about our assertion of 'connectivity maintained'
across the seventh and early eighth centuries, an assertion that
has obvious repercussions for McCormick's discerning the
'early growth of the European economy'[7] during the Carolin-
gian period rather than after it Peters, however, does no more
than mention our section on the early medieval depression, the
'Pirenne period'. This is presumably because—*à la* Pirenne—
for him the Mediterranean economy has to 'hit bottom' (p. 50)
in order for the northern European economy to come to life.
And we are interpreted as portraying the Pirenne period as

---

[4] Squatriti 271 n. 22 does not offer a huge bibliography of what we missed.
Compare *CS* 567–9.

[5] Squatriti 272. Compare M. McCormick, *Origins of the European Economy: Communications and Commerce AD 300–900* (Cambridge, 2001), 170,
199, 233, 264, 428–9, 519, 768. McCormick's dossier of early medieval travellers suggests that the dangers of pirates have been overestimated; but that
does not affect our argument that open-sea piracy, quite clearly attested in the
period, is some index of *minimum* levels of seafaring.

[6] There is a brief but highly informed discussion in Fentress and Fentress
215–17.

[7] We allude to G. Duby's 1974 monograph of that title (in translation).

'only' a depression, as 'a slight dip', even though (*CS* 154) we explicitly characterize the period as one that makes audible the 'background noise' of Mediterranean connectivity when the 'strident commercial networks' are silenced. If we use 'depression' and 'abatement' in portraying the period, this should not be taken to mean that we treat such phenomena as mere blips. It means simply that—to change metaphor—our 'degree zero' of Mediterranean exchange is a little higher than that of most other students of the period (even though it is not so high as McCormick's).[8] This is an instance of a problem of presentation for which we bear full responsibility: our pursuit of generalization across three thousand years led us throughout to give the impression of damping down the intensity of change. There is nothing, however, in our model to deny remarkable peaks of intense connectivity or equally deep troughs, though we persist in enjoining caution on those who wish to predicate such extremes of the whole basin.

By contrast, the reaction of the third of the large constituencies among the readership we hoped for—the 'high' or 'central' medieval constituency—has, disappointingly, been briefer, less detailed, far less willing to engage. There has been no real exploration of the possible implications, for the study of the medieval Mediterranean, of our discussions of connectivity, technology, and the control of microecologies.[9] Nor have our comparisons of ancient and medieval economies been tested from the medieval end. We expected, indeed would have welcomed, more resistance here. David Abulafia, from whose works on medieval commerce we have learned so much, virtually ignores these topics in his review, apart from chiding us (p. 10) for disdaining the westward movement of the banana

---

[8] We do not understand Peters' comment in his n. 3: 'Horden and Purcell accept the later [= *c*.1000] beginning of the European economy, but for indifferent [*sic*] reasons'. We are not aware of thinking in that way at all. We simply *contrast* the Pirenne period with the high Middle Ages.

[9] See now also D. Abulafia (ed.), *The Mediterranean in History* (London, 2003), which emphasizes conflicts and connections across the sea without, after an opening chapter on the physical setting, paying much attention to the circum-Mediterranean environment, and without offering any fresh explanation of high medieval economic expansion in Mediterranean Europe.

after the rise of Islam (though see *CS* 258–9 on Arab agronomics and their place in Mediterranean history).[10] Thomas Glick, whose writings were our gateway to much of the newest scholarship on water technology, glides past our response to that work in chapter VII.2.[11]

The interest shown by archaeologists in *CS* has been comparably restrained—with the exception of Cyprian Broodbank's gratifying suggestion that we extend our 'corruption' further back into prehistory (see further below).[12] Squatriti, a historian who knows his archaeology, considers that we evince 'a basic shyness before textual evidence' (of which we had thought we cited rather a lot)[13] and that archaeology is our 'most congenial' resource. By contrast, some archaeologists seem to have resented what they take to be our historical emphasis. In truth we were conscious that our own skills lie in history rather than in archaeology, and this made us reluctant to advance ambitious claims for the latter. We regret having given the impression of considering archaeology an ancillary discipline.[14] We hoped, moreover, to have acknowledged fully our huge debt to field survey; we shall, we trust, make it still plainer in *LC*, in our discussion of settlement patterns. It remains nonetheless a debt of a general nature. The findings of survey are very specific, and in a work of this scope we could not describe dozens of

---

[10] Molho explicitly (p. 492) confines his review to the opening section of *CS*. On this theme see now D. Zohary, 'The Diffusion of South and East Asian and of African Crops into the Belt of Mediterranean Agriculture', in H. D. V. Prendergast, N. L. Etkin, D. R. Harris, and P. J. Houghton (eds.), *Plants for Food and Medicine* (Kew, 1998), 123–34.

[11] He does, more encouragingly, conclude that we have made historical ecology 'accessible to the general medievalist' (557). We may mention in passing here the forthcoming publication, by F. Beltrán Lloris, of an inscription from the middle Ebro valley containing a Roman imperial regulation of river-fed irrigation systems. It conclusively establishes the scale and complexity of at least one pre-Islamic Iberian hydraulic landscape.

[12] C. Broodbank, 'Before Corruption' (unpublished, a prolegomenon to his forthcoming monograph on the Mediterranean in prehistory).

[13] It is only the romantic tradition in Mediterranean writing to which we are averse.

[14] Thus van Dommelen winces at our estimate of what archaeology can tell the historian, inclining to attribute this to ignorance rather than caution. B. Knapp and S. E. Alcock in public debate have made a similar point.

settlements or farmsteads, scores of microregions. We therefore eschewed the piling up of descriptions of individual estates or territories and their fortunes—descriptions that might have been drawn from field archaeology, from ancient inscriptions or literary texts, or from the later documentary record. Where we did display four localities as examples (chapter III), survey contributed heavily and explicitly to our analysis. We note that to do justice to the data of survey can be hard even for archaeologists: a recent reviewer of a series on Mediterranean survey speaks of 'archaeological method... demoted to a kind of anthropological geomorphology'.[15] His complaint is that by adopting a tightly focused and environmentally orientated survey technique, looking inwards at small areas, Mediterranean survey archaeology elucidates large interaction less well than do the techniques and models used by archaeologists working in Asia and America, and does not amount to proper regional analysis. We hope at least to have avoided such introversion.

On the archaeological front, our major regret is that Barry Cunliffe's *Facing the Ocean*, like McCormick's monograph, was not published either a little earlier than *CS*, so that we could draw parallels and contrasts between his Atlantic world and our Mediterranean, or a little later, so that Cunliffe could have included some response to *CS*. Cunliffe's mode of exposition is different from our own. But we share a stress on the primacy of responses to the sea and ease of communications across it as combining to generate coherent zones throughout long stretches of prehistory and history; and the European Atlantic periphery, as Cunliffe maps it, is our western neighbour. In that basic geographical sense, we are not in conflict. We wish only that Cunliffe had gone further chronologically. It remains to build bridges between Cunliffe's archaeological vision, which does not seek to elucidate periods more recent than 1500, and the increasingly lively early modern historiography of the Atlantic.[16]

---

[15] R. E. Blanton, 'Mediterranean Myopia', *Antiquity* 74 (2001), 629.

[16] D. Armitage, 'Three Concepts of Atlantic History', in id. and M. J. Braddick (eds.), *The British Atlantic World, 1500–1800* (Basingstoke and New York, 2002), 11–27; O. Ribeiro, *Portugal, o Mediterrâneo e o Atlântico: esboço de relações geográficas*, 4th edn. (Lisbon, 1986).

2. *LES AUTEURS NE SE NOIENT JAMAIS DANS LEUR
   MÉDITERRANÉE:*[17] THEORY AND SCOPE

We turn now from reviews that have not been written, or not
written from all the disciplinary standpoints that we had hoped
for, to the reviews as they are. Paradoxically some of the most
complimentary passages are the ones that, for us, raise the most
troubling questions about the purposes and scope of *CS*. Gratifyingly, we have been seen as advancing a novel theory of
Mediterranean history: 'a genuinely new thalassology' (Peters
2003: 56); 'un ouvrage phare' (D'Hautcourt 2001: 221); 'a
substantial new approach' (Fentress and Fentress 2001: 203),
etc. But then, very reasonably, we are taxed with the ways in
which the enterprise thus described does not quite work, at least
as an all-embracing theory (e.g. Fentress and Fentress 2001:
210–11; Shaw 2001: 434 ff.). Perhaps we should first try to
remind our readers (and ourselves) what we thought we were
attempting.

At the very least we were, in the words of the ninth-century
author of a history of the Britons known as Nennius, 'making a
heap' of all that we had found. We wanted the illustrative
vignettes in the chapters and the parallel discussion of the
Bibliographical Essays to have a value independent of the arguments advanced. At the next level up, we hoped to offer illuminating comparisons across the various supposed divisions
between prehistory and history, history and anthropology, and
(above all) Antiquity and the Middle Ages. Our aim was to
discover on what basis one might treat ancient and medieval
Mediterranean history as a single field of enquiry and how far
an approach derived ultimately from Braudel enabled us to
cross the boundaries that scholarship seemed to have erected.
To that extent we thoroughly endorse Herzfeld's verdict in this
volume. To think in terms of Mediterranean history is, for us,
an 'excuse' for 'creating new [scholarly] alliances and agglomerations to generate novel and interesting heuristic options'. It
is an 'excuse' to undermine the now, on the whole, more usual
agglomerations of European and Middle Eastern, and ancient
and medieval, historiography by (re)creating a *tertium genus*.

---

[17] D'Hautcourt 221.

The strategy, moreover, seems to have worked. So far no one has insisted, against our project, that the ancient and medieval Mediterraneans really have been so radically different that there is no point in taking the long view. Similarly, as we noted earlier, no one has asserted the utter dissimilarity of European and Islamic Mediterraneans.

At a 'higher' analytical level we attempted to develop a framework for interpreting certain aspects of Mediterranean history that shed light on the big questions of unity, distinctiveness, and continuity in the region. That conceptual framework included a fragmented topography, the mutable microecology, two-way interaction between humanity and environment, connectivity (especially, of course, by sea), and a contrast between history 'in' and 'of' the region. We are well aware that none of these ingredients was our invention. All relied on terminology appropriated from the disciplines of ecology, anthropology, geography, and, in the case of 'connectivity', mathematics.[18] Naturally, we hope that we have, by combining the ingredients, developed a distinctive and, more importantly, useful approach. It is, as Shaw writes (2001: n. 39), not exactly a model, but 'an historical description and analysis of how things actually happen in a Mediterranean world'—a summary that (despite our rash Toynbeean subtitle) we would qualify only by adding '*some* things'. It is a way of looking at a few of the lowest—and perhaps not so low—common denominators of human ecology in the Mediterranean. It is not, or at least not directly, even a way of looking at the whole of Mediterranean history (*CS* 2), and emphatically not a programme for how all Mediterranean historical writing should be undertaken.

---

[18] *Pace* Squatriti 267 n. 10, 'connectivity' was not a political neologism of the 1990s (whatever currency it then achieved) but a rather older term of art in mathematics and by extension human geography. Cf. W. L. Garrison, 'Connectivity of the Interstate Highway System', *Papers and Proceedings of the Regional Science Association* 6 (1960), 121–37. The diagnosis of being inspired by New Labour phraseology seems to have become a topos of academic invective: see A. Cameron, 'Ideologies and Agendas in Late Antique Studies', in L. Lavan and W. Bowden (eds.), *Theory and Practice in Late Antique Archaeology* (Leiden, 2003), 16–17, responding to similar accusations.

That is why we invoked a distinction (already drawn by others) between history 'in' and 'of' the region.[19] It is, admittedly, not a wholly satisfactory distinction. 'History of' does suggest the all-encompassing, though we intended it to refer to 'indispensable frameworks' of the region, such as the micro-ecological ensemble (*CS* 9): it was history of the whole in a particular *geographical* sense, not history of all conceivable Mediterranean *subjects*. On the other hand, history 'in' the region is hardly the ideal way of conveying what 'history of' leaves out. History 'in' the Mediterranean was, we wrote, only contingently or indirectly Mediterranean. That is, as we should now prefer to put it, reference to microecologies would need to come in the *extreme* background of analysis or explanation. It would for example, be the point (which we shall not, ourselves, now try to identify) at which the historian finds the ineluctable Spanishness of the Spanish Civil War—Spanishness in a geographical sense, rather than the cultural or psychological essentialism beloved of an older national historiography. We should perhaps not have implied that any history within the region was, for historians, utterly detachable from its Mediterranean setting.

In *CS*, chapter III, we referred to this 'other' history—which we were not trying to survey fully—under the heading 'Theodoric and Dante'. Aspects of almost everything for which those two resonant names might stand—political power, civic culture, religious beliefs, and so forth—find their way from time to time into 'our' microecologies. (The grip of the powerful on the productive landscape is the most frequent and obvious.) But the converse is not true; microecologies do not embrace or explain everything. That is why early medievalists should not for example expect to find a discussion of Byzantine iconoclasm simply because that is an important aspect of the period. We, the two authors, each write different kinds of history ourselves and have never supposed or (intentionally) implied that the microecological approach of *CS* was an exclusive alternative to other kinds.

[19] It is, for instance, explored by Y. Shavit, 'Mediterranean History and the History of the Mediterranean: Further Reflections', *Journal of Mediterranean Studies* 4 (1994), 313–29, which we regret not having noticed earlier. We are grateful to Irad Malkin for drawing it to our attention.

CS was an attempt to provide a backdrop against which those other kinds of history could be written. Many reviewers have regretted that more extended attention was not given to social, economic, and cultural forms held to have been characteristic of the Mediterranean coastlands; and indeed, social and economic change in the region can hardly be sensibly modelled without including these culturally more specific elements. On the other hand, the social variables have often seemed so very varied as to make wide-ranging comparisons unhelpful, and our search was for the common denominators that would promote comparison.

Doubtless we took that as an excuse to miss out too much. One of the most arresting criticisms of our picture (as e.g. by Shaw 2001: 441) is the absence from *CS* of the state—especially by comparison with our project's great inspiration and progenitor, Braudel's *Mediterranean and the Mediterranean World*.[20] The implication is perhaps that our omission is both unjustifiable and convenient: history can hardly do without such institutions, and, had we attempted to say more about them, we should have faced far greater difficulty in defending the comparability of very different epochs. We confess, naturally, to a degree of omission. The state is not in fact wholly absent from our index and is more widely present than its entry there would suggest because it is subsumed by our wider category of 'managers' of microecologies: the 'powerful' who direct production. But on a Braudellian yardstick our treatment is of course brief and unsystematic. Our aim was to seek precisely those structures and continuities that are camouflaged by the glitter of diversity in this most culturally complex and *mouvementée* of regions. And our reluctance to pursue in detail, for a hundred different societies, how this may be worked out is therefore the product simply of the constraints of scale and available time.[21] Elsewhere in this volume, Purcell tries to show how the gap may be bridged, through the study of a 'middle-order' historical phenomenon, halfway between the ecological foundations and the culturally specific structures.

[20] Even though many critics of Braudel have noted that his political narrative in vol. 2 is somewhat detached from his historical ecology in vol. 1: *CS* 41–2.

[21] One striking example is offered by S. K. Cohn, *Creating the Florentine State: Peasants and Rebellion, 1348–1434* (Cambridge, 1999).

3. DOUGHNUTS IN CYBERSPACE: FINDING THE METAPHOR

From the vocabulary that we have just been using, it will be clear why some of the very different metaphors that *CS* has prompted in reviewers do not seem helpful. This is because they all suggest a greater scope for *CS* than it was ever intended to possess. We are not describing a 'doughnut' with a defining hole in the middle (Fentress and Fentress), a hole that is like 'cyberspace' (p. 204).[22] The homogeneous and stodgy doughnut seems to us a singularly inapposite metaphor for our mutable and variable microecologies, but, still more, it implies a totality to which we do not aspire. So too does the characterization of our perspective as 'a post-modern, turn-of-the-twenty-first century conception of historical writing' (Molho 2002: 488). Our local realities are indeed, as Anthony Molho writes, 'infinitely complex' (*CS* 53). And our commitment to register the genuinely two-way interaction of the human and the natural can admit a degree of social constructionism—'la fertilité comme rapport social', etc. (*CS* 231). But our attempt to develop an analytical framework that can be applied across three millennia of history, and our trust that the complexity is genuinely 'out there', are alike far removed from the all-subsuming post-modern style. Our Mediterranean is partly discourse, with the *Odyssey* as its creator (*CS* 43)—but only partly.

Again, comparison (by Shaw 2001: 427) of our approach with Kuhn's paradigms and Foucault's epistemes or discourses seems inappropriate. For all the similarities—'out of a series of units, patterns are formed that are characterized by strong continuities'; the creation of power shifts with intensification and abatement, and so forth (ibid.)—there are two facets of the comparison which we do not find congenial. The lesser one is that we would, unlike Kuhn and Foucault, admit genealogical links (and indeed evolutions) between successive paradigms or epistemes. The major objection is, again, that paradigms and epistemes are all-embracing; our microecologies are not.

---

[22] Cf. N. Purcell, 'The Boundless Sea of Unlikeness? On Defining the Mediterranean', *Mediterranean Historical Review* 18 (2003), 9–29.

Later in his review (2001: 447), Shaw switches analogy to the Mandelbrot series, the fractal geometry in which, the more one 'zooms in', the more complex and endlessly variable every outline seems.[23] Our picture is 'so fluid and so dynamic that it consequently impedes the understanding of relatively fixed systems and structures'—such as 'the city, the state, the army, and the church and mosque'. We hope that we have not in fact impeded understanding, and we wonder, in *CS* chapter IV, at what level '*the* city' has existed as a fixed structure. But, as we have already said with respect to 'the state', we do not consider such institutions except here and there where they fall into the 'gravitational pull' of the microregions.[24] We rather prefer the metaphor of a chess game (Fentress and Fentress 2001: 210) or our own repeated image of a kaleidoscope. There is a world outside the chessboard. A kaleidoscope is a small contraption that one peers into. One can lift one's eye from the board or the contraption. In neither case is the particular object likely to be mistaken for the whole of reality.

In this and the previous section, we have been rehearsing ways in which our type of Mediterranean historiography touches on some major subjects while omitting others. In so doing we have also started to formulate a response to those critics who mention other topics on which we might—ideally, should—have had more to say. Our detailed illustrations of our approach are no more than that: illustrations. Evidence was, as we said (*CS* 5), chosen to exemplify a theme rather than fill out a dossier. (In that respect, as well as many others, our approach differs from McCormick's wonderfully exhaustive cataloguing.) We have not, to our knowledge, been accused of an unrepresentative selection of material—a relief. Indeed, Shaw (2001: 420 n. 7) imputes to us a western Mediterranean and Roman focus, whereas we foresaw the possible cavil that much of our material was derived from, and best suited to, the Aegean. We have, doubtless, too little to say about the Black Sea,

---

[23] By contrast, Abulafia suggests that, in effect, we offer a stratospheric view, and that we need more people in our analysis.

[24] Cf. Fentress and Fentress 209, on those 'pedestrian' enough to want a 'straight account of exchange or pastoralism'. To do so is not pedestrian; it is simply to require a book other than *CS*.

about Middle Eastern frontiers of the Mediterranean, about Anatolia, about Egypt south of the Delta (Shaw 2001: 424, 426–7, 448; D'Hautcourt 2001: 223; Squatriti 2002: 278; although compare Abulafia (2000: 9) using Egypt to open his summary of our argument!). We were not concerned to demonstrate our approach or to establish the horizono of its applicability in every direction (except perhaps in chapter XII on honour and shame). *CS* could not go in detail into all the periods, peoples, and places on which it touches. If we have a personal regret, it is that we did not have the time, even after too many years' work, properly to get to grips with the evidence for the Ottoman Mediterranean world.

4. FALSIFIABILITY

In framing the book in the way we chose, and in mounting the foregoing defence of it, have we written ourselves a blank cheque? We can be original to the extent that suits us, but not so much that we offer a whole new Mediterranean history and render ourselves vulnerable to charges of omission. We can leave subjects out or touch on them briefly and only in the way we want. Since we eschew systematic coverage our examples can be serendipitous rather than representative.

The list of ways in which we have our cake and eat it could be extended.[25] In our microecologies all is mutability. So any change can be subsumed under the heading of 'normal variability'. Discontinuity is also normal, thus becoming another kind of continuity. We welcome the formulation of Fentress and Fentress (2001: 210): 'the question is not whether or not discontinuities exist, but whether or not they exist as singularities'. But then we are brought up short by another penetrating summary (p. 217):

The issue might seem simply this: when are the discontinuities clamorous enough to justify a period change? Yet this turns out to be a false question, for the authors have formulated their notion of discontinuities in such a way that the answer to the question can only be 'never'.

---

[25] Indeed has been, orally, at a conference in London by Michael Crawford, to whom we offer gratitude for the provocation.

Let us try to put our response to these criticisms at its most general by asking ourselves the Popperian question: is our view of the Mediterranean susceptible to falsification?

First, we should stress again that what we offer is only a perspective on the subject, a synthesis of analytical tools—it is hardly amenable to quantification. That is, no one (least of all ourselves) can, for example, specify how much variability or discontinuity is outside what we conceive as the normal range and could therefore invalidate our picture of the broad Mediterranean continuum. Our perspective either carries conviction as a way of relating diverse aspects of Mediterranean history or it does not.

Of course, the model can be rejected outright, but only by denying its major parameters. Of these the most important, fragmentation and connectivity, seem to us to be fairly robust and to have been accepted by virtually all reviewers. But they are not so obvious as to be commonplaces. Many archaeologists and anthropologists of the Mediterranean have found it necessary to elaborate the microregional structure of their areas of study; and new and constructive research on the precise nature of interdependence in all periods of Mediterranean history is being published every year.

In this context, a further significant aspect of *CS* is that our approach has been accepted as yielding results across many different chronological periods, from the Bronze Age to the Renaissance. This is surely a long enough span to establish what has broadly been normal. Our approach could be falsified by showing for instance that the nexus of connectivity and fragmentation in the Middle Ages radically differed from that of (say) the Roman Empire. Yet, as we suggested above, while medievalists have not, in reviews, engaged with *CS* as fully as we had hoped, they do not seem to have denied the fundamental applicability of its approach. At the ancient end of our period, downplaying of the interconnectedness of Roman economies has often relied on what one might call the missing wheelbarrow argument: the ancient world had no windmills, double-entry bookkeeping, whatever. Shaw suggests (2001: 431) that, in attacking arguments of this kind, and thereby asserting the closer comparability of Roman and medieval, we are actually tilting at windmills rather than denying their relevance. Yet, despite its obvious vulnerability, distinguished scholars have often used this form of argument. We await a more solidly founded restatement of the ineluctable differences between the ancient and medieval Mediterraneans, and we are heartened by the fact that the only reviewer known to us to have doubts about our chronological 'levelling' (Shaw again, p. 446) has to reach into the early modern period before Mediterranean conditions that look different from our presentation begin to be readily documented. Pending further assaults of that type but using earlier (i.e. medieval) evidence, we take it that our approach to Antiquity and the Middle Ages has gained broad assent; and we interpret that in turn as an absence (so far) of major falsification.

Far from seeing the time-span that we cover as too long, as smoothing out divisions between periods, and as thus calling our approach into question, some have thought it not long enough. Our reluctant obituary of 'the corrupting sea', killed off by the political reconfigurations of the second half of the last century, by economic globalization, etc., has sometimes been read as too cautious. We are heartened that our approach might after all have something to offer the student of the modern, even the contemporary, Mediterranean as it is (re?)unified by its reaction to tourism and its reinventions of tradition (cf. Driessen 2001: 530).[26] Meanwhile, at the other chronological extreme, Broodbank has suggested[27] that we were too timid in our incursions back into prehistory and that we should have extended our coverage more thoroughly into the second millennium BC. Indeed, some prefiguring of the Mediterranean patterns that we identify and treat as central can be discerned still earlier than that.[28]

---

[26] We acknowledge here most warmly the informal (unpublished) welcome extended to our anthropology by Thomas Hauschild. See also D. Abulafia (ed.), *The Mediterranean in History*, 283–312, concluding that the two later twentieth-century agents of transformation in the region have been the aeroplane and the bikini.

[27] Broodbank, 'Before Corruption'. See also M. Suano, 'The First Trading Empires', in Abulafia, *The Mediterranean in History*, 67–93.

[28] If A.T. Grove and O. Rackham, *The Nature of Mediterranean Europe: An Ecological History* (New Haven and London, 2001), 150, are correct, however, the climatic element in the distinctive regime of risk that we find in the Mediterranean has been present only since the aridization of (broadly) the fourth millennium BC.

All this, we assume, constitutes an endorsement of our approach. But if, in each case, a converse argument had been offered, the validity of the microregions-plus-connectivity 'formula' would have been seriously in question. In these respects our depiction of the long-term Mediterranean past—'our flexible friend' as the title of the *TLS* review by Abulafia had it—is not infinitely flexible. It can be tested to breaking point.

The falsification could be conducted in geographical ways, as well as by questioning our chronological span. Critics have been keen to point out similarities between our *modus operandi* and Braudel's—to establish our intellectual paternity. And they have done this, gratifyingly for us, by noting the points at which Braudel clearly anticipated our twin emphases on microregional variability and connectivity (Molho 2002: 490). They have not reasserted the master's more obvious way of proceeding by ecological types—mountains, plains, etc. (although Shaw (2001: 450) does uphold an enduring east–west distinction in the Mediterranean and postulates a strange 'median geographic sieve'). Such a reassertion of analytical categories intermediate in scale and kind between the whole region and our tiny fragments could quite conceivably have been undertaken. It could have been buttressed by examples of how Mediterranean ecologies have worked chiefly at this level rather than at that of our usually far smaller and very different units, which admit of structural resemblances but not of types. It would then have constituted another falsification of our approach.

Beyond these, so far hypothetical, ways of undermining *CS* we hope to have offered, in effect, some falsifications of our own. We thought it important to note certain times and places which have departed notably from the more pronounced display of 'our' Mediterranean parameters—and indeed, in our remarks on abatement, have claimed that reductions in the intensity with which our model applies are entirely to be expected (*CS*, chapter VII.4). There are places that have deliberately tried to withdraw from connectivity, as the Corsicans did under the rule of Genoa; or that have succeeded, as the Cretans did in those periods when they turned *façades aveugles à la mer*.[29] Our conception of

---

[29] E. Kolodny, 'La Crète: Mutations et evolutions d'une population insulaire grecque', *Revue géographique de Lyon* 3 (1968), 227–90.

Mediterranean history would be falsified if such examples could be hugely multiplied instead of clearly constituting exceptions. There are also places within the region that may form more lasting exceptions to our connective and fragmented world. Once again a way of falsifying our picture would be to demonstrate that they are too numerous and widespread to be seen as exceptions. We have been taken to task by scholars of post-colonial disposition for failing to listen hard enough for the suppressed, subaltern voices of those excluded from the benefits of Mediterranean interaction.[30] Parts of the interior of prehistoric Spain are given as an instance of those who were not 'well connected'. This may be true, and certain kinds of history may own ethical obligations to give prominence to such isolated histories. But we should note first that connectedness can be very hard to assess. Take a set of studies of the Jebel Hawran, the mountainous tract on the fringes of the desert south of Damascus, in which both the Roman and the modern phases of occupation have been explored. The Hawrani strain of *triticum durum*, very drought-resistant and of the highest quality, was exported to southern Europe on a considerable scale in the nineteenth century; but 'even when export was booming, the bulk of production was nevertheless consumed in Hawran'.[31] Nearby is the strange igneous landscape of the lava flows of the Lajā, a natural labyrinth which was the normal home of brigands; here also, the local cereal farmers were apt to withdraw as a form of resistance to the government which depended on their produce, especially for feeding the Haj.[32] This 'definite place'

[30] Michael Dietler, at a conference at the University of Chicago in 2002; see also Keenan. By contrast, Driessen 529 credits us with a subaltern perspective because of our concern with the small producer and the *caboteur*. It is said (by Keenan 93–4) that our theorizing of the structures of slavery seems inhuman. But we are investigating the rationale of those who manage microecologies, and fail to see how else we can integrate the phenomenon into the very much wider picture that we seek.

[31] L. S. Schilcher, 'The Hawran in Late Roman and Ottoman Times: Three Models for Comparative Research', in D. Panzac (ed.), *Histoire économique et sociale de l'Empire Ottoman et de la Turquie (1326–1960): actes du sixième congrès international tenu à Aix-en-Provence du 1er au 4 juillet 1992* (Paris, 1995), 705–17 at 707, 715.

[32] N. N. Lewis, 'The Lajā in the Last Century of Ottoman Rule', in Panzac (ed.), *Histoire économique et sociale de l'Empire Ottoman*, 631–40 at 633–6.

combined—in the nineteenth century(!)—precarious and invo-
luted behaviour with many classic traits of 'the corrupting sea',
above all those occasional and opportunistic engagements with
different kinds of redistribution. The area happens to be rich in
remains of a prosperous, surplus-producing agrosystem of the
Roman period, based on a network of large villages and thriving
cities. It would be much harder to read stories of Mediterranean
corruption solely from the archaeology of its late Ottoman
phase. In any case, as far as *CS* is concerned, just as some topics
lie 'above' the reach of our microregional conception ('ultravio-
let'), so others are 'infrared'. Those areas entirely cut off from
connectivity or unable to manage production in the ways that
we have taken as characteristic are indeed set apart from the
Mediterranean world: 'in' the region, but not 'of' it, perhaps. If
they are relatively few they tend to confirm our picture. If on
the other hand, the difficulties of interpreting the evidence of
connectivity and isolation could be overcome and their ubiquity
could be demonstrated, then they would naturally undermine
our project.

Finally, our Mediterranean world has frontiers, even if they
shift, are mostly 'fuzzy', and can be nearly imperceptible (as in
the Middle East). In a way, these frontiers provide a perpetual
falsification of our approach. If they reached too far, or too
often, into the region, we should be proved mistaken. We have
said little about frontiers in *CS* but promise to return to them in
LC in our discussion of the Mediterranean and a wider world.[33]

In *LC* we shall also take the opportunity, under that same
heading, to juxtapose the Mediterranean and comparable regions. The question has been raised: have we produced a universal solvent (Shaw 2001: 452)? Could the same approach not
be applied to the Baltic world (Molho 2002: 489, Hodges 2001:
378, van Dommelen 2000: 231) or to the Indian Ocean? Is the
Thames Valley not a fragmented landscape held together by
waterborne communications (D'Hautcourt 2001: 223)? Yes,

---

[33] For a preliminary statement, however, see Purcell, 'Boundless Sea of
Unlikeness?'. We have sometimes been charged with deflecting criticism of
our omissions with the response that they will be repaired in *LC*. But apart
from explicitly allowing ourselves space there to respond to critics (as in the
opening quotation above) the contents of *LC* are outlined in the Introduction
to *CS*.

indeed—and stated in very brief abstract terms our approach is clearly applicable to many parts of the globe. But the difference is in the details, in the particulars of risk regimes, forms of connectivity or whatever, to which it is applied. Our approach is not beyond falsification because it is adaptable. Moreover, we expect some of the other 'liquid continents' found across the world to be different from the Mediterranean, because of their degree or type of connectivity, their level of fragmentation, or the diversity of productive opportunities evident on their shores. Even if analogous corrupting waters could be identified in the Baltic or Black Seas, the Caribbean, or the Philippines (or the Thames Valley), that would not falsify our approach to the Mediterranean. It would not unmask it as a *universal* solvent that, capturing anything or anywhere, explains nothing. Rather, we propose, it would show its value as a heuristic tool for the study of a set of environments that is still, in global terms, very limited.

5. MONSTROUS SQUID OR CALAMARI?[34]

If our approach has been thought too generalized and adaptable to be contradicted by the evidence, it has also been seen as too nice: the 'flexible *friend*'. First, our description of the geographically all-round and chronologically all-year-round connectivity of the sea itself has been seen as anachronistic projection of contemporary frictionless communication onto the Mediterranean past. We hope never to have underestimated the dangers of Mediterranean seafaring represented both anecdotally and in the shipwrecks that have been found. The dangers were at no time an absolute deterrent, however; not even in the early Middle Ages, as the researches of McCormick have shown through numerous examples.[35] To our surprise, the Elephantine palimpsest does reveal commercial shipping in the fifth-century BC eastern Mediterranean in all except two winter

[34] See Squatriti 268 on the perceived danger to early medieval shipping of monstrous squid, which for us, supposedly, are mere calamari.
[35] McCormick, *Origins*. Even our pirates have been thought too nice because we are taken to imply (something we never intended) that they, like pastoralists, exist in symbiosis with those whose lives they disrupt (Fentress and Fentress 214).

months. If our argument for potential—only potential, by no means always achieved—all-round connectivity is to be met head on, it must be through a challenge to our discussion of John H. Pryor's work on Mediterranean winds and currents, not by recounting marine horror stories. No such challenge has yet been made.[36] Meanwhile work goes on, steadily demonstrating the skill and fearless ingenuity of Mediterranean seafarers.[37]

A related criticism is that the Mediterranean 'system', as we present it, is benignly homeostatic: 'a zero-sum balance' (Shaw 2001: 438). 'As Rome's population declines that of Constantinople rises'. Or again: 'one cannot simply re-interpret this [the 'early medieval depression'] as a fixed quantity of connectivity that has somehow been dispersed elsewhere in the system.' Indeed not. We are not aware of having argued this at all and regret any lack of clarity on the matter. People and goods move around our Mediterranean, perhaps more freely than some of our critics find acceptable. Producers diversify and store and redistribute in the face of omnipresent risk. But none of this entails the rarity of shortage and famine. It is precisely because of their endemic nature that all the precautions described in *CS* chapter VI have been so essential. Their success is hardly guaranteed, however (compare Fentress and Fentress (2001: 210), recalling the 'invisible hand' of Adam Smith and Talcott Parsons's 'equilibrium theory', neither of which we ever intended to evoke). We present a precarious world in which the effects of the insurance mechanisms of producers are always likely to be skewed by the interests of the powerful. There have been few if any periods or places of equilibrium (*CS* 185 and *passim*; cf. Squatriti 2002: 268).

[36] McCormick, *Origins*, 450–68, esp. 467: 'early medieval land and sea travelers moved in all seasons'. Shaw 432 similarly implies that we overestimate connectivity, asks how the sea both isolates and connects, and suggests that while the few enjoy seaborne connectivity, the many are denied it. This seems to us take insufficient account of *cabotage*.

[37] J. P. Oleson, 'Ancient Sounding Weights: A Contribution to the History of Ancient Mediterranean Navigation', *JRA* 13 (2000), 293–310; H. T. Wallinga, 'Poseidonios on Beating to Windward (FGH 87 F 46 and Related Passages)', *Mnemosyne* 53 (2000), 431–47; H. R. Neilson III, 'Roman Sailing: Offshore Navigation by Wind Direction', *Athenaeum* 89 (2001), 235–9.

Perhaps our working ecological metaphor has been misleading in this respect. It has created the impression that Mediterranean people have lived in harmony with their environment (*CS* 473). If there has been homeostasis it has been on only the very longest of timescales; but that is in no respect to diminish the devastation of environmental catastrophes, political impositions, or regional abatements in the medium term. Our analysis does not allow much space to particulars of violence, racism, or war in the Mediterranean (D'Hautcourt 2001: 222), for reasons already given. But we do not 'optimistically' (ibid.) deny that violent competition has been the 'dark face' of connectivity. The title of *CS*, with its genealogy in the epigraphs, points to the 'grim view' that we take of the world we describe and the acquisitive greed of its entrepreneurs—which greed we are, *pace* Squatriti, happy to see as a transhistorical category (Squatriti 2002: 265, 270).[38]

6. DOING WITHOUT TOWNS

The tendency attributed to us to smooth our subject out finds obvious but, we hope, superficial justification in the few chapters in *CS* that, unlike the rest, each focus on one particular subject of a textbook kind, rather than sweep up a myriad topics into a microecological bricolage. The first of these is chapter IV, on towns and cities.

This argued that, since there are no clear criteria for separating out one particular kind of larger, more diverse settlement, towns presented no special obstacles for microecological history. If we are considering population density then we should be comparing items all the way along the spectrum of possibilities from the hermitage to the metropolis. If we are looking into population diversity then we should proceed analogously. For each degree of settlement complexity there is, in principle, even if the evidence does not enable us to calculate it, an exchange of biomass between settlement and territory—the latter often

---

[38] Perhaps naively, we had not expected any present-day inhabitant of circum-Mediterranean lands to find the title offensive. But see the review by P. Hurtado at http://www.mmsh.univ-aix.fr/SeminaireCommun/seance_inaugurale.asp.

being, so we argued, a 'dispersed hinterland' (Glick 2002: 556). But none of this, we believe, challenges an ecologizing discussion of Mediterranean settlement.[39]

The chapter on towns comes early on in *CS*, after the preliminary 'model building' and the primary exemplification of 'definite places', because towns and cities might have seemed highly resistant to the type of history we were pursuing. The chapter was a piece of 'ground clearing' for the more comprehensive discussion of demography and settlement that we postponed to *LC* because of the obvious responsiveness of the topic to the wider context, *LC*'s focus.[40] We denied neither the cultural dominance of elites in many parts of our period nor the specific cultural forms (such as civic benefaction in the ancient world: Shaw 2001: 436–7) that control of 'urban production' might involve. Our plea was very simply that, in ecological terms, towns should not be treated as *a priori* a special case but should be blended into a large field of investigation (to be called, e.g. settlement studies). We hoped that, in a crisper formulation than our own, 'there is nothing very mysterious about this . . . from some perspectives cities may appear as significant entities while from others they may not' (Fentress and Fentress (2001: 211) who also refer (p. 212) to our 'authentic radicalism', which we hope is a compliment). Historical geographers (e.g. Astill) have taken this radicalism 'on the chin'. Early medievalists, for whom the question of the survival of the ancient city has often been an unprofitable distraction, may have welcomed what we hope was a liberating perspective (Squatriti 2002: 273). Shaw, for ancient history, rightly raises important questions about our attempted demolition of models such as 'the consumption city'. Yet his comparanda—Tokyo, London, Amsterdam—seem to make our point for us. Their geographical and chronological remoteness from the ancient

---

[39] We are grateful to Driessen 530 for the suggestion that the 'agrotown' is a distinctive Mediterranean settlement and will return to it in *LC*. R. Ellenblum, *Frankish Rural Settlement in the Latin Kingdom of Jerusalem* (Cambridge, 1998), 12–14, not known to us when completing *CS*, has some apposite remarks on how awkward the idea of a town is for sensible enquiry into the sociology of settlement.

[40] In which we shall heed the strictures of Walter Scheidel in a paper read at Chicago (see n. 30) concerning our incautious demographic remarks in *CS*.

Mediterranean leaves our assault on typologies applying where we want it to apply. (See Shaw (2001: 445–6) arguing for the autonomous city-state as '*the* sign [author's italics] of Mediterranean unity in the pre-modern period'; if 'pre-modern' means 'pre-Amsterdam' that is a very large claim indeed).

7. MANAGING MONOTHEISMS

The second chapter in *CS* which deals at length with one main topic is that on the geography of religion (chapter X). This chapter was hard to write in a balanced way. By comparison with the literature on the ancient world there are few studies of the geographical aspects of Christianity and Islam for us to draw upon; this seems to us an undeveloped aspect of the subject. Because of that, and still more because what we discussed was only one very particular aspect of the subject of Mediterranean religious practice, we stand accused (rather harshly, we feel) of 'little understanding how the coming of the three great monotheistic religions transformed the religious life of the Mediterranean' (Abulafia 2000: 10, giving no supporting example).[41]

By contrast, Shaw, while largely accepting and indeed developing our analysis, returns to the special place of towns and cities in the landscape. He implies that the reassuring familiarity of the standardized architecture of Christian basilicas (e.g. in late Roman North Africa) 'offers a rather different relation to a local system of topography than do the network of springs, groves, rivers, and caves'—a network on which we focus because of our alleged predilection for the natural and the exotic (Shaw 2001: 450). The essential difference *in geographical-ecological terms* between church and grove remains, however, to be demonstrated. And a precondition for that demonstration will, at least in part, surely be a comparison of the flows of people and objects into, through, and away from the two different kinds of cult centre and the relation of both to wider systems of movement. We do not claim to have 'explained' the basilica any more than to have explained the expansion of Islam. Yet

---

[41] Nor do we learn more about this from Abulafia, *The Mediterranean in History*, which is essentially a maritime history.

we do think that our focus on the microecological aspect of any such phenomenon offers one way forward—one of many. We are not, by the same token, intentionally 'reductionist', seeing pilgrimage as '*just* connectivity in disguise' (Squatriti 2002: 275–6, our italics; compare *CS* 445). Connectivity helps us to understand pilgrimage (and vice versa) even though pilgrimage must always be interpreted in the light of the relevant theology and eschatology.[42] A far more telling and accurate criticism here is made by Fentress and Fentress (2001: 218–19). We need to address the question of why topography is enshrined in religious perceptions and rites in the ways we describe.

Why should the practical, hard-working people of the Mediterranean interrupt their *cabotage* in order to translate their topological knowledge into flights of mythological fancy, unless, of course . . . by re-inscribing their topological knowledge in this manner, they were preserving it in ways that made more sense to them—more socially meaningful and easier to remember? . . . Sacred landscapes are loci of social memory relating communities to their real or mythological history.

8. RENDER UNTO CAESAR: IN QUEST OF NARRATIVE

Fentress and Fentress argue that our religious history should have taken account of diachronic variables, and the point can be generalized. It can be turned into a judgement of *CS* that brings together a number of criticisms rehearsed above and adds a few more. The overall judgement is that the book lacks a narrative. This is a judgement that we take very seriously—so much so, indeed, that we are not going to respond to it here. This is because the scale of any adequate response would be too large for the present context and we are not yet ready to make it. We hope to offer something more considered in *LC*. Meanwhile, our task, and our interim contribution to the debate, is to try to characterize our omission.

First, the underlying point seems to be that we have not clearly enough integrated cultural variables at the particular points at which they are drawn into our account of microecol-

---

[42] Cf. McCormick, *Origins*, part II generally, for pilgrimage as an index of connectivity.

ogies. We have not made clear the 'outreach' of our 'micro-analysis' into the more conventional world of 'Theodoric and Dante'. In terms of political history, we have not adequately rendered 'unto Caesar'. Oddly, no reviewer seems to have made this point about our Four Definite Places in chapter III. But many critics have expected to find familiar landmarks in later chapters: they want 'the city', 'the state', and, if not 'the Church', then some large consideration of religious change. That request arises from our viewing cultural history in the widest sense from the remote vantage point of microecologies. In chapters XI and XII, we to some extent cut loose from microecologies and venture into cultural anthropology. We are then vulnerable to the charge that we do not fully analyse the links between culture and ecology from the cultural end. Shaw (2001: 452) asserts that we make no connection between honour and risk. We do in fact try (*CS* 518–19), but the attempt is admittedly brief and—to shift the blame a little—reflects the fact that the ethnographers on whom we draw have been of surprisingly little help in this respect.

A second aspect of the critique is that we lack a theory—or if not a theory, then some basic conception—of agency. We again have our cake and eat it. On the religious front, we steer a course between Marx and Durkheim: to our critics, an uncertain course; to us, a pragmatic one. More generally, we rely on vague assertions of two-way interaction between humanity and the environment. We have no consistent means of encapsulating the relation between the two in such a way as to show how the environment is controlled and the cultural variables mediated by the decisions of individual producers or individual representatives of 'the powerful'.[43] It has been suggested to us that Bourdieu's quasi-Aristotelian concept of *habitus* might offer a working metaphor here,[44] not least because it is, for him, exemplified in, and perhaps derived from, his own ethnography in Algeria.[45]

---

[43] Parker 227: 'on their model, human initiative is heightened rather than dwarfed by ecology.' *CS* is, we think, full of people; it is just that many of them are now anonymous.

[44] By Megan Williams, in conversation.

[45] P. Bourdieu, *Outline of a Theory of Practice* (Cambridge, 1977). For context see J. Parker, *Structuration* (Buckingham, 2000).

Third, a point repeatedly made—and well made—by Shaw:[46] over time and space, power and capital (both symbolic and material) are concentrated and dispersed in various ways in the Mediterranean, not least by the state. There is not, on this score, the even continuum that we have (mistakenly) been held to present. Therefore, of course, some analysis is needed of the 'mechanism' of concentration and dispersal beyond generic references to greed and 'intensification'. Moreover, whether or not an explanatory theory is possible here, some overarching account is required to link the major concentrations of power together into a sequence that would show both their chronology and their relative size.

Fourth and last, then, we need a master narrative. What could such a narrative look like? It might, like Wittgenstein's philosophy, 'leave everything as it is'. That is, our ecological account may, on the whole, reflect the micro-foundations of what is already known about the rise and fall, the conflict and coexistence, of polities, empires, and cultures in and around the Mediterranean. But that ecological history does not necessitate any 'surface' change in what the textbooks say. Such an outcome is conceivable. We now have a sophisticated and up-to-date instance of such a political and economic narrative in David Abulafia's edited volume, *The Mediterranean in History*, which perhaps dispenses us from going over the same 'ground' in *LC*.[47]

The alternative—a narrative written on our own primarily ecological terms—is hard to envisage. Clearly it would not be simple and linear. We have been correctly diagnosed as 'resolutely anti-historicist' (Fentress and Fentress 2001: 213). We share Braudel's 'vision... résolument non téléologique'.[48] There is plenty of room in our Mediterranean for *événements*, well beyond what most would call humming and buzzing—but there is no evolution (Fentress and Fentress 2001: 217). A master narrative can, of course, have themes and turning points without being teleological. To isolate them at the political,

---

[46] Esp. 434, 345, 349, 441–2, 443, 447.

[47] See also J. Carpentier and F. Lebrun (eds.), *Histoire de la Méditerranée* (Paris, 1998), which we were not able to cite in *CS*.

[48] A. Molho and D. Ramada Curto, 'Les réseaux marchands à l'époque moderne', *Annales* 58 (2003), 569–79 at 571.

economic, and cultural level remains the challenge. And new evidence keeps changing the nature of the task. We have learned recently that ancient Mediterranean livestock were up to twice the size of their descendants or successors—until the eighteenth century.[49] How should we integrate that into the story we tell?

---

[49] G. Kron, 'Archaeozoological Evidence for the Productivity of Roman Livestock Farming', *Münstersche Beiträge zur antiken Handelsgeschichte* 21 (2002), 53–73.

SELECT BIBLIOGRAPHY

Abella, I. and Troper H., *None Is Too Many: Canada and the Jews of Europe 1933–1948* (Toronto, 1982).

Abou-Zeid, A., 'Honour and Shame among the Bedouins of Egypt', in J. G. Peristiany (ed.), *Honour and Shame: the Values of a Mediterranean Society* (London, 1966), 243–59.

Abulafia, D., 'L'economia mercantile nel Mediterraneo occidentale (1390 *ca*–1460 ca): Commercio locale e a lunga distanza nell'età di Lorenzo il Magnifico', *Schola Salernitana* 2 (1997), 21–41; repr. in *Mediterranean Encounters, Economic, Religious, Political, 1100–1550* (Aldershot, 2000).

—— 'East and West: Comments on the Commerce of the City of Ancona in the Middle Ages', in M. P. Ghezzo (ed.), *Città e sistema adriatico alla fine del Medioevo. Bilancio degli studi e prospettive di ricerca* (*Atti e memorie della società Dalmata di storia patria* 26) (Venice, 1997), 49–66; repr. in *Mediterranean Encounters, Economic, Religious, Political, 1100–1550* (Aldershot, 2000).

—— 'Industrial Products: The Middle Ages', in *Prodotti e tecniche d'Oltremare nelle economie europee, secc. XIII–XVIII. XXIX Settimana dell'Istituto Internazionale di Storia economica 'F. Datini'* (Florence, 1998), 333–58; repr. in *Mediterranean Encounters, Economic, Religious, Political, 1100–1550* (Aldershot, 2000).

—— (ed.), *The Mediterranean in History* (Los Angeles, 2003).

Alcock, S. E. (ed.), *The Early Roman Empire in the East* (Oxford, 1997).

—— Cherry, J. F., and Davis J. L., 'Intensive Survey, Agricultural Practice and the Classical Landscape of Greece', in I. Morris (ed.), *Classical Greece: Ancient Histories and Modern Archaeologies* (Cambridge, 1994), 137–70.

Alföldy, G., 'Inscriciones, sacrificios y misterios: El santuario rupestre de Panóias / Portugal', *Mitteilungen des Deutschen Archäologischen Instituts—Abteilung Madrid* 36 (1995), 252–8.

Alföldy, G., 'Die Mysterien von Panóias (Vila Real, Portugal)', *Mitteilungen des Deutschen Archäologischen Instituts—Abteilung Madrid* 38 (1997), 176–246.

Allport, G. W., *The Nature of Prejudice*, abridged edn. (Garden City, NY, 1958).

Altman, A., 'Trade Between the Aegean and the Levant in the Late Bronze Age: Some Neglected Questions', in M. Heltzer and E. Lipinski (eds.), *Society and Economy in the Eastern Mediterranean (c.1500–1000 B.C.)* (Louvain, 1988), 229–37.

Álvarez-Millán, C., 'Practice versus Theory: Tenth-Century Case Histories from the Islamic Middle East', *Social History of Medicine* 13 (2000) (special issue, *Medical Practice at the End of the First Millennium*, ed. P. Horden and E. Savage-Smith), 293–306.

Amit, D., Patrich, J., and Hirschfeld ,Y. (eds.), *The Aqueducts of Israel* (*JRA*, Suppl. 46) (Portsmouth, RI, 2002).

Amouretti, M.-C. and Brun, J.-P. (eds.), *La Production du vin et de l'huile en Méditerranée* (*Bulletin de Correspondance Hellénique*, Suppl. 26) (Athens and Paris, 1993).

Ampolo, C., 'Greci d'Occidente, Etruschi, Cartaginesi: Circolazione di beni e di uomini', in *Magna Grecia, Etruschi, Fenici, Atti del trentatreesimo Convegno di Studi sulla Magna Grecia, Taranto 1993* (Naples, 1996), 223–52.

Andreades, A. M., *A History of Greek Public Finance* (Cambridge, Mass., 1933).

Andreau, J. and Schnapp, A., 'Ettore Lepore, la colonisation et l'écriture de l'histoire ancienne', in E. Lepore, *La Grande Grèce: Aspects et problèmes d'une colonisation ancienne* (Naples, 2000), 7–15.

—— and Virlouvet, C. (eds.), *L'Information et la mer dans le monde antique* (Rome, 2002).

Angelomatis-Tsougarakis, H., *The Eve of the Revival: British Travellers' Perceptions of Early Nineteenth-Century Greece* (London, 1990).

Argoud, G., Marangou, L. I., Panagiotopoulos, V., and Villain-Gandossi, C. (eds.), *L'Eau et les hommes en Méditerranée et en Mer Noire dans l'antiquité* (Athens, 1992).

Armitage, D., 'Three Concepts of Atlantic History', in D. Armitage and M. J. Braddick (eds.), *The British Atlantic World, 1500–1800* (Basingstoke and New York, 2002), 11–27.

Armstrong, C. D., 'Progress in the Age of Navigation: The *Voyage-Philosophique* of Julien-David Leroy' (Ph. D. thesis, Columbia University, 2003).

—— 'De la théorie des proportions à l'expérience des sensations: l'*Essai sur la Théorie de l'Architecture* de Julien-David Le Roy, 1770,' forthcoming in *Annales du Centre Ledoux* 5 (2003).

Arribas, A., Trias, G., Cerdá, D., and de Hoz, J., 'L'Épave d'El Sec (Mallorca)', *Revue des Études Anciennes* 89 (1987), 3–4, 13–146.

Arrizabalaga, J., 'The Death of a Medieval Text: The *Articella* and the Early Press', in R. French, J. Arrizabalaga, A. Cunningham, and L. García-Ballester (eds.), *Medicine from the Black Death to the French Disease* (Aldershot, 1998), 184–220.

Aubet, M. E., *The Phoenicians and the West*, 2nd edn. (Cambridge, 2001).

Augustinos, O., *French Odysseys: Greece in French Travel Literature from the Renaissance to the Romantic Era* (Baltimore and London, 1994).

Austin, J. L., *How To Do Things with Words*, 2nd edn., ed. J. O. Urmson and M Sbisà (Cambridge, Mass., 1975 (1962)).

Austin, M. M. and Vidal-Naquet, P., *Economic and Social History of Ancient Greece: An Introduction* (Berkeley and Los Angeles, 1977).

Ayoob, J. C., *Ancient Inscriptions in the New World; Or Were the Phoenicians the First to Discover America?* (Pittsburgh, 1951).

Bagnall, R. S., *Reading Papyri, Writing Ancient History* (London, 1995).

Balty, J.-C., 'Problèmes de l'eau à Apamée de Syrie', in P. Louis, F. Métral, and J. Métral (eds.), *L'Homme et l'eau en Méditerranée et du Proche Orient* iv. (Paris and Lyon, 1987), 11–23.

Bammer, A., *Das Artemision von Ephesos: das Weltwunder Ioniens in archaischer und klassischer Zeit* (Mainz, 1996).

Banfield, E. C., *The Moral Basis of a Backward Society* (Glencoe, Ill., 1958).

Barber, E. J. W., *Prehistoric Textiles: The Development of Cloth in the Neolithic and Bronze Ages* (Princeton, 1991).

Barker, G., with R. Hodges and G. Clark, *A Mediterranean Valley: Landscape Archaeology and* Annales *History in the Biferno Valley* (Leicester, 1995).

Bartoloni, G., Colonna G., and Grotanelli, C. (eds.), *Atti del convegno internazionale Anathema. Regime delle offerte e vita dei santuari nel mediterraneo antico, Roma 15–18 Giugno 1989* (*Scienze dell'antichità* 3–4) (1989–90).

Barton, C., *Roman Honor* (Berkeley and Los Angeles, 2001).

Barton, S. C. and Horsley, G. H. R. ,'A Hellenistic Cult Group and the New Testament Church', *Jahrbuch für Antike und Christentum* 24 (1981), 7–41.

Bayliss-Smith, T., 'Prehistoric Agriculture in the New Guinea Highlands: Problems in Defining the Altitudinal Limits to Growth', in

J. L. Bintliff, D. A. Davidson, and E. G. Grant (eds.), *Conceptual Issues in Environmental Archaeology* (Edinburgh, 1988), 153–60.

Beal, R. H., 'Hittite Military Organization', in J. M. Sasson (ed.), *Civilizations of the Ancient Near East* (New York, 1995), 545–54.

Bean, G. E., 'Notes and Inscriptions from Caunus', *Journal of Hellenic Studies* 74 (1954), 10–35.

Beckett, J., comment in *Current Anthropology* 20 (1979), 85–6.

Behr, C. A., *Aelius Aristides and the Sacred Tales* (Amsterdam, 1968).

Ben-Ami, S., 'Foreword', *Mediterranean Historical Review* 1 (1986), 5–7.

Bennett, D., 'Medical Practice and Manuscripts in Byzantium', *Social History of Medicine* 13 (2000) (special issue, *Medical Practice at the End of the First Millennium*, ed. P. Horden and E. Savage-Smith), 279–91.

Bent, T. J., 'On Insular Greek Customs', *Journal of the Royal Anthropological Institute* 15 (1886), 391–403.

Berend, N., *At the Gates of Christendom: Jews, Muslims and 'Pagans' in Medieval Hungary*, c.*1000*–c.*1300* (Cambridge, 2001).

Bergdoll, B., *Léon Vaudoyer: Historicism in the Age of Industry* (Cambridge, Mass., 1994).

Bichler, R., *Herodots Welt* (Berlin, 2000).

Bintliff, J. L. (ed.), *The* Annales *School and Archaeology* (Leicester and London, 1991).

Birch, D. J., *Pilgrimage to Rome in the Middle Ages* (Woodbridge, Suffolk, 1998).

Blanton, R. E., 'Mediterranean Myopia', *Antiquity* 74 (2001), 627–9.

Bloch, M., *The Historian's Craft*, trans. P. Putnam (New York, 1953); original edn.: *Apologie pour l'histoire, ou Métier d'historien*, (Paris, 1949).

Blok, A., 'Rams and Billy-Goats: A Key to the Mediterranean Code of Honour', *Man* (NS) 16 (1981), 427–40.

Born, K. and Van Orsdel, L., 'Searching for Serials Utopia', *Library Journal* 126/7 (2001), 53–8.

Bourdieu, P., *Outline of a Theory of Practice* (Cambridge, 1977).

Bourque, N., 'An Anthropologist's View of Ritual', in E. Bispham and C. Smith (eds.), *Religion in Archaic and Republican Rome and Italy: Evidence and Experience* (Edinburgh, 2000), 19–33.

Bradbury, S., 'Julian's Pagan Revival and the Decline of Blood Sacrifice', *Phoenix* 49 (1995), 331–56.

Braham, A., *The Architecture of the French Enlightenment* (Berkeley and Los Angeles, 1980).

Braudel, F., *The Structures of Everyday Life* (1. *Civilization and Capitalism*), trans. S. Reynolds (London 1979); original edn., *Les Structures du quotidien* (Paris, 1979).

—— *Les Mémoires de la Méditerranée: Préhistoire et antiquité* (Paris, 1998), trans. by S. Reynolds as *The Mediterranean in the Ancient World* (London, 2001).

Braund, D. C., 'Piracy under the Principate and the Ideology of Imperial Eradication', in J. Rich and G. Shipley (eds.), *War and Society in the Roman World* (London, 1993), 195–212.

Bresson, A., 'Aristote et le commerce exterieur', *Revue des Études Anciennes* 89 (1987), 217–38; repr. in *La Cité marchande* (Bordeaux, 2000).

—— 'Les Cités grecques et leurs *emporia*', in A. Bresson and P. Rouillard (eds.), *L'Emporion* (Paris 1993), 163–226.

—— *La Cité marchande* (Bordeaux, 2000).

Broc, N., *La Géographie des philosophes: Géographes et voyageurs français au XVIIIe siècle* (Paris, 1975).

Brogiolo, G. P. and Ward-Perkins, B. (eds.), *The Idea and Ideal of the Town between Late Antiquity and the Early Middle Ages* (Leiden, 1999).

Broodbank, C., *An Island Archaeology of the Early Cyclades* (Cambridge, 2000).

Brown, H., *Scientific Organizations in Seventeenth-Century France (1620–1680)* (New York, 1934).

Brown, N. B. and Phillips, J., 'Price Indexes for 1981: U.S. Periodicals and Serial Services', *Library Journal* 106/13 (1981), 1387–93.

Brown, P., *Society and the Holy in Late Antiquity* (London, 1982).

—— *Poverty and Leadership in the Later Roman Empire* (Hanover and London, 2002).

Brownan, D. L., 'High Altitude Camelid Pastoralism of the Andes', in J. G. Galaty and D. L. Johnson (eds.), *The World of Pastoralism: Herding Systems in Comparative Perspective* (New York and London, 1990), 323–52.

Brun, P., 'La Stèle des céréales de Cyrène et le commerce du grain en Égée au IVe s. av. J.-C.', *ZPE* 99 (1993), 185–96.

Brunschvig, R. (ed.), *Deux récits de voyage inédits en Afrique du nord au XV siècle* (Publications de l'Institut d'études orientales de la Faculté des lettres d'Alger, 7) (Paris, 1936).

Bruun, C., 'The Antonine Plague in Rome and Ostia', *JRA* 16 (2003), 426–34.

Buarque de Hollanda, S. ,*Visão do Paraíso* (São Paulo, 2000 (1959)).

Burford, A., *The Greek Temple Builders at Epidauros* (Liverpool, 1969).

Burkert, W., 'Katagógia-Anagógia and the Goddess of Knossos', in R. Hägg, N. Marinatos, and G. Nordquist (eds.), *Early Greek Cult Practice: Proceedings of the Fifth International Symposium at the*

Swedish Institute at Athens, 26–29 June, 1986 (Stockholm, 1988), 81–7.

—— *Creation of the Sacred: Tracks of Biology in Early Religions* (Cambridge, Mass., and London, 1996).

—— 'Fitness oder Opium? Die Fragestellung der Soziologie im Bereich alter Religionen', in F. Stolz (ed.), *Homo naturaliter religiosus: Gehört Religion notwendig zum Mensch-Sein?* (Bern, 1997), 13–38.

Burnett, C. and Jacquart, D. (eds.), *Constantine the African and 'Ali ibn l-'Abbas al Magusi: The 'Pantegni' and Related Works* (Leiden, 1996).

Burr, V., *Nostrum Mare. Ursprung und Geschichte der Namen des Mittelmeeres und seiner Teilmeere im Altertum* (Stuttgart, 1932).

Burstein, S. M., 'A Contested History: Egypt, Greece and Afrocentrism,' in S. M. Burstein, R. MacMullen, K. A. Raaflaub, and A. M. Ward, *Current Issues and the Study of Ancient History* (Claremont, Calif., 2002), 9–30.

Butel, P., *The Atlantic* (London and New York, 1999).

Buxton, R., *Imaginary Greece. The Contexts of Mythology* (Cambridge, 1994).

Buzoianu, L., 'Types d'amphores hellénistiques découverts à Callatis', in Y. Garlan (ed.), *Production et commerce des amphores grecques en mer Noire* (Aix-en-Provence, 1999), 201–21.

Cahen, C., 'Douanes et commerce dans les ports méditerranéens de l'Égypte médiévale d'après le Minhadj d'al-Makhzumi', *Journal of the Economic and Social History of the Orient* 7 (1965), 217–34.

Cameron, A., 'Ideologies and Agendas in Late Antique Studies', in L. Lavan and W. Bowden (eds.), *Theory and Practice in Late Antique Archaeology* (Leiden, 2003) 3–24.

Campbell, J. K., *Honour, Family and Patronage : A Study of Institutions and Moral Values in a Greek Mountain Community* (Oxford, 1964).

Cardinal, R., 'Romantic Travel', in R. Porter (ed.), *Rewriting the Self: Histories from the Renaissance to the Present* (London and New York, 1997), 135–55.

Carpenter, K. H. and Alexander, A. W., 'Price Index for U.S. Periodicals', *Library Journal* 116/7 (1991), 52–9.

Carpentier, J. and Lebrun, F. (eds.), *Histoire de la Méditerranée* (Paris, 1998).

Carrier, J. G. (ed.), *Occidentalism: Images of the West* (Oxford, 1995).

Casson, L., *The Ancient Mariners*, 2nd edn. (Princeton, 1991).

—— *Ships and Seafaring in Ancient Times* (London, 1994).

Catastini, A., 'Il mostro delle acque: Reutilizzazioni bibliche della funzione di un mito', *Mediterraneo Antico: Economie, Società, Culture* 4 (2001), 71–89.

Cawkwell, G., 'Early Colonisation', *Classical Quarterly* 42 (1992), 289–303.

Chaniotis, A., 'Plutarchos, praeses Insularum', *ZPE* 68 (1987), 227–31.

—— 'Amnisos in den schriftlichen Quellen', in J. Schäfer (ed.), *Amnisos nach den archäologischen, topographischen, historischen und epigraphischen Zeugnissen des Altertums und der Neuzeit* (Berlin, 1992), 51–127.

—— 'Reinheit des Körpers—Reinheit der Seele in den griechischen Kultgesetzen', in J. Assmann and Th. Sundermeier (eds.), *Schuld, Gewissen und Person* (Gütersloh, 1997), 142–79.

—— 'Ritual Dynamics: The Boiotian festival of the Daidala', in *Kykeon: Studies in Honour of H. S. Versnel* (Leiden, 2002), 23–48.

—— 'Foreign Soldiers—Native Girls? Constructing and Crossing Boundaries in Hellenistic Cities with Foreign Garrisons', in A. Chaniotis and P. Ducrey (eds.), *Army and Power in the Ancient World* (Stuttgart, 2002), 99–113.

—— 'Old Wine in a New Skin: Tradition and Innovation in the Cult Foundation of Alexander of Abonouteichos', in E. Dabrowa (ed.) *Tradition and Innovation in the Ancient World* (Krakow, 2002), 67–85.

—— 'Der Kaiserkult im Osten des Römischen Reiches im Kontext der zeitgenössischen Ritualpraxis', in H. Cancik and K. Hitzl (eds.), *Die Praxis der Herrscherverehrung in Rom und seinen Provinzen: Akten der Tagung in Blaubeuren vom 4. bis 6. April 2002* (Tübingen, 2003), 3–28.

—— 'Zwischen Konfrontation und Interaktion: Christen, Juden und Heiden im spätantiken Aphrodisias', in C. Ackermann and K. E. Müller (eds.), *Patchwork: Dimensionen multikultureller Gesellschaften* (Bielefeld, 2002), 83–128.

—— 'Negotiating Religion in the Cities of the Eastern Roman Provinces', *Kernos* 16 (2003), 177–90.

Chaudhuri, K. N., *Trade and Civilisation in the Indian Ocean from the Rise of Islam to 1750* (Cambridge, 1985).

—— *Asia before Europe: Economy and Civilisation in the Indian Ocean from the Rise of Islam to 1750* (Cambridge, 1990).

Cherry, J. F., 'Frogs Round the Pond: Perspectives on Current Archaeological Survey Projects in the Mediterranean Region', in D. R. Keller and D. W. Rupp (eds.), *Archaeological Survey in the Mediterranean Area* (Oxford, 1991), 375–416.

—— and Knapp, A. B., 'Editorial', *Journal of Mediterranean Archaeology* 12 (1999), 3–6.

Cherry, J. F. and Renfrew, C., 'Epilogue and prospect', in C. Renfrew and J. F. Cherry (eds.), *Peer Polity Interaction and Socio-political Change* (Cambridge, 1986), 149–58.

Ciano, C., *La Pratica di mercatura datiniana (secolo XIV)* (Milan, 1964).

Clauss, M., *Kaiser und Gott: Herrscherkult im römischen Reich* (Stuttgart and Leipzig, 1999).

Cline, E. H., *Sailing the Wine-dark Sea: International Trade and the Late Bronze Age Aegean* (Oxford, 1994).

Coggins, R., 'Jewish Local Patriotism: The Samaritan Problem', in S. Jones and S. Pearce (eds.), *Jewish Local Patriotism and Self-Identification in the Graeco-Roman Period* (Sheffield, 1998), 66–78.

Cohen, D., *Law, Sexuality, and Society in Classical Athens* (Cambridge, 1991).

——*Law, Violence and Community in Classical Athens* (Cambridge, 1995).

Cohn, S. K., *Creating the Florentine State: Peasants and Rebellion, 1348–1434* (Cambridge, 1999).

Constantine, D., *Early Greek Travellers and the Hellenic Ideal* (Cambridge, 1984).

Cracco Ruggini, L., 'Eforo nello Pseudo-Aristotele, *Oec.* II', *Athenaeum* 53 (1966), 199–236.

Craddock, P. B. (ed.), *The English Essays of Edward Gibbon* (Oxford, 1972).

Crary, J., *Techniques of the Observer* (Cambridge, Mass., 1990).

La Cristianizzazione della Lituania. Atti del Colloquio internazionale (Vatican City, 1989).

Cristofani, M., 'Il testo di Pech-Maho, Aleria e i traffici del V secolo a.C.', *Mélanges de l'École Française de Rome, Antiquité* 105 (1993), 833–45.

Cunliffe, B., *Facing the Ocean: The Atlantic and its Peoples* (Oxford, 2001).

Dalley, S., 'Ancient Mesopotamian Military Organization', in J. M. Sasson (ed.), *Civilizations of the Ancient Near East* (New York, 1995), 413–22.

Daunton, M. J., *Progress and Poverty: An Economic and Social History of Britain 1700–1850* (Oxford, 1995).

Davis, J., *People of the Mediterranean: An Essay in Comparative Social Anthropology* (London, 1977).

Day, J., *Les Douanes de Gênes, 1376–1377* (Paris, 1963).

de Certeau, M., *The Practice of Everyday Life*, trans. S. F. Rendall (Berkeley, 1984).

Decourt, J.-Cl., 'Le Plomb de Pech Maho: État de la recherche 1999', *Archéologie en Languedoc* 24 (2000), 111–24.

De Laet, J., *Portorium: Etude sur l'organisation douanière chez les romains, surtout à l'époque du haut-empire* (Bruges, 1949).

Demand, N., *Birth, Death, and Motherhood in Classical Greece* (Baltimore, 1994).

DeMaris, R. E., 'Demeter in Roman Corinth: Local Development in a Mediterranean Religion', *Numen* 42 (1995), 105–17.

De Pina-Cabral, J., 'The Mediterranean as a Category of Regional Comparison: A Critical View', *Current Anthropology* 30 (1989), 399–406.

Descat, A., 'La Cité grecque et les échanges: Un retour à Hasebroek', in J. Andreau, P. Briant, and A. Descat (eds.), *Les Échanges dans l'antiquité: Le Rôle de l'état*. *Entretiens d'archéologie et d'histoire* (Saint-Bertrand-des-Comminges, 1994), 11–30.

Descoeudres, J.-P., 'Preface: Australian and New Zealand Contributions to the Archaeology of the Mediterranean World: A Preliminary Sketch', *Mediterranean Archaeology*, 2 (1989), 1–8.

De Spens, R., 'Droit international et commerce au début de la XXIᵉ dynastie: Analyse juridique du rapport d'Ounamon', in N. Grimal and B. Menu (eds.), *Le Commerce en Égypte ancienne* (Cairo, 1998), 105–26.

Diakonoff, I. M., 'The Structure of Near Eastern Society before the Middle of the 2nd millennium B. C.', *Oikumene* 3 (1982), 7–100.

—— (ed.), *Early Antiquity* (Chicago, 1991).

Di Castri, F., 'An Ecological Overview of the Five Regions with a Mediterranean Climate', in R. H. Groves and F. di Castri (eds.), *Biogeography of Mediterranean Invasions* (Cambridge, 1991), 3–16.

Dickie, M. W., 'The Learned Magician and the Collection and Transmission of Magical Lore', in D. R. Jordan, H. Montgomery, and E. Thomassen (eds.), *The World of Ancient Magic: Papers from the First International Samson Eitrem Seminar at the Norwegian Institute at Athens, 4–8 May 1997* (Bergen, 1999), 163–93.

Dickinson, O., *The Aegean Bronze Age* (Cambridge, 1994).

Dilke, O. A. W., 'Graeco-Roman Perception of the Mediterranean', in M. Galley and L. Ladjimi Sebai (eds.), *L'Homme méditerranéen et la mer* (Tunis, 1985), 53–9.

Dini, B., *Una pratica di mercatura in formazione (1394–1395)* (Florence, 1980).

Dirlmeier, U., 'Mittelaltliche Zoll- und Stapelrechte als Handelhemnisse', in H. Pohl (ed.), *Die Auswirkungen von Zöllen und anderen Handelshemnissen auf Wirtschaft und Gesellschaft vom Mittelalter bis* zum Gegenwart (*Vierteljahrschrift für Sozial- und Wirtschafts-geschichte*, Suppl. 80) (Stuttgart, 1987), 19–39.

Douglas, M., *Purity and Danger: An Analysis of Concepts of Purity and Taboo* (London, 1966).

Dover, K. J., rev. of D. Cohen, *Law, Sexuality and Society*, *Gnomon* 65 (1993), 657–60.

Duby, G., *The Early Growth of the European Economy*, trans. H. B. Clarke (Ithaca, NY, 1974); original edn.: *Guerriers et paysans, VII–XIIe siècle* (Paris, 1973).

Dugat, M. G., 'Études sur le traité de médecine d'Abou Djàfar Ah'mad', *Journal Asiatique*, 5th ser., 1 (1853), 287–353.

Duncan-Jones, R. P., 'The Impact of the Antonine Plague', *JRA* 9 (1996), 108–36.

Durliat, J., 'Taxes sur l'entrée des merchandises dans la cite de Car-ales-Cagliari à l'époque Byzantine (582–602)', *Dumbarton Oaks Papers* 36 (1982), 1–14.

Eco, U., *Lector in Fabula: la cooperazione interpretativa nei testi narrativi* (Milan, 1979).

Edel, E., *Die ägyptisch-hethitische Korrespondenz aus Boghazköi in babylonischer und hethitischer Sprache* (Opladen, 1994).

Edelstein, L., 'The Dietetics of Antiquity', repr. in translation in his *Ancient Medicine* (1967, abbreviated edn., Baltimore and London, 1987), 303–16.

Editorial Working Group, 'Foreword', *Journal of Mediterranean Studies: History, Culture and Society in the Mediterranean World* 9 (1999), 147–54.

Edzard, D. O., 'Die Beziehungen Babyloniens und Ägyptens in der mittelbabylonischen Zeit und das Gold', *Journal of the Economic and Social History of the Orient* 3 (1960), 37–55.

Eisner, R., *Travelers to an Antique Land: The History and Literature of Travel to Greece* (Ann Arbor, 1991).

Ellen, R., *Environment, Subsistence and System: The Ecology of Small-scale Formations* (Cambridge, 1982).

Ellenblum, R., *Frankish Rural Settlement in the Latin Kingdom of Jerusalem* (Cambridge, 1998).

Elsner, J. and Rubiès, J. P. (eds.), *Voyages and Visions: Towards a Cultural History of Travel* (London, 1999).

Engelmann, H., *The Delian Aretalogy of Sarapis* (Leiden, 1975).

—— and Knibbe, D., 'Das Zollgesetz der Provinz Asia: Eine neue Inschrift aus Ephesos', *Epigraphica Anatolica* 14 (1989), 1–206.

Étienne, R. and Le Dinahet, M.-T. (eds.), *L'Espace sacrificiel dans les civilisations méditerranéennes de l'antiquité: Actes du colloque tenu à la Maison de l'Orient, Lyon, 4–7 juin 1988* (Paris, 1991).

Fedeli, P., *La natura violata: ecologia e mondo romano* (Palermo, 1990).

Feldman, M. H., 'Luxurious Forms: Redefining a Mediterranean "International Style"', 1400–1200 B.C.E.', *Art Bulletin* 84 (2002), 6–29.

Fentress, E. and J., rev. of Horden and Purcell, *CS, Past and Present* 173 (2001), 203–19.

Fernandez, J. W., 'Consciousness and Class in Southern Spain', *American Ethnologist* 10 (1983), 165–73.

Fernández-Armesto, F., *Before Columbus: Exploration and colonisation from the Mediterranean to the Atlantic, 1229–1492* (London, 1987).

Finley, M. I., *The Ancient Economy* (second edn., Berkeley and Los Angeles, 1985).

Finucane, R. C., *Miracles and Pilgrims: Popular Beliefs in Medieval England* (London, 1977).

Fishwick, D., 'Votive Offerings to the Emperor?', *ZPE* 80 (1990), 121–30.

Flemming, R., *Medicine and the Making of Roman Women* (Oxford, 2000).

Flint, V. J., *The Imaginative Landscape of Christopher Columbus* (Princeton, 1992).

Forbes, H., 'The Uses of the Uncultivated Landscape in Modern Greece: A Pointer to the Value of Wilderness in Antiquity?', in J. B. Salmon and G. Shipley (eds.), *Human Landscapes in Classical Antiquity: Environment and Culture* (London, 1996), 68–97.

Fotiadis, M., 'Modernity and the Past-still-present: Politics of Time in the Birth of Regional Archaeological Projects in Greece', *American Journal of Archaeology* 99 (1995), 59–78.

Foxhall, L. and Forbes, H., '*Sitometreia*: The role of grain as a staple food in Classical Antiquity', *Chiron* 12 (1982), 41–90.

France, J., 'Les Revenus douaniers des communautés municipales dans le monde romain (république et haut-Empire)', in *Il capitolo delle entrate nelle finanze municipali in occidente ed in oriente: Actes de la Xe Rencontre franco-italienne sur l'épigraphie du monde romain, Rome, 27–29 mai 1996* (Rome, 1999). 95–114.

——*Quadragesima Galliarum: l'organisation douanière des provinces alpestres, gauloises et germaniques de l'Empire romain (1er siècle avant J.-C.-3er siècle après J.-C.)* (Rome, 2001).

Francotte, H., *Les Finances des cités grecques* (Liège, 1909).

Frazer, J. G., *The Golden Bough. A Study in Magic and Religion*, i. *The Magic Art and the Evolution of Kings*, 3rd edn. (London, 1913).

Friedl, E., *Vasilika: A Village in Modern Greece* (New York, 1962).

Friedländer, L., *Roman Life and Manners under the Early Empire*, trans. L. A. Magnus, J. H. Freese, and A. B. Gough (London, 1907–13); original edn.: *Darstellungen aus der Sittengeschichte Roms*, 7th edn. (Leipzig, 1907), 4 vols.

Gale, N. H. (ed.), *Bronze Age Trade in the Mediterranean* (Jonsered, 1991).

——Stos-Gale, Z. A., and Gilmore, T. R., 'Alloy Types and Copper Sources of Anatolian Copper Alloy Artifacts', *Anatolian Studies* 35 (1985), 143–73.

Gallant, T., *Experiencing Dominion: Culture, Identity, and Power in the British Mediterranean* (Notre Dame, Ind. 2002).

Garant, J.-M., 'Jacques-Nicolas Bellin (1703–1772): Cartographe, hydrographe, ingénieur du ministère de la Marine, sa vie, son œuvre, sa valeur historique' (MA thesis, Université de Montréal, 1973).

García-Ballester, L., 'On the Origin of the "Six Non-Natural Things" in Galen', in G. Harig and J. Harig-Kollesch (eds.), *Galen und das Hellenistische Erbe*, *Sudhoffs Archiv* Beiheft 32 (Wiesbaden, 1993), 105–15.

Garlan, Y., 'Réflexions sur le commerce des amphores grecques en mer Noire', in Y. Garlan (ed.), *Production et commerce des amphores grecques en mer Noire* (Aix-en-Provence, 1999), 131–42.

Garnsey, P., *Famine and Food Supply in the Graeco-Roman World* (Cambridge, 1988).

Garrison, W. L., 'Connectivity of the Interstate Highway System', *Papers and Proceedings of the Regional Science Association* 6 (1960), 121–37.

Geary, P., *Furta Sacra*, 2nd edn. (Princeton, 1990).

Gebbard, E. R., 'The Gods in Transit: Narratives of Cult Transfer', in A. Y. Collins and M. M. Mitchell (eds.), *Antiquity and Humanity: Essays on Ancient Religion and Philosophy presented to D. Betz on his 70th Birthday* (Tübingen, 2001), 451–76.

Gelles, P. H., 'Equilibrium and Extraction: Dual Organization in the Andes', *American Ethnologist* 22 (1995), 710–42.

Gentili, B. and Perusino, F. (eds.), *Le orse di Brauron: Un rituale di iniziazione femminile nel santuario di Artemide* (Pisa, 2002).

Giannaras (Yannaras), C., Ορθοδοξία και Δύση στη Νεότερη Ελλάδα (Athens, 1992).

Gibbon, E., *History of the Decline and Fall of the Roman Empire*, ed. D. Womersley (London, 1994 (1776–88)), 3 vols.

Gilmore, D. D., 'Introduction: The Shame of Dishonor', in D. D. Gilmore (ed.), *Honor and Shame and the Unity of the Mediterranean* (Washington DC, 1987), 2–21.

—— 'On Mediterraneanist Studies', *Current Anthropology* 31 (1990), 395–6.

Gil-Sotres, P., 'Modelo teórico y observación clínica: las pasiones del alma en la psicología médica medieval', in *Comprendre et maîtriser la nature au Moyen Age: Mélanges d'histoire des sciences offerts à Guy Beaujouan* (Geneva, 1994), 181–204.

—— 'The Regimens of Health', in M. D. Grmek (ed.), *Western Medical Thought from Antiquity to the Middle Ages* (Cambridge, Mass. and London, 1998), 291–318.

Gladigow, B., 'Mediterrane Religionsgeschichte, Römische Religionsgeschichte, Europäische Religionsgeschichte: Zur Genese eines Faktkonzeptes', in *Kykeon: Studies in Honour of H. S. Versnel* (Leiden, 2002), 49–67.

Glotz, G., 'Le Prix des denrées à Délos', *Journal des Savants* (1913), 16–29.

Goddard, V. A., Llobera, J. R., and Shore, C., 'Introduction: The Anthropology of Europe', in V. A. Goddard, J. R. Llobera, and C. Shore (eds.), *The Anthropology of Europe* (Oxford and Providence, RI, 1994), 1–40.

Gofas, D. C., 'Les Carpologues de Thasos', *Bulletin de Correspondance Hellénique* 93 (1969), 337–70.

Goitein, S. D., *A Mediterranean Society: The Jewish Communities of the Arab World as Portrayed in the Documents of the Cairo Geniza* (Berkeley and Los Angeles, 1967–93), 6 vols.

Goldenberg, D., 'Scythian-Barbarian: The Permutations of a Classical Topos in Jewish and Christian Texts of Late Antiquity', *Journal of Jewish Studies* 49 (1998), 87–102.

Gordon, C. H., *Before Columbus: Links between the Old World and Ancient America* (New York, 1971).

Gouldner, A. W., *Enter Plato: Classical Greece and the Origins of Social Theory* (London, 1967).

Gourdin, P., 'Présence génoise en Mediterranée et en Europe au milieu du XVe siècle: L'Implantation des hommes d'affaires d'après un registre douanière de 1445', in M. Balard and A. Ducellier (eds.), *Coloniser au Moyen âge* (Paris, 1995), 14–35.

Graf, F., 'Bemerkungen zur bürgerlichen Religiosität im Zeitalter des Hellenismus', in M. Wörrle and P. Zanker (eds.), *Stadtbild und Bürgerbild im Hellenismus* (Munich, 1995), 103–14.

—— *Gottesnähe und Schadenzauber: Die Magie in der griechisch-römischen Antike* (Munich, 1996).

—— 'Zeichenkonzeption in der Religion der griechischen und römischen Antike', in R. Posner, K. Robering, and T. A. Sebeok (eds.), *Semiotik. Ein Handbuch zu den zeichentheoretischen*

Grundlagen von Natur und Kultur (Berlin and New York, 1997), 939–58.

Gras, M., *Trafics tyrrhéniens archaïques* (Rome, 1985).

—— 'Pour une Méditerranée des *emporia*', in A. Bresson and P. Rouillard (eds.), *L'Emporion* (Paris 1993), 103–12.

Greenberg, J., 'Plagued by Doubt: Reconsidering the Impact of a Mortality Crisis in the 2nd c. A. D.', *JRA* 13 (2003), 413–25.

Greenblatt, S., *Marvellous Possessions: The Wonder of the New World* (Oxford, 1991).

Griffin, M., *Seneca* (Oxford, 1976).

Grove, A. T., and Rackham, O., *The Nature of Mediterranean Europe: An Ecological History* (New Haven and London, 2001).

Gruner, O. C., *A Treatise on the Canon of Medicine of Avicenna, Incorporating a Translation of the First Book* (London, 1930).

Gruzinsky, S., *La guerra de las Imágines* (Mexico City, 1994).

Guarducci, M., 'Ordinamenti dati da Gortina a Kaudos in una iscrizione inedita di Gortina', *Rivista di Filologia* 8 (1930), 471–82.

Guilaine, J., *La Mer partagée: La Méditerranée avant l'écriture 7000–2000 avant Jésus-Christ* (Paris, 1994).

Guiraud, P., *La Main-d'oeuvre industrielle dans l'ancienne Grèce* (Paris, 1900).

Gupta, R., *The Rig Veda: A History Showing how the Phoenicians had their Earliest Home in India* (Chittagong, 1904).

Halstead, P., 'Traditional and Ancient Rural Economy in the Mediterranean: Plus ça change?', *Journal of Hellenic Studies* 107 (1987), 77–87.

Hamlin, A. T., *The University Library in the United States: Its Origins and Development* (Philadelphia, 1981).

Harris, E. M., 'Notes on the New Grain-tax Law', *ZPE* 128 (1999), 269–72.

Harris, W. V., *Ancient Literacy* (Cambridge, Mass., 1989).

—— 'Between Archaic and Modern: Some Current Problems in the History of the Roman Economy', in W. V. Harris (ed.), *The Inscribed Economy* (*JRA*, Suppl. 6) (Ann Arbor, 1993), 11–29.

—— *Restraining Rage: The Ideology of Anger Control in Classical Antiquity* (Cambridge, Mass., 2002)

—— 'Roman Governments and Commerce, 300 BC—AD 300', in C. Zaccagnini (ed.), *Mercanti e politica nel mondo antico* (Bari and Rome, 2003), 279–309

Hartog, F., *The Mirror of Herodotus: The Representation of the Other in the Writing of History*, trans. J. Lloyd (Berkeley and Los Angeles, 1988); original edn.: *Le Miroir d'Hérodote: Essai sur la représentation de l'autre* (Paris, 1980)

Heinzelmann, M., *Translationsberichte und andere Quellen des Reliquienkultes* (Turnhout, 1979).

Herman, G., rev. of D. Cohen, *Law, Violence and Community*, *Gnomon* 70 (1998), 605–15

Herzfeld, M., 'Honour and Shame: Problems in the Comparative Analysis of Moral Systems', *Man* 15 (1980), 339–51.

—— *Ours Once More; Folklore, Ideology, and the Making of Modern Greece* (Austin, 1982).

—— 'The Horns of the Mediterraneanist Dilemma', *American Ethnologist* 11 (1984), 439–54.

—— *Anthropology through the Looking-Glass: Critical Ethnography in the Margins of Europe* (Cambridge, 1987).

—— *A Place in History: Social and Monumental Time in a Cretan Town* (Princeton, 1991).

—— *Cultural Intimacy: Social Poetics in the Nation-State* (New York, 1997).

—— 'Factual Fissures: Claims and Contexts', *Annals of the American Academy of Political and Social Science* 560 (1998), 69–82.

—— 'Performing Comparisons: Ethnography, Globetrotting, and the Spaces of Social Knowledge', *Journal of Anthropological Research* 57 (2001), 259–76.

—— *The Body Impolitic: Artisans and Artifice in the Global Hierarchy of Value* (Chicago, 2004).

Hirschon, R., 'Open Body/Closed Space: The Transformation of Female Sexuality', in S. Ardener (ed.), *Defining Females* (London, 1978), 66–88.

Hohlfelder, R. L. and Vann, R. L., 'Cabotage at Aperlae in Ancient Lycia', *International Journal of Nautical Archaeology* 29 (2000), 126–35.

Holton, R. J., *Cities, Capitalism and Civilization* (London, 1986).

Holub, R. C., *Reception Theory: a Critical Introduction* (New York, 1984).

Hong, S., Candelone, J. P., Patterson, C. C., and Boutron, C. F., 'History of Ancient Copper Smelting Pollution during Roman and Medieval Times Recorded in Greenland Ice', *Science* 272 (1996), 246–9.

Hopkins, K., 'Rome, Taxes, Rent and Trade', *Kodai* 6/7 (1995/6), 41–75.

Horden, P., 'Musical Solutions', in P. Horden (ed.), *Music as Medicine: The History of Music Therapy since Antiquity* (Aldershot, 2000), 4–40.

Horden, P., 'Religion as Medicine: Music in Medieval Hospitals', in
P. Biller and J. Ziegler (eds.), *Religion and Medicine in the Middle
Ages* (Woodbridge, Suffolk, and Rochester, NY, 2001), 135–53.

—— 'The Earliest Hospitals in Byzantium, Western Europe and
Islam', *Journal of Interdisciplinary History* forthcoming, 361–89.

—— 'Household Care and Informal Networks: Comparisons and
Continuities from Antiquity to the Present', in P. Horden and
R. Smith (eds.), *The Locus of Care: Families, Communities, Institutions, and the Provision of Welfare since Antiquity* (London and New
York, 1998).

Huddleston, L. E., *Origins of the American Indians: European Concepts, 1492–1729* (Austin, 1967).

Hughes, J. D., *Pan's Travail: Environmental Problems of the Ancient
Greeks and Romans* (Baltimore, 1994).

Gli Inizi del Cristianesimo in Livonia-Lettonia. Atti del colloquio internazionale (Vatican City, 1989).

Iser, W., *Der Akt des Lesens* (Munich, 1976).

Iskandar, A. Z., *A Catalogue of Arabic Manuscripts on Medicine
and Science in the Wellcome Historical Medical Library* (London,
1967).

Jackson, M., *Paths toward a Clearing: Radical Empiricism and Ethnographic Inquiry* (Bloomington, Ind. 1989).

—— (ed.), *Things As They Are: New Directions in Phenomenological
Anthropology* (Bloomington, 1996).

Jameson, M. H., 'Private Space and the Greek City', in O. Murray and
S. Price (eds.), *The Greek City from Homer to Alexander* (Oxford,
1990), 171–95.

Jashemski, W. F. and Meyer, F. G. (eds.), *The Natural History of
Pompeii* (Cambridge, 2002).

Jauss, H. R., *Rezeptionsästhetik* (Munich, 1975).

Johnston, S. I., 'Sacrifice in the Greek Magical Papyri', in P. Mirecki
and M. Meyer (eds.), *Magic and Ritual in the Ancient World*
(Leiden, 2002), 344–58.

Jones, C. P., *Kinship Diplomacy in the Ancient World* (Cambridge,
Mass., 1999).

Judson, L., 'Aristotle on Fair Exchange', *Oxford Studies in Ancient
Philosophy* 15 (1997), 147–75.

Kallet-Marx, L.. *Money, Expense, and Naval Power in Thucydides'
History 1–5.24* (Berkeley, 1993).

Kantor, H. J., 'The Aegean and the Orient in the Second Millennium
B. C.', *American Journal of Archaeology* 51 (1947), 1–103.

Keay, S. and Terrenato, N. (eds.), *Italy and the West: Comparative
Issues in Romanization* (Oxford, 2001).

Kemp, B. J., *Ancient Egypt: Anatomy of a Civilization* (London, 1989).

Kessener, P., 'The Aqueduct at Aspendos and its Inverted Siphon', *JRA* 13 (2000), 104–32.

Kilian, K., 'Mycenaean Colonization: Norm and Variety', in J.-P. Descoeudres (ed.), *Greek Colonists and Native Populations* (Canberra and Oxford, 1990), 445–67.

Kirby, D., *Northern Europe in the Early Modern Period: The Baltic World 1492–1772* (London, 1990).

Knapp, A. B., 'Editorial Statement', *Journal of Mediterranean Archaeology* 1 (1988), 3–10.

——— 'Ethnicity, Entrepreneurship, and Exchange: Mediterranean Inter-island Relations in the Late Bronze Age', *Annual of the British School at Athens* 85 (1990), 115–53.

——— and Cherry, J. F., 'Editorial Comment', *Journal of Mediterranean Archaeology* 7 (1994), 3–4.

Kolodny, E., 'La Crète: Mutations et evolutions d'une population insulaire grecque', *Revue géographique de Lyon* 3 (1968), 227–90.

Kowaleski, M., *The Local Customs Accounts of the Port of Exeter 1266–1321* (Exeter, 1993).

Kron, G., 'Archaeozoological Evidence for the Productivity of Roman Livestock Farming', *Münstersche Beiträge zur antiken Handelsgeschichte* 21 (2002), 53–73.

Kuhrt, A., *The Ancient Near East c.3000–330 BC* (London and New York, 1995).

Kula, W., *An Economic Theory of the Feudal System: Towards a Model of the Polish Economy, 1500–1800*, trans. L. Garner (London, 1976); original edn.: *Teoria ekonomiczna ustroju feudalnego* (Warsaw, 1962).

Lane Fox, R., 'Ancient Hunting: From Homer to Polybius', in J. B. Salmon and G. Shipley (eds.), *Human Landscapes in Classical Antiquity: Environment and Culture* (London, 1996), 119–53.

Laronde, A., *Cyrène et la Libye hellénistique: Libykai Historiai* (Paris, 1987).

Launey, M., *Recherches sur les armées hellénistiques*, new edn. with addenda by Y. Garlan, Ph. Gauthier, and Cl. Orrieux (Paris, 1987).

Lebessi, A., 'Flagellation ou autoflagellation? Données iconographiques pour une tentative d'interpretation', *Bulletin de Correspondance Hellénique* 115 (1991), 103–23.

——— and Muhly, P. M., 'Aspects of Minoan Cult: Sacred Enclosures: the Evidence from the Syme Sanctuary (Crete)', *Archäologischer Anzeiger* (1990), 315–36.

Lederman, R., 'Globalization and the Future of Culture Areas', *Annual Review of Anthropology* 27 (1998), 427–49.

le Houérou, H. N., 'Impact of Man and his Animals on Mediterranean Vegetation', in F. di Castri, D. W. Goodall, and R. L. Specht (eds.), *Mediterranean-type Shrublands* (Amsterdam etc., 1981), 479–521.

Lendon, J. E., *Empire of Honour: The Art of Government in the Roman World* (Oxford, 1997).

Leveau, P., 'La Ville antique et l'organisation de l'espace rurale: *villa, ville, village*', *Annales ESC* 38 (1983), 920–42.

Lewis, N. N., 'The Lajā in the Last Century of Ottoman Rule', in D. Panzac (ed.), *Histoire économique et sociale de l'Empire Ottoman et de la Turquie (1326–1960): Actes du sixième congrès international tenu à Aix-en-Provence du 1er au 4 juillet 1992* (Paris, 1995), 631–40.

LiDonnici, L., 'Burning for it: Erotic Spells for Fever and Compulsion in the Ancient Mediterranean World', *Greek, Roman, and Byzantine Studies* 39 (1998), 63–98.

Liebeschuetz, J. W. H. G., *The Decline and Fall of the Roman City* (Oxford, 2001).

Lister, M., *The European Union and the South: Relations with Developing Countries* (London, 1997).

Liverani, M., 'Ras Shamra. Histoire', *Supplément au Dictionnaire de la Bible* (Paris, 1979), ix. 1333–42.

——*International Relations in the Ancient Near East, 1600–1100 B.C.* (New York, 2001).

Lockwood, D. P., *Ugo Benzi: Medieval Philosopher and Physician 1376–1439* (Chicago, 1951).

Loizos, P., *The Greek Gift: Politics in a Cypriot Village* (Oxford, 1975).

Lombard, D. and Aubin, J., *Asian Merchants and Businessmen in the Indian Ocean and the China Sea*, new edn., (New Delhi and New York, 2000) (first edn., Paris, 1988).

Lombard, M., *Les Métaux dans l'ancien monde du Ve au XIe siècle* (Paris and The Hague, 1974).

Long, L., Pomey, P., and Sourisseau, J.-Chr., *Les Étrusques en mer: Épaves d'Antibes à Marseille* (Marseilles, 2002).

Lonie, I. M., 'A Structural Pattern in Greek Dietetics and the Early History of Greek Medicine', *Medical History* 21 (1977), 235–60.

Lopez, R. S., *The Commercial Revolution of the Middle Ages, 950–1350* (Englewood Cliffs, NJ, 1971).

Loucas-Durie, E., 'Simulacre humain et offrande rituelle', *Kernos* 1 (1988), 151–62.

Ma, J., 'Black Hunter Variations', *Proceedings of the Cambridge Philological Society* 40 (1994), 49–80.

McCormick, M., *Origins of the European Economy* (Cambridge, 2001).

—— 'Rats, Communication, and Plague: Toward an Ecological History', *Journal of Interdisciplinary History* 34 (2003–4), 49–61.

McVaugh, M. R., 'Arnald of Villanova's Regimen Almarie (*Regimen castra sequontium*) and Medieval Military Medicine', *Viator* 23 (1992), 201–13.

—— 'Medical Knowledge at the Time of Frederick II', *Micrologus* 2 (1994), 3–17.

Maddison, F. and Savage-Smith, E., *Science, Tools and Magic, i. Body and Spirit, Mapping the Universe* (London, 1997).

Malamut, E., *Sur la route des saints byzantins* (Paris, 1993).

Malay, H., *Researches in Lydia, Mysia and Aiolis* (*TAM*, Ergänzungsband 23) (Vienna, 1999).

Mallowan, M. E. L., 'Phoenician Carrying-Trade, Syria', *Antiquity* 13 (1939), 86–7.

Manganaro, G., '*SGDI* IV 4 n. 49 (*DGE* 707) e il bimetallismo monetale di Creso', *Epigraphica* 36 (1974), 57–77.

Manning, J. G., 'Irrigation et état en Égypte antique,' *Annales HSS* 57 (2002), 611–23.

Margueron, J.-C., 'Fondations et refondations au proche-orient au bronze récent', in S. Mazzoni (ed.), *Nuove fondazioni nel vicino oriente antico: realtà e ideologia* (Pisa, 1994), 3–27.

Mas Latrie, J. M. J. L., *Traités de paix et de commerce et documents divers concernant les relations des chrétiens avec les Arabes de l'Afrique septentrionale au moyen âge* (Paris, 1866).

Masson, P., *Histoire du commerce français dans le Levant au XVIIe siècle* (Paris, 1896).

—— *Histoire des établissements et du commerce français dans l'Afrique barbaresque (1560–1793) (Algérie, Tunisie, Tripolitaine, Maroc)* (Paris, 1903).

—— *Histoire du commerce français dans le Levant au XVIIIe siècle* (Paris, 1911).

Mastrocinque, A., 'Alessandro di Abonouteichos e la magia', in *Imago Antiquitatis. Religions et iconographie du monde romain: Mélanges offerts à Robert Turcan* (Paris, 1999), 341–52.

Mattingly, D. J., 'First Fruit? The Olive in the Roman World', in J. B. Salmon and G. Shipley (eds.), *Human Landscapes in Classical Antiquity: Environment and Culture* (London, 1996), 213–53.

Menzies, G., *1421: The Year China Discovered the World* (London, 2002), repub. as *1421: The Year China Discovered America* (New York, 2003).

Merkelbach, R., *Abrasax III. Ausgewählte Papyri religiösen und magischen, Inhalts III* (Opladen, 1992).

—— and Stauber, J., 'Die Orakel des Apollon von Klaros', *Epigraphica Anatolica* 27 (1996), 1–54.

Merrillees R. S. and Evans, J., 'Highs and Lows in the Holy Land: Opium in Biblical Times', *Eretz Israel* 20 (1989), 148–54.

Meuli, K., 'Griechische Opferbräuche', in *Phyllobolia für Peter von der Mühll zum 60: Geburtstag am 1. August 1945* (Basle, 1946), 185–288.

Mézin, A., *Les Consuls de France au siècle des Lumières (1715–1792)* (Paris, 1997).

Mikkeli, H., *Hygiene in the Early Modern Medical Tradition* (Helsinki, 1999).

Millard, A., 'The Phoenicians at Sea', in G. J. Oliver, R. Brock, T. J. Cornell, and S. Hodkinson (eds.), *The Sea in Antiquity* (Oxford, 2000), 75–9.

Miller, P. C., *Dreams in Late Antiquity* (Princeton, 1994).

Molho, A. and Ramada Curto, D., 'Les réseaux marchands à l'époque moderne', *Annales* 58 (2003), 569–79.

Moscati, S., *The Phoenicians* (Milan, 1988).

Mosse, G. L., *Respectability and Abnormal Sexuality in Modern Europe* (New York, 1985).

Mrozek, S., 'Le Fonctionnement des fondations dans les provinces occidentales et l'économie de crédit à l'époque du Haut-Empire romain', *Latomus* 59 (2000), 327–45.

Mukarovsky, J., *Structure, Sign, and Function: Selected Essays* (New Haven, 1977).

Murray, O., 'Ho archaios dasmos', *Historia* 15 (1966), 142–56.

—— and Price, S. (eds.), *The Greek City from Homer to Alexander* (Oxford, 1990).

Ñaco del Hoyo, T., 'Roman *Realpolitik* in Taxing Sardinian Rebels (178–75)', *Athenaeum* 91 (2003), 531–40.

Naumann, R., *Architektur Kleinasiens von ihren Anfängen bis zum Ende der hethitischen Zeit*, 2nd edn. (Tübingen, 1971).

Neilson III, H. R., 'Roman Sailing: Offshore Navigation by Wind Direction', *Athenaeum* 89 (2001), 235–9.

Nicolet, C., *Tributum: Recherches sur la fiscalité directe sous la république romaine* (Bonn, 1976).

Nieto, X., 'Le Commerce de cabotage et de distribution', in P. Pomey (ed.), *La Navigation dans l'Antiquité* (Paris, 1997), 146–58.

Nilsson, M. P., *Griechische Feste von religiöser Bedeutung mit Ausschluss der attischen* (Lund, 1906).

——*Geschichte der griechischen Religion*, i. 3rd edn. (Munich, 1967).

Nixon, L., rev. of Horden and Purcell, *CS, Journal of Roman Studies* 92 (2002), 195–7.

——and Price, S. R. F., 'The Size and Resources of Greek Cities', in O. Murray and S. R. F. Price (eds.), *The Greek City* (Oxford, 1990), 137 70.

Nutton, V., 'Continuity or Rediscovery? The City Physician in Classical Antiquity and Mediaeval Italy', in A. W. Russell (ed.), *The Town and State Physician in Europe from the Middle Ages to the Enlightenment* (Wolfenbüttel, 1981), 9–46.

——'The Drug Trade in Antiquity', *Journal of the Royal Society of Medicine* 78 (1985), 138–46.

——'Les Exercises et la santé: Hieronymus Mercurialis et la gymnastique médicale', in J. Céard, M. M. Fontaine, and J. C. Margolin (eds.), *Le Corps à la Renaissance* (Paris, 1990), 295–308.

Nutton, V., 'Galen and the Traveller's Fare', in J. Wilkins, D. Harris, and M. Dobson (eds.), *Food in Antiquity* (Exeter, 1995), 359–70.

O'Boyle, C., *The Art of Medicine: Medical Teaching at the University of Paris, 1250–1400* (Leiden, 1998).

O'Connor, D., 'New Kingdom and Third Intermediate Period, 1552–664 BC', in B. G. Trigger, B. J. Kemp, D. O'Connor, and A. B. Lloyd, *Ancient Egypt: A Social History* (Cambridge, 1983), 183–278.

——'Egypt and Greece: The Bronze Age Evidence', in M. R. Lefkowitz and G. M. Rogers (eds.), *Black Athena Revisited* (Chapel Hill, 1996), 49–61.

Oleson, J. P., 'Water-lifting Devices at Herculaneum and Pompeii in the Context of Roman Technology', in N. de Haan and G. C. M. Jansen (eds.), *Cura aquarum in Campania* (*Bulletin Antieke Beschaving*, Suppl. 4) (Leiden, 1996), 67–77.

——'Ancient Sounding Weights: A Contribution to the History of Ancient Mediterranean Navigation', *JRA* 13 (2000), 293–310.

Olmsted, J. W., 'The Académie Royale des Sciences and the Origin of the First French Scientific Expeditions, 1662–1671' (Ph. D. thesis, Cornell University, 1944).

Olson, G., *Literature as Recreation in the Later Middle Ages* (Ithaca, NY and London, 1982).

Ortner, S. B., 'Theory in Anthropology in the Sixties', *Comparative Studies in Society and History* 26 (1984), 126–66.

Orvietani Busch, S., *Medieval Mediterranean Ports: The Catalan and Tuscan coasts, 1100 to 1235* (Leiden, 2001).

Osborne, R., *Classical Landscape with Figures: The Ancient Greek City and its Countryside* (London, 1987).

Pakkanen, P., 'The Relationship between Continuity and Change in Dark Age Greek Religion: A Methodological Study', *Opuscula Atheniensia* 25–6 (2000–1), 71–88.

Palmer, R. E. A., 'Customs on Market Goods Imported into the City of Rome', *Memoirs of the American Academy in Rome* 36 (1980), 217–34.

Pare, C. F. E., 'Bronze and the Bronze Age', in C. F. E. Pare (ed.), *Metals Make the World Go Round* (Oxford, 2000), 1–38.

Parker, A. J., *Ancient Shipwrecks of the Mediterranean and the Roman Provinces* (Oxford, 1992).

Parker, J., *Structuration* (Buckingham, 2000).

Parry, J. H., *The Discovery of South America* (New York, 1979).

Peacock, D. P. S. and Williams, D. F., *Amphorae and the Roman Economy* (London, 1986).

Pébarthe, C., 'Thasos, l'Empire d'Athènes et les emporia de Thrace', *ZPE* 126 (1999), 121–54.

Pébarthe, C., 'Fiscalité, empire athénien, et écriture: Retour sur les causes de la guerre de Péloponnèse', *ZPE* 129 (2000), 47–76.

Peristiany, J. G. (ed.), *Honour and Shame: The Values of Mediterranean Society* (London, 1965).

—— 'Honour and Shame in a Cypriot Highland Village', in J. G. Peristiany (ed.), *Honour and Shame: The Values of Mediterranean Society* (London, 1965), 173–190.

Pignatti, S., 'Human Impact in the Vegetation of the Mediterranean Basin', in W. Holzner, M. J. A. Werger, and I. Ikusima (eds.), *Man's Impact on Vegetation* (The Hague, etc., 1983), 151–61.

Pingaud, L., *Choiseul-Gouffier: La France en Orient sous Louis XVI* (Paris, 1887).

Piolot, L., 'Pausanias et les Mystères d'Andanie: Histoire d'une aporie', in J. Renard (ed.), *Le Péloponnèse: Archéologie et Histoire, Actes de la rencontre internationale de Lorient, 12–15 mai 1998* (Rennes, 1999), 195–228.

Pirenne, H., *Mohammed and Charlemagne*, trans. B. Miall (London, 1939); original edn.: *Mahomet et Charlemagne* (Paris and Brussels, 1937).

Pitt-Rivers, J. A., 'Honour', *Proceedings of the British Academy* 94 (1997), 229–51.

Pleket, H. W., 'Notes on a Customs-law from Caunus', *Mnemosyne* 11 (1958), 128–35.

—— 'Models and Inscriptions: Export of Textiles in the Roman Empire', *Epigraphica Anatolica* 30 (1998), 117–28.

Pomeranz, K., *The Great Divergence: Europe, China, and the Making of the Modern World Economy* (Princeton, 2000).

Posener, G., *Les Douanes de la Méditerranée dans l'Egypte Saïte* (Paris, 1947).

Potter, P., *Short Handbook of Hippocratic Medicine* (Quebec, 1988).

Potts, D. T., *The Archaeology of Elam* (Cambridge, 1999).

Price, S. R. F., *Rituals and Power: The Roman Imperial Cult in Asia Minor* (Cambridge, 1984).

Pulak, C. and Bass, G. F., 'Uluburun', in E. Meyers (ed.), *The Oxford Encyclopedia of Archaeology in the Near East* (New York and Oxford, 1997), v. 266–8.

Purcell, N., 'Colonization and Mediterranean History', in H. Hurst and S. Owen (eds.), *Ancient Colonizations: Analogy, Similarity and Difference* (London, forthcoming).

—— 'The Boundless Sea of Unlikeness? On Defining the Mediterranean', *Mediterranean Historical Review* 18 (2003), 9–29.

—— 'Fixity', in R. Schlesier and U. Zellmann (eds.), *Mobility and Travel in the Mediterranean from Antiquity to the Middle Ages* (Münster, 2004), 73–83.

Purpura, G., 'Il regolamento doganale di Cauno e la lex Rhodia in D. 14,2,9', *Annali del Seminario Giuridico della Università di Palermo* 38 (1985), 273–331.

Quigley, C., 'Mexican National Character and Circum-Mediterranean Personality Structure,' *American Anthropologist* 75 (1973), 319–22.

Rackham, O., 'Ecology and Pseudo-ecology: The Example of Ancient Greece', in J. Salmon and G. Shipley (eds.), *Human Landscapes in Classical Antiquity* (London, 1996), 16–43.

Ramos, B. de Azevedo da Silva, *Catálogo da Coleção Numismática* (Rome, 1900), 4 vols.

Renfrew, C., 'Introduction: Peer Polity Interaction and Sociopolitical Change', in C. Renfrew and J. F. Cherry (eds.), *Peer Polity Interaction and Socio-political Change* (Cambridge, 1986), 1–18.

Renfrew, C. and Wagstaff, J. M. (eds.), *An Island Polity* (Cambridge, 1982).

Ribeiro, O., *Portugal, o Mediterrâneo e o Atlântico: esboço de relações geográficas*, 4th edn. (Lisbon, 1986).

Ricciardelli, G., 'Mito e performance nelle associazioni dionisiache', in M. Tortorelli Ghedini, A. Storchi Marino, and A. Visconti (eds.), *Tra Orfeo e Pitagora. Origini e incontri di culture nell'antichità. Atti dei seminari napoletani 1996–1998* (Naples, 2000), 265–82.

Ridgway, D., 'The First Western Greeks and their Neighbours, 1935–1985', in J.-P. Descoeudres (ed.), *Greek Colonists and Native Populations* (Canberra and Oxford, 1990), 61–72.

Ridgway, D., 'Final Remarks: Italy and Cyprus', in L. Bonfante and V. Karagheorgis (eds.), *Italy and Cyprus in Antiquity: 1500–450 B.C.* (Nicosia, 2001), 379–93.

Robert, L., *Hellenica XI–XII* (Paris, 1960).
—— *Monnaies grecques: Types, légendes, magistrats monétaires et géographie* (Geneva and Paris, 1967).

Rojas Mix, M., *América Imaginária* (Barcelona, 1992).

Rosivach, V. J., 'Some Aspects of the Fourth-Century Athenian Market in Grain', *Chiron* 30 (2000), 31–64.

Rostovtzeff, M. I., *Social and Economic History of the Roman Empire*, 2nd edn. (Oxford, 1957), 2 vols.
—— *Social and Economic History of the Hellenistic World* (Oxford, 1941), 3 vols.

Rowell, S. C., *Lithuania Ascending: A Pagan Empire within East-Central Europe, 1295–1345* (Cambridge, 1994).

Ruiz Rodríguez, A., Molinos, M., and Castro López, M., 'Settlement and Continuity in the Territory of the Guadalquivir Valley (6th Century B.C.–1st Century A.D.)', in G. Barker and J. Lloyd (eds.), *Roman Landscapes: Archaeological Survey in the Mediterranean Region* (London, 1991), 29–36.

Saadé, G., *Ougarit. Métropole Cananéenne* (Beirut, 1979).

Säve-Söderbergh, T., *The Navy of the Eighteenth Dynasty* (Uppsala, 1946).

Said, E. W., *Orientalism* (New York, 1978).

Sakellarakis, J., 'The Idean Cave: Minoan and Greek Worship', *Kernos* 1 (1988), 207–14.

Saldit-Trappmann, R., *Tempel der ägyptischen Götter in Griechenland und an der Westküste Kleinasiens* (Leiden, 1970).

Sallares, R., *The Ecology of the Ancient Greek World* (London, 1991).

Salviat, F., 'Le Vin de Thasos: Amphores, vin et sources écrites', in Y. Garlan and J.-Y. Empereur (eds.), *Recherches sur les amphores grecs* (*Bulletin de Correspondance Hellénique*, Suppl. 13) (Paris, 1986), 145–96.

Samons, L. J., *Empire of the Owl: Athenian Imperial Finance* (Stuttgart, 2000).

Sant Cassia, P., 'Authors in Search of a Character: Personhood, Agency and Identity in the Mediterranean', *Journal of Mediterranean Studies* 1 (1991), 1–17.
—— 'Editorial Foreword'. *Journal of Mediterranean Studies* 1 (1991), pp. v–vi.

Sassmannshausen, L., *Beiträge zur Verwaltung und Gesellschaft Babyloniens in der Kassitenzeit*. Baghdader Forschungen 21 (Mainz, 2001).

Sasson, J. M., 'Canaanite Maritime Involvement in the Second Millennium B.C.', *Journal of the American Oriental Society* 86 (1966), 126–38.

Sauer, C. E., *The Early Spanish Main* (Berkeley and Los Angeles, 1966).

Schachter, A., *Cults of Boiotia* (London, 1981–94), 4 vols.

Scheidel, W., 'Progress and Problems in Roman Demography', in W. Scheidel (ed.), *Debating Roman Demography* (*Mnemosyne*, Suppl. 211) (Leiden, 2001), 1–81.

Schiaparelli, L. (ed.), *Codice diplomatico longobardo* (Rome, 1929).

Schilcher, L. S., 'The Hawran in Late Roman and Ottoman Times: Three Models for Comparative Research', in D. Panzac (ed.), *Histoire économique et sociale de l'Empire Ottoman et de la Turquie (1326–1960): Actes du sixième congrés international tenu à Aix-en-Provence du 1er au 4 juillet 1992* (Paris, 1995), 705–17.

Schlesier, R., 'Menschen und Götter unterwegs: Ritual und Reise in der griechischen Antike', in T. Hölscher (ed.), *Gegenwelten zu den Kulturen Griechenlands und Roms in der Antike* (Munich and Leipzig, 2000), 129–57.

Schwennhagen, L., *Fenícios no Brasil: antiga história do Brasil, de 1100 a.C. a 1500 d.C.: tratado histórico* (Rio de Janeiro, 1976).

Scott, T., *Regional Identity and Economic Change: The Upper Rhine, 1450–1600* (Oxford, 1997).

Sebald, W. G., *On the Natural History of Destruction*, trans. A. Bell (London and New York, 2003); original edn: *Luftkrieg und Literatur* (Munich, 1999).

Sergi, G., *La decadenza delle nazioni latine* (Turin, 1900).

Sewell W. H., 'Marc Bloch and the Logic of Comparative History', *History and Theory* 6 (1967), 208–18.

Sfameni Gasparro, G., 'Alessandro di Abonutico, lo "pseudo-profeta" ovvero come construirsi un'identità religiosa I', *Studi e Materiali di Storia delle Religioni* 62 (1996) [1998], 565–90.

—— 'Alessandro di Abonutico, lo "pseudo-profeta" ovvero come costruirsi un'identità religiosa II', in C. Bonnet and A. Motte (eds.), *Les Syncrétismes religieux dans le monde méditerranéen antique: Actes du colloque international en l'honneur de Franz Cumont* (Brussels and Rome, 1999), 275–305.

Shanks, M., *Art and the Greek City-state: An Interpretive Archaeology* (Cambridge, 1999).

Shavit, Y., 'Mediterranean History and the History of the Mediterranean: Further Reflections', *Journal of Mediterranean Studies* 4 (1994), 313–29.

Shaw, B. D., rev. of Horden and Purcell, *CS*, *JRA* 14 (2001), 419–53.

Shaw, I., *The Oxford History of Ancient Egypt* (Oxford, 2000).

Shepherd, R., *Ancient Mining* (London and New York, 1993).

Sherratt, A. and S., 'From Luxuries to Commodities: The Nature of Mediterranean Bronze Age Trading Systems', in N. H. Gale (ed.), *Bronze Age Trade in the Mediterranean* (Jonsered, 1991), 351–86.

Silverman, S., *Three Bells of Civilization: The Life of an Italian Hill Town* (New York, 1975).

Smith, W., 'Fuel for Thought', *Journal of Mediterranean Archaeology* 11 (1998), 191–205.

Snodgrass, A. M., 'Survey Archaeology and the Rural Landscape of the Greek City', in O. Murray and S. Price (eds.), *The Greek City from Homer to Alexander* (Oxford, 1990), 113–36.

—— 'The Euboeans in Macedonia: A new Precedent for Westward Expansion', in *Apoikia: Scritti in onore di Giorgio Buchner* (= *Annali di archeologia e storia antica*, NS 1), (Naples, 1994), 87–93.

Sobrequés i Callicó, J. and Riera i Viader, S., 'La lleuda de Barcelona del segle XII', *Estudis universitaris catalans* 26 (1984), 329–46.

Souyri, J.-F., *The World Turned Upside Down: Medieval Japanese society*, trans. K. Roth (New York, 2001/London, 2002).

Spencer, T., *Fair Greece, Sad Relics : Literary Philhellenism from Shakespeare to Byron* (New York, 1973).

Spiteri, A., 'Preface', *Journal of Mediterranean Studies: History, Culture and Society in the Mediterranean World* 11 (2001), 1–9.

Sporn, K., *Heiligtümer und Kulte Kretas in klassischer und hellenistischer Zeit* (Heidelberg, 2002).

Squatriti, P., rev. of Horden and Purcell, *CS*, *Early Medieval Europe* 11 (2002), 263–79.

Stafford, B. M., *Voyage into Substance. Art, Science, Nature, and the Illustrated Travel Account, 1760–1840* (Cambridge, Mass., 1984).

Stancliffe, C., 'Red, White and Blue Martyrdom', in D. Whitelock, R. McKitterick, and D. Dumville (eds.), *Ireland in Early Medieval Europe* (Cambridge, 1982), 21–46.

Stewart, F. H., *Honor* (Chicago and London, 1994).

Stirling, P., *Turkish Village* (London, 1965).

Stos-Gale, Z. A. and Gale, N. H., 'New Light on the Provenience of the Copper Oxhide Ingots Found on Sardinia', in *Sardinia in the Mediterranean: Studies in Sardinian Archaeology Presented to Miriam S. Balmuth* (Sheffield, 1992), 317–37.

Suano, M. 'The First Trading Empires', in D. Abulafia (ed.), *The Mediterranean in History* (Los Angeles, 2003), 67–93.

Subrahmanyam, S., *The Political Economy of Commerce: Southern India, 1500–1650* (Cambridge, 1990).

Sudhoff, K., 'Ärztliche Regimina für Land- und Seereisen aus dem 15. Jahrhundert', *Archiv für Geschichte der Medizin* 4 (1911), 263–81.

Tadmor, H., 'The Decline of Empires in Western Asia ca. 1200 B.C.E.', in F. M. Cross (ed.), *Symposia Celebrating the Seventy-fifth Anniversary of the Founding of the American Schools of Oriental Research (1900–1975)* (Cambridge, Mass., 1979), 1–14.

Tandy, D. W., *Warriors into Traders: The Power of the Market in Early Greece* (Berkeley and Los Angeles, 1997).

Temkin, O., *The Falling Sickness: A History of Epilepsy from the Greeks to the Beginnings of Modern Neurology*, second edn. (Baltimore and London, 1971).

Thiel, J. H., 'Zu altgriechischen Gebühren', *Klio* 20 (1926), 54–67.

Thomasset, C., 'Conseils médicaux pour le voyage en mer au moyen âge', in C. Buchet (ed.), *L' homme, la santé et la mer* (Paris, 1997), 69–87.

Thompson, D. J., 'Philadelphus' Procession: Dynastic Power in a Mediterranean Context', in L. Mooren (ed.), *Politics, Administration and Society in the Hellenistic and Roman World: Proceedings of the International Colloquium, Bertinoro 19–24 July, 1997* (Louvain, 2000), 365–88.

Traina, G., 'Hellenism in the East: Some Historiographical Remarks,' *Electrum* 6 (2002), 15–24.

Trombley, F. R., *Hellenic Religion and Christianization, c.370–529* (Leiden, 1993–4), 2 vols.

Tsetskhladze, G. R. and De Angelis, F. (eds.), *The Archaeology of Greek Colonisation: Essays Dedicated to Sir John Boardman* (Oxford, 1994).

Turville-Petre, G., *The Heroic Age of Scandinavia* (London, 1951).

Tziovas, D., *The Nationism of the Demoticists and its Impact on their Literary Theory (1881–1930)* (Amsterdam, 1986).

Ullmann, M., 'Neues zu den diätetischen Schriften des Rufus von Ephesos', *Medizinhistorisches Journal* 9 (1974), 23–40.

—— *Islamic Medicine* (Edinburgh, 1978).

Vagnetti, L., 'Les Premiers Contacts entre le monde égéen et la Méditerranée occidentale', in G. Pugliese Carratelli (ed.), *Grecs en Occident: De l'âge mycénien à la fin de l'Hellénisme* (Milan, 1996), 109–16.

van Berchem, D., 'Du portage au péage: Le Rôle des cols transalpins dans l'histoire du Valais celtique', *Museum Helveticum* 13 (1956), 67–78.

van Cleve, T. C., *The Emperor Frederick II of Hohenstaufen: Immutator Mundi* (Oxford, 1972).

Van De Mieroop, M., 'Revenge, Assyrian Style', *Past and Present* 179 (2003), 3–23.

van Effenterre, H. and Ruzé, F. (eds.), *Nomima: Recueil d'inscriptions politiques et juridiques de l'archaïsme grec* (Rome, 1994–5), 2 vols.

Vélissaropoulos, J., *Les Nauclères grecs: Recherches sur les institutions maritimes en Grèce et dans l'Orient hellénisé* (Geneva, 1980).

Vergé-Franceschi, M., *La Marine française au XVIIIe siècle* (Paris, 1996).

Versnel, H. S., *Inconsistencies in Greek and Roman Religion* (Leiden, 1990–3), 2 vols.

Verschuer, C. von, *Le Commerce extérieur du Japon des origines au XVIe siècle* (Paris, 1988).

Victor, U., *Lukian von Samosata, Alexander oder Der Lügenprophet* (Leiden, 1997).

Vita-Finzi, C., *The Mediterranean Valleys* (Cambridge, 1969).

Wachsmann, S., *Seagoing Ships and Seamanship in the Bronze Age Levant* (College Station, Tex., 1998).

Wack, M. F., *Lovesickness in the Middle Ages: The 'Viaticum' and its Commentaries* (Philadelphia, 1990).

Waddell, L. A., *The Phoenician Origin of Britons, Scots and Anglo-Saxons Discovered by Phoenician and Sumerian Inscriptions in Britain, by Pre-Roman British Coins and a Mass of New History* (London, 1931).

Walcot, P. *Greek Peasants Ancient and Modern: A Comparison of Social and Moral Values* (Manchester, 1970).

Wallinga, H. T., 'Persian Tribute and Delian Tribute', in *Le Tribut dans l'Empire Perse* (Paris, 1989), 173–81.

—— 'Poseidonios on Beating to Windward (FGH 87 F 46 and Related Passages)', *Mnemosyne* 53 (2000), 431–47.

Watrous, L. V., *The Cave Sanctuary of Zeus at Psychro: A Study of Extra-Urban Sanctuaries in Minoan and Early Iron Age Crete* (Liège, 1996).

Watson, J. L., 'Introduction: Transnationalism, Localization, and Fast Foods in East Asia', in J. L. Watson (ed.), *Golden Arches East: McDonald's in East Asia* (Stanford, 1997).

Wells, P. S., rev. of *Mediterranean Archaeology* and *Journal of Mediterranean Archaeology*, *Antiquity* 65 (1991), 1006–7.

Whitehead, D., *The Demes of Attica* (Princeton, 1986).

Whittaker, C. R. (ed.), *Pastoral Economies in Classical Antiquity*: Proceedings of the Cambridge Philological Society, Suppl. 14 (Cambridge, 1988).

Wiebenson, D., *Sources of Greek Revival Architecture* (London, 1969).

Wilhelm, G., 'Marijannu', *Reallexikon der Assyriologie* 7 (Berlin and New York, 1987–90), 419–21.

Williams, R., *The Country and the City* (London, 1973).

Wink, A., 'From the Mediterranean to the Indian Ocean: Medieval History in Geographic Perspective', *Comparative Studies in Society and History* 44 (2002), 416–45.

Wöhrle, G., *Studien zur Theorie der Antiken Gesundheitslehre* (*Hermes* Einzelschriften 56) (Stuttgart, 1990).

Wrigley, R. and Revill, G. (eds.), *Pathologies of Travel* (Amsterdam and Atlanta, 2000).

Xenakis, D. K. and Chryssochoou, D. N., *The Emerging Euro-Mediterranean System* (Manchester and New York, 2001).

Yaser, J., *Fenicios y árabes en el génesis americano* (Córdoba, Argentina, 1992).

Yiakoumaki, V., ' "The Nation as Acquired Taste": On Greekness, Consumption of Food Heritage, and the Making of the New Europe' (Ph.D. diss., Department of Anthropology, The New School University, New York, 2002).

Young, G. K., *Rome's Eastern Trade: International Commerce and Imperial Policy, 31 BC–AD 305* (London and New York, 2001).

Youtie, H. C., *Scriptiunculae* (Amsterdam, 1973).

——*Scriptiunculae Posteriores* (Bonn, 1981).

Zaccagnini, C., 'Pferde und Streitwagen in Nuzi, Bemerkungen zur Technologie', *Jahresbericht des Instituts für Vorgeschichte der Universität Frankfurt a. M.* (1977), 21–37.

——'Prehistory of the Achaemenid tributary system', in *Le Tribut dans l'Empire Perse* (Paris, 1989), 193–215.

Zohary, D., 'The Diffusion of South and East Asian and of African Crops into the Belt of Mediterranean Agriculture', in H. D. V. Prendergast, N. L. Etkin, D. R. Harris, and P. J. Houghton (eds.), *Plants for Food and Medicine* (Kew, 1998), 123–34.

——and Hopf, M., *Domestication of Plants in the Old World: The Origin and Spread of Cultivated Plants in West Asia, Europe and the Nile Valley* (3rd edn., Oxford, 2000).

INDEX

Abulafia, D. 8, 344, 352–3, 371
Adam of Cremona 197
Adrianople 288
Adriatic 67
Aegean 67–8; Bronze-Age 122,
  126; archaic 216; mapping of
  in eighteenth century
  253–67
Aelius Aristides 186
Aeschylus, *Oresteia* 40
affiliations, imaginary 294–313
Agatharchides 144
agriculture, specialization in 71
Ahhiyawa 121–2
Akhetaten (El-Amarna) 128–9
Akkadian as an international
  language 135
Alcock, S. E. 2, 343
Alexander of
  Abonouteichos 163–4
Alexandria 34, 214
Almohads 69
Alponos 208
Amarna, El-: *see* Akhetaten
Amazon 297–301
Ambracia 216
American School of Classical
  Studies in Athens 342–3
Americas 294–313
amphorae, Roman 110
Anazarbus 208
Anthimus 183
anthropologists: use of the
  Mediterranean construct 1,
  47; anthropology, trends in
  30, 53, 54–5
Arabic, ignorance of 343
Arcadia 105

architecture, Greek 258–63
Aristotle 170, 217, 218–19;
  ps.-Aristotle 229
Armstrong, C. D. 339, 341
Arnald of Villanova 197–8
art: *see* 'international style'
Arzawa 121
Assyria 120, 132
astronomy 242
Athenaeus 143
Athens 102, 145, 151–2, 223–5,
  275
Atlantic 108–111; Atlantic
  'Mediterranean' 80–2
Attica 106
Austin, J. L. 50
Australian scholarship on the
  Mediterranean 328–30
autarky: *see* self-sufficiency
Avicenna: *see* Ibn Sina

Babylonia 120
Baltic-North Sea complex 66,
  76–80
Barcelona 73, 215
Bernard, Jean-Frédéric 239–40
Biqa valley 6 n.
Black Sea 11, 68, 99, 175, 177
Bloch, M. 5, 11
Blok, A. 61
Boccaccio 211, 232
Boeotia, ritual sacrifice of eels in
  144; festival of Daidala and
  155–60
Boyle, Robert 237
Braudel, F. 3, 5–6, 7, 10 n., 13,
  21–2, 30, 32–3, 65, 66, 68,
  90–1, 93, 94, 117, 166, 202,

Braudel, F. (*cont.*)
  221, 269, 312, 321–2, 327,
  358, 364
Brazil 294–313
Bresson, A. 202
bronze 25
Brown, P. 20
Bruges 79
Buarque de Hollanda, Sérgio
  298–9
Buffon, Georges-Louis Leclerc,
  comte de 235, 252
Burkert, W. 158–9, 160
Burton, Robert 188–9
Byzantine Empire 68

cabotage, caboteurs 16, 96, 221
Caelius Aurelianus 187–8
Cahen, C. 214
Cairo: see Geniza
C. Calpurnius Rufinus 163
capital cities, new 128–9
Carales 208
Caribbean shortly before and
  after first European
  contact 82–5
carrying capacity 14
Carthage 102
Cartier, R. 201
cartography 235–67
Cassini, Gian Domenico 242
Catalonia 213–14
catastrophes 35
Caunus 209–10, 213, 219–20,
  221, 225
Celsus 182
Chabert, Joseph-Bernard,
  marquis de 248–52, 263
chariots, charioteers 130,
  132–3
Chaudhuri, K. 66, 90–1
Chazelles, Jean-Mathieu de
  246–7, 250

China in medieval Japan 85–90;
  Chinese 173–4
Choiseul-Gouffier, G.-F.-A.,
  comte de 263–7, 278–90
Christianization of Norway and
  the Baltic 78
chronometers 242, 251–2
cities 34; open and closed spaces
  in 55; perceived as
  corrupting 56
Claudius Damas, Ti. 152–4, 163
climate 21
Cohen, D. 28
coinage 207 n.
Colbert, J.-B. 246, 347
colonization 19–20, 33, 77, 81
comparative history 91–2;
  method 41
'connectivity', connectedness 8,
  24–5, 94–114, 356, 368
Constantinople 68
continuity 27–8, 36; between
  antiquity and the Middle
  Ages 71; alleged, in Greece
  268–93
copper 35, 136
Corinth 102, 207
corruption 55, 62
Crete 135, 208 n.
cultural unity 20, 26–9
Cunliffe, B. 109, 354
customs, exaction of 200–32
Cyrenaica 6 n., 34
Cyzicus 207

Daidala, festival of 155–60
dancing, ancient and modern
  Greek 284
Davis, J. 49, 50
decadence of modern
  Greeks 270–87
deforestation 9–10, 12, 35–6
Delisle, Guillaume 243–6

Delos 216–17
Delphi 207
De Pina-Cabral, J. 26, 30
Descat, R. 217
deserts 65
De Thoron, E. O. 309
diffusionism 307, 309
dining rituals 143
Diocles of Carystus 191–2
Dover, K. J. 27
Driessen, H. 350
Duby, G. 312
Duncan-Jones, R. P. 35
Durkheim, E. 51, 373

east–west orientation 167–78
ecological unity 21–22
economic history 25
Egypt 4, 12, 18, 25, 100–1,
    122–3, 125, 128, 138, 176,
    187, 339–47
Egyptian deities 161, 162; *and see*
    Sarapis
Egyptology in modern
    America 343
Elam 119, 126
Elephantine palimpsest 209,
    210–11, 367
elites, nature of in medieval
    Italian cities 72
emperor cult 165 n.
Emporion 96
Enlightenment 235–67
ephebes, Athenian 151–2
Ephesus 206–7
Essenes 178
Ethiopia 172–3
ethnographic present 27
ethnography, world-wide 41;
    imaginary 298
Etruria, southern 6 n.;
    Etruscans 68, 99, 102–3
Eudoxus of Cyzicus 108–9

exchange 17–19, 136
exercise 189–90
Exeter 212–13

falsifiability of Horden-Purcell
    theses 361–7
famines 35
Fatimids 214–15
Fentress, E. and J. 349, 350, 372
Fernández-Armesto, F. 81
Finley, M. I. 19, 220
Florence 72
Fontenelle, Bernard le Bouvier
    de 244, 263
France, state administration of
    235–67
France, J. 227
Frayn, J. M. 13
Frazer, J. G. 157, 160
Frederick II of Sicily 71
Fustel de Coulanges, N. D. 311

Gades 169
Galen 185–6
Gallant, T. 55
games: ball games in central
    America 84
Gaul 227–8
Geniza letters 70
Genoa, Genoese 68, 70, 74, 212,
    215
Gibbon, Edward 168–9, 171
Gilchrist, Ebenezer 187
global Mediterranean 92
globalization 59
Goitein, S. 30, 70, 93, 322, 339,
    341
Goldenberg, D. 172
Gordon, C. 309
Gouldner, A. W. 268
Gras, M. 204
Gratarolo, Guglielmo 198–9
'Great Sea' 15, 64

Greaves, John 239
Greece, modern 56–7, 58–9;
    alleged continuity in 268–93;
    contrasted with Italy 49, 58;
    image of contemporary
    Greece from the sixteenth
    century to the nineteenth
    268–93; travel to 235–93
Greek conceptions of the
    Mediterranean Sea 15–16;
    diplomacy 145–6; expansion
    in the Mediterranean 102–3;
    fiscality 206–11, 218–20,
    223–6, 230; hinterland 105;
    history, boundaries of 343–4;
    medicine 185, 187, 189,
    191–2; rituals 141–66;
    settlement patterns 31; *and
    see* cartography; colonization;
    Mycenaeans
Guiraud, P. 219
Guys, Pierre-Augustin 271, 280,
    281–2, 284, 285, 289

Hakata (Japan) 86, 87
Hanno 108
Hansa 77
harbour-taxes 200–32
Hatti: *see* Hittites
Hattusa 128
Hawran 365–6
Hecataeus 15
Hellenistic monarchies 345
hero, myth of, as possible
    Mediterranean feature 312
Herodotus 143
Herzfeld, M. 1, 26, 339, 341,
    345, 346, 347, 349–50
Hesiod 16, 97, 269
hierarchy: *see* structure, social
(pseudo-)Hippocrates,
    Hippocratic corpus 181–2,
    185, 198

history, ritualized use of 145
history in/ history of, distinction
    between 3, 5, 7, 94, 99–100,
    202, 342, 357
Hittites 121, 124, 138
Hodges, R. 351
Homer 16, 206, 254–6
honour 26–7, 28–9, 39, 54, 61
Horden, P. 1–42, 45–6, 49, 52,
    55, 57, 65, 94, 104, 117,
    142–3, 161, 167, 168, 179,
    321–2, 339–42
horses 133
hospitals, earliest 183
hunting 188
hydraulic engineering 17; *and see*
    water management
Hyksos 122, 124

Ibn al-Jazzar 184
Ibn Sina (Avicenna) 193, 194,
    197
immobilism, immobility 9–10
India 113
Indian Ocean 66, 90–1, 111–13
inland economies 105
'inscriptions' in Brazil 303–11
'international style' in Late
    Bronze Age 134–5, 136
Islam, penetration of black Africa
    by 75
Italy, contemporary 58–9

Japanese 'Mediterranean' 85–90
Jews, in medieval Provence and
    Catalonia 73; Jewish
    merchants 74–5; alleged
    urban proclivities of 56
*Journal of Mediterranean
    Archaeology* 320, 325, 330–1
*Journal of Mediterranean
    Studies* 331–3
journals, academic 314–35

Kyme, Aeolic 207–8

land-transport 97–8, 106; *and see* Sahara
Leclerc, Georges-Louis: *see* Buffon
Lederman, R, 47, 59
Lemnos 206
Leroy, Julien-David 236, 258–63
Leveau, P. 33
Levi, Carlo 10
literacy 41–2
Lithuania 78
livestock, ancient Mediterranean 375
Loizos, P. 60
Lopez, R. S. 76
Lucan 173

Madaba map 170
al-Makhzumi 214
Malthusian checks 14
Manaus 302, 310–11
Maniots 273–4, 282, 286
Mansa Musa, emperor of Mali 75
maps: *see* cartography
Marajoara ceramics 305–6
C. Marius 227
Marx 373
Massalia 227
Maurepas, Jean-Frédéric, comte de 247–8, 347
Maynus de Mayneriis (fourteenth-century medical writer) 194–5
McCormick, M. 351
measurement 235–67
medicine 179–99
Mediterranean Archaeology 320, 328–30

Mediterranean
consciousness 51;
identity 49–50, 52 (in modern Egypt) 345–6
Mediterranean Historical Review 326–8
Mediterranean region,
boundaries of 11–12, 21, 117, 118, 229, 361, 366;
distinctiveness of and its limits 4, 45, 92, 142, 161, 162, 203, 229–31, 312, 366;
ecology of 4–5; names for, lack of in antiquity 15–16;
stereotypical characteristics of 60; traumas of, at the present day, 335; supposed unity of 4–5, 20–9, 69–70, 141–2, 332; unity of eastern Mediterranean world in Late Bronze Age 119; wish for connections with 294–313
Mediterranean Sea, ancient conceptions and names of 15, 208; perceptions of 138–40; representation of in eighteenth century 242–52
Mediterraneanism 1, 2, 38–42, 45–63, 117, 271, 295–6
Mediterraneans 64–93
Méditerranée 316
Mediterraneo Antico 333–4
Megara 152
Melanesia 46–7
Melos 4, 6 n.
mercenaries 133–4
Mercuriale, Girolamo 198
Meuli, K. 159
microecologies, microregions 6, 30, 34, 357, 359;
microregional trade connections 96–8

Miletus 152–3
mineral resources 18
Mittani 120–1
mobility 179–99, 203–6
Molho, A. 359
Montagu, Lady Mary Wortley
    271, 287–8
Motya 102
Mycenae, Mycenaeans 25, 101,
    122, 128, 138

Naucratis 208, 211
Naxos 254, 281
Necho II 108,
Nectanebo II 208
neo-classicism 310, 311
networks 223
New Zealand, Mediterranean
    and 328–30; Phoenicians in
    297
Nile delta 214; valley 340
Nilsson, M. P. 157
North Sea: *see* Baltic
north–south axis 167–78

obsidian 4, 98
Oedipus in Freudian
    psychoanalysis 313
oikoumene 16, 171
olive, olive-trees 4, 13, 21, 22
Orellana, Francisco de 299–300
Oribasius 190–1
Oropos 151

'pagan' revival 152, 165–6
palaces of Late Bronze Age 129
Palestine 125
palm-trees 21
Panóias (Portugal) 163
Pare, C. F. E. 25
pastoralism 218
pasturage taxes 217–18
Paul of Tarsus 172

'peer polity interaction' 127,
    132, 134, 137
Peiresc, N.-C. F. de 246
Persian Empire 230, 345
Peters, E. 351
Petra 346
*Peuples Méditerranéens/
    Mediterranean Peoples* 316
Peutinger Table 170
Phoenicia, Phoenicians 19–20,
    68, 69, 101–2, 140, 206, 297
pilgrims, pilgrimage 196, 197
piracy 17, 69–70, 88, 139, 351
Pirenne, H. 30, 350
Pisa 70
Plataea 155–60
Plato 11, 217
Plutarch 170–1
polis 216, 229–30
Pompeii 13
population 14–15
portoria 200–32
Portuguese in west Africa 109; in
    the Indian Ocean 112–13; in
    Brazil 310
pre-Columbian history and
    archaeology 302–11
Pryor, J. H. 368
Ptolemaic history 342–3
Ptolemy II 347
Purcell, N. 1–42, 45–6, 49, 52,
    55, 57, 65, 94, 104, 117,
    142–3, 161, 167, 168, 179,
    321–2, 339–42

Quadragesima Galliarum 229
Qumran 178
Qusta ibn Luqa (medieval
    medical writer) 195–6

Rackham, O. 16–17, 35
Ramos, Bernardo 301–11
Razi (Rhazes) 193–4

religion 141–66; alleged
continuity in Greek 284–5
Renfrew, C. 127
revenge 39–40
Revett, Nicholas 259, 263
Rhodes 209–10, 226; Rhodian
Sea Law 225
Riedesel, J. H. van 275–87,
289–90
Rio de Janeiro 309, 310
risk 23, 34
rites of passage 151
rituals 141–66
Roman Empire 29; economies
of 362; geographical horizon
of 173–4; said to be 'multi-
polarized' 103; olive-oil
consumption under 22;
settlement patterns in 30–1,
33; timber in 35–6; typicality
of Egypt in 346
romantics 287–90
Rome, contemporary 58; fiscal
policies of classical 226–30;
importation of grain from
Egypt to 18; imports from
provinces 99
Rooke, Lawrence 237–8
Rostovtzeff, M. I. 30
Royal Society 236, 237, 238, 263
Rufus of Ephesus 185, 195
rural population 31, 40, 105

sacrifices, blood- 165–6
Sahara 66, 75–6
Said, E. 48, 52
Samaritans 162
Sarapis 163
Sarmatia 172–3
'satrapal' economies 229
Schachter, A. 157
Schwennhagen, L. 310
Scythia 172–3

sea-sickness, how to avoid 194
sea-transport 203–4
sea-voyages as therapy 187, 188
self-sufficiency 104, 106, 217
serials: *see* journals
sex in port cities 211
shame 39, 54
Shardanes, allegedly Sardinians
101
Shaw, B. D. 349, 356, 362–3,
370–1, 374
ships, Bronze-Age 4–5, 97, 138;
shipwrecks, Bronze-Age
107
Sijilmasa 75
Siphnos 288
Solomon ben Amar 75
Souyri, J.-F. 89
Sparta 155
Spon, Jacob 238–9, 240, 270,
274–5
Squatriti, P. 349, 350, 353
state 358; state-sponsored
research 240–52; *and see*
taxation, taxes
states, territorial, growth of in
Late Bronze Age 123–7
stereotyping, self-
stereotyping 45–63, 145,
268–93
Strabo 176
structure, social, in Late Bronze
Age 128–31
Stuart, James 259, 263
Sudhoff, K. 195
survey archaeology 353–4
syphilis 195

taxation, taxes 200–32
technology 19, 138
Tell el-Daba'a (Egypt) 135
Tell Kabri (Palestine) 135
tents 162

Thasos 222–3, 226
Theocritus 287–8, 289
theory of Mediterranean
    trade 74–5
therapy 179–99
Timbuktu 75, 76
time 8–9, 141
tin 136
Tinos 288
Tournefort, Joseph Pitton
    de 253–4, 276, 278, 280,
    284–5, 286–7
towns 29, 30, 31, 32–4, 54,
    369–71
trade 17–19, 64–114, 136,
    200–32
transhumance 22–3
travel, travellers 179–99, 268–93;
    traveller-observers 253–63
Turkish conquest, effects on
    Greece of 272, 278
Tyrrhenian Sea 99

Ugarit 132, 139
Ulu Burun wreck 107, 136–7
Unamon 106–7, 139
urbanization 30, 70

Van De Mieroop, M. 9, 344–5

van Gennep, A. 160
Vélissaropoulos, J. 219
vendetta 40
Venice 67, 68, 70, 71, 73
Verlinden, C. 81
Vernon, Francis 238
Verschuer, C. von 88
Vindolanda 346
vine, vine-trees 4, 21, 22
voyageurs-philosophes: see
    traveller-observers

Wake Forest University 303 n.
Walcot, P. 268–9
war, warfare 24, 369; between
    Etruscans and Syracuse
    68–9; in Late Bronze Age
    132–4
water management 13, 353 n.
Wen-Amun: see Unamon
Wheler, George 238–9, 240, 270,
    274–5
Williams, R. 56
Wink, A. 111
Wood, Robert 236, 255–8, 290

Yam, the Sea, in Ugaritic
    literature 139
Youtie, H. C. 41, 343–4